# WILLIAM HENRY GOSS

Nicholas Pine
Lynda Pine

*William Henry Goss with his youngest daughter Florence in the garden at Ashfield Cottage, Stoke-on-Trent, in 1897*

# WILLIAM HENRY GOSS

# THE STORY OF THE STAFFORDSHIRE FAMILY OF POTTERS WHO INVENTED HERALDIC PORCELAIN

## Lynda and Nicholas Pine

MILESTONE PUBLICATIONS

Published in Canada by
Fitzhenry & Whiteside
195 Allstate Parkway
Markham
Ontario L3R 4T8

Design Brian Iles

Photography Michael Edwards

Jacket front photograph David Flynn

Typeset by The Monitor, Hayling Island, Hampshire

Film origination Thomas Campone, Southampton, Hampshire

Printed and Bound in Great Britain by
RJ Acford, Industrial Estate, Chichester, Sussex

British Library Cataloguing in Publication Data
Pine, Nicholas
William Henry Goss : The story of the Staffordshire
family of potters who invented
Heraldic Porcelain
1. Goss, William Henry   2. Porcelain industry
——England——Stoke-on-Trent (Staffordshire)——
Biography
I. Title   II. Pine, Lynda
338.7′6665′0924   HD9612.5

ISBN 0-88902-967-9

Published in Great Britain by
Milestone Publications
62 Murray Road, Horndean
Portsmouth, Hants PO8 9JL England

*Other books by Nicholas Pine*
The Price Guide to Goss China
1st Ed. 1978 Milestone Publications
2nd Ed. 1981 Milestone Publications
3rd Ed. 1984 Milestone Publications
4th Ed. 1986 Milestone Publications
Goss China Arms Decorations and Their Values
1st Ed. 1979 Milestone Publications
2nd Ed. 1982 Milestone Publications
Goss and Other Crested China 1984 Shire Publications
*and with Sandy Andrews*
The Price Guide to Crested China
1st Ed. 1981
2nd Ed. 1984

*To*

BEVERLY
DAN
DICK
GRAHAM
JOHN
JOHN
NORMAN
TREVOR

*whose friendship, dedication and*
*encouragement has spurred us on*

*The St. Martins Cross, Iona memorial to William Henry Goss in Hartshill Cemetery, Stoke-on-Trent.*
*This postcard view was one of many sold throughout the potteries in 1906 and for some time after William's death, by Latham and Bott, photographers of Longton*

# Contents

WILLIAM HENRY GOSS

The Story of the Staffordshire Family of Potters who invented Heraldic Porcelain

# KEY TO BACK COVER ILLUSTRATIONS

```
┌──────────┬──────────┬──────────┐
│          │    2     │          │
│    1     ├──────────┤    3     │
│          │    4     │          │
├──────────┼──────────┼──────────┤
│          │          │          │
│    5     │    6     │    7     │
│          │          │          │
├────┬─────┴───┬──────┼─────┬────┤
│  8 │         │      │  11 │    │
├────┤    9    │  10  ├─────┤    │
│ 12 │         │      │  13 │    │
└────┴─────────┴──────┴─────┘
```

1. Plaque bearing the Goss family arms affixed to every original cabinet.
2. Beachy Head, Portland, Eddystone and Longships Lighthouses.
3. Elephant with Howdah.
4. Queen Charlotte's Favourite Windsor Kettle.
5. Preserve Pot and lid with grapefruit decoration.
6. Pear shaped highly decorated vase with sepia transfer of Windsor Castle.
7. Milk Jug with colour transfer of Bournemouth from West Cliff.
8. Bulbous medium crinkle-top Violet Vase with seaweed decoration.
9. Flower Girl, Miss Prudence.
10. Minster Ancient Ewer with Arms of Minster.
11. Goodwin Sands Carafe with the Burgee of Royal Clyde Yacht Club, Hunter's Quay.
12. Egyptian Water Jar with badge of the Honourable Artillery Company.
13. The Peace Plate, 1919.

# Acknowledgements

This book has taken some six years to research, write and publish and could not have been completed without the assistance of many individuals to whom we are extremely grateful.

We would like to thank the following people and organisations for their help, encouragement, information and, where appropriate, the loan, gift or sale of material used for research and for permission to quote from books, letters, obituaries, reports, reviews and other printed material and to reproduce letters and photographs.

Whilst we have endeavoured to include everybody, there may inadvertently be some omissions, for which we apologise in advance.

## The Family In Great Britain
We are indebted to all the members of the family who threw open their doors and welcomed our intrusion into their lives, who patiently answered our probing questions and who extended to us gracious hospitality.

The information provided by Major W.R. Goss, great-grandson of William Henry, the founder of the famous pottery, provided us with a clear insight into the personalities of Adolphus, his brothers and father who were between them responsible for the firm which was in family ownership between 1858 and 1929. Louise, widow of John Goss, grandson of the founder, was a mine of information, as were Doreen Ashton, Rosemary Cooper and Joy Goss, who had spent many hours listening to the stories of Ethel Goss, elder daughter of Adolphus.

Ethel realised the importance of her father and grandfather, and had kept useful papers and letters and instructed they be stored even after her death.

## The Family In The Falkland Islands
We have corresponded with a number of Goss family members in the Falklands who have provided much information unobtainable elsewhere. We are grateful for the trouble so many of them have taken to search out and send information and to those who visited us at Horndean.

We are indebted to the late Horace L. Bound whose help with the preparation of the Falklands branch family tree has been invaluable and who has since sadly died, and Mae Glen whose hard work has made this tree so detailed.

## The Family In America
Nicholas travelled America for one month visiting every descendant of the Goss family that he could trace. Everywhere he went he was made most welcome and no effort was spared to assist with the project and supply information, much of which proved invaluable.

The highlight of the tour was a family reunion in Kansas attended by some 70 members of the family, as a result of which, many cousins are now in touch with one another.

Berniece and Arnold Rausch have been particularly helpful as have Virginia Goss, Betty Carlson and Joy Wilson and many members of their families. Dorothy and Harold Goss went out of their way to make Nicholas welcome and to assist, resulting in much valuable information being obtained. We thank also Lydia Mae and Earl Robertson and Mr & Mrs Cliff Goss.

Clara Goss has carefully preserved much original material which has been researched by her sons David and Don Goss. We are indebted to them for making their material available to us and also for assistance with photography and for being warmly welcomed in all three homes.

Nicholas was pleased to meet Sadie Goss and her family all of whom he thanks.

Valentine Taggart is the daughter of Florence Murdock (née Goss) and the only surviving granddaughter of William Henry. Nicholas was delighted to meet her and extends his thanks to Vallie and her family for their hospitality and assistance.

The Hurlin family warmly welcomed Nicholas and provided much useful material. In particular we thank Georgiana Peavey and her son, and Henry Hurlin and family. John and Ann Peavey have researched their family tree and generously made it available to us.

## The Historians
Michael Willis-Fear MA, made available his thesis on Goss china which has proved invaluable. He also magnanimously allowed us unhindered access to his unpublished book on the subject, his extensive files and information resulting from interviews with the late Noel and John Goss.

Alex Shaw, a historian of Alsager, and his wife Betty could not have been more kind, helpful and full of encouragement, going to great lengths on our behalf obtaining photographs and other information. Their intimate knowledge of the Gosses' especially Ethel, have enriched this book enormously.

## The Museums, Libraries And Organisations
We thank Norman Emery FLA; the staff of the Horace Barks Reference Library, Hanley; the Town Clerk of Stoke-on-Trent; the William Salt Library, Stoke-on-Trent; Keeper and staff of the Public Record Office, London; Director General of the Ordnance Survey, and Superintendent Dr H.M. Wallis and staff of the Map Room, Ordnance Survey; V. Tyrrell, FLA, Principal Area Librarian, City General Library, Hanley; Dr Celoria and the Gladstone Pottery Museum, Longton, and Jeremy Smith, former Mayor of Alsager.

## Collectors, Friends and Descendants
We are grateful to the many collectors and friends who have given their time and assisted in so many diverse ways.

John Magee, John Galpin, Sylvia Munday, Pauline Dobson, Michael Palmer and Stephen Godly have all made many useful contributions.

We also extend our thanks to Mrs G. Ash, Derek Ashton, Mrs D. Burgess, Rev. B. Goss, Eric Goss, Mrs M.E. Goss, Prof. A. Pollard, C. Hollinshead, Jane Kimbell, Margaret Latham, Mrs R. Norris, Mrs. E. Norris, Patrick Rawlings, Robert Sephton, Sam Shaw, T. Skerratt, Robert Southall, Mrs Joy Stones, Mrs B. Sellek, Ken Taylor and the late John Willis.

## The Wordsmiths
Lt. Cdr. Norman Pratten, FCIS, RD, RNR, has carefully edited the text and we are indebted to him for his scholarly assistance, advice and friendship. We owe an especial debt of gratitude to Beverly Shepherd for editorially advising on the text and also to Patricia Pearson and Vanessa Amis. Our many thanks also to the typists Margaret Wooding and Debbie Webb who were transformed into Goss enthusiasts by the end of their work!

## Photographic Acknowledgements
We thank those who have supplied, arranged for or allowed us to take photographs for this book.

In particular Clara Goss, Louise Goss, Jocelyn Goss, Valentine Taggart, Major W.R. Goss, Dorothy and Harold Goss, Joy Stones, Don Goss and David Goss.

M.J. Willis-Fear, MA has provided many rare and important photographs for which we are especially grateful.

Douglas Goodlad and The Leicester Mercury and Portsmouth & Sunderland Newspapers PLC.

The Controller of H.M. Stationery Office for photographs of plans of the factory based on Ordnance Survey Maps.

Alex Shaw has tirelessly taken and provided many photographs and to him we extend a particular thank you.

*For reasons of authenticity original spellings and punctuations have been retained in all quotations and extracts.*

# Introduction

As a young man, William Henry Goss displayed talents verging on the genius, but as he grew older these traits developed into eccentricities. He was a redhead with a terrible temper, and not at all easy to live with. He lived apart from his wife Georgiana for most of their married life, their children helping to prevent any confrontation between them which would give their father the excuse to officially separate from her. Even so, they did not speak to one another for the last twenty years of their lives.

From a promising start as a literary student, William used the important contacts and friends he made in London to carve a career in the potting industry, becoming Copeland's chief artist and designer by the time he was only 21. By the age of 22 he had opened up his own factory and never looked back. With his son Adolphus they advanced from a limited production range of busts and classical figurines to inexpensive mass produced souvenir heraldic ware, and started a new collecting craze which swept the nation. It was hard times for the potting industry and almost all the other Staffordshire pot banks followed suit with successful heraldic lines, although none rivalled Mr. Goss's special parian and enamels, for they were his own perfected recipes, being a trained chemist.

Blessed with a generous nature and a need to help others, never being short of money and living in a poverty stricken area where he loved to help and was highly regarded, he should have lived an idyllic life. However, William was the victim of his own paranoia for ultimate perfection, but life was not perfect, and he suffered, and his family suffered with him.

Although loyal to him in public, within the privacy of their own circle his children aired their complaints. They were incensed that their father appeared to prefer the company of the children of his good friend Llewellynn Jewitt to his own, and that he spent his money on his acquaintances and weird antiquities instead of them. Yet in many ways they were similar in temperament and personality to their father, and all had their own eccentricities.

It is unfortunate that Victor met with a fatal accident in 1913. Had he lived to steer the factory through the financial crisis of the war years, the firm could probably have survived. He may have eventually had his own family and kept up the pottery, however, his younger brother Huntley sold up in 1929 and although the new owner kept up production of heraldic ware for a few more years, tastes had changed and the market for crested china had by then entered its terminal decline.

Adolphus, Victor and Huntley Goss played a far greater part in the manufacture of heraldic ware than their father. In particular, Adolphus, who was ahead of his time, guided the firm towards the mass production of souvenir ware in order to fulfil a nation's need. Much of our research has been aimed at the three brothers who between them influenced the style of the product after 1880 and for most of the firm's life.

The collecting of Goss china became a craze that swept the nation and it is thought that in Edwardian times some 90% of all homes contained Goss porcelain miniatures, a higher incidence than telephones or television sets enjoy today. After the craze had died in the 1920's, the nation spent the next forty years throwing crested china away. Now, after languishing unwanted in junk shops for years, Goss china has found its way back into its rightful place in the best china cabinets of Britain. In recent years the factory, situated in Sturgess Street off London Road, Stoke, has been used for clothing manufacture, but in the early 1980's was sold to the adjoining Portmeirion Pottery who have since demolished the majority of the original buildings, with the exception of the two glost ovens, still standing and protected as listed buildings, as does the enamel and printing warehouse built by Adolphus, Victor and Huntley between 1902 and 1905.

The stone Goshawk can still clearly be seen inset in the gable of the warehouse building and William's former home, Ashfield Cottage, now let, still overlooks the site below, but sadly lacking its former glory.

# CHAPTER ONE

# The Early Years

*When a man has more than usually distinguished himself in Art, in Literature, in Science,
or in any of the other special walks in life to which he has devoted himself, his time, and his energies,
there springs up in the minds of most of his fellows a widespread and wholesome desire to know something
of his personal history; of the struggles through which he has passed in the attainment of
the proud position he has at length achieved; and of the means he has adopted for the cutting out for himself
the path through the world's jungle, that has ultimately led him to the 'fair plains of sweet success',
where his labours have met their reward in the admiration of his fellow-men.*

Llewellynn Jewitt, 1882: The Life and Works of Jacob Thompson

Descended from a middle class Middlesex family based in Shoreditch, with his grandfather a merchant and his father a weaver and painter, William Henry Goss went to great lengths to keep his background and family intensely private, and never revealed the birth and marriage dates of his parents and elder brothers and sister to his inquiring children. For years after his death they wrote to their relations and one another trying to discover them, thinking he had something to hide.

William was born in Wheler Street, London on 30 July, 1833, the fourth child of Richard and Sophia Sarah (née Mann), and baptised on 27 October the same year in the impressive baroque Christchurch, Spitalfields, the same church in which his parents had married 19 July, 1821.

William's father, Richard Victor was also born in London, in 1791 and being orphaned when quite young, was reared by his grandparents Thomas and Anne and attended the Bluecoat School, Christ's Hospital. The young Richard had a terrible argument with his grandparents over the eating of potatoes, or so the story goes according to descendants, and in a temper left home for good. His grandfather was considered a tyrant by the rest of his family so sympathies were with the young lad. Leaving behind his younger brothers, he joined the crew of the battleship HMS Bellerophon, and was bosun when Napoleon I surrendered himself on 8 August 1815 to Captain Maittand of that ship en route to St. Helena, after his disastrous stand at Waterloo. The capture of Napoleon made a great impression on the mind of Richard and in commemoration of the event he decided to name his future family accordingly. In later years he called his eldest son Jacob Napoleon who in turn named his first son Richard William Napoleon. Jacob was the second child, born 17 June 1825, and was baptised at St. Leonards Church, Shoreditch on 1 October 1826. William's second

brother Richard died young about 1828, and his third brother Richard William was christened 30 May 1830 at Christchurch, Spitalfields along with his only sister, Sophia Mary who was born some two years earlier. It was common practice over a century ago in those days of large families for parents to wait until there were several infants

*William Henry Goss as a young student at Somerset House, London.*

*Napoleon boarding HMS Bellerophon in 1815, en route to St. Helena.*

to baptise at once as it was cheaper to christen en masse! Richard William, like his brother William, married at the age of 19 on 15 July 1849, a cousin, Mary Ann Mann at Christchurch, Hoxton. Their first son they named Jacob Napoleon after his uncle. Possibly William did not approve of his uncle marrying their Mother's niece, for there was no evidence of any contact between the two families. William's fourth brother Abner Mitchener was born 10 June 1838 when the family lived at 4, Harts Lane, London. He worked for the Goss factory in its early days as foreman whilst lodging with William, but later left and went with his wife to live in Colchester. He died in 1924 leaving behind a large family.

As a child, William loved Sophia more than anyone else. She was his guiding star and he adored her company. She personally took a hand in his upbringing, and as she was eleven years older, considered herself to be almost a mother to him. He once said that she taught him to pray as he knelt in her lap. He was always grateful for the encouragement she gave him in his youth and told his own children that he owed her 'an incalculable debt' but alas his children never had the chance to meet her. In 1842 she married the Rev. Charles Hurlin. Three children and ten years later they emigrated to Maine, U.S.A. on 4 June, 1852. They were never to return. Amongst William's precious personal belongings was a large old gold brooch with a glass front revealing a soft curl of hair which he had labelled 'The hair of my darling only sister.'

The Goss family can be traced back as far as the twelfth

*HMS Bellerophon, William's father Richard Goss was the bosun on this battleship.*

century when a Peter Goss was Sheriff of Lincolnshire in 1164-5, recorded in Latin as *Petrus de Gossa*. Over the centuries the surname varied in spelling, Gosse or Goss being predominant. William's mother's side of the family, the Manns, were traced to one of the Huguenot families who were exiled from France at the time of the repeal of the Edict of Nantes.

The Goss branch of the family tended towards tradition. Although there were Gosses living in different parts of the country, whenever William Henry had chanced to meet anyone with the same surname he could not help noticing how similar they all were. Even if they were not blood relations, in any person named Goss or Gosse he found certain characteristics repeated, such as red hair, a temper to match, good health and fine artistic tastes. Thus the Goss clan appeared to be retaining its peculiar characteristics in every way which pleased William immensely. The emblem of the Goss family was a goose, which was later to play its part in the production of Goss china. There was no ancient Goss family coat of arms as the family were not members of the nobility or gentry, so William designed his own, the motto being *Se Inserit Astris* — 'It is written in the stars.'

During his youth William's achievements were remarkable. At the age of 16 he was sent to the Government School of Design at Somerset House, according to *The Art Union* in February, 1840, 'instituted for the purpose of affording instruction to those engaged in the practice of ornamental art, and in the preparation

*Sophia Mary Hurlin, William's only sister, in 1874.*

*William in his early twenties.*

*The Rev. Charles Hurlin in 1874, who emigrated with his wife Sophia and three children to the U.S.A. in 1852.*

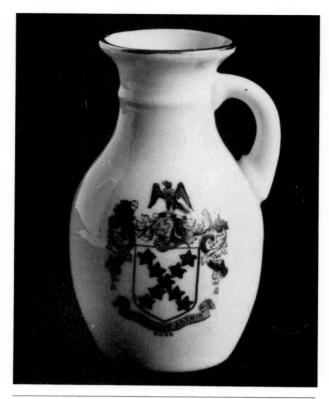

*Goss model of a Newcastle Jug bearing the Goss Arms*

*Richard Redgrave, RA, one of William's art masters at Somerset House, London, 1849-52*

of designs for the various manufactories of this country'. The fees for morning school which William attended were 4/- per month, while evening classes were 2/-. An Art Union monthly journal of 1846 praised the Government Schools of Design:

'They are largely assisting to enable our manufacturers to compete with foreign producers; they are giving sound and useful education to a large number of youths, and they are gradually but certainly improving public taste, and leading to a more general appreciation of what is true and excellent in art.'

William, a keen and natural student, exceptionally devoted to his books, read vast amounts of literature, from the great works and classics to history, and conceived his own opinions as to the origin of man, which differed from those of Charles Darwin. Like his family, he was devoutly religious and an ardent churchgoer. He would spend much of his leisure time at Somerset House, where he earned many awards and became a talented artist.

While residing in London, William made some long lasting friendships with influential people. He frequented the museums and galleries which existed in the great capital, educating himself to a high degree and meeting similarly minded students. Before he was 19 he had formed a circle of young intellectuals who regularly met weekly at one another's homes for the research and study of science and the development of literary faculties. Their first meeting was on 5 March 1852 when he delivered a long lecture in which he outlined the advantages of their proposed Society, the importance of perseverance in the pursuit of learning and wisdom, the extension of their obtaining information through the medium of books and elsewhere, the attainment of fluency and boldness of utterance and the need for fertility of thought. He later observed:

'The Literary Society which I established here two years ago is in a most flourishing condition. Its Art Exhibitions are quite interesting, and its literary productions are probably Amaranths. I purpose to form a publishing establishment by & by, in connection with it, but this is only in embryo at present.'

With the exception of an early poem, his publishing ambitions were never realised until the last few years of his life when he published several volumes of his own letters and essays. William gave himself entirely to work, and he put any necessary leisure time second to his quest for knowledge. Whenever he took a holiday or had a change of scenery it was usually in order to study geology, natural history or another form of science. He was gathering up 'the fragments that nothing be lost', as he liked to say.

William found a fatherly friend in the eminent person of Samuel Carter Hall, FSA, and his wife Anna Marie, who were both prolific authors. He felt particularly indebted to S.C. Hall for the encouragement he received in his literary efforts and for his financial support. Hall, thirty years his senior, gave him mature advice which William reciprocated with son-like love and affection. Hall introduced him to Llewellynn F. Jewitt, the famous author and engraver and both men were to remain good to him for the rest of their lives.

During his teens he was poetically motivated and it was obvious he was enjoying life. His only published poem was *Ralph and Priscilla*, written when he was 17, and based on his romance with Georgiana Goldswain of Marlow, whom he later married. He wrote excitedly to Sophia and his brother-in-law Charles Hurlin:

'The poem has done well; its success is quite signal for a *poem* and the *first* publication of its author. Some of the best of our aristocracy have become its patrons and commendors. I have letters from — the Duchess of Sutherland, Earl of Shaftesbury, Lord Viscount Barrington, Lord Bishop of Chichester, the Lord Mayor, besides some of our first rate ministers and literary men.'

Unfortunately he could not resist a jibe at his younger brother, Abner, for whom he found work, which apparently included the selling of his book, because he quipped:

"But Ab. has not made *his* future out of the discounts for he only sold *three*."

Always hypercritical, William was a difficult employer to work for and Abner's employ did not last long.

In the poem, William is Ralph and Georgiana is Priscilla whom he loved passionately — at that time! He had met the wealthy Georgiana when he was only 16 and moved in with her as a lodger at 44, Milton Street, St. Marylebone. She was four years older than him, being born in 1829. William married her just seven months after his dear sister Sophia emigrated, although he was only 19 years old. It is possible the businesslike William simply used Georgiana to replace the gap in his affections. For some reason he refused to state his age on their marriage certificate of 25 March, 1853. Shortly after they married, the couple moved to Homer House, St. Marylebone.

Exactly nine months later, less four days, their first child Adolphus was born. William let his sister know immediately of his marvellous news:

'It is my turn now to say "Don't *you* boast about your little 'uns". You don't 'speck' that I've got a little Willie to match your little Georgy! I left Georgy this morning very poorly, came home just now at half past one o'clock to see how she is, and lo, find a little Willie lying on her dear bosom. He's a precious little fellow already. It's brave, patient mother seems to be going on very nicely as far as we can judge at present.'

That Christmas holiday at Homer House was one of the happiest he had ever enjoyed and in a gay mood described it as follows:

*Samuel Carter Hall who guided the young William Goss through his studies. Photograph taken 1851*

*Professor Llewellynn F. Jewitt when a young man*

*Mrs William Henry Goss, the former Georgiana Goldswain of Marlow, aged about 30*

'Christmas day has fallen on a Sunday, and to make up for it, the English people are going to make a general holy day of tomorrow, that there shall be no excuse for the desecration of the Sabbath by those who wish to keep up the festival as a jolly, gay holiday.'

One shadow on the horizon was the imminent departure of his parents to the Falklands in response to his eldest brother Jacob's invitation to them to join him out there.

'Mother has made up her mind to go to the Falklands, if the invitation continues to wear the aspect of a "Call" as she terms it, meaning a *Providential* call. I have written to Jacob commending him for his kind remembrance of our parents. Father dined with us at Homer House last Sunday, he is full of the matter, and looks forward with delight to the voyage. He thinks the change of scene and position will make him comparatively a happy man, and so I think, as regard temporal matters.'

Why Jacob Napoleon Goss first ventured out to the Falklands, a tiny group of wind-battered islands isolated in the South Atlantic, which suffered severe winters, is not clear but the first settlers were transported there by a Captain Stanley Goss, a relative who perhaps sowed the seed of the idea which was later to germinate. He must have regularly sailed the passage as Port Stanley, indeed the Falklands capital was named after him.

Another important figure in directing William's life and career was the learned, interesting and the then Lord

*William in his late twenties, sitting in his smoking chair*

*Georgiana's sister, Miss E. Goldswain of Marlow in 1877*

Mayor of London, Alderman W.F.M. Copeland whom he met while still in his teens. Being much older than the young student, Copeland looked on him rather like a son and under his guidance William learnt the art of potting and advanced skills of chemistry which were later to prove invaluable. Ald. Copeland and S.C. Hall financed William's studies and experiments and introduced him to some important contacts with whom he made a good impression. In later years he was to continually express his thanks for their moral and material support, eventually writing Hall's biography after his death.

Alderman Copeland owned the famous Copeland Spode china works at Stoke-on-Trent. He offered the young William an apprenticeship at the London branch, and, after training, offered him a job at his Stoke factory where he was trained further in the art of potting and advanced chemistry and was quickly promoted to the position of chief artist and designer.

His work at Copeland Spode aroused attention for its skill and mastery across a wide range, but he left the firm in 1858 following disagreements over managerial decisions. In truth, William needed to be his own boss. He founded his own firm the same year in John Street (now non-existent), at Lock Pottery, a very small pottery of 250 sq. ft, according to the 1877 ordnance survey, with a kiln at the end of John Street adjacent to the Cock Inn, backing onto Ald. Copeland's Spode works.

William had rewarded his generous friend by setting up a rival firm producing similar products in premises adjoining those of his former employer!

*The croquet lawn on the terrace in the rear garden of Rode Heath, with William reading as usual and Florence nearby, taken in 1884*

# CHAPTER TWO

# The Move To Stoke.
# The Goss Clan Enlarges

Heaven lies about us in our infancy!
Shades of the prison-house begin to close
Upon the growing boy,
But he beholds the light, and whence it flows,
He sees it in his joy;
The youth, who daily farther from the east
Must travel, still is Nature's priest,
And by the vision splendid
Is on his way attended;
At length the man perceives it die away,
And fade into the light of common day.

**Wordsworth: 'Intimations of Immortality'**

William Henry Goss fell in love with the century old Ashfield Cottage from the time he first moved there in 1857. Although not particularly large, it had a kind of splendour, with its own sweeping drive flanked by a superb pair of white, gated pillars to match the Victorian architecture. He originally leased it from Mr. Campbell of Campbell's Tile Works, whom he befriended, eventually purchasing the house in later years.

From the time William first lived at Ashfield Cottage the surrounding area took on a great change. His daughter, Eva Adeline, poetically described the scenery as it was in 1857:

'What a different prospect then. London Road was bounded on both sides by green fields and well-wooded hedges. All around Ashfield Cottage were lovely giant trees, and an ash-tree bordered drive running down to London Road. Clear springs made music, and found their natural level in several winding streams, courses marked by all kinds of charming bushes and wild flowers. Fruit and nut trees were in abundance and at the top of the cottage kitchen garden there stands today (1907) an ancient pear tree, a solitary relic of those days which yearly has white blossom but too ancient to produce fruit.'[1]

The cottage faced east and overlooked the magnificent countryside of the Trent valley. The only building visible between it and Longton was Fenton Hall, set in woods and partly hidden. There was no town of Fenton before 1860, just trees and fields as far as the eye could see. To the south it faced the village of Hanford and further on nestled Trentham and Barlaston. These two areas had not altered much during William's lifetime although, of course, they have since his death in 1906. To the north of his home stood Shelton Church with its tall tower hovering over Stoke village. He adored this house which he kept for the rest of his life, and although he had other properties over the years, he always referred to Ashfield as 'home'. He made much use of the garden which was very ornate with little paths and steps, lawns at different levels and the flower beds teeming with colour most of the year round. Within this setting he thought himself in absolute paradise, for he was a loner, preferring his own company, sitting and walking for hours observing birds, insects and plant life. Throughout his life he took a daily walk in the surrounding countryside regardless of the weather. Adeline remembered that:

'He conceived a deep love for the cottage which never after left him, even during the long interval which ensued after the then owner had required the house for another, until circumstances permitted him to purchase the property, from which time until his death, it was the house he best liked to live in, although one would suppose that the rural quiet of Barthomley would have been more congenial to him.'[1]

*1901 view of Ashfield Cottage, Stoke. William had moved there from London in 1857*

*Ashfield Cottage in 1962. Remains of his stone paths are still visible*

The pottery towns of Stoke, Shelton and Hanley, Longton, Tunstall, Fenton and Burslem sprang up along the same turnpike route in the centre of Staffordshire over a century before William's time, using the local clays, coal and water power. The middle towns of Stoke, Etruria, Shelton and Hanley were renowned for the manufacture of the more expensive and costly wares, and of course William was based at Stoke. The towns north and south were associated with cheaper goods, especially Longton, once known as Lane End and the dirtiest of the pottery towns, but the inhabitants set to and cleaned the place up and renamed it Longton. It was an area where sparsely populated farming country surrounded the densely populated towns with their gardenless terraced houses packed together amongst hundreds of smoking bottle ovens causing an almost permanent smog, which hung over the area like a black cloud. William never failed to be fascinated by the area and its natives, whose language and way of life he observed on his daily walks.

William and Georgiana's first child was Adolphus William Henry, born 27 December, 1853 at Homer House, Homer Place, Marylebone Road whilst they were still living in London. Bearing his father's name within his own, he was brought up to follow in his father's footsteps. Adolphus does not appear to be a family name, but possibly was selected because of William's fascination for an historic character, the King of Sweden, Gustavus Adolphus, who

*William and Georgiana's first child, Adolphus William Henry*

*Their eldest daughter, Georgiana*

*Godfrey William aged about five. Through leaving school at ten, his future was affected by his lack of education*

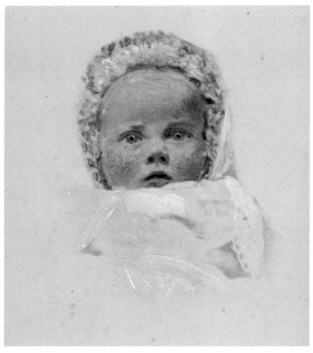

*Evangeline, who lived only eight months. Her father immortalised her in porcelain as an angel. Taken in 1861*

was a Russian Ahaseurus and noble young warrior who delivered Europe from the Austrian peril. The next child was Georgiana, affectionately called Georgie, who came two years later on her father's birthday in 1855, and was destined to be his favourite. After their move to Stoke came Godfrey William on 31 January, 1857, born at Ashfield Cottage. A fourth child, Evangeline, a sickly infant, died in her first year in 1860. She was probably named after the subject in Longfellow's poem which appeared in the *Art Journal* in 1850. Eva Adeline was next in line appearing on 8 March, 1863, the fifth child in ten years! The twins were born 12 May, 1865 and were christened Victor Henry and Edith Maria. William Huntley arrived two years later on 23 September and their ninth and last child, Florence, known as Florry, was born on 18 May 1870. It was Florence's head with a rose in her hair, which was the model for a Goss china wall pocket vase. The luckless Evangeline was immortalised on the lid of a casket, appearing as a baby reclining on a cushion. William also made a bust of his daughter Georgiana, after her early death. This was not for general sale but examples were given to Edwin Jewitt her husband, to various members of the Goss family, and to certain employees who shared his grief at her loss.

William's marriage did not prove to be a happy one, and although they never divorced, their lives were so separate they might just as well have been. The task of rearing eight children as well as years of taking second place in his affections to all his other loves took its toll on Georgiana

*Victor Henry, sixth child and twin of Edith. Taken in 1887*

and William and they grew further apart as the years progressed. The year after their last child Florence was born, the Census in 1871 recorded the Goss family as living at Alsager with the exception of William and second son Godfrey, so it appears they parted some time between 1870 and 1871.

Only a matter of a few years after their parting and as a result of a tremendous argument, possibly about 1877, they never spoke to each other again. It was most uncomfortable for others to be in their company together, with communication between them being in the form of written notes and the use of children to mediate. The story of the cause of the argument was passed on down the family over the generations as something they ought to know but never talk about.

William was fanatical about the privacy of his study. All his personal belongings, ancient coins, antiques, collections of medieval tiles, engravings and private letters and albums were contained in this one room. No-one was allowed inside unless invited by him. It was never properly dusted or cleaned, and was arranged entirely to suit himself. He felt comfortable in there, enjoying his own company, and safe from intrusions from his nagging wife, eight noisy children and the bustle of servants. One day, the gardener, who had been cleaning the outside windows, had left the ladder up against the side of Ashfield Cottage, exactly at the locked study's open window. It was the

*Adolphus in 1860*

*Florence and Edith, aged five and ten respectively in 1875*

*Mrs Georgiana Goss with her youngest child Florence*

window immediately over the front door. Mrs. Goss took her chance and, with her duster and polish, shinned quickly up the ladder. Her husband was at the factory a short distance away and she thought she would have time to clean the room for since 1870, when William bought Ashfield Cottage, the study had not been spring-cleaned. Whether he saw her from his office window or whether he just happened to arrive home earlier than usual is uncertain, but he caught his wife in his hideout and was enraged. After a fierce and bitter exchange of words they did not speak to one another for the rest of their lives. To have spoken to her again would have meant he had forgiven her, and this he found he could not do.

No doubt many of the family's friends and acquaintances knew and understood that they lived separate lives because they had so little in common with each other. He was an intellectual and she, as her surviving letters show, was no brilliant scholar. Maybe it was her beauty that had captivated him in the beginning, or her French Huguenot origins like his mother, or the fact that she strikingly resembled his dear sister Sophia. Divorce was out of the question because William did not want any scandal or gossip, and in any case, no one else was involved. The split was never openly discussed by the Goss children because theirs was a very private family and, especially in Victorian times, one was discreet. The children, while obedient to their father, though often reluctantly, were at the same time protective and affectionate towards their mother.

Despite having a Queen reigning over them, Victorian gentlemen considered themselves so much more important than their women. The Goss children accepted that their father's decisions were final because he was the head of the family, and presumed their mother had failed to live up to their father's expectations. After the parting, William removed all his wife's photographs from his albums. He succeeded in destroying every photograph he had of her and, strangely, none of Georgiana senior turned up amongst the belongings of the decendants of her children in England. It was from America and the descendants of Godfrey that several portraits were finally obtained.

Georgiana seems to have been a strong willed woman, who had a superb bone structure, a good figure and a fine head of black hair. The few photographs which exist show her, despite having borne eight children, as slim and expensively dressed. She was a good mother and devoted her life to the upbringing of her children but the lack of a loving husband turned her into a rather hard and bitter person. When the children were old enough they accompanied their father wherever he went, particularly the girls when they were home from boarding school. It was most important to their father that his children be well educated. The sons were sent to school locally at Newcastle-under-Lyme but none of them stayed at school longer than was necessary. Godfrey left at ten years of age, his lack of education alienating him from his own family, and his work on the factory floor led him to believe he was closer to the workers than to his own brothers and sisters. Indeed, a paintress called Jane, who he worked alongside in the enamelling room, was looked upon as a sister.

William constantly reminded his children (and work force too) about the necessity to work to the best of their ability and never to try to shirk or delay work. When in a good mood or feeling pleased with any of his children, he showered them with gifts, invited them to share his company, and encouraged them to read and not assist in household chores. But when he was crossed, or felt any members of his family were being lazy, he would avoid their company and set them many tasks. There was always one person who was 'flavour of the month'. Surviving letters written by his children often revealed who was the latest to be favoured. When she began to grow into a young woman, the youngest, Florry, was close to her father. He gave her a gold watch, paid for extravagant dresses and superb jewellery, whilst the other daughters received very little. He was exceptionally tough with his sons. Punishment for the slightest misdemeanour was to deprive them of home comforts, making them sleep on the floor on sacks instead of their beds, and banning them from the factory and from his company.

He denied his daughters the chance of attending parties and balls as a matter of course, unless they were organised by his best friends, the Jewitts. Georgiana, Adeline, Edith, and later Florry were regularly invited via their father to functions, but he rarely used to pass on the information. When they did find out, the girls were considerably displeased and often complained about their unreasonable father in their letters. On one occasion, their father's friends, the Skenes, gave a party at nearby Lawton Hall and invitations were duly sent to William for the whole family, but he failed to mention the invitation to them. Edith met the Skenes in the street shortly before the event and they discussed it with her, not realising she knew nothing about it. She was pleased that they were amazed at her father and told a friend, 'It serves him right that the Skenes know of his duplicity!'

During the 1880's the three elder daughters took turns to live with their father for one week at a time in order to keep house; Florence was too young having only been born in 1870.

As the Goss children grew older, they found their father's various punishments intolerable. He was especially unkind to Godfrey, whose illiteracy he found unbearable. Godfrey felt he was the black sheep of the family and although he had always been close to Adolphus and his mother, imagined they had all turned against him when he began courting Alice Buckley who was a paintress at the factory. It is possible that Godfrey worked as a foreman or checker in the enamelling room, but he had a good grounding in all the various processes of pottery manufacture. A handsome young man himself, he had taken out several

*Godfrey William, the third child who was to emigrate to America in 1882*

young ladies who were all employees, but fell in love with tiny Alice whom he considered beautiful, with her blue eyes, blonde locks, and delicate bone structure.

All his family made it quite clear they did not approve of the match and endeavoured to point out the reasons why, but he would not listen. He just thought they were attempting to poison his mind and this made him turn against them all, and although he informed Victor and Adolphus of his intention to emigrate it came as a shock to the others when he finally did. Only these two brothers accompanied him to Liverpool to see him off on the *Indiana* in May, 1882. He suffered a rough voyage with dreadful food, eventually landing at Philadelphia. At the age of 24 he had left behind everything he owned, and had to begin again, penniless in a foreign country.

Florry used to say that it seemed to be the rule in their family to run away. It certainly appears that the Gosses had a stubborness in their character. William's own father ran away when quite young, then his own second son, and it was to be that Adolphus's second son would also run away when of a similar age. Even Godfrey's second son, Archie, was to run away.

In terms of personality, Godfrey was more like his father than any of his brothers; he was a very intense person who, once he had been crossed, found it very hard to forgive. When he emigrated in 1882, he had little idea of what life had in store for him. Had he known Alice would not be following him out for another four years, he probably would not have gone, for his letters, several a week without fail, revealed his intense love for her. He hardly bothered to write to his own family, who only learned his latest news through relations of other emigrants. His family found this humiliating, especially his mother who felt his loss the most. We do not think Alice helped him to keep in contact with home, for by keeping him paralysed with worry about her ever making the decision to follow him, largely based on her parents unwillingness to let their youthful 16 year old emigrate to marry a lad they had never seen, the poor lovesick Godfrey had no thoughts for anyone else, and found it difficult to concentrate on earning a living. Alice also wrote about the lack of friendliness by her future in-laws which angered him.

Poor Godfrey may have felt there was too much trouble within his family to keep in touch more than he did. An unfortunate facet of the letters from Victor, Edith, Adeline and Florry was that they used their pens to have a good moan and groan about life at home, and constantly dwelt on the bad rather than the good news. Conversely, it was quite noticeable that the two elder children, Adolphus and Georgiana, rarely mentioned anything disagreeable about home, and only spoke well of their parents. The young Huntley hardly ever wrote, perhaps because of the 12 year age gap Godfrey and he were not very close, but in any case, Huntley was never to be a keen writer.

Victor was very forthright and said some outrageous things. One letter to America told Godfrey:

*Victor's twin sister Edith, about 1880, seated in a hammock*

'Oh, you remember that letter you sent him some time ago, in which you signed yourself 'Your obedient son', well, the old beggar told lots of folks about that and said that there was a touch of repentance in it. Of course *we* all saw at once that you were having a poke at *him*; for we all know that you never did anything to him to be sorry for. By George, I should rather fancy that *he* is the one to feel sorry. If you write to me send it to Rode Heath, or else the old man will be sure to look at it and criticise it and find some evil in it like he usually does.'

About 1885 there appeared to be some form of major disagreement between William and his two middle daughters, possibly because he spoilt their fun preventing them meeting young men at parties, but more likely by treating Florence and Georgiana as his favourites, giving special treats while Adeline and Edith kept house. That year Edith said of her father:

'Papa is something *awful* to live with, his temper is *terrible*. We had a fine row last week, he scarcely *ever* speaks to any of us unless he is obliged to and has told us that he does not want our kisses so we never kiss him now. Adeline and I are going to work for our living when I am 21 which will be in 12 months tomorrow. He promised to bring us three tricycles the other week but won't get any now although Mr. Pedley has gone to the expense of twenty pounds to build a stable in the back lane for us next to his coach house.'

In July of that year their father went on a Field Naturalists excursion for nearly a week and Edith described his absence to her absent brother Godfrey as:

'Such a treat to be without him for he is still unkind to us all. Adeline has been invited to stay with the Chadwicks at The Towers, Matlock, for a short time but he won't let her go. You can't think how cruel and horrid he is to us, you did the best piece of work in your life when you left him darling, but we *do miss you*. Papa never lets us girls go out together when we are here. He won't be left alone for fear he should want anything. We can't even go to see our friends, isn't he selfish?'

However, when staying at Rode Heath with their mother and their brothers they had more freedom.

### Reference

1. *Fragments from the life and Writings of William Henry Goss* by Eva Adeline Goss. Hill & Ainsworth 1907

# CHAPTER THREE

# The Family Grows Up

Children begin by loving their parents.
After a time they judge them.
Rarely, if ever, do they forgive them!

Oscar Wilde: 'A Woman of No Importance'

Despite the strict discipline and clashes with their father, the Goss children had a relatively happy childhood, living in comfortable homes in privileged circumstances, meeting many famous people of their time. They enjoyed many years as a family growing up together, before the rift between their parents later on.

The eldest, Adolphus, bearing his father's illustrious name within his own, was a good scholar and showed artistic promise. His name was teutonic and meant 'Noble Wolf'. He had inherited William's looks and features, and echoed his cold and businesslike manner.

He went straight from leaving school to full time work in the Goss factory, but never really achieved anything of note until 1880 when he entered the management at the somewhat late age of 26 years. William was only 47 years of age himself and as the years went by this age gap narrowed until they were almost like rivals. This problem was resolved by Adolphus becoming the firm's traveller. When the business expanded, his younger brother Victor joined him and they worked the British Isles and Ireland between them.

As a person, Adolphus was confident, upright, observant and shrewd with a strong personality. His principle was 'Make up your own mind and let nobody alter it.' He was a hard worker and enjoyed many activities in his leisure time, including photography, sketching, poetry and heraldry, all of which were to be vital in his career and in the progression of the firm and the resulting products.

Like his father, he was a heavy smoker and was not noted for dressing to attract women, unlike his younger brother Victor. Since they were childhood friends, Adolphus had courted the plump and friendly Sarah Ellen Dale, known as Nellie. She had been a school friend of his sister Georgiana and lived nearby at Holly Cottage, Smallwood, Cheshire. Her parents John and Anne Dale were close to his parents. Indeed, John Dale often used to accompany William and his sons on day trips and on holidays with their other friends the Jewitts in Derbyshire. It was always thought that Adolphus and Nellie would one day marry; it was just a question of when.

*Georgiana, sister of Adolphus, companion to her father, in 1878*

\* \* \* \* \* \* \* \* \* \* \* \* \*

Georgiana, the eldest daughter, was a very mature young woman, and we can see from her many letters that she was gentle and loving, did not care to criticise and always looked on the brighter side. Those who knew her loved her, and although, like her brothers and sisters, she suffered her father's temper, she did not complain about him to others. She was not entire happy to live quietly at Rode,

*The porcelain plaque made for Georgiana by her father William, possibly when at Copelands*

attending to her needlework, painting on canvas and satin, and took to spending long weekends with the Jewitts in Derbyshire. She was the best of friends with Adele Jewitt, and was very close to Adele's brother Edwin.

The Jewitts were a large and happy family, who were very relaxing to be with. They enjoyed life and stimulated the most interesting conversations. They held regular parties and tennis afternoons, at which were entertained the leading authors, poets and artists of the day. Their home was a hive of activity. Adeline complained in 1885 'Georgie is still at Jewitt's. She has been there 13 weeks today.' Edith used to say her sister more or less lived there.

Georgiana was very close to her mother and had helped her with the younger ones for many years. With her dark hair swept back and parted at the front, her curls reached her shoulders. She was a remarkably good looking young lady with a gentle and kind personality. An ideal nurse, she went to look after Mrs. Jewitt for many weeks when she bacame ill,and helped her to recover. She went back again when the old lady was dying, and cared for her until the end. Georgiana's family missed her company, especially her father, who had become accustomed to having her as his companion both socially and when walking. By accompanying William before her marriage she knew his literary friends and was intellectually accomplished. William had only been 22 years old at the time of her birth so there was not much of an age gap. She became particularly close to his friends the Stamers, the Halls and the Crappers among many, and joined in their charity work. Her favourite charity was 'Our Dumb Friends League', the badge of which was used as a Goss decoration.

\* \* \* \* \* \* \* \* \* \* \* \* \* \*

After emigrating to America in 1882, Godfrey wrote to his mother only three times during three and a half years. Alice, ironically, did not reply to his regular missives for the first six months, but she eventually wrote in January

1883. Her letters to him were cool and short, because she was practical, and not romantically inclined.

He suffered agonies when he wrote to Alice's parents asking for her hand in marriage and received negative replies. He sent their letters to Alice for her to read; she returned them to him secretly. He wrote to her in 1884:

'You were right about Adolphus wanting to break our engagement and that made me mad and I did not answer his letters he said you were noisy and not suitable for my wife.'

*Harriet Jewitt, friend Florrie, Georgiana Goss and Nellie Dale in 1878 on holiday at Barrow in Furness*

On an outing to Cloud Hill with the Goss works employees, Edith informed her brother that she could not help noticing how much plainer Alice Buckley looked compared to what she used to. He had three letters from England telling him that Alice was going out with another man, 'but I burn them as soon as they come for they are all lies.' Godfrey was furious at the sabotage attempts of others to part Alice and himself and this interference had the opposite effect.

Although William was displeased with Alice for her relationship with his son, after Godfrey left England he could not have been nicer. Alice, who lived with her parents at 2, Clyde Street, Shelton, Hanley, and who worked as a paintress at the Goss pottery, observed in a letter to her fiancé that 'Mr. Goss was having most of the decorating done at Stoke' and 'we are getting quite a large firm.'

Alice stayed faithful and wished her parents would allow her to go to Godfrey. 'If I could get enough wages to satisfy my mother at painting I should go somewhere else and then they would not know when I come to you.' She felt very uncomfortable working for members of Godfrey's family, knowing their opinion of the match, even though she was treated generously by William.

Godfrey repeatedly wrote to her parents, whom he had never met, asking for her hand in marriage, but they always turned him down. Alice's father wrote to him:

'You know that your father has been very kind to Alice on many occasions and we think it would be a great injustice to him not to let him know she was coming out to you as I am quite convinced he is cognisant of your attachment to her, and also that it might lead to a reconciliation between you, he is your father after all, and emnity between parents and children is a sad thing'.

By the following year in 1885 Godfrey was still at his wits end trying to persuade the Buckleys to let his darling Alice come to him, and also to earn enough to be able to look after her. He wrote to Alice:

'And if your mother still refuses to let you come you can come without her consent by starting in the morning, as if you were going to work and taking the first train to Liverpool and the ship agent would meat you at Liverpool and see you all safe on the ship and I could get Jane to tell your mother the same night and then you would be gon to far for her to fetch you back and besides your older enough to please yourself if I wait for the 18 months she will still require just the same so make up your mind to come Darling or you be sorrie for it is a shame that we are unhappy just to please your mother. I did intend to come over to England this year but I have lived nearly 4 months without doing any work and things are verry bad so that it is impossible for me to think of it I had to sell one of my horses to reduce my expenses. . . So chear

*Nellie Dale and Annie Hilton, school friends of Georgiana Goss, who eventually became members of the Goss family themselves*

up my Darling and rember the old sayend true love never rund smothe.'

\* \* \* \* \* \* \* \* \* \* \* \* \* \*

After Georgiana's marriage in 1886, Adeline took over her role as their father's travelling companion at the age of 23 years, Florence being too young and Edith not particularly close to him. She enjoyed his company and perhaps because she so rarely went out socially without him she failed to marry. She was attractive and always stylishly dressed, often in identical outfits to her sisters. The fashion was to have a waspish waist, with the aid of bone corsets and a bustle. She was mentally quick and alert, confident, businesslike and rather sharp with people; it was always upheld in the family that it was a shame she could not work in the pottery, for she could have possibly made an excellent job of managing it.

Adeline had an active, energetic, industrious personality, much like her father. Their long walks together; her weekly swim at the local Baths and cycle rides with her brothers, ensured her good health, this she never wrote about, unlike Nellie and Alice, who constantly reminded their friends

*W.H. Goss, bottom right hand corner, with his friends the Jewitts, the Fairholts and their children. Mrs Samuel Carter Hall is top left*

*The Gosses and the Jewitts playing at being servants. L to R: Llewellynn with a broom, William cleaning his shoes, Clara, Mrs Brittlebank, Adeline, Georgiana, Elizabeth Jewitt and Benjamin Brittlebank*

of their current state of wellbeing. She had a serious cycling accident whilst out with Adolphus and Victor up in the Pennines, one day in 1896. She lost control of her machine when going down a steep hill, hitting a low stone wall and shooting over it, landing in a bog. She spent two months recovering in nearby Buxton, and Adolphus believed that it was 'only the purity of her blood which saved amputation.' We wonder what he meant!

Adeline loved family games and dressing up parties. One photograph taken in 1891 depicts her as a Pharaohs' daughter; other photographs show the Goss and Jewitt families together playing charades in the back garden of Winster Hall, the Jewitts' Derbyshire home. The families are all dressed as servants, with William polishing his shoes, Mrs. Brittlebank wringing out a sponge in a bucket of water on a chair and Llewellynn Jewitt himself wielding a broom!

Adeline's 21st birthday was a memorable occasion, with her best present coming from the work force. It was a splendid photograph album with silver-plated clasp and inscribed '8 Mar 1883 to Miss Adeline Goss. Please accept this small present as a token of love from the work-girls.' The album contained a photograph of every female worker with their signatures appended. The factory had a party that day to celebrate her coming of age; she was a regular and very popular visitor to the works.

In March 1885 she attempted to decorate some Goss bag-ware porcelain:

'I have been trying my hand at painting in enamels and have succeeded very well. Father says I can have as many things as I like from the works for my own property if I like to paint them and the ivory porcelain is just the thing to show my flowers off well.'

There still exists a melon cup beautifully decorated with intricate green ferns, signed on the base 'E.A. Goss.'

\* \* \* \* \* \* \* \* \* \* \* \* \*

A Goss melon cup with blue handle decorated with green ferns by E. Adeline Goss

Eva Adeline, fifth child of Georgiana and William. She was to write her father's memoirs after his death

Adeline's signature on the base

*Victor Henry in his early twenties*

*View of part of the Goss home at Rode Heath, Cheshire, in 1884*

*The same view a hundred years later. This house is now 'Rode Terrace' and home to several families*

In their late teens, Victor and Huntley began to rebel against their father, with Victor yearning to go to sea and Huntley at one stage considering packing his bags and joining Godfrey, who was trying to start an enamel business in the American 'Potteries'; Trenton, New Jersey. Victor believed that if Huntley did join Godfrey, he would be useful because he had been studying the enamel recipes and had been making up the colour washes for the firm at the time. They comforted each other with schemes and plots:

> 'We are both going to leave the old man at the same time and maybe he won't be in much of a fix; but I guess he *will*, for he won't get fellows in a hurry who will stand as much rot as his own sons have done'.

His sisters loved Victor's company and were proud of their good looking brother. In 1882 when Victor and his friend Gyran Kirkham went on a cycling tour, Adeline described her brother upon his return as 'like a nigger in the hands and face.' When he began worshipping at Astbury Church in 1883, he made several heads turn in the congregation and a Mrs. Colyer even made enquiries about him as she thought he would be an ideal husband for her daughter. This made his sisters very indignant but he was most amused. He was so dashing, usually dressed in brown leggings and the latest fashionable clothes, and was considered locally a most eligible young man. He was quite unlike his father who wore a suit until it was threadbare. A young lad, now a retired stonemason, living in the London Road used to look out his window each morning to see what Victor was wearing for work as he strode past to the factory.

Victor was living with his father and learning the ropes at the 'Falcon' Works in the early 1880's but things were not working out. 'I don't seem to be able to 'hit it' with my Father any better than you did', he wrote to Godfrey, 'and I think that if I went home every night (to his mother) we should be able to agree much better, don't you?' He wanted to go to sea but William wouldn't let him, so Victor was purposely difficult. When his father finally relented, he worked his passage to New Zealand and all the family fretted until he was safely home again. He got back in April 1884 and recounted his adventures on board. The voyage seemed to have satisfied his yearning for excitement and the sea, and he settled down to being a traveller for the firm. William later sent the 1st and 2nd Mates and the cook from Victor's ship a present each as Victor had spoken so highly of them. Mrs. Goss hoped he wouldn't go to sea again and thought that her husband would 'be *much* put about' if he did. Adeline believed that her brother Victor had, by 1885:

'grown into such a handsome young man, but father is very nasty to him because Vic defends his mother as far as he can.'

He was 20 years old by then, but not in the best of health. He had an abcess in his leg which meant he had to take time off from work, stay at home and be looked after by his mother and sisters. He was more or less an invalid all year, and when he did improve, there remained a hole in his thigh.

Huntley and Victor went on a cruise to Rotterdam and Antwerp during Wakes week to assist his recuperation from the abcess. When they returned William gave Victor a year's contract to sleep at Rode, near Alsager, every night that year, and to work at the factory which Adeline thought foolish. Victor travelled to work by the first train in the morning, and went home by the fly (a light carriage). Their mother believed that their father intended splitting the two brothers up, and eventually he asked Huntley to move in with him at Stoke, leaving Victor living at Rode. Victor proved so good in management that his father appeared to be as afraid of him as he was of Adolphus being the 'Goss Boss', a name Adolphus used for himself which irritated William intensely.

*Huntley, William's youngest son, about 1887*

When he had regained his full health, Victor was once again instructed to go back 'on the road', and their father insisted it was because he was a first-rate traveller. Their mother believed that if Victor had not gone, William was going to send Huntley away to school, but because Victor had gone, their father took 'Willie' (Huntley) into the management at the works. He was 18 years old by then.

Victor again became unwell in 1886 with lumbago and another abcess, this time in the hip and sailed to New Zealand in April of that year in order to improve his health. His twin sister Edith was worried about him and had asked him if he wanted to join herself, Lucy and Mary Kirkham on holiday in Harrogate.

'Victor is so poorly again, the poor lad is so bothered with Papa, he is so nasty and unkind to him we asked him to come to us here for a few days. . . it would do him much good.'

\* \* \* \* \* \* \* \* \* \* \* \* \*

The youngest son, William Huntley, his mother called 'Willie' but he preferred to be known as 'Huntley'. It seems likely he was named after William Huntley of Huntley and Palmer's biscuits, a friend of his father's. Adeline described him to Godfrey:

'Huntley has just sworn an awful swear. He has an awful peppery temper. He is very fond of messing in the colours and makes all that are used. You would not know him, he has grown into such a great fellow.'

We know he was not very artistic, nor imaginative, and was probably the least suitable of the sons to have worked with Goss porcelain. He was, however, good with his hands and mechanically minded.

In April 1884 a neighbour's cat at Rode killed a dove Godfrey had given Huntley. He was so incensed he poisoned it and when the owners of the cat found its dead body they hung it up for nearly a week in their yard on a long pole. Huntley had a bit of spirit and he did not like others to get the better of him so ignored the dangling cat. He had obtained justice.

\* \* \* \* \* \* \* \* \* \* \* \* \*

Edith, Victor's twin, was another lovely redhead, and possessed her father's and brothers' temper. She was close to Adeline and the Kirkham girls, and they all used to hope one day to marry one of the local curates who made their Sunday worshipping much more interesting.

Although in the opinion of some, Edith was not as beautiful as Georgiana or Florry, she was attractive to men. At the Field Naturalists Excursion on 19 April 1883 which

*William's American niece, Mary Brown of Kansas, elder daughter of Sophia and Charles, 1882*

*Georgiana Lucy, fifth child of Sophia and Charles, taken in America, 1872. Note the similarity to William's Georgiana*

*Lizzie (Elizabeth Harriet) Harmon of America, second daughter of Sophia and Charles, in 1887*

*John Brackett Hurlin, the sixth child, taken in 1885*

*Charles Hugo Hurlin, nephew of William, son of Sophia and Charles, taken in America, 1874*

*Arthur Merle Hurlin, William's great-nephew when two years old in 1885. Arthur visited his Falklands relations in his old age*

she attended with her father and Adeline, Gwynn Kirkham 'followed Edith about like a little dog.' (The Kirkham childrens' father owned the Goss works which William rented). 'I expect he will propose' remarked Adeline, perhaps with a tinge of jealousy. That particular day was Beaconsfield's Day and all Conservatives wore primroses in their coats.

Like her brothers, Edith enjoyed cycling and eventually in 1892 was given a tandem, which she used with Victor or Adeline to visit Annie Burne in Manchester. This was a considerable 30 miles away from Rode. The Burne family were friends of the Gosses, Annie having been at school with Georgiana and Nellie.

Edith was obsessed with money and she thought it a blatant waste when her father took some of the family and the Jewitts on holiday in July 1885:

'Papa, Sis (Georgiana) and Florry are going to Rhyl for a fortnight. Pa is taking Mr. and Mrs. Jewitt with him. They are going tomorrow morning by the 12.15 train, it will cost him a fine lot of money for he is having a special carriage (first class) put on for them so they will not have to change at any of the stations.'

It hurt her that she was not invited on that occasion, for he found room for Ted and Beattie Jewitt for one weekend as well.

On another, sadder visit to the seaside, she recalled:

'Papa has gone to Bournemouth with Mr. Kirkham for a week, they went on Friday. Lucy is very ill and has been staying here for some months. She is in consumption and the doctor does not think she will get better, when she has been in Bournemouth another month she has to go to some mountainous district for the winter and then to Ventnor for the summer, it will cost Mr. K a fine lot.'

In 1890 her father took all the Jewitts on holiday again, leaving behind his own family:

'Father has been staying in Southport for a week, he took all the Jewitts down there, you cannot think what a sneak Ted is, so is Beattie — how I detest the family, they are a continual expense to him. I don't mean that Ted is poor — but you know how father is always giving such expensive presents to outsiders but never helps his own sons as he ought.'

But Victor once said sarcastically, 'And yet, forsooth, he would have been rolling in riches but for his children.'

* * * * * * * * * * * * *

Born when her father was 37 years old, Florence, known as Florry, was a baby when her father chose to live away from his wife and family. A very attractive redhead, she was clothes conscious and adored expensive jewellery, and by keeping in her father's good books, he showered her with gifts of that kind. Her sisters, Adeline and Edith, felt that Florry, being very close to her mother and the baby of family, was spoiled at her mother's home also.

In 1883 she attended Miss Brodie's school locally, living with Adolphus and Nellie in the week and coming home to Rode at weekends. In 1888 she was sent to boarding school at Colwich for a year but found the restraint unbearable. When she came back Adeline considered Florry had:

'Grown into a very handsome girl, but I don't get on with her like I do with Edith. Many people think Edith is much prettier than F. She seems to have more in her. Flo would just glory in a gay life with plenty of parties and you know father keeps up his old objections to dancing so won't let her go to any.'

He forbade her to go to the Lynam's party and not even to the Johnson's who lived at the local mansion 'Rode House'. Florence occupied her time painting, taking afternoon tea with friends, tennis, and the obligatory weekly rota with her sisters of spending a week at Stoke with their father. She was a good artist and her work adorned the walls of the family homes.

*Victor Henry in 1887*

# CHAPTER FOUR

# Just William

See deep enough, and you see musically;
the heart of Nature being everywhere
music; if you can only reach it.

Carlyle

However difficult William was to live with, he taught his family an appreciation of the countryside and seaside, taking them for long rambling walks, and for many holidays. Their lives were privileged ones, and they suffered none of the hardships that they were especially surrounded by in the Potteries; poverty, starvation, ill health and early death through the unhealthy work and lack of heating. They had time and the opportunities to study what really interested their father most — nature itself.

The seaside offered a never ending scope for nature study and they frequently visited it in winter especially at Rhyl and Llandudno. At the water's edge William found great wonders in small things that to the unenlightened mind were not visible. The more he studied and learned about nature the more he was struck with the wonder of it all. One of his poems on the seaside begins:

'Oh where can fancy reach or eye survey
Through all this scene, but joys and beauty are,
And wonders infinite.'

Holidays were spent walking during the daytime and writing in the evening.

He insisted that the sea gave him inspiration, and in his book *Review of Modern Science and Modern Thought*[1] he included reminiscences of his visits to Rhyl sands. He and his family gathered seashells and seaweeds whilst beachcombing, which they used to create shell and seaweed pictures, arranging them artistically on a mount and framing them for display. These were used as presents for friends and relations; Queen Victoria had made the hobby popular and William's study walls were lined with such pictures. The results were fascinating and showed a remarkable variety of shades and hues, and he said they gave him more pleasure to look at than rare works of art. He hung them where he could most easily see them and also taught his children to use fragments from their marine expeditions to decorate Christmas cards; gluing pretty little leaves, pressed flowers and seaweeds, twigs and shells into little miniature paintings. These cards were intended to be framed later by the recipients and it is disappointing that none of them appear to have survived. His shell pictures were displayed among portraits of eminent friends such as General Gordon, S. C. Hall, Llewellynn Jewitt, Charles Swain, William Fairholt and C. Roach Smith. William's study was a room dedicated to love and friendship and was crammed with souvenirs and memorials, as well as valuable antiquities. Adolphus wrote to Godfrey in 1886:

*A poignant poem by Adolphus Goss in his own hand, surrounded by pressed leaves, entitled 'The Old Stone Wall'*

'You ought to keep up your correspondence with your father and if you are hard up mind you let us know. Dad makes plenty of money now and you might as well have a bit if you want it for he only spends it on curiosities. The Stoke House is just like a museum now with mummies of cats and leather bottles, old swords, spears, pictures, old china, and ivory carvings and Egyptian idols etc. etc.'

After 1870 he spent vast amounts of money on ancient relics to put into his museum in his study at Ashfield Cottage. He made his friend Dr. McAdrine an honorary curator of his museum along with himself, and the doctor and his sister spent hours helping him and Adeline to arrange the exhibits. After his friend Jewitt's death, Edwin Jewitt his son, gave all the Jewitt treasures to William to add to his museum. William was able to announce in 1886 that:

'My museum is growing into a most important affair, having had all Jewitt's antiques added to it, and all his splendid china. It is now, far ahead, the finest museum in North Staffordshire.'

Almost the entire contents of this museum are now incorporated in the Hanley Museum, founded by William's friend Dr. Robert Garner, an eminent surgeon, who was a fellow member of the North Staffordshire Field

*Dr. Robert Garner, F.R.C.S., F.L.S., a fellow member of the Field Naturalists' Club with William*

*William's three beautiful daughters who accompanied him on his walks and who kept house — Edith, Florence and Adeline*

Shadows of the evening steal across the sky

*The potteries firing up of an evening*

Naturalists' Club and an intellectual of some note. William gave him a plain white unglazed parian wall plaque of Garner in bas-relief which his factory had produced especially, and in 1877 presented terracotta versions to members of the Geological Society. Coloured and gilded versions were on sale to the public after that date but today they are scarce.* Garner and William were quite close, and shared the same charitable interests in helping the poor, the widowed and the fatherless. Garner's daughter, Mrs. Lynam, became her father's companion for most of his later life, and enjoyed intellectual company, including William's.

A report in the *Staffordshire Sentinel* dated 9 February 1891, outlined Garner's life story and achievements. He was a native of Longton and had been a consulting surgeon for over 25 years and author of *The Natural History and Antiquities of Staffordshire*. Mr. J. Nash Peake, a famous local artist, painted a portrait of him to hang in the Museum Gallery in Pall Mall.

A keen walker all his life, William explored the Staffordshire, Cheshire and Derbyshire countryside far and near. He owned pocket maps of his favourite counties; one exists still of Staffordshire, with the various levels of ground coloured in ink in his own hand. He had his favourite well-trodden routes around his Rode Heath, Barthomley and Stoke homes. Looking at glass photographic plates made

* The white wall plaque, as well as a coloured version of Robert Garner, can be found in the Hanley Museum.

by Adolphus Goss, we noticed that Barthomley (in Cheshire) has not changed much and were pleasantly surprised to meet villagers who still remember the Goss family, particularly Geoffrey and Noel, sons of Huntley. Rode Heath is nearby and although now more populous, still retains its rural charm. William was a frequent visitor there and in order to see his children, but not his wife, would take them off into the countryside for hours on end. His other regular retreat was in Derbyshire at the home of Mr. & Mrs. Llewellynn Jewitt, first at Winster Hall, Winster, near Darley Dale, and later at The Hollies, Duffield. He adored the Derbyshire countryside, which is still just as beautiful, and on his lengthy hikes would exhaust his children and the Jewitt clan, but not himself. He admired Llewellynn Jewitt's father, Arthur, who considered a thirty mile walk short!

Walking was really William's main recreation until the last few years of his life when his walks were restricted to the boundaries of Ashfield Cottage. But for many years his usual daily afternoon outing come rain or shine would be to take some of his children to Stoke Station, board a train and get out of the city leaving the smoke behind them. The dirt and grime that used to pour out of the potbank chimneys caused considerable harm to the health of the local inhabitants, and a short life span of 40 years was common. The Goss family liked to halt mid-walk in order to rest and take afternoon tea. They had their favourite hostesses at each place they walked; it was essential to William that these hostesses be clean and homely, class did not matter to him at all. Adeline recalled how when these women saw her father coming up to their door, their faces would light up with pleasure as they were all so fond of him:

'In summer, a homely though dainty tea would be set for us in the garden, but in winter the cottage kitchen would furnish an acceptable retreat, being the only room with a fire in it. How charming is a scrupulously clean kitchen in an old-world cottage! The red-tiled floor, the quaint black beamed ceiling, the bright grate with its glittering steel fender, and the mantelpiece set off with all the tin lids and copper vessels of the establishment, worn to a dazzling smoothness by constant polishing. The old 'Grandfather' clock (always kept half an hour too fast), generally flanked by the family heirloom par excellence, the copper warming pan, shining like burnished gold in the firelight, and a few framed memorials in black and silver of departed relatives. A roomy settle covered with some brightly hued chintz, rush bottomed chairs, a rocking easy chair, table covered with marbled oil cloth, and a hearth rug made of fragments of all the garments ever worn by the family, and stitched into some semblance of design and with some regard for contrast in colour. Such a room furnishes beauty enough in harmony, and refinement enough in expression to satisfy the most fastidious if only the housewife be sufficiently impressed by the value of cleanliness. Happily, such homes as these are common among our rural population both in Stafford-shire and Cheshire and to take tea in one of them after an afternoon's walking always gave father pleasure. In his intercourse with these humble, kindly hostesses the true gentleness of his character was again revealed.'[2]

Adeline also observed that whenever her father was in the midst of rural countryside it was wonderful to watch his obvious appreciation and enjoyment of it, and was thankful that they as children were always willing and keen to accompany him on his expeditions, as he would not go on his own.

Whilst on his walks, whether walking or resting, it was his habit to remain silent for long periods of time, as though seeking inspiration for his work or writings. At these times his companions always kept quiet so as not to interrupt him until he had fixed the train of his thoughts. Then later he would be in a lighter mood and make jokes and laugh. A favourite local walk of his was over the Barlaston Downs, and he especially liked to venture out there when the heather was in bloom, and survey the beautiful scenery from the hills:

'What an inspiring sight it is to stand on one of these gorgeous hills and let the eye wander over miles and miles of undulating country covered with purple and gold. Purple with heather and gold with fading bracken. Not a sign of smoke, no more indication of human occupation than an occasional farm dotted here and there, who could imagine they were within a very few miles of the great 'ceramic' industry. I can never see heather without recalling my father's great appreciation for this enchanting spot. He would walk about with a look of perfect happiness upon his face, and often assist me to tie up bunches of heather destined to cheer some of the busy toilers in the town, whose duties kept them prisoners there, he never forgot to provide string for the purpose, for he would put dozens of little neatly rolled up pieces in his pocket before he left home.'[2]

After these longer walks he would be much refreshed and relaxed mentally and physically, and would spend the evening at home writing. A favourite winter walk was at Trentham. He liked to go through the woods to Tittensor and Barlaston and marvel at the changes the seasons would bring. In autumn he loved the golds, browns and shades of green; in winter he marvelled at the structure of the majestic trees, laid bare from their foliage. It was a great treat to his artistic eyes to study these forms.

In spring he would walk amongst the heavenly bluebells as though enchanted, and used to say the wood was 'carpeted with the blue sky'. In summer the bracken and rhododendrons had replaced the bluebells and these were almost as wonderful to him with their vivid shades of green. He was very grateful to the owner of the land, the Duke of Sutherland, for allowing the public access to these woods for enjoyment. In return he did not pick any flowers or specimens — not even a bluebell, as it was against the rules in Trentham to gather anything. Other good walks of his were around the outskirts of Leek, Wall Grange, Stone, and, in summer other North Staffordshire places further away, like Cannock Chase. In Cheshire, which he loved, he had many favourite spots, like the hills of Congleton Edge and Mow Cop, from where could be seen the thickly wooded and fertile Cheshire valley, and Wales, shrouded in blue mist in the distance.

It was during weekends at Mow Cop that he wrote some of his most important works. He made endless visits to Sandbach, and the Sandbach crosses of which he made a magnificent model, were of untiring interest to him. Adeline remembered on one occasion when they were standing looking at the crosses as usual, their attention was interrupted by two small boys having a fierce argument. They were urchins and uneducated. Eventually one of them turned to her father and, using him as arbitrator asked: "Maester, inner that God?", indicating the crosses, " 'e says it inner!" She could not remember her father's reply unfortunately but it was apparent to him that it was an example of sun worship of these prehistoric crosses in much the same way as others must have done in ancient times before their symbolism had changed. These ancient stones were a typical example of the sort of historical

*Trentham Gardens near William's home, where he regularly walked*

subject he loved to meditate on and research the origins of and write about. He also wrote a long article on the Sandbach crosses for the North Staffordshire Field Club Journal.

Apart from his writing, which is discussed more fully later, William's other interests were archaeology and collecting fossils, ancient artefacts and information relating to them. In his *Review of Modern Science and Modern Thought* and *Primitive Man and His Work*, he marvelled at the wonders of nature and tried to examine their origins. He was a leading member of the North Staffordshire Field Club along with several of his closest friends. The club had a much publicised annual outing which experienced members took in turns to organise and prepare a lecture for. On 22 March, 1882 it was William's turn and he chose Cloud Hill as the venue for this the seventeenth annual meeting. His lecture was a major success. He had researched and studied the area's rocks, coal seams, marine troughs and the chemistry of the air in the carboniferous period and his lecture was printed in the *Staffordshire Sentinel* three days later. In his sphere of fellow enthusiasts he was well respected for his knowledge. He was a Fellow of the Geographical Society and a Fellow of the Royal Meteorological Society and took a keen interest in observing the weather and recording rainfall. A friend, Clement L. Wragge, used to ascend Ben Nevis daily to compile meteorological records; the pair used to correspond, discussing tidal flows, air pressures and more

controversially, condemning Darwin's theories. William's letters to the *Staffordshire Sentinel* about the great eruption of Krakatoa and the volcanic dust theory were printed in 1884 and 1885.

The 'volcano' letters he wrote whilst on holiday at Penmaenmawr, another of his favourite haunts. What he most liked here were the ruins of the old sun temple, the Cerrig-y-Druidon. Other regular trips were made to Lee Moor in Devon and St. Austell in Cornwall. He often visited Llangollen, and this place featured in many of Adolphus's photographs taken on holiday. On one occasion William was the guest of the one remaining 'Fair Maids of Llangollen.' immortalized by Charles Matthews. She was then an elderly lady and passed away shortly after his visit. One of his companions in Llangollen was General Yorke who had his leg crushed at Balaclava. William also liked to roam the beautiful expansive sands at Rhyl and the adjoining coastline, describing these sands as 'pages of gold, all mosaiced with hieroglyphic gems' (shells).

His newspaper was *The Daily Telegraph*. He once said:

'I well remember those sheets being started as a so-called Liberal paper when I was a Conservative youth in London. I remember taking a fancy to it the first day of its publication, and remarking to friends that I found it more interesting to hear and watch the sayings and doings of the best intelligence of the opposite party, than to labour through more reflections and reiterations of one's own thoughts and opinions.

*Huntley, William and Adeline on the terrace at Ashfield Cottage, Stoke-on-Trent, in 1901*

*A view by Adolphus Goss of Church House, Barthomley, Cheshire, his father's holiday home in the country*

*A china cabinet at Church House. A Goss bust of Lady Godiva stands on a small table whilst the cabinet contains William of Wykeham, a jewelled vase and other favourite pieces*

As I have never found time to read two daily papers I have neglected all but *The Daily Telegraph*, which has been as conservative as I can ever wish, and as well written and instructive in the affairs of the world as ever.'

Other journals he regularly read were the *Pottery Gazette*, to which he regularly contributed, *Punch*, *The Reliquary* edited by Llewellynn Jewitt and *The Art Journal*, edited by Samuel Carter Hall.

\* \* \* \* \* \* \* \* \* \* \* \* \* \*

All the Gosses without exception liked their gardens, were known to be protective towards trees, and would give home grown produce and flowers to those they thought would most appreciate it.

William took a keen interest in the gardens at all their various homes and the grounds of the Goss factory were magnificent. Even when he no longer lived with his family at Rode Heath he gave instructions as to when the geranium plants had to be taken out of the greenhouse that Godfrey built. Adeline, who was in charge of that garden often did not agree on the timing and argued she thought it still too cold, but always complied with her father's wishes, if reluctantly.

From the 1880's William took on long term lease, a holiday home in Barthomley, Cheshire. This tiny rural hamlet resplendent with black timbered cottages with white walls, remains virtually unchanged today except for the nearby motorway. Church House, a large property compared to his other homes, afforded him peace and quiet whenever he needed it. It was just a train ride away and he would go there to see Paddy his dog for long weekends. In 1884 he moved to Bank House, Stoke, and he was still there as late as 1900; one of his daughters described the back yard as being the size of two square yards, so no doubt he took greater pleasure in the larger garden at Barthomley. Although the present owners have since altered the layout of the garden, remains of his winding paths of wood and stone with little steps that he was so fond of, still exist.

Even though he owned Ashfield Cottage, after 1870 he did not fully reside there until 1900 when he began writing his books. For some time during his life he owned three residences — Rode Heath, Bank House and Ashfield Cottage, and he rented Church House in Barthomley as well. The 1861 Census listed the whole family at 10, Stoke Villa but by 1867 he and his growing family were living in Princes Street, according to Keate and Ford's *Annual Directory of the Potteries and Newcastle*. The 1881 Census listed the Gosses living at Rode Heath, just north of Alsager, with the exception of Adolphus who had just bought his own house and was trying to persuade his sweetheart Nellie to marry him. To all these properties were attached pleasant gardens. Ashfield Cottage in particular was a sizeable plot of four acres of orchard and pasture, and William no doubt spent much of his precious time organising the layout with the gardener who he prevented from weeding out the wild flowers in the beds, as he did not like a regimented orderliness with plants, preferring to see them grown naturally in haphazard clumps, effecting blazes of colour from cultivated bushes to the neutral tints of the wild ones. Many consider daisies on the lawn as weeds and prefer to be rid of them but William described them in his books as 'babies of the sun'. Daisies were famed for all time in Burns' poem composed when ploughing a field. William compared his daisies to jewels that starred. No daisy rake was permitted on his grass! He was very fond of 'rayed' flowers like dandelions and forget-me-nots, and thought sunflowers 'simply glorious'. When studying the decorations on the porcelain he produced, forget-me-nots in particular are prominent, especially in his favourite shade of turquoise blue. They were generally known as 'Goss's gems'.

During one year he raised some abnormally large sunflowers in a corner of the kitchen garden. While they were in their prime, he sat beside them in a basket chair, smoking and telling his children stories, including the one about Clytie (produced as a Goss bust), and admiring the sunflowers at the same time.

The story of Clytie originates in Greek mythology, and is about an ordinary nymph who falls in love with the great Apollo — the god of poetry, the sun, music and love and all things wonderful. He could not stoop from his powerful

*The dining room at Church House*

*The rear view of Ashfield Cottage, Stoke, with Adeline, Elizabeth Kingston, Huntley and William*

*The magnificent lower drive and gates of Ashfield Cottage, now Sturgess Street, with Adeline and Huntley in the background*

*Ashfield Cottage today*

*Adeline in the superb gardens at Ashfield Cottage. The path led to the factory below*

position to love so lowly and simple a nymph but he felt a deep compassion for her. He showed his feelings for her by turning her into a sunflower, so she could always turn to him in adoration. The firm of Copeland began producing busts of Clytie in 1859; the *Art Journal* described the bust as having 'hair brought down so low on the forehead and the figure represented as if rising from a bud of the lotus.' The later Goss bust of Clytie is remarkably similar to the Copeland example.

William's study window above the front door at Ashfield Cottage faced the prettiest part of the garden, and the gardener always put the most colourful and eye-catching plants in that area. The gardener doubled the brilliance by placing pots of flowers brought on under glass, in between the existing plants in the flowerbed, and as the potted flowers finished flowering he would change them over with others so that the master could always see a pretty display and a good effect could always be maintained in summer. Those closest to William could see how much these little effects gave him pleasure and in the spring an extra number of bulbs was always planted outside his window. Daffodils and narcissi had a special meaning for him, as they signalled the coming of warm weather and sunshine. He believed the sun to play an important part in our health and happiness. In good weather he liked to watch the sunrise from the front of the house and view

the sunset in the back garden in all seasons and never failed to marvel at its effects. There are many references to the sun in his books especially *Review of Modern Science and Modern Thought*.

Letters sent by his children often described the flowers currently in bloom, the loveliness of the local woods, which wild flowers they had seen on their travels and the plants in their own gardens. Rode Heath in particular was often described as being completely covered with bluebells in the spring.

Adeline summed up his love of nature:

> 'In looking back over my father's life and thinking of all the joys and sorrows which make up the sum of it, there is one part, merely to think upon, lifts up the heart with gratitude. This is the intense joy he experienced from the contemplation of nature, because the Great Master planned His works so wonderful and so fair, and gave some of His worshippers enought light to appreciate and reverence them. This blessing was vouchsafed to my father in a marked degree, so it is impossible to over-estimate the amount of divine pleasure that must have been added to his years by the study of the elevating subject alone.'[2]

\* \* \* \* \* \* \* \* \* \* \* \* \* \*

William was a devoutly religious man who had a noble reverence for every form of life from the humblest to the highest and his doctrine was the primeval righteousness of things. The argument proposed in his books is that the human race ever grows towards God whom he worshipped through the laws of the universe. In his *Hebrew Captives of the Kings of Assyria* he confided, 'When groping in the dimness, I whisper, "Give me light that I may discern truth". He appeared to find light in his lifetime 'behind the veil'. This phrase was a favourite one of his; he used it often because there was so much he could not understand in the ways of God. He lifted it from Tennyson's *In Memoriam* and used it to portray life after death. He vehemently believed that there was an evident veil of mystery about death, and the fact that there was a veil existing gave faith to an existence behind the veil. As life on this side of the veil was such a blessing, he was inspired to think that death on the other side would also be a blessing.

He was a Protestant, but found other religions fascinating, particularly Buddhism. He thought 'Our unavoidable deaths, like those of all other living creatures, are just part of the natural cycle created by God, and are an economy rather than a waste.' Atheists and agnostics were much the same to him and he had no time for either of them:

> 'While the Agnostic eats his orange, his pineapple, and his peach, he declares there is no beneficent design in their provision for his use. Yet when he was a poor

labourer he returned thanks for his potato, his turnip, and his cabbage, as blessings evidently designed for his benefit, and worthy of gratitude. Still more remarkable than the potato is the indulgent beneficence and its design in the richer gifts, and man's inborn tastes to enjoy them. And when you next look into the interior of an orange, behold there the evidence of the design for the future production of oranges in the presence of the pip-beneficent design. Yes; truly Allah is Allah.'[1]

His books were written in this poetic way because of his glorious feeling for God and nature. He had instructed his children to leave a little joy with the people they met, through some kind word or deed. It cost nothing, but meant so much, and how fuller their lives would be, spreading love to all the people they met. Adeline asked:

'How can people say that the world is growing worse? My father never thought so, and he was able to speak from actual experience, for he came into contact with so many people. I often think how much good he must have done during his life, even if the magic power of his love and kindness had only touched those of his fellows who had worked for him.[2]

His conclusion of life written the year before he died was:

'Life, with all its drawbacks, is worth living, and that to have been born in a civilised country in the nineteenth century is a boon for which a man can never be sufficiently thankful. Some may find it otherwise through no fault of their own; more by their own fault; but the majority of men and women may lead useful, honourable, and on the whole fairly happy lives, if they will act on the maxim which I have always endeavoured, however imperfectly, to follow — FEAR NOTHING; MAKE THE BEST OF EVERY-THING.'[1]

He believed the Bible to be a wonderful book, and as an evolution of a very early civilisation truly marvellous, but thought mistakes could have occurred in the text over the hundreds of centuries the Bible has survived. He disagreed with Darwin's theory that man descended from apes, but argued that man evolved from the giants which once haunted this planet, along with dinosaurs and other extinct gigantic creatures.

To love one's neighbour as one's self, was, in his opinion, progressing towards Godhood. He was very much against slavery and often took part in local debates on the subject. His argument was that negro slaves, given education and the same benefits as white people, would become just as capable; that it might take a generation or two, but it could be done. He later befriended two upper class negresses who spoke perfect English, French and German. Their singing and playing in his drawing room impressed him and he found their appreciation of works of art that of connoisseurs. He had this to say on slavery:

'It is my belief in time the negro will grow revengeful against the children of his old masters, and resentful of the contempt of the children of his deliverers, and will ultimately claim and seize a part of the New World for an Empire of his own; and may prove a formidable neighbour; and turn the tables upon the race of his old masters. I believe that Providence controls all things and turns all events to ultimate right and good; and this may possibly be the providential outcome of the cruel wrongs done to the African when he was torn from his home, dark as that home was, and sold into slavery in regions of light — all his blood and bone and sinew and brain — for money.'[2]

As a Conservative, he believed people should receive their just deserts; if a person wanted something badly enough, then he should have to work for it. He opposed the left inclined newly-elected M.P. for Stoke-on-Trent, Dr. Kenealy, and had this letter published in the local newspaper to express his views and to expose the impossibilities of what was virtually Communism:

'A woman who manufactures certain articles used by potters, made a call upon one of her customers for an order. I happened to be calling upon the potter who was my friend, and I overheard what follows. On passing out through the warehouse her glance lighted upon some parian bust, when she observed to her customer, 'I reckon yer mane that theer fur a statue of Kenealy?'
" 'No,' he replied; 'I don't make one. Are you a Kenealyite?'
" 'I *arm*,' emphatically. 'What art thay?'
" 'That's coming to close quarters. I suppose you are for Magna Charter, then?'
" 'I *arm* .'
" 'What is Magna Charta; can you tell me?'
" 'The lady paused a moment and replied, 'I dunna exactly know; but I reckon its summat fur us aw bay on a level; an' its time it wur so. Look at that youth (the then Prince of Wales) stuffin' (etc.) out ther i' Indy at our expense. An' as to his mother I'd bring her down to the washing jow' raght sharp if I'd my wey.'
" 'Then I suppose you are not in favour of the aristocracy?'
" 'I anna!' with excitement. 'If I mun rule I'd jest have aw ther yeds cut off sharp.'
" 'Then you're for having all *level*.'
" 'I *arm*.'
" 'After some further remarks, a little astray, the customer asked, 'Is business pretty good with you?'
" 'Pretty tidy, I reckon.'
" 'I suppose you've done pretty well at it, on the whole?'
" 'Well, I've managed save jest a little property — jest two or thre' little housen principly, and I've had tur work fur it.'
" 'Well,' he replied, I've worked hard for it too; but I have not managed to get any houses yet. As we should

all be level, suppose you divide yours with me?'

" 'Git out!' replied the lady, 'you're a 'aving mey on!' and departed, casting another doubting glance at the bust which she had mistaken for that of her hero.

"Such are the people who read this kind of literature, and such are the effects of this kind of literature upon the people, who, but for it, and better guided, would be happy, loyal and contented with their own prosperity. At the same time other demagogues, both petticoated and trousered, are preaching to those women that they should, and shall, have a vote in the managment of imperial affairs.'

William was a perfectionist who suffered neither fools nor dishonesty in any form. Staff who could not keep up standards were not with him long. In a letter to Godfrey in 1883 Adolphus told him, 'Our father has sacked old George Till and John Stubbs is firing the kilns now.' Any slovenly workmanship upset their boss because he was such a perfectionist himself.

As a local magistrate he was used to judging others and doling out punishment. He believed it did not matter what their station was in life or to which family they belonged as each individual had his or her appointed work be it physical or mental. If they did not conscientiously carry out their allotted work then they would have to account for it in some future life in heaven. This doctrine of the dignity of labour must have seemed terrifying for the simple, uneducated work folk and he certainly pressed the point home to them. He would say that it was a crime to be idle and doing no good to anyone, and that one day, sooner or later, they would have to answer for it and make amends for the wasted time and opportunities missed. It is noticeable that most of his men stayed with him for the whole of their careers. Apprenticeships started at about 13 years of age, lasting for seven years. Sometimes pottery artists received their art college education in the evening after a full day's work. Life was certainly much harder for an employee in those days, but life with William was not as unpleasant as with some other masters. It is strange, therefore, that he was so difficult to live with at home. He treated his daughters fairly well, but his sons often found life with him unbearable, and his wife put up with a great deal. He appeared to be kinder to his work force than he was to his own family.

Although he was always reserved in manner, William did not think of himself as being superior to his workers, and indeed, often kept their company. His rule was the 'golden rule of love' and it was said by Adeline that his work force gained their greatest pleasure out of pleasing him. However, anyone working for him who failed to keep these standards was sent for with the likelihood of a severe reprimand. If the same person was sent to him a second time it would mean being threatened with dismissal and a third time would certainly be the end. It was not known to happen very often because he was very careful whom he would employ in the first place. He strived to encourage

good relations with his workers. He was a remarkable man in his time, when a lack of factory rules and regulations led many unscrupulous employers to exploit their unfortunate work force. But William looked upon his employees as his mutual helpers and as friends. It was considered that this personal benevolence on the factory floor was not duplicated in any of the other potteries at the time. Those workers who had worked elsewhere before joining Goss said how much nicer it was to work for him and how kind and generous he was. Adeline described her father as:

'having an affectionate interest and sympathy for those dependant on him, and from the employees, a love returned which found expression in their best efforts in his service. It was always thus throughout all the forty-eight years during which he employed labour, and so he was always able to secure people for his service whose characters were irreproachable, and whose daily lives were high examples of pure living.'[2]

He liked to get to know his own people, and in some cases he employed all the working members of a family which meant that he got to know them all very well indeed, further cementing the bond of friendship. Examples of this were the Myatt and Mollart families among many.

* * * * * * * * * * * * *

William could never bear to see animals being ill-treated or suffering unnecessarily. It troubled him to see the pain animals experienced when being slaughtered for food and once tried to draw attention to it publicly and to get slaughterhouses to use an anaesthetic on the animals beforehand. He was joined in this venture by Sir. W. Fergusson and Lady Burdett-Coutts. They succeeded in causing much public discussion about it in the press at the time, but were unsuccessful in making the slaughterers change their methods, and so the animals continued to suffer. He often saw cruelty around him, especially in the market places where live hens were laid out in bundles, tied by the legs and smaller varieties of poultry were crowded into tiny baskets with no room to move. He disliked seeing dogs chained up with no water, especially on hot days and treated his own dog, Paddy, as a friend, taking him with him on the train and out for walks, attributing to him human characteristics and a personality of his own. His love of animals extended to a respect and understanding of insect life, and if he ever saw flies, moths etc. in difficulty, perhaps drowning in a puddle, he would interrupt whatever he was doing and attempt to save the wretched insects. He never destroyed life but preserved it when possible. He daily inspected his rain water butts to check nothing was trapped in them. Adeline once caught him with a bee in a rain tub, appearing to be trying to drown it! However, she found he was giving it a wash to get rid of the stickiness on its wings — it had fallen into his jam pot! He succeeded in his task and the bee later flew off. Many of his letters describe events he witnessed with tiny insects and animals, explaining reasons for the ways they behave. One day he found a spider in the wash-hand bowl in his office at the Goss works. He always kept it filled with fresh water and so would have felt responsible if anything had drowned in it, such as this particular spider:

'I never hurt spiders wilfully, but often rescue them from drowning; and know something of their ways. The other day I saved one and was rewarded. I found her in the wash-hand bowl of my office, apparently drowned in the clear water with which the bowl was supplied ready for use. But I know their ways. She had all her eight eyes upon me while pretending to be dead. I lifted her out tenderly and placed her on a little shelf outside the door in the open air.'

He watched the creature run along the shelf when suddenly, out from behind a web leapt another spider whose home it was. He believed angry words were exchanged between the spiders, but he could not hear them. Although the intruding spider was twice the size of the owner of the web, it jumped off the shelf when the smaller one snapped at it, just in the same way as big dogs run away from smaller dogs when they know they are in the wrong. He could see the fun in this incident and insisted:

'That little shelf was *mine*, and did not belong to the spider. I believe I fixed that shelf about twenty years ago, with my own hands. I am sure it is mine.'

His moral in this tale was that we humans all lay claim to our various little territories on God's planet, and yet the land also belongs to other creatures who also mark out their own boundaries.

He did not agree with the way collieries treated the draught-horses which pulled the coal carts. Where he lived in Stoke he saw many, and it was known for these horses to sometimes collapse and die in the street through the sheer weight of their load and the exhaustion of climbing hills. He often tipped a 'jaggar' or driver of these loads to let his horse have frequent rests up Hartshill Bank which was incredibly steep. If he saw drivers lashing their horses with whips, or tugging at their bridles to make them go faster, he would go over and plead nicely with them because he knew it had more of the desired effect than if he had become angry and lost his temper. He once knew a rich coal owner in the north, but they were not friends as he was quick to point out, who boasted that as a businessman, he found it paid best to overwork his horses and get the maximum out of them each day. Although this shortened their lives, and they had to be replaced more often, the coal owner found he gained financially in the long run. William often wondered what the poor horses had done to be condemned to that 'hell-upon-earth treatment.'

*Hanley market place. William scoured the local markets to check livestock were not kept without food or water*

Paddy, William's dog, preferred to live in Barthomley, his Cheshire home near Alsager in later years. He liked the country and would only suffer Ashfield Cottage for a couple of days before whining continually to go back to Barthomley. He was a real friend to his master, sensing his moods or intentions which used to quite startle William. Paddy would sit beside him on the garden benches, not on the ground, indicative of his elevated status in the Goss household. In his books William recalled some amusing incidents involving Paddy, such as his clairvoyance. William conducted an experiment with Kate Millward, their maid, on the other side of a closed door to where he was with Paddy. She was to perform a series of movements and he wanted to watch Paddy's reactions. In disbelief he saw the dog move and turn his head in similar directions as the maid moving in the other room. Paddy had not actually seen the maid in the next room, but Adeline had whispered her name in his ear. This to William was clairvoyance.[1]

On another occasion Paddy managed to escape from Ashfield Cottage after having had enough of it for one visit, and crossed the path of Joseph Myatt, a factory employee, as he came up the drive. Joe gave chase for two miles through a maze of busy narrow streets filled with traffic, but eventually lost him. However, Joe noticed that the direction he took was for Cheshire, and although the dog had only ever travelled there by train, and had not walked that way before, he clearly knew by instinct which way to take. The dog arrived at the Goss home in Barthomley in just over an hour, having covered ten miles.

Every time William visited his country home from Stoke he brought Paddy a present of raw beef, a treat for these occasions only. Such presents he carried in his little brown leather briefcase which he took everywhere with him. Inside were his writing materials and his latest manuscript, so he could work if kept waiting at railway stations etc, or if he had a good idea he wanted to record, when away from home.

Another of Paddy's loves was milk. Georgiana senior had never considered it necessary for a dog to have milk in his daily diet, but William used to secretly reserve half of his own allowance and put it in a bowl in his study where Paddy used to sidle up and drink it on the sly. Paddy died only a few weeks before his master and he was buried at Barthomley. His tombstone was inscribed 'For sixteen years a devoted and beloved friend in the family of W.H. Goss.' William often wondered what became of dogs' souls 'behind the veil'. We searched the graveyard of St. Bertoline's Church, Barthomley, but could not find Paddy's gravestone. It is possible that he was buried in the garden of 'Church House', their home next door, but as this garden has been altered considerably in the last twenty years it is possible that the stone has been dug up and disposed of.

Whilst walking through Hanley one day William spotted

*Adeline, Victor and Paddy before Victor left to fight in the Boer War*

a retriever diligently carrying his master's dinner from home to the workshop in a covered tin can which was swinging by the handle from the dog's mouth. Before he had delivered his master's meal, another dog rushed out to meet him and challenged him to a fight. The two stood square on, with clenched teeth growling at one another, until the bully dog slunk off. William deduced from this that both dogs realised that delivering a working man's lunch had priority over their brawl, however much they both wanted to fight.

Another favourite experiment of his was to use raw meat to attract flies, then watch their eggs hatch into the larvae and examine the result. How his wife must have hated such hobbies. No wonder he kept a lock on his study door to prevent her interference.

His penfriend Mr. Mark Wentworth Goss of Peoria, Mexico, sent him a pair of Mexican jumping beans which William received on the 15 August 1894. For well over a year he carried the beans around with him, keeping a diary of their movements. Jumping beans were being marketed in America as magical beans from Mexico, but they only contained a worm which caused the bean to move according to the movement of the worm. His obsession was so great that he interrupted his books, which were written in the form of letters, with continual reports on the beans, a fine example perhaps, of his eccentricity.

* * * * * * * * * * * * *

Despite his sober outward appearance, William had a sometimes wicked sense of humour. He devised many successful practical jokes during his life, always playing them on those he felt deserved some sort of punishment. For example, when staying at his Barthomley country cottage one winter in thick snow, he learned of a villager who had beaten his son for violating the Sabbath because he had rounded up the chickens and put them in a shed thinking they might die in the unusually deep snow. William also believed in not working on the Sabbath, but had common sense enough to see how sensible the lad had been. He thought he would teach this gloomy Christian a lesson. The following Saturday an extra fall of snow presented an ideal opportunity. William and his sons waited until the boy's family had gone to bed and then crept up to the house and completely blocked off both front and back doors with snow. This meant that the next day the 'Christian' had either had to miss Sunday church service — a sin indeed! — or dig himself out through the snow. The victim chose the latter but was heard by neighbours to say, 'He had no idea Mr. Goss was a man of *that* sort.'

In his discourse on *Magic and Gothic Magi*, he wrote a far-fetched tale but presented it in his normal prose and sent it to Mrs. Anderson who was completely deceived by it. Mrs. Anderson was the sister of General Gordon and she and William exchanged letters for many years. Her friendship with him was very formal and she assumed he only ever wrote factual essays and non-fiction. When he gave a copy of the tale to Adeline, she took it away and read it, brooding over it for some time because she thought he must have gone mad. Finally she realised it was a joke and started laughing; her father rushed out of his room and was highly delighted to find she too had been taken in at first, and laughed heartily with her at the joke's success.

William kept up a long tradition with his best friend Llewellynn Jewitt, of sending each other ridiculous letters. He kept Jewitt's letters in his possession until his death, so they must have meant a great deal to him. In a short note to Jewitt after going to a concert at Milford in Derbyshire in 1881, where 'funny little rabbits' prominently featured, he asked the question, 'Which is the most sublime couplet of the two?

'The bunny little rabbits
With their funny little habits;

or

'The funny little rabbits
With their bunny little habits?'

Jewitt, ever ready to enter into such nonsense, and indeed often initiating it, immediately sent back an extremely long, cleverly written reply, beginning:

*One of William's favourite walks at Barlaston*

The Hollies
February 24th 1881

'My dear Mr. Goss,
The question which you have propounded is one of vast magnitude and import; and demanding such extreme erudition to solve, that I approach it with a feeling of awe, and with a deep sense of my own utter unfitness and unworthiness to have been selected from among all the great and learned professors of the earth to attempt its solution!'

He continued in this way at great length and obviously enjoyed himself doing so.

An amusing story which William loved to tell occurred when he stayed at 'The Hollies' in Duffield, Derbyshire one evening in the 1870's when on holiday at the Jewitt home. He had difficulty in sleeping that particular evening because he could hear clinking buckets and chattering on the streets below. It was a Saturday night and he remembered thinking how stupid the housewives were to be out washing their steps in the middle of the night. He eventually slept, then awoke, to hear they were still at it and thought 'You Duffielders are duffers to be working this late.' He went back to sleep, awoke again, only to discover they were yet still busy with their buckets. He believed he had been asleep for hours but it was less than an hour when he awoke after dawn and found the noise still unabated. He thought he had better investigate so he stretched his head out of the window and had to shake himself in case he was dreaming. What he took to be a river was the street. The Jewitt's house appeared to be on the edge of the waters of Venice, but they were really the waters of the Ecclesbourne, which had flooded the streets of Duffield instead of flowing to the Derwent!

William liked to study human faces and behaviour patterns when in crowds wherever he happened to be, especially where he was unknown and would be unlikely to be interrupted or recognised.

One Christmas in his old age when living the life of a hermit, he was very amused at one of his sons writing a verse about his behaviour, in the form of a Christmas Card to him, which went thus:

'What can I wish for your Christmas-tide
And the New Year — close at hand — beside?
For festive fare you do not care;
From circles gay you hide away;
And nowt appals like ladies' calls;
You will not try through air to fly,
And so don't like the healthful bike;
But choose a walk and quiet talk
With darling Addie and willing Paddy;
And knowledge gain in field and lane,
By stream and pool in Nature's school,
You study too, ye Ancient Man,
And write about him all you can;
And prove at least, he was no beast
For fiercest beasts before him ran

And here you find my wish at last —
May those two volumes go so fast
That type may wear, and printers swear
Because they have to *work* 'so fast.' '

William framed and kept it, labelling it with Adolphus's name and the date, as he always did with anything pleasingly written or handmade especially for him.

Keen on riddles, the following were extracted from his ideas notebook, dated 1865, when he was 32:

Why is St. Paul's like a hay loft?
Because it rests on a stable foundation.

Why is Adolphus like a clergyman?
Because he is a Pa's son (Parson).

What celebrated song and plant is represented when a lady hastens from her dressing room to be introduced to company?
The Mizzle-to-bow (Mistletoe bough).

Why is a kiss in the dark like an Irish seaport?
Because it is a Sligo.

What great London Building was I reminded of when the beautiful Princess Louise accepted the heart of the noble Marquis of Lorne and yielded him her own return?
The Royal Exchange.

What is the difference between a gentleman who indulges in his bottle, and an impatient dog who is waiting for his dinner?
No difference. They'll probably wine after their dinner.

The King of beasts
at parties and feasts
Tho' in dress superb
a contemptible hub
What is it? The Dandy-lion.

William regularly received the magazine *Punch*, and he was on good terms with the editor of the day, Mark Lemon. Inscribed under Lemon's photograph in his album, William had written:

'Mark Lemon, in writing to me about a bust of Punch which I had modelled, said "The Head is Capital". Of *course* it was. All *heads* are *capital* . Especially Mark's.'

William produced a white parian model of 'Mr Punch' in 1861 which still resides in the London offices of Punch magazine.

One story William cut out from *Punch* and treasured was the following:

'A smoker short of a match to light his pipe approaches a group of comrades and says to one: "An yer onny matches on yer Mate?" "No; I anner". Then addressing the group the first speaker says, referring to the desiderated match; "An onny onyer onny onyer?" William noted that when this is spoken it sounds thus, 'Anonnyonyeronnyonyer?' and that those who spoke this dialect would understand instantly that it meant, 'Have any of you any upon you?".

William used to feel quite pleased with himself when he deciphered any of the local dialects, which amused him no end.

During the 1860's and 1870's, he had a series of letters published in Staffordshire and Cheshire newspapers, called *The White Elephant Letters*. The purpose of these was to speak up for the poor and needy. A satirical sketch by Linley Sambourne appeared in a Fleet Street journal in summer 1875, depicting William as an elephant with his tusks decorated with forget-me-nots. He thought this tremendously amusing and appropriate, reminding readers in his next letter to forget-me-not those about whom he cared.

When William first moved to Staffordshire he could not understand the dialect of the natives, and felt he needed an interpreter as if he were in a foreign land. Gradually, over the years he spent there, schools and railways began to change all this. Shortly after he first moved to Stoke he overheard two boys talking; one saying to his friend, "Ile githay slap chops!" the other replying "Grout; they wunner!" William managed to get this translated as "I will give you a slap on the face!" and the reply being, "Get out; you will not!" Although he had difficulty understanding the Staffordshire dialect, the locals naturally all understood each other instantly. Another example occurred when William was passing two cyclists who had crossed and stopped in the lane to gossip. One was telling the other that a friend no longer stopped at a certain public house, and the other replied, "Wizzygoo?" (Where does he go?")

\* \* \* \* \* \* \* \* \* \* \* \* \* \*

William firmly believed that people should live within their means, and he appreciated there were many poor though decent folk who, although they were honestly employed and never shirked work, could not afford all they needed in the way of food, clothing and rent. Jobs in the country were especially badly paid, but he kept a fatherly, watchful eye on his own workers, often adding a little extra to certain wage-packets if he knew they needed something. Laura Schofield, an ex-employee of the Goss factory, recalled during an interview with collector John Galpin in 1971, that her boss sometimes added a roll of Swiss chocolate croquettes or other delicacies to their wages. He once even added a few pence extra (worth so much in those days) to cover the cost of some new hair ribbon she had just bought and which he had noticed her wearing.

William was a firm believer in everyone saving a little each week to add to their nest egg for old age, but realised that those who had large families were unable to do so because they struggled to make ends meet from day to day. Those with whom William came into contact and who

were deserving causes were often given, or unconditionally loaned sums of money to help them out so that they could at least buy food and not starve. The only condition was that the gift should remain anonymous, the recipients telling no one. He did not always receive a 'thank you' for such generous acts, but his view was that 'if our part was conscientiously performed without hope of reward, the result in no way affected the righteousness of the act.' He kept all his charity work secret, and we have been unable to ascertain for certain which charities he supported. Occasionally his name appeared on subscription lists for various organisations' fund raising appeals, but he only permitted use of his name if this also led to the urging of other Stoke gentlemen to offer financial help.

William was very fond of visiting Hanley Public Park, and ever since his first visit there he wondered how he could contribute to its adornment as a way of expressing his gratitude for being able to ramble in such a lovely area, all provided free. One of his favourite phrases was 'Thanks are justly due for things got without purchase.' Eventually he donated eye-catching fountains and laurel vases, which were erected on the terrace in the Cauldon grounds, an area of Hanley Park, all in bronzed iron, manufactured by the Coalbrookdale Co., and set on stone bases. The fountains were eight feet high, with plinths ten feet in diameter, surmounted by a water carrier, with three merboys below, beside bullrushes and dolphins. The vases were six feet high, each was planted with palms arranged alongside columns which were included in the donation. One of his schemes to improve the world about him was always to take a full interest in and perhaps reward anyone who worked for him or any of their families and friends who showed bravery, honesty, self-sacrifice or devotion to some cause or person. He also went out of his way to pass the time of day with any tramps he met in the street, and to give them a little money. As most people avoided tramps, possibly even his words meant as much as any money to them.

William adored his own garden and took great interest in its produce. He loved to give away vegetables and flowers to those who had no garden of their own and believed it was beneficial to regularly pick the fruits because it meant that the bushes would bloom longer and redirect goodness to other parts of the tree or plant. William would pick bunches of flowers according to season, especially roses and sweetpeas, before travelling to the heart of the Potteries and distributing bunches of them to whomever he thought would like them, together with kind words. The 'courteous railway servants' on the North Staffordshire Railway regularly received flowers from the Gosses, dividing up the blooms between the number of workers at each station.

Much of the original Potteries have now disappeared and been replaced with modern development, but at one time the area was packed with rows of tiny gardenless terraces for the Pottery population. It was to this populace that

*Etruria Park, Hanley, providing some breathing space in the smoky Potteries of Staffordshire*

the head of the Goss clan sent out various members of his family with bags of windfall apples and any other excess fruits and vegetables in their garden, donating them to the poor in the streets. Fruit was particularly expensive at that time and William knew it was a necessary part of a person's diet. In her book about her father, Adeline recalled his many gifts to the needy, and how grateful most recipients were. A railwayman once told her that he was keeping the new Crown that her father had given him as an heirloom, and not even the direst poverty would make him or his family spend it!

Although he was free with his gifts to strangers who were deserving cases, he abhorred wastage and no-one in his factory dared waste anything. In his office he always re-used wrapping materials; string was untied from parcels coming in and re-used for parcels going out, and also for his heather picking expeditions. The backs of used envelopes were office notepads — indeed some of his notes still exist. We also found a note written by Adolphus amongst his photographic plates — written on the back of a used envelope! He was economical at home, always wearing out his own clothes until they were threadbare, very rarely spending anything on his own wardrobe. Yet he allowed his children to have any new clothes they wanted — within reason, providing that every time they bought material and had a new outfit made, they gave an old one away to someone less fortunate than themselves.

Odd rules like these may seem eccentric but upon reflection appear sensible and full of common sense, bearing in mind the poverty at the time.

He never wasted anything that could be of use to someone. Newspapers and journals, before being thrown away, were carefully searched and any interesting essays or articles cut out to add to his hoard of useful cuttings, or pictures given to children to make into scrapbooks or for decoration of screens. Any new coins from the bank he retained to use as presents because being so bright he considered they were just like treasure.

'And so on all through his life, he gathered up the fragments, and recognised his responsibilities to his fellows, as much in the little acts of graciousness, and trifling gifts, as in the more vital deeds of love and good-fellowship. And what a huge sum-total the often wasted fragments of kindness make, in a lifetime, when gathered up like this!'[2]

\* \* \* \* \* \* \* \* \* \* \* \* \*

William's standard for women was so high that few measured up to it. He had the greatest respect for Mrs. Anderson, sister of General Gordon; Mrs. Lynam; Mrs. Llewellynn Jewitt and Mrs. Samuel Carter Hall, and loved his daughters, but not, sadly, his wife. We can see from his choice of lady friends whose company he sought, that it was important for a woman to be intelligent, a good listener, to think before speaking and not to chatter unnecessarily, in addition to having good breeding and kindly ways. He thought that if women were as God had planned them to be, then they were responsible for the moulding of the minds of their children — the next generation — and for influencing their husbands, brothers and fathers and any men they met during each day.

His own marriage followed the pattern described by Freud of a typical 19th Century middle class union. William, in keeping with the narcissistic image of the great lover with his long romantic verses chasing his future bride, the conquest and then marriage, changed when he became a husband, to showing a lack of interest in his wife both intellectually and affectionately, treating her as a mere possession. Since Georgiana was property, she was expected to be inanimate, like many other wives in her situation; the propriety character of a bourgeois marriage conditioned her to be cold towards him, although loving and gentle to her children.

In his opinion marriage was a success only when the man was manly and the woman womanly. He discussed women and his fear of the emancipated woman in *The Life and Death of Llewellynn Jewitt*. His omission of any mention of his own wife could only indicate in his prudish Victorian manner that his marriage was not happy and that he did not feel he could praise Georgiana. Although she had been a dutiful mother to the best of the knowledge of other members of the Goss family and had brought up her eight children splendidly, William felt she did not share his interests nor did she earn his respect. Probably she saw little of him, as for most of his career he worked in the factory in the mornings, took his children for long walks in the afternoons, spending his evenings alone in his study reading or writing. This did not leave much time for her which undoubtedly made her bitter as she grew older. Their children mentioned her in correspondence from time to time as 'their affectionate mother.'

In a letter to Mrs. Anderson in 1892 he discussed a quote from his Shakespearian Calendar hanging on the wall above his desk:

'What a piece of work is a man! how noble in reason! how infinite in faculty! in form and moving how express and admirable! in action how like an angel! in apprehension how like a god!'

(Hamlet II, 2)

He wrote:

' 'The angel' smile belongs more to woman than to man. Woman is the prototype of the ideal angel; of whom and of whose form we know nothing; but we give him an ideal resemblance to the sweetest and most divine form of which our conception is capable — woman!'

It is just as well that he lived in the last century; his illusions of women would be shattered today!

*The polluted atmosphere of the potteries. William would send fresh produce and flowers from his gardens to those who had no gardens*

Although he believed all human beings were equal in this life, he certainly had strong views about whose company he wished to share and whose he wished to avoid. The type of woman who chattered unceasingly was to be strictly avoided: any meetings with such women were duly noted and no further invitations were ever issued to them. To listen to endless idle chatter used to shatter his tranquillity and render it impossible for him to think clearly, and therefore write, until he had time to recover.

The strongest form of love in William's opinion was the bond between a mother and her child. It amazed him how much work children caused their poor mothers, how difficult young ones could be, and how mothers devoted themselves to their offspring. He thought that unlike animals who neglect the weakest of the litter and concentrate on the fittest, women who had sickly infants spent more love, anxiety and cherishing care on them than they would otherwise have done if their babes were healthy.

A poem entitled *Women*, Adeline felt was particularly applicable to her sister Georgiana, as she passed away at an early age, but not before establishing a record of gracious womanliness. The poem was written by Samuel Carter Hall and published in a volume dedicated by command of Queen Victoria, to her grandchildren. S.C. Hall penned it to describe his friend Llewellynn Jewitt's wife's character, and yet it was equally applicable to her daughter-in-law Georgiana.

*Miss Neilson, William's 'pin-up girl', a beauty of her day*

## WOMEN.

Men are what women make them: Age and Youth
Bear Witness to that grand — Eternal — Truth!
They steer the bark o'er Destiny's dark wave,
And guide us from the cradle to the grave.

Away with women of new-fangled schools —
God pardon them — who would unsex the sex:
of all her natural 'Rights' make ghastly wrecks;
And let none rule who does not show she rules!
Shadow for substance giving — where they bring
A taint more deadly than an adder's sting.

Contrast! — Friend, counsellor, companion, wife,
Cherished for love, in this, and after life:
Reflective, prudent, wise, and sweetly kind:
A generous heart, a liberal hand and mind:
Giving a ready help to all who need:
Though to her 'household' first, wise and just:
Yielding with grace, and not because she must:
While she, of greater troubles, takes her share,
She treats the lesser as the garden weed,
To be removed, and yet with gentle care,
That flowers as well are not uprooted there.

Such women will be always in their prime:
Goodness is beautiful at every stage:
The soul is never old, and knows not Time:
For wedded love — in youthhood, so in age —
Is love that lasts through *all* a chequered life —
Strong in the sunshine as when tempest-tossed:
The husband found, a lover is not lost,
The Sweetheart still remains — a Sweetheart Wife!

Know ye not such wives,
Who to such duties dedicate their lives?"

Samuel Carter Hall

### References
1.  *Review of Modern Science and Modern Thought* by William Henry Goss F.G.S., F.R.M.S. & C. Vyse & Hill, Stoke-on-Trent.
2.  *Fragments from the Life and Writings of William Henry Goss* by Eva Adeline Goss. Hill & Ainsworth 1907.

# CHAPTER FIVE

# Friends and Mentors

From quiet homes and first beginnings
Out to the undiscovered end
There's nothing worth the wear of winning
But laughter and the love of friends.

Hilaire Belloc

William's closest friend for most of his life was Llewellynn Jewitt, a Fellow of the Royal Society of Arts. William modelled a gigantic bust of Jewitt in 1875 in parian ware, when Llewellynn was aged 59. A photograph of Jewitt in the Goss family album, taken in 1874, was the original from which the bust was modelled.

Three copies of this bust were commissioned by Jewitt, with a steel-plate engraving of one appearing as the frontispiece to the first (1878) edition of Jewitt's *Ceramic Art of Great Britain*. The bust is undated, impressed in upper and lower case across the back 'Llewellynn Jewitt, F.S.A.', with both bust and plinth impressed 'W.H. GOSS.' The sculptor, W.W. Gallimore, had signed his name towards the lower left rear of the shoulder .Although the bust itself is correct, the steel-plate engraving which appears in the *Ceramic Art* has been reversed, an unfortunate error. In the book Jewitt is looking to dexter instead of sinister and his waistcoat button is reversed.

Jewitt spent most of his years at Duffield, in Derbyshire, but in his younger days he went to London in 1838 to join Fairholt, the well-known artist, working as an engraver and artist to Charles Knight, Chambers and others in illustrating popular literature of the day. In 1843 he moved to Derby and started the *Derby Telegraph*, first as a penny monthly, then as a weekly. He then helped launch *The Reliquary* in London in 1846 before moving back to Derbyshire where he concentrated on writing rather than drawing. Among his best drawings was an architectural diorama of London from Hyde Park Corner to Aldgate pump. West End mansions were represented as 1″ to 1½″ height and the whole picture measured 40″ long.

Born at Kimberworth near Rotherham on 24 November, 1816, Llewellynn was the youngest of seventeen children of Arthur and Martha Jewitt. Martha was the daughter of Thomas Sheldon and was connected to the family of Archbishop Sheldon. Arthur Jewitt was the latest of a long line of Arthur Jewitts — all heads of the family for many generations. William recalled that many great ages were recorded within the Jewitt family.

Llewellynn's father did not carry on the long family tradition of manufacturing cutlery at Sheffield. When twenty-one years old, and at last able to make his own career decisions, he scorned the freedom of the Cutlers Company and started an academy in Chesterfield in 1793, after having first spent many years educating himself to a high standard in a variety of subjects. He also married Martha that same year. William considered the Sheffield cutlery trade as 'honourable' and believed it to be more worthy than his own pottery trade. He also insisted that Arthur had been perfectly respectable in serving his cutlery apprenticeship, according to the wishes of his father, until he had become of age and able to go his own way.

In 1813 Arthur became master at Kimberworth School near Rotherham. At that time Arthur was writing local guide books for Lincoln, Buxton and the Peak District, as well as books on geometry and perspective. Three years later his last child Llewellynn, was born.

Arthur Jewitt was the sole tutor of his children. William described him as:

'A man of remarkable energy and activity and stern firmness of will. He was also a man of strong constitution, and a despiser of all doctors' stuffs. Whenever he felt himself getting out of sorts, his custom, even in old age, was to put aside his work, have his saddle bag filled with a few necessaries of travel, mount his horse and ride away, anywhere, until he was weary, then rest at an inn, and so on for days, and sometimes weeks, until his health was restored, when he would return home.'

Arthur died in 1852 and his memoir appeared in the *Gentleman's Magazine*. His birthday was 7 March, so was his wedding day, and so was the day he died — at the age of 80 years exactly. He died at Headington near Oxford and was buried in the churchyard there.

*The Goss bust of Llewellynn Jewitt*

*Llewellynn Jewitt, fatherly friend of William Henry Goss, who, together with Samuel Carter Hall, introduced him to the leading literary figures of the day. Taken in 1874*

Llewellynn's eldest brother was the Rev. Arthur George Jewitt and he too was a literary man. His poems were dedicated to HRH George, Prince of Wales, and he also wrote, *Wanderings of Memory, Self Knowledge* and had many sermons published. Another brother, Orlando, seventeen years older than Llewellynn, and a clever and renowned artist, was the most famous wood engraver of his time and brought fame to the family. In W.H. Goss's opinion Llewellynn became an equally skilled artist and engraver.

Llewellynn was a diligent worker and to save working time it was arranged that his wedding to Elizabeth Sage should take place on Christmas Day 1838. They travelled back from the wedding at Derby to home in London the same day. He was so devoted to his wife, he insisted they did not have a single quarrel in their long marriage. William explained:

'They treated each other and each other's opinion, uniformly, with such loving deference, that they never differed to the extent of one arousing anger.'

Jewitt worked for many years at home, not completely shut up and secluded in his study writing, but in and around the house, always enjoying his wife's company. Even William concluded they coped well considering how most wives and husbands tire of each other's company if they spent their days as well as their evenings together. William recalled:

'I remember once asking him, in later years, to join me in some outing; but his wife was not well enough to go, and thus he concluded his letter in reply: 'I shall never go away without her. I have scarcely ever left her in my life and only then there was no help for it, and now she is so much more feeble, and we are both old together, we shall just never leave each other, but help one another down the hill we have had such hard life-work to climb. Thank you so much from us both for your loving kindness, which I feel intensely.'

Llewellynn's first book was written soon after his marriage. It was called the *Handbook of British Coins* which survived several editions and was the definitive work on the subject. He became an eminent draughtsman and artist, sketching for the *Pictorial Times, Illustrated London News, Literary World* and *Saturday Magazine*. He also contributed poems to these magazines.

One of his few short-lived attempts to keep a diary was in June 1845 when he spent many days at Buckingham Palace, preparing sketches of the various dresses, shoes, hats, buckles, swords etc. to be worn by the guests at the grand bal masqué given by the Queen; he also sketched the various rooms used. Because photography had not yet been invented, it was necessary for artists such as Llewellynn to make the wood engravings for the illustrations the day before an event was to be featured in a newspaper. Llewellynn strongly criticised the architecture and interior decoration of Buckingham Palace (to his close friends only) and was disappointed that some of the minor details, such as the brass borders of the door frames, were not fit for such a wonderful young Queen as theirs. He had such very good taste himself in these matters and in his diary he wrote:

'June 3rd — The Palace again. Here I have been all day in the midst of all the paraphernalia of royalty, walking through the rooms and ranging the whole place, almost fancying myself a king. What empty vanities these kingly titles are, yet how necessary for the common good of mankind. My loyalty has been excited both yesterday and today to the highest pitch by the sight of the lovely figure of our Queen. I have seen her two or three times today. She has been practising the Minuet de la Cour with the ladies of her court in the room next to mine. She dances well and gracefully.'[1]

Llewellynn spent the next decade travelling to sketch his various assignments, and in his diary he often recorded in detail the costs of the coach trips, meals and nights spent at inns, all for the matter of a few pence at a time. He wrote clear descriptive assessments of the places he visited and the people he met and often sketched and engraved for royalty and the gentry. His diary records that on Friday, 8 August, 1845, he was ready to go to Germany the next day with the Queen after she was to have completed the proroguing of Parliament, his task being to sketch places she was to visit. On Saturday, 9 August he recorded:

'The Queen is gone, but I am not. The only Rhine I shall see is a beautiful German model, from which I am making a drawing. At the prorogation of Parliament today, the Lord. . ., in carrying the crown before her Majesty, fell, and broke the crown to pieces. A pretty exposé for his lordship.'

Jewitt also worked on drawings for Mr. Pratt, producer of pottery meat and fish paste containers with colourful covers known as Pratt ware or pot lids.

Llewellynn Jewitt was well acquainted with the leading artists of his day, including writers and antiquaries such as Samuel Carter Hall, Roach Smith, Frederick William Fairholt and Thomas Wright. William made a bust similar to that of Llewellynn's of Samuel Carter Hall, as a mark of respect. He greatly admired Hall and his wife Anna Marie, and they feature in several photographs in the Goss family album. Everyone enjoyed Llewellynn's wit; William always said he was wit by personality and wit by name.

Much of Llewellynn's sketching during the mid 1800's was for railway companies, the newspapers being full of advertisements for them at that time. He inspected many newly invented locomotives, with an apparent understanding of the way they worked, and could add ideas of his own. The coming of the railways allowed easy access to most parts of the country, all within the space of a few years, and this enabled Llewellynn and William to travel

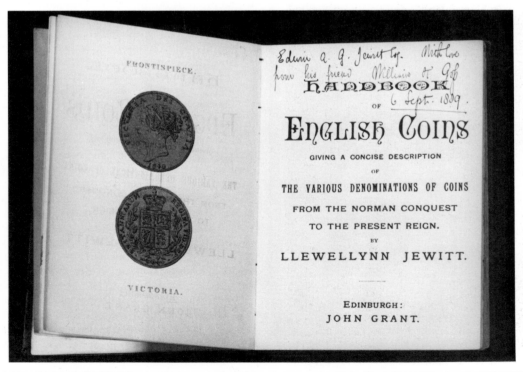

*William gave Llewellynn's book of coins to the author's son as a gift*

to dig up barrows, old graves and burial grounds. This appeared to be their favourite hobby and they made personal collections of Saxon, Roman, Celtic and Norman bones, coins, ornaments, flints and tools. Thus it can be seen why the Goss factory fell naturally to reproducing ancient shapes in porcelain miniatures.

After spending the first few years of his life in London and not really appreciating flora and fauna — in his own words Llewellynn said he didn't know how a cabbage grew! — he moved to Oxfordshire, then on to Plymouth where he accepted the post of chief librarian at Plymouth Public Library. William Henry Goss wrote:

'At once he identified himself energetically with the various literary and scientific associations of the west of England. Through his contacts with renowned historians with collections of rare books, he managed to get many collections donated to the library. At a time when Llewellynn could tour Yorkshire for three weeks for £2.4s.6d., he managed to obtain the William Cotton collection of rare books and works of art, valued at no less than £18,000 at that time, as a gift to the Plymouth Library.'[1]

Llewellynn like William, was interested in archaeology and toured the country giving lectures on the subject, following them up with drawings of his Celtic, Romano-British and Anglo-Saxon finds. When he was about to leave Plymouth, all its newspapers sounded his praises and expressed thanks to him.

*Samuel Carter Hall, who treated William like a son and financed his studies. Taken 1875*

He considered it each man's duty to enrol himself as an active member of The Corps. He said:

'It is a duty each man owes to his Queen, his country and his family, and it is a duty which each one ought to feel it to be a high privilege to owe, and a source of sincere pleasure to discharge. The movement ought to progress until there is not a man who is not perfect in the use of a rifle, and who is not thus prepared to defend our fatherland, our national rights, our Queen, and our homes.'

At this time he had been editing *The Reliquary* and also writing regularly for the *Art Journal* to which he contributed for nearly a quarter of a century.

His energy for life and work was quite astounding. His diary for 1861 and 1862 records his tasks of writing the history of various china factories including the Worcester Porcelain Works, Dr. Wall, Chelsea, Coalport, Wirksworth China, Salopian, Lowestoft and Swansea china. He also needed to see samples of the various factory's products, past and present, in order to criticise them; to do which necessitated the writing of many letters to the managers of the potteries.

Goss remembered that one of his friend's particular dislikes was the stupidity of pottery manufacturers in not promptly furnishing replies to his letters. An entry in Llewellynn's diary dated 30 March 1876 shows he feared missing out vital information in his *Ceramic Art of Great Britain* which he was due to publish the following year.

*The Goss bust of Samuel Carter Hall*

He recorded:

'Unfortunately I find some — nay many, of the manufacturers who are too blind, or too lazy, or too ignorant to reply to my enquiries. So, from many, although I write twenty letters to one firm perhaps, I really can get no response. It arises, surely, from a want of attention, but it is very awkward, and makes it difficult to get all houses in. I fear I may, quite unintentionally, omit some.'

In 1862, he noted that he sent 37 letters on 23 February, 23 letters on 4 February, 21 letters on 5 February and so on. William explained that Llewellynn could do the research and write-up of a factory's history all in one day, yet wait weeks for replies to his letters to clarify minor details. William purported that when Llewellynn was unwell that year:

'This invalid accomplished before breakfast what an ordinary healthful man would consider a fair day's work.'

Sixteen years later, in 1878, he published the *Ceramic Art of Great Britain* which included a laudable report on the Goss factory! He had studied every British pottery firm, reviewed its wares and recorded its history in order to write that mighty tome which was and is still the definitive work on the subject.

William Henry Goss received the very first copy of *The Ceramic Art of Great Britain* straight from the publishers, as a gift from the author. William kept inside the front cover of his copy, the letter from the author informing him that he was going to receive the first copy as a 'little gift' from him on his sixty-first birthday. When William, by way of receipt wrote to thank him for the book in November 1877, Llewellynn replied saying that he himself had still not yet set eyes on a copy, the publishers not being able to bind them up quickly enough to supply demand — so as author he was being left until demand had been satiated.

Llewellynn had shown W.H. Goss the rough draft of the introduction for his approval before printing, sending it by post with a note:

'Please look at and return the enclosed introduction. I could not let it pass without thanks to you in it. Others I give in the lump. You I heartily thank for all your help.'

William informs us that:

'The introduction here referred to was the 'proof' of the Introduction to his *Ceramic Art of Great Britain* in which he had rendered him some slight help. He would be at any pains and at a loss of much valuable time to search out answers to questions for me; he would thoroughly weary himself in searching among his rare books to furnish me with information, and if he could not accomplish the object in one day he would go at it again and again until he succeeded. Yet if I gave him some slight help in return, he never put his own services in the scale contra, and could never show enough gratitude and sense of indebtedness.'

Jewitt had amassed a personal collection of pottery samples during his research, many examples of which he gave away to his friends as gifts. An entry from his diary, dated 23 March 1862, reads:

'At Norwich. Started, along with Mr. Lucas and Mr. Norman, to Lowestoft at 9.30 a.m. Saw Sir Henry Tyrwhit's china. He gave me a cup with the arms of Potter. Saw Lady Smith, and staid some time with her, talking about the old Lowestoft china works. She is eighty-seven years old, and a nicer, more intelligent and attractive old lady I never saw. Saw Mr. Seego, the town clerk's collection. He gave me two cups of Lowestoft china and a mug of Lowestoft earthenware. Saw also the collections of Mr. Curtis, Mr. Browne, and Mrs. Johnson. Dined at the 'Crown'. Got back to Norwich at ten p.m. Very tired.'

'March 24th — At Norwich. Spent the early part of the day in sketching and noting Mr. Norman's specimens. Went to the Cathedral and the Castle. Called on Mr. James Mills. Saw through his museum. He has a splendid collection of antiquities. He gave me a 'mustard' Worcester cup and saucer, and a Bristol cup. He gave Mr. Lucas a beautiful piece of Spode ware. Made some sketches. Went to the Museum.'

His Lowestoft china article was for the *Art Journal*.

In 1864 Llewellynn was writing his *Life of Josiah Wedgwood*, having paid several visits to the Wedgwoods and receiving much help and assistance from the family. The book was published the following year in 1865. Son Herbert was taken by his father to the Derby China works to discuss his learning the trade. He later tried potting for some weeks and did not like it. Of the same china works William wrote:

'When the time shall come for the publication of my geological volume there will be found in that section of it which is entitled *The Constituents of English Pottery*, mention of John Mountford, who served his apprenticeship at Bloor's Old Derby China Works, and who remained there until its close. He then came to Stoke and was engaged as a figure-maker at the Works of the great potter Alderman William Taylor Copeland, and was the first to compound the porcelain body called 'Parian' and 'Statuary'. He afterwards returned to the Old Derby Works, or what remained of it, which was carried on by Sampson Hancock, and he is there still, a very aged man. A few days ago he called upon me in Stoke, and I asked him if he knew Herbert Jewitt. He replied that he remembered him very well, as they both worked together during the time of the trial. He speaks of him as a most amiable and lovable boy, who, while on his trial (apprenticeship), was employed in making little china figures.'[1]

*Llewellynn and Elizabeth Jewitt in the late 1870's*

*The Jewitt crest on a plate from their dinner service. This crest surmounted their family arms*

Herbert was the least successful of Llewellynn's children. Only three sons and four daughters survived out of the fifteen born; these children, Clara Adele Maud, Florence, Edwin Augustus George, Beatrice, Harriet, Isaac Herbert Sheldon and Llewellynn Frederick William have their photographs, taken in their late teens and early twenties, in the Goss family album, positioned alongside William's own children, demonstrating his fondness for them.

Clara appears to have been a particularly beautiful young woman, and there are several views of Florence including her wedding day and holding her newborn baby Florence Elizabeth Sibley Greene. William was obviously fond of his own daughter Georgiana, there being more photographs of her inscribed 'My daughter Georgiana' than there are of her sisters and brothers. Of Llewellynn's children, Herbert was the black sheep of the Jewitt family although not loved any the less. He longed for the sea and did not persevere at any of the jobs which his father found for him. He even ran away from home once, after an argument with his mother and sisters, but was soon found. Eventually he got his own way and signed on with the Navy, sailing in the 'Shackamaxon' for several years before becoming an officer. Whilst serving his first officer's duty in April 1869 on his return from India, he had an accident on deck and died hours later. William wrote:

'It is not possible to describe, nor, happily, to conceive the mental agony of the family at Winster Hall when the dreadful tidings reached them. When Llewellynn Jewitt read the terrible news his mind seemed to become suddenly dazed, and for a considerable time he was quite bereft of all power of speech, while the anguish depicted in his countenance was terrible to behold. His poor wife too — such a loving mother! — was struck with a dire amazement and bitter sorrow, most pitiable. So it was with all the circle.'

William remembered that Herbert's mother's hair turned from brown to white, with the original colour returning in the course of time. Only a few months after the loss of their beloved Herbert, young Llewellynn came home unwell one day, and despite being attended to night and day by a skilful physician, he also died'. Herbert had been twenty and Llewellynn junior twenty-three. They were buried together under one monument in Winster Churchyard. On the memorial card for young Llewellynn, his father wrote 'One of the best of sons and most brilliant of intellects.'

William observed that these losses stamped deep lines on the father's sad face. 'But', he said, 'it was a sorrow that further ennobled his already noble nature'. The youngest son Edwin later married William's eldest daughter Georgiana, a marriage which provided deep satisfaction for her father, but which met with disapproval from her

*Llewellynn Frederick William Jewitt, the son who died young*

*Florence S.A. Jewitt on her wedding day 17 February 1874, to Mr. Geo. Sibley Greene*

*Miss Harriet Jewitt, friend of Georgiana*

*Isaac Herbert Sheldon Jewitt who met an untimely death at sea. He was the black sheep of the family*

*Miss Clara Adele Maud Jewitt in 1874, also a good friend of Georgiana Goss*

*Beatrice A. Jewitt, the youngest member who became Adeline Goss's firm friend*

# Goss & Crested China Limited

*Return to:*
62 Murray Road
Horndean, Hants PO8 9JL
Tel: (0705) 597440

## PLEASE LIST YOUR CHOSEN PIECES IN ORDER OF PREFERENCE

| Month of Catalogue | Page | Item No. | Piece | Crest | £ | p |
|---|---|---|---|---|---|---|
|  |  |  |  |  |  |  |
|  |  |  |  |  |  |  |
|  |  |  |  |  |  |  |
|  |  |  |  |  |  |  |
|  |  |  |  |  |  |  |
|  |  |  |  |  |  |  |
|  |  |  |  |  |  |  |
|  |  |  |  |  |  |  |
|  |  |  |  |  |  |  |
|  |  |  |  |  |  |  |
|  |  |  |  |  |  |  |
|  |  |  |  |  |  |  |
|  |  |  |  |  |  |  |
|  |  |  |  |  |  |  |
|  |  |  |  |  |  |  |
|  |  |  |  |  |  |  |

Add Postage & Packing charge (see over)

## TOTAL REMITTANCE

£

☐ Tick box for your FREE illustrated catalogue of inexpensive wall display cabinets, acrylic stands and platewires.

☐ We offer INTEREST-FREE credit on all orders over £50.00. Please tick box for details.

WE TRY TO DESPATCH ALL PARCELS BY RETURN BUT PLEASE DO NOT QUERY NON-DELIVERY UNTIL 28 DAYS AFTER SENDING/TELEPHONING YOUR ORDER.

# EASY ORDER FORM

Simply tick the relevant boxes below, list your chosen pieces overleaf and return to:

**Goss & Crested China Ltd**
**62 Murray Road, Horndean, Hants PO8 9JL Tel: (0705) 597440**

*PLEASE TICK BOX*

☐ Please send me the item(s) listed overleaf in order of preference.

☐ This confirms my telephone order

☐ The maximum amount I wish to spend is £ _____

☐ I enclose Cheque/P.O./Cash for £ _____
**OR**

☐ I have paid to your National Girobank A/C No. 244 3252

on_____ the sum of £ _____
**OR**

☐ Please charge my Access/MasterCard/Eurocard/Barclaycard/Trustcard/Visa/

Diners Club/American Express No._____

Signature_____ Expiry date_____
(Overseas cards only)

**OR**

☐ Please send my order on 14 days approval

---

If any items are not available, please:

☐ Substitute identical crests or decorations

☐ Substitute identical pieces – crest unimportant

☐ Offer me suitable alternatives

☐ Credit my account with any surplus amount
IF NONE OF YOUR SELECTED PIECES ARE AVAILABLE,
YOUR REMITTANCE WILL BE CREDITED TO YOUR
ACCOUNT UNLESS STATED OTHERWISE

**IMPORTANT PLEASE COMPLETE THIS SECTION**

---

U.K. and Europe add £1.00 for postage and packing.
Australasia, N. America and other overseas, would you like your
order sent either:

☐ by SURFACE MAIL? If so add £2.00 per parcel
**OR**

☐ by AIR MAIL? If so add £1.00 per piece (£3.00 minimum per parcel)

ALL PARCELS DESPATCHED BY RETURN AT OUR RISK

MY NAME IS (Mr/Mrs/Miss/Ms) _____
BLOCK CAPITALS ONLY

ADDRESS_____

_____

_____

_____

Telephone orders accepted Monday - Saturday between
8.30 a.m. - 7.00 p.m. during the first week of every month and
between 8.30 a.m. - 5.30 p.m. during the remainder of the month.

brothers and sisters, who rather disliked Edwin and thought him 'a sneak.'

In his contribution to *The Reliquary* for July 1866 Llewellynn Jewitt mournfully recorded the loss of four of his literary friends all within three months. These were Frederick William Fairholt, Charles Henry Cooper, the Rev. J.M. Gresley of Exeter College, Oxford, and Lord Vernon of Kinderton, Chester. William recorded the family tree of the Vernons which was a long and noble line. They took the name Vernon from their estates in Normandy upon which they founded monastries. They came over with the Conqueror, and were ennobled as Lords of Shipbroke and of Haddon. He considered the fifth Baron, who succeeded his father the fourth Baron in 1853, as being unimpeachable for nobleness and patriotism. Lord Vernon was descended from Sir Thomas Vernon, brother to George Vernon, 'the King of the Peak of Haddon Hall', and father of Dorothy Vernon whose arms appear on Goss porcelain.

Mrs. Llewellynn Jewitt was very pleased with a paper William had written on an opening of a barrow in 1877 by her husband. William remembered that:

'we were having a happy picnic up among the Druidical rocks at Birchover, near Winster — or rather, a large party of us, all guests of Llewellynn Jewitt, were having a happy time up there picnic fashion — among the rocking-stones, the stone-chairs, the menhir, and various megaliths, when Mrs. Jewitt called me aside to sit beside her against one of the rude stone monuments, and said she wanted to ask a favour.

*The grave of Llewellynn junior and Isaac Herbert Jewitt at Winster churchyard in Derbyshire. This fine memorial is now the churchyard gardener's favourite bonfire site!*

favour. Would I send her a copy of the paper containing the account of the barrow opening? She liked it very much and would like to have a copy to keep for herself. Then Llewellynn Jewitt came stealthily towards us, and peeping round the corner exclaimed in his pleasant serio-comic way, "Look here! I've caught them at it. He's courting my wife here, round the corner!"

He was never more gratified than when his friends paid special court and homage to his adored wife.

William exhibited some of his better porcelain at Winster Hall, which was three miles from Darley Dale near Matlock Bath. Llewellynn had a high opinion of Goss's porcelain, describing it as 'eggshell porcelain'.

One of the pieces William exhibited at Winster Hall was his spill holder of Dr. Kenealy, the lawyer who represented the infamous 'Tichborne Claimant'. William spoke of:

'the talented and eccentric Dr. Kenealy, who for a brief time made a great noise in the world as a member for Stoke-on-Trent, and who styled himself 'The Lion of Britain.'

The porcelain caricature figure of Edward Kenealy was published on 5 November 1875, with leonine mane and beard, and is referred to in the following letter:

Durham, 28th October, 1877

'My dear Sir, (to W.H. Goss)

I received this morning the very happy account of our not very happy opening of the barrow on Hart Hill Moor, with 'On Arbor Low'. Pray accept my best thanks. I hope some day we may meet again over the burial mound of some ancient of days, with more success. Anyhow, urns or no urns, I shall be glad to meet you by a British barrow, or anywhere, except by the side of the pseudo-British Lion. I am glad to say that by this time I believe my 'British Barrows' is issued from the Clarendon Press —

Yours very truly,
W. Greenwell'

(The Lion referred to is Kenealy).

William and his contemporaries despised Dr. Kenealy; William would certainly not have made a spill holder featuring Llewellynn Jewitt or Samuel Carter Hall! There are two photographs of Kenealy in the Goss family album alongside a satirical sketch showing the figure of Kenealy with an outsized head and beard and the caption 'That's the sort of man I am'. The cartoon is signed 'Geo. Bernascuni'. The umbrella and top hat which feature on the spill holder are also included in this sketch. Maybe featuring Kenealy as a vessel for spills was William's way of showing that he thought he had an empty head! The two photographs show first Kenealy as a young man wearing his graduate's gown and secondly the Goss parian

*A Geo. Bernascuni cartoon of Dr. Kenealy captioned*
'THAT'S THE SORT OF MAN I AM'

*William's Kenealy spill holder in parian, depicting him as an empty headed vessel, which he called 'Dewdrops' because of Kenealy's dripping nose. William disliked this lawyer and M.P. and his left wing views*

*Dr. Edward Kenealy the defending lawyer of the Tichborne claimant who failed in his bid to claim a noble title and was transported to Australia*

spill head labelled in William's own handwriting, 'My Kenealy Spill' — with a few spills inside it and matches in the top hat held in the subject's hand.

When his unfortunate victim passed away in 1880, shortly before the Jewitts' removal to Duffield, Kenealy's death was only alloted two sentences from Llewellynn's pen when writing to William. These were, 'Poor Kenealy, I see by yesterday's papers, is dead. I am heartily sorry, for with all his faults and short-comings and far-goings he was a clever man. . ' This letter was dated 18 April 1880.

Llewellynn had a strong friendship with Baron Nicholas Casimir de Bougouschevsky, a Russian high in favour with the Czar and a member of the Imperial Archaeological Society, and with whom he corresponded regularly and affectionately. William enjoyed any contacts with royalty and was proud to report 'On one occasion I remember the Baron conveyed a message from the late Emperor Alexander II, inviting Llewellynn Jewitt to settle with his family in Russia, and promising to confer upon him an estate if he would do so. "But" as Llewellynn Jewitt observed to me, "what would be the use of an estate to me out there, with a climate that would kill me?" '

William did not meet Llewellynn until the latter was approaching middle-age, but enjoyed his company and friendship for the rest of Jewitt's life. Llewellynn wrote to William on 15 August 1882 inviting him and his daughters (with no mention of William's estranged wife) to a picnic at Birchover. William replied politely excusing himself due to his work, but accepted on behalf of his daughters. He immediately penned a reply, 'No, my dear Mr. Goss, it won't do at all! and we won't stand it! We mean to have you all three, and we will have you! There! Nonsense apart, we can't and won't let you off.' Needless to say William was persuaded to go and he doubtless enjoyed the outing.

William looked forward to his trips to Winster and it was always an adventure getting there. There were at least three miles of rugged country, all uphill, to climb before reaching the Jewitt home. In the Particulars of Sale when the Winster Hall Estate was split up and auctioned off in 1926, the 'old-world village' was described as being 2½ miles from Darley Dale, 4½ miles from Matlock, and 5½ miles from Bakewell Railway Stations (London Midland & Scottish Railway). We stayed the night at this house, now an hotel, in 1983 and were very sad to see how much it had changed according to even the 1926 particulars. During the First World War it was taken over for military purposes and used as a factory. Then, after changing hands a few times, it became an hotel. The delightful old panelled reception rooms with decorated ceilings having paintings portraying 'The Seasons', believed to have been painted by Benjamin West, a President of the Royal Academy, had been stripped and artexed, and the large elegant rooms divided with false walls to provide many smaller rooms as hotel bedrooms.

The Jewitts had entertained the author and traveller Hubert Smith, who was so taken by their hospitality he penned the following lines:

'TO MR. AND MRS. JEWITT

I enter'd through the pillar'd gate;
Passe'd stately hawthorn on my right;
And found the entrance door undone,
As if to show that I was one
To whom, by some auspicious fate,
Was ready welcome for the night.

The hall was deck'd with pictures rare
Whence to a panelled room I went —
Passing the staircase quaint and wide —
When host and hostess 'Welcome' cried,
And damsels Beatrice and Clare
Came in like angels heaven-sent.

I've wander'd through the garden's maze,
All toned with grey and mossy age,
O'er box-edged walks, down steps of stone
With feet of generations worn,
And distant woodlands met my gaze
As there I wander'd all alone.

When I recall the fine old Hall,
Thoughts pleasant will come with it, ever —
Of guests, with many a famous name,
And host, of even greater fame.
'Twill be with pleasure I'll recall
All here, from which I sadly sever!'

For most of his life Llewellynn rose at 5.30 a.m. and began writing as soon as he could, and retired to bed at 11 p.m. William always said that Llewellyn's general happiness depended upon the amount of work he was able to get through his head and hands, and expressed amazement at the remarkably long hours he worked daily.

Llewellynn had an enjoyable trip with William to the Isle of Man, then a fairly inaccessible place. They went with the North Staffordshire Field Naturalists' and Archaeological Society and were received like V.I.P.s with worthy mentions in the Manx newspapers. Jewitt commenced writing a book on the trip but never completed it. He wrote on his return, 'On Thursday June 12th, 1884, my dear wife and myself left home by the 12.17 train, leaving Derby at 1.55 and arriving at Stoke-upon-Trent at 3.05 where we were met at the station by our good friend Mr. Goss, and leaving the bulk of our luggage at the station, walked with him through the town (meeting his bright young son Victor on the way) to his residence, Bank House.' Later it continued 'Next morning, Friday, June 13th, 1884, we left immediately after breakfast, in a fly, for the station — Mr. and Miss Goss and our two selves — and left there in a saloon carriage, with a goodly

*At Winster Hall, standing: Llewellynn, Adeline, Clara, William, Mrs Brittlebank. Seated: Elizabeth, Benjamin Brittlebank and Georgiana*

party of the North Staffordshire Naturalists' Field Club and Archaeological Society.'

When Llewellynn's wife Elizabeth grew very weak and ill during the early autumn of 1885, young Georgiana Goss spent many weeks in the Jewitt household tending the sick woman and her presence cheered them all greatly. However, when Elizabeth Jewitt rallied, Georgiana returned home. Within a month Elizabeth grew frail again and lingered on her deathbed until she died in March 1886. Her husband was beside himself with grief and wrote to William begging him to come. He replied that he would and Llewellynn sent this acknowledgement by return, 'Thank you, thank you a thousand times, my dear Mr. Goss, for your promise to come to us in our trouble tomorrow'.

William wrote of him:

'For over forty years I have been happy and proud to call Llewellynn Jewitt my friend; a man who possessed a vast amount of rare knowledge, employed continually and invariably for the instruction and benefit of all human kind, as well as to the honour and glory of God.'

William's daughter Adeline, who knew her father's thoughts better than anyone else, believed that:

'A man may possess many friends, but there is always one, above all the others, to whom he gives his fullest confidence, and highest friendship, one, whose mental attributes and aspirations accord most completely with his own, and such a one, may be more accurately described as a soul friend. In 1886 a crushing sorrow fell upon my father, for the friend who filled this place in his affections passed away in the person of Llewellynn Jewitt, F.S.A.'

William mourned the loss of his best friend and missed their regular correspondence. Jewitt's family asked William to write his biography; he agreed, and this work was to be the only book he wrote which showed his own more private, personal side.

\* \* \* \* \* \* \* \* \* \* \* \* \*

Samuel Carter Hall first met William in London in the 1850's and they became close friends from that time on, remaining so until Hall's death in 1889 at the age of 89. He was a barrister and author and instrumental in furthering William's education and in introducing him to the right people. Hall was a good deal older, as indeed were most of William's friends. Hall's wife Anna Marie Fielding was also a celebrated author and came from a famous Irish family; those who knew her adored her. The Halls were very gracious people, who lived well, had high standards and were prolific writers, producing over 500 books between them. In William's biography of Llewellynn Jewitt, he took the opportunity to publicly thank his friend Hall for all he had done for him. Hall was duly gratified and the two exchanged letters about the book. S.C. Hall wrote in 1888:

My dear Mr. Goss,

What can I say in the way of grateful thanks for the honour you have done me, and the gratification you have given me, by the twenty-sixth chapter of your most beautiful book? Prouder I ought to be of it than I could or should be if the Queen had made me a belted earl! What a joy I received this morning. (The book). The blessing of God be with you, very dear friend W.H. Goss. I shall read it again tomorrow, being Sunday, and give thanks to God who has given me such a friend at the close of my long life. I will add nothing to this letter of grateful affection, but treat some other topics tomorrow. I am thoroughly enjoying the sea breezes. Ever your attached and grateful friend.

S.C. Hall'

William replied to him:

'I am indeed thankful that the boy who looked up to you with reverence in 1847, as his literary critic, and guide, is able to afford you pleasure in 1888 by means of his pen. It is indeed delightful.'

W.H. Goss'

William addressed his friends by their surname which was deemed to be the correct form in those days. Goss, was spelt Gofs by those who wrote to him, and he spelt it that way himself, in the mode of the period. Samuel, who was devoted to his wife Anna Marie, was especially pleased with the tributes William afforded him in the Jewitt biography because it recorded the Hall's Golden Wedding which was a public commendation for them. Literary men, 41 in all, who knew Samuel organised a committee to present a written testimonial to him. He was a charitable man, and with his wife started up many benevolent funds, one being the 'Florence Nightingale Fund' which raised £48,000, no mean sum in those days, as a memorial to Miss Nightingale on her return from the Crimean War. It was used to found an institution to train nurses, to replace the 'Mrs Gamp régime'. Samuel's father was Colonel of a regiment quartered in Ireland during the Rebellion. In County Kerry no man was hanged or shot during the six years they were there; this Samuel believed, reflected much credit on his father. Perhaps it was due to this Irish connection that he knew so many Irish jokes, and he often coloured his conversation with them.

S.C. Hall and other Fellows of the Royal Society of Arts were aware of the drop in aesthetic standards in the production of pottery. After the original genius of Josiah Wedgwood, more recent firms had declined in taste in general potting, with domestic ware hideously shapeless in the eyes of many. A renaissance slowly resulted from the later influence of the Prince Consort, acting through the Society of Arts and the Schools of Art. Improvement in style and beauty was encouraged among the main firms of Copeland, Minton, Worcester, Ridgway, Coalport and

Alcock among others. S.C. Hall, countenanced by the Prince, selected examples monthly of the most successful results of a competition, and illustrated and commented upon them in the *Art Journal*. Eventually this led to the more commonly used copied oriental designs giving way to classical and stylish patterns.

Hall was born on 9 May 1800, about the time when the two houses of Parliament in Ireland signified to the British Parliament their willingness to accept the provisions of the Union of the two kingdoms, and married Anna Marie in 1824. She had come to London at the age of sixteen, and married at twenty-four. They were both involved in fund-raising for Irish people including the 'Poor Clares' of Kenemara. Their first joint book was *The Amulet*, an elegant volume.

Alice King, the blind writer, wrote in *The Argosy* of Anna Marie's home:

'Mrs. S.C. Hall's drawing-room was one of those favoured rooms where a spell of ease and freedom seems always to be at work; drawing everyone that enters its beneficient influence and yet harmonising all into one blended whole, whatever widely differing elements may be there, men and women always looked their best and talked their best, and were, in short, their very best selves. In that room met all the wit and genius which, through more than fifty years, made the world laugh and weep, and sent streams of amusement and instruction flowing hither and thither in the land.'

Anna Marie enjoyed tokens of royal favour and received presents of portraits from the Queen and Prince Consort and a pension of £100 per annum.

Hall once said that at the age of eighty-two he had known personally nearly all the leading statesmen and literary men of his century, 'men who have been, men who can never die, for their works live after them'. One of his most important jobs was Editor of the *Art Journal*, a task which he undertook for forty-two years. Samuel and Anna Marie Carter Hall both lived to ripe old ages, with his wife reaching the age of 81 and Hall himself passing away in his 89th year.

Samuel and William regularly corresponded with one another. They often exchanged gifts, Samuel giving William treasures to add to his museum, including pictures, plate, family mementoes and presentation books signed by their authors. One of the most touching little treasures was a sealed envelope which, when held up to the light, revealed a small fragment of dried broom. On the front of the envelope Anna Marie had written 'From my darling Mother's grave, Monday, March the 9th, 1857.' William intended to keep it sealed. The last book Hall wrote was an anthology of poetry for children dedicated as follows:

'To my dear and valued friend William Henry Goss, F.G.S. & co of Stoke-on-Trent. Who has in many ways, augmented my sources of happiness and enjoyment in extreme old age, and who is emphatically the Friend of 'Little Children', I dedicate this book.'

S.C. Hall

* * * * * * * * * * * * *

*Left to right, Joseph Myatt, Fanny Slater (fiancée), Harriet Ellen Myatt (Joe's sister) and friend, probably a fellow Goss paintress*

Harry Myatt, 1879 - 1955, potter's caster for William Henry Goss

Frederick Myatt, a dipper for Goss

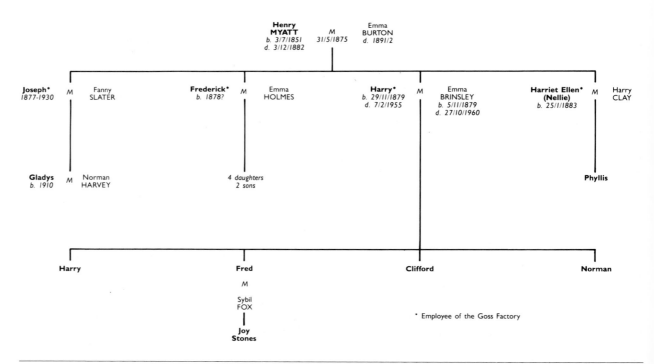

The Myatt family tree

Joseph Myatt was William's most favoured employee, having engaged him straight from school and been responsible for his training. They were to spend the greater part of their lives together at the works.

Years later in 1970, when writing to Dolly Harpur, granddaughter of William Henry Goss, Joseph's daughter Gladys Harvey described their friendship:

'There was a firm bond of affection between your grandfather and my father, irrespective of the great difference in their social positions. Mr. W.H. Goss was a man of brilliant intellect, wealthy, with diverse talents while dad was poor, orphaned at a very early age, with the responsibility of two young brothers and a sister, all of whom worked at Goss's as they grew older. Perhaps it was father's generous disposition, his ambition to work hard and prosper, his strict honesty and absolute integrity which appealed to his employer; at any rate he taught him the art of kiln-firing, at which he became most skilful. My mother's description of your grandfather was always 'a perfect gentleman' with which most of his contemporaries would agree'.

Gladys's recollections included the days when she lived in Ashfield Cottage between the ages of 5 and 20 years, some time after the death of William Henry Goss. Edith (Goss) Mountford often came to stay there with her daughter Mildred. Huntley Goss, for whom her father continued to work after 1906, frequently visited the Myatts with his sons Noel, Geoffrey and Jack (John). Jack she remembered particularly as he used to help her with her algebra and Capt. Victor Goss had a large red motor car and a huge Great Dane dog which the Myatts used to look after when Victor went on his travels.

The Myatts themselves once had a superb collection of Goss china which was highly prized, but Joe was such a kind hearted and generous person that he rarely entertained visitors without making them a parting gift of pieces of it, which he usually forgot to replace, much to his wife's chagrin, although they managed to retain a forget-me-not tea service which was passed on to Gladys. Even the Goss doll she was given in 1918 when aged eight was given away to an admirer. Joseph held the position of Manager, and was a dependable and reliable employee for many years until he developed appendicitis. His refusal to take time off work for treatment led to peritonitis which in turn led to an early death.

Myatt's wife was Fanny Slater who worked for Goss until her marriage, William called her the 'bright-eyed girl'. Joe's brothers Frederick and Harry were also Goss employees, Frederick being a dipper and Harry a potter's caster. Harry spent all his working life at the factory until it closed.

Their father, Henry Myatt the Town Crier, suffered an early death due to phthisis pulmonalis, which is Potters Dust on the lungs and his death certificate described him as a potter. His son Harry was only three at the time, and he did not even live to see his daughter Harriet Ellen born.

The whole family was left destitute; his widow Emma was shown in the Rate Book in 1886/7 as being exempt from payment. She remarried a man with six children and a love of drink and died in 1891 leaving four poor orphans. Joseph took his little sister to live with their maternal grandparents, the Burtons in Peel Street, Stoke, leaving Fred and Harry with their stepfather. Harry eventually grew up to marry Emma Brinsley, whose mother, also Emma, worked at Goss's sometime during the years when Joseph was manager and was one of the paintresses who decorated china with forget-me-nots.

* * * * * * * * * * * * * *

William's other favourite employees, both of whom predeceased him, were Thomas Boden, and foreman Joseph Astley. Boden was the maker of eggshell porcelain, the finest, thinnest and most delicate porcelain ever made, whilst Astley was a skilled modeller in portraits and artistic forms. 'His sudden death about 5 years ago was a great trouble to my father, and in the workshops he is greatly missed for he was much respected there,' wrote Adeline in her biography of her father. She also described other employees for whom he had affection. William Mollart rendered honourable and skilful service and was well respected by his bosses. He refused the office of foreman after Astley's death, and so the job went to his brother Alfred Mollart. Both brothers were taken on at the Falcon works from childhood and never found cause to leave. Astley's son, John W. Astley, also came to work for Goss. Harry Myatt worked alongside the Mollarts and was a particular friend of William Mollart. Alfred Mollart, a modeller for Goss for 42 years, was born in 1864 and died in 1924. He remained single, practised as a Wesleyan preacher and lived in London Road next to the works.

* * * * * * * * * * * * * *

Sir Lovelace Stamer's contact with William began when he was Rector of Stoke-on-Trent in 1858, the year after William had moved there himself. It was Stamer's most important preferment to date, and during that period until his consecration, he was Rural Dean and Archdeacon of Stoke for eleven years. He was born at York in 1829, the son of Sir William Stamer, Lord Mayor of Dublin and was educated at Rugby and Trinity College, Cambridge, gaining a 2nd class in Classical Tripos and a B.A. degree in 1853, proceeding to M.A. in 1856. On his consecration to the episcopate, his university offered him a degree of D.D. Honoris Causa. He was ordained Deacon of Lichfield in 1853, by the Bishop of Ely in the Cathedral of St.

Ethelfreda and in 1857 married Ellen Isabel, only daughter of Joseph Dent, and they had a son who later became Major Lovelace Stamer of the 16th Lancers.

In his album William had labelled his signed photograph of his friend, 'Sir Lovelace T. Stamer, Bart. received from Sir Lovelace 9/1/75' and this was printed by the Queen's photographer in London, John Watkins of Parliament Street. Lovelace went on to lead a varied clerical life after leaving Stoke as Suffragen Bishop of Shrewsbury, and remained in contact with William.

His wife, Lady Stamer, was a hard worker for local charities during her years in Stoke. In the early 1880's William's daughter, Georgiana, assisted with grand bazaars which Lady Stamer had organised locally. The Goss family donated many possessions to these charitable events. and the Goss girls tended the stalls.

*William made a porcelain plaque of Sir Lovelace Stamer, Bt., who was an important Clerical friend. Taken in 1875*

\* \* \* \* \* \* \* \* \* \* \* \* \* \*

One of William's favourite haunts was Biddulph, near Congleton, owned by wealthy landowner Robert Heath, D.L., J.P., C.C. who was the local M.P. and lived at Biddulph Grange, a beautiful Italianate mansion. William received a signed photograph from Mr. Heath in 1857, the year of his death, and as this was displayed in his album alongside his own family he must have had a high regard for him. We have no evidence of any friendship with Heath's son, also Robert, although this was a possibility. The father married Anne Beech of Tunstall, and their son was born in 1851, going on to Rugby and Trinity to gain his M.A. He lived at Greenway in Stoke and took over his father's firm of Robert Heath & Sons, and as well as undertaking magisterial duties for 30 years, he was also M.P. for Stoke after his father. The size of the firm can be gauged by the fact they paid over £11,000 in wages per week during the 1890's. In memory of his father, the son built a convalescent home at Llanfairfechory intended for the workmen of their firm, but it also opened its doors to other poor residents of North Staffordshire.

*Robert Heath, M.P. for Stoke in 1875*

\* \* \* \* \* \* \* \* \* \* \* \* \* \*

Inserted by hand in the front of some copies of *Review of Modern Science and Modern Thought* was the following extract:

'From the London 'Daily Chronicle' July 8th, 1895, DAILY CHRONICLE OFFICE, Monday morning.

As considerable interest has been felt with regard to the novelist 'Mary Anderson' we are glad to be able to reveal the identification of that lady, who, as already stated, is not Mrs. Navarro, née Mary Anderson, the famous actress. She is niece, by marriage, of General Gordon, the hero of Khartoum, being the wife of Major William Anderson, whose mother is Mrs. Wilhelmina Harriet Anderson, sister of General Gordon. Her first literary work was *A Son of Noah*, which quickly attained a great selling success. Mrs. Anderson was so much encouraged by this she wrote 'Othello's occupation', which has recently been published. The authoress has been much amused at the numerous paragraphs attributing these books to her distinguished namesake. It was to Mrs. Anderson, her mother, that Mr. W.H. Goss wrote his *Review of Modern Science and Modern Thought*, in the form of letters.'

Mrs. Anderson senior and William were constantly in contact with one another over a long period. William had, in his own library, ten bound volumes of her philosophy of life, all in her own handwriting. They contained some letters by her brother General Gordon, and also some watercolour illustrations. She had given these to William as a record of her life's thoughts, when she stopped writing a few years before her death. There is reported to be in existence a scarce Goss parian figure of General Gordon standing on a square base, although not seen by us to date. Perhaps this was made by the factory as a gift from William to Mrs. Anderson. A 190mm high bust of Gordon on a two-stepped plinth was produced commercially and was a successful line.

William described her volumes as 'a collection of sublimities' and treasured them. He also held in high regard some relics she sent him of her brother, such as the signed portrait of the 'Ever Victorious Army' of Gordon in the Tai-ping Rebellion and his silk Chinese Flag. She passed away in her sleep in November 1899 and the following day a parcel arrived containing a present she had ordered to be given to him. It was a pencil made out of a relic of the battle of Omdurman, showing that some of her last thoughts were for him. Her sister Mrs. Moffitt brought it to him, thanking him for the extreme kindness he had shown her late sister, and how much pleasure he had given her with his letters.

The shared philosophy of William, Mrs. Anderson and General Gordon, was that happy people were better than precious stones, or any other valuables. Instead of cherishing possessions people should cherish other people, especially the weak, the ill and infirm and the poor.

\* \* \* \* \* \* \* \* \* \* \* \* \*

Dr. J.S. Crapper of Hanley, a Doctor of Dental Surgery, was the founder and managing director of the Dental Manufacturing Company Ltd. of London and Manchester. He was a Freemason in Stoke and the oldest member of the Menturia Lodge, holding various important positions. He was also a member of the Board of Guardians of Stoke-on-Trent, and contributed to the provision of entertainment for the inmates of the workhouse including arranging and financing trips for them to Hanley, and dips in the public baths. He would also feed them at his home 'The White House' before sending them back to Stoke. The Doctor was a magistrate for the borough of Hanley from 1875 until his death in 1891 and served for several years as a member of the Town Council.

Besides being an occasional contributor to the monthly dentistry magazines, he published in 1876 a *Brief History of the Ancient Corporation of Hanley*. Another of his interests was attending science classes established by the committee of the Potteries Mechanics' Institution. Like William Goss he was a staunch Conservative and was one of the vice-presidents of the Conservative Club. Apart from sharing interests in science, history and potting,

William and Dr. Crapper possibly collaborated on the production of porcelain teeth, some of which were exported to Africa for natives to make into necklaces, supplies of the real thing having become almost unobtainable due to the abolition of cannibalism.

A young dentist working in Dr. Crapper's local practice later married Edith Goss, William's fourth daughter.

*Dr. J.S. Crapper, who manufactured porcelain false teeth, commissioned a series of oval wall plaques from William Goss*

\* \* \* \* \* \* \* \* \* \* \* \* \*

As photography progressed in the 1870's it became a new national hobby to keep albums and to send to eminent persons for their photographs. Many of the famous at that time were featured in William's album, including the politicians Earl Granville, the Rt. Hon. John Bright, the Earl of Derby, the Earl of Beaconsfield and nobility and royalty such as the Duchess of Sutherland and the Princess of Wales.

William Savage, a celebrated Winchester photographer and Goss's first agent, was an old friend and sent his portrait as early as 1862. On the back of this photograph which was pasted on to a rectangular piece of cardboard, as they all were at the time, was an oval seal printed in gold 'Wm. Savage, photographer, 97, High Street, Winchester'. Another print, also on card, had the Manners Makyth Man motto, on the reverse, as depicted on Goss china. The address is further down the same street, at No. 58, called 'The Wykeham Studio'. In pencil on the back 'With best respects, W.S.' in Mr. Savage's handwriting, and in William's, 'Rec'd June 1880'. The portrait of Savage was that of an elderly man, with a long white beard and an eyeglass perched on the end of his nose.

In 1836 Savage's parents opened a fancy goods and wool shop at 12, The Square. His mother was a competent

*A page from William's photograph album, showing Edwin Jewitt, Sir Wilfrid Lawson, the Earl of Derby and the Earl of Beaconsfield. Of both Earls he made parian busts and also a terracotta Keystone of the Kingdom of the latter*

knitter and the authoress and publisher of a book on the subject. Later they moved to 107, High Street, where they advertised locally as a 'Depot of Winchester Memorials' from which customers could obtain decorative needlework, sewing materials and fancy goods in papier-mâché. Their son became a photographer, establishing himself quickly at an early age. Later he became a publisher and produced steel engravings of his negatives of Winchester architecture taken over a decade. He sold these pictures at the local bookshop as well as his Wykeham Studio and next added china ornaments bearing brown transfers of views of Winchester taken from his own prints. On the base of each piece was printed 'Wm. Savage', or 'Made for Wm. Savage of Winchester', the Copeland factory of Stoke being one of his earliest suppliers. William met Savage when working for Copelands, who specialised in supplying Winchester Flagons and Bushels. Later the firm of W.H. Goss were to choose him as their Winchester agent. There are numerous Goss Models from this city, including the Winchester Bushel, Flagon, Black Jack, Pot, Quart, Warden's Horn and Font, as well as magnificent figures of the Trusty Servant, taken from a painting on the outer wall of the College Kitchen, and William of Wykeham, who founded the college in 1282, both brilliantly executed in colour. A letter Adolphus wrote to his wife Nellie in 1889 was on scrap paper used for an order from their Winchester Agent. The order was as follows:

*Charles Swain the poet in 1870, with whom William corresponded*

*William Savage of Winchester in 1862. He sold souvenir ware including Copeland china Jacks with Winchester motifs*

'My dear Father,

Please send me prices of —
s/s (small size) Winchester bushells
l/s Do Do
Figures of Trusty Servant
4½ plaques m m m and bust
s/s Winchester Font
l/s Do Do
Prices can be added to above and returned to me'.

It was never finished and the paper was turned over and used as a letter to Nellie. Another example of Goss thrift!

\* \* \* \* \* \* \* \* \* \* \* \* \*

Sir Edwin Saunders, for many years dentist to the Royal family, and William were more acquaintances than friends, but both shared the same charitable causes, Sir Edwin being a liberal benefactor of the public institutions connected with his own profession of medicine.

Inscribed in William's own handwriting 'Received at his house March 18th, 1876,' Saunders' large signed photograph is above a newspaper clipping carefully glued to a page of its own in William's album, announcing in the British Medical Journal that the honour of a knighthood had been offered to Mr. Edwin Saunders, F.R.C.S.

William rented part of Mr. Kirkham's pottery and grinding mills for many years. He and his daughters were very friendly with the Kirkhams' their son Gyran and girls Polly and Lucy, and for years they accompanied each other on trips to the seaside and for holidays. In October 1888 poor Polly died after undergoing an operation

*Sir Edwin Saunders, F.R.C.S. in 1876. Dentist to the Royal Family, he worked for charitable causes with William*

for some internal disease, whilst Lucy, the youngest girl, caught pneumonia and was sent to Bournemouth for the winter, and eventually in desperation to Switzerland as she was not expected to last out the winter if she stayed in Stoke. As we can find no further mention of her in the Goss letters we presume she did not live to see 1889. Sudden death in all age groups was an all too common occurrence in those days. Even the clever and wealthy Dr. Crapper lost his young son Norman who was found dead in bed in January 1886.

William made oval wall plaques depicting in bas-relief

*The Goss wall plaque of Eugene Rimmel, surmounted by turquoise trimmed porcelain ribbon*

*Eugene Rimmel, the famous Victorian perfumier, who purveyed his exotic perfumes in William's jewelled scent bottles*

the busts of the Prince of Wales, Oakley Coles, Eugene Rimmel, Dr. J.S. Crapper, Dr. Robert Garner and the Rev. Lovelace T. Stamer. These were people he either greatly admired or knew and loved as friends.

Eugene Rimmel was a perfumier who created beautiful novelties and scents, and was world famous in his time. His porcelain, metalwork and straw mosaic boxes were given a favourable review in *The Reliquary* in 1873-4.

*Dai Aberdaron, self-taught Welsh linguist, who could converse in 35 languages. Although a tramp, William admired him enormously*

*Mr. and Mrs. William Huntley in 1860. He was part founder of Huntley and Palmers biscuits, after whom William named his youngest son Huntley*

He imported Japanese art-work products and displayed them alongside his novelties and perfumes in his stores across Europe. His shop in London was at 96, The Strand and he was William's main customer for jewelled scent vases and bottles, sold in London, Paris, Rome and New York.

William's friends were very important to him and he carefully nurtured and attended to his friendships, often at the expense of his own family. His children frequently complained about what they considered was the excessive amount of time William devoted to his companions and there is little doubt that they were a major influence in his life, but by 1900 almost all these friends were dead and irreplaceable. After he became a recluse he would only see immediate family, his staff and a female friend, a Miss Marshall, whom he held dear.

## Reference

1.  *The Life and Death of Llewellynn Jewitt* by W.H.Goss, Henry Gray, London 1889.

# CHAPTER SIX

# The Educating Author

Those who most cultivate their intellectual powers should also be
most happy; for such persons not only attain the best temper of mind, and
the highest perfection of their own nature; but they are also the most
pleasing in the sight of the Divinity.

Aristotle

William Henry Goss was a prolific writer all his life, producing romantic and heart-searching poetry in his youth and maintaining regular exchanges of letters with friends on important topics in depth throughout his life. He regularly contributed articles to local newspapers and the *Pottery Gazette*, and in later life retired to his study to write his books.

His only published poem, in 1853, a book of 120 pages, was *Ralph and Priscilla*, inspired by his love for Georgiana, when he was a young man of seventeen, this mammoth work written in rhyming couplets reveals a romantic intellectual. This is a short extract from the beginning of the book:

'Since that auspicious day when Ralph was born
Full eighteen times around the spring of day
Had earth her circuit roll'd, when thus one morn
Upon his bed he dreamt: A garden gay
And beauteous he paced with happy mind,
The sun display'd most charmingly to sight
Majestic trees, and flow'rs of sweetest kind,
And walking by his side his heart's delight,
With love's surpassing charms, made joy complete.'

We have since found William's handwritten text of an unpublished addition to this poem, which he penned a few years later. In the front of the published poem, William had printed:

'While writing it, I thought nothing of the scrutinising eye of a literary public; I thought little of the public ever hearing its title, but went on writing, merely because I found happiness in it — as the lark delights to soar up into the heavens, and pour forth its strains of joy; — until it was finished, and had received the commendations of some kind literary friends; then I thought it might afford a few hours profitable amusement to some of my peers in age, and wrote *The Minstrel's Invitation*, placed at the commencement,

to which I now solicit their attention, trusting, that after these preliminary remarks they will not be disappointed.'

William, no doubt seeing himself as some kind of minstrel providing entertainment for others of an artistic kind, began *The Minstrel's Invitation* with the following lines:

'Come! lover of my art,
A little while forsake the busy throng
Of Mammon's worshippers — prepare thy heart,
For purer thoughts, and listen to my song.'

When he was 19 William composed a patriotic poem, moderately short by his standards, entitled *An Embassy*, which commenced:

'Ye British youths on whom depends the sheen
Of dear Britannia's glory, ye who now
As sons of the majestic Ocean-queen
Must her uphold upon her native rock;
Whose courage lion-like, if war be hurled
Against her sacred coast, must break the shock!'

This was quickly followed by *Balm for the Bleeding Heart*:

'My spirit strolling forth in reverie
By chance had wandered to the ocean-side,
Where only dreary rocks, and sound, and sea,
And vaulted sky, composed the prospect wide,
Hushed were the winds, and waves, and mute I stood,
Profoundly musing on the wide display.'

In September 1852 William sent his sister Sophia and her husband Charles Hurlin a long, poignant poem he had composed to commemorate their emigration the previous March, which they undoubtedly cherished. This is the first verse:

'Have your forgotten when three months ago
Amid the busy crowds of parting friends
We met to say 'farewell?' I doubting then
If ever we should meet on earth again,
Though now believe some kind Providence intends,
That soon we *shall* again meet here below.'

William's letters were a joy to read. This description of the weather and London in the fog he penned in November 1853:

'The winter has set in very severely, it is bitter frozen weather. The sun has been obscured all the day by a dense fog. Its density has increased this evening, so that looking out from the window of Homer House with the road (the New Road), vehicles and passers-by are invisible. I perceive the glimmer of numerous torches passing by, and hear the cautious tread of horses, the shrieks of females. It looks dense enough to swim in. "Look out!" they are shouting perpetually — "Look out! Look out!" in every key. A *cube foot of the atmosphere is about as opaque as a piece of china* now, — since I began these remarks about three minutes ago, even the blaze of the torches passing by has become invisible: not one glimmer is perceptible all around, tho' there are numerous gas lights on each side, some only a few feet from my window. The streets are a perfect labyrinth to horses, men without torches, men with torches, ladies following torches, — and everything that has eyes.' [The next day he again observed the conditions around him,] 'The fog has continued all the day, and the description of last evening will apply to this. I have passed as many as forty torches in one street. At times I could not see the ground on which I walked and could only ward against danger by means of my stick. This dark weather brings out into our streets hundreds of a class medium between men and devils — the refuse of Society, who are often one — (and *all* ) all the way along the streets with torches, to sell them at five hundred per cent, or hire themselves as escorts *thro'* the streets. The incessant shouts all around were quite animating "A light! a light! a light!" "who wants a light! a light! a light!?" is the many-voiced reply. Then there is the shouting in the midst of the road, and a dozen of these link-devils rush in to throw a light upon the subject, but their dozen links and dozen shouts are almost insufficient to mend the matter. I call these fellows 'devils' because they would as leave pick your pockets as sell you a link. They are mostly pick-pocket thieves, house thieves, beggar thieves — and all styles of thieves. The omnibuses have ceased to run this evening, for last night they could not run a journey without some blunder, turning down wrong streets, or guiding their horses onto the pavement and nearly 'walking into' some shop front by mistake. Home is

'home sweet home' this weather most particularly; — tho' with myself, since GOOD-Friday it has "all'ays" been so.'

When aged 23 he wrote *Jack Slow Boy*,[1] a laboriously long poem, all in rhyming couplets, being in a style quite unlike his other writings. It was an amusing and entertaining account in verse of the adventures of *Jack Slow Boy* in the domains of a giant world. Jack was meant to be Ald. Copeland's son, Alfred who was laid up in bed recovering from a long illness, and the poem was dedicated and sent to him with an accompanying letter on the 10 July 1856. Some of William's descendants believed that Alfred Copeland was not particularly pleased to have been compared to a half-witted slow giant and years later in 1899 he sent the poem back to the author saying that he had found it whilst moving house and thought William deserved it.

This is how the introduction of JACK SLOW BOY began:

'My sick friend asked me for some tale or poem
Of mine own writing, to beguile his time:
'Too dry', said I. Then my esteem to show him,
I thought I'd try my hand at comic rhyme;
Since all my works were dry, this I would do,
Good thought! — I'd write for him a book brand new.'

The only copy of the poem is written in William's own neat and tidy hand, and is dated July, 1856.[1]

Other works were *Query! A Word for the Muse*, written in 1854 the only known copy as yet untraced, and *The Heavenly Pilgrimage* is believed to have been published but to date unseen.

His favourite poem, written by himself *Morning*, first appeared in *Good Words* and was later printed in various other magazines. Critics hailed the poem a beautiful one: 'I like the poem greatly; it is very powerful; harmonious; highly poetic and altogether good in sentiment and feeling.' Another said, 'From those elegant verses, I find that poetry and pottery are nearer akin than I supposed.' Other favourable comments were 'The lines of 'Morning' ' are truly beautiful, and most beneficial to the heart and intellect to contemplate. The reference to the wondrous works of God to be unveiled in the coming future, especially struck me' and *The Ode to the Morning* is a gem, unsurpassable for the purity and beauty of thought, gracefulness of conception, and ease and perfect harmony of flow.'

The last five verses of the poem were chosen to be engraved on the massive Iona Cross monument at the head of William's grave in Hartshill cemetery, Stoke-on-Trent:

O where can fancy reach or eye survey
Through all this scene, but joys and beauties are
And wonders infinite? Stay, Fancy, stay!
Lead not my spirit to that warning star;
'Tis vain for human thought to penetrate so far!

Of earth — among the astral host a grain —
Speck of that gold-dust sprinkled o'er the sky —
Man seeks to grasp the knowledge all in vain.
Vain were it then for human thought to try
To solve the wonders of the countless orbs on high.

But when my soul shall quit terrestrial mould
And soar restraintless to the Spirits' Home,
Then, comprehensive, free, fatigueless, bold,
And wing'd with speed as swift as thought I'll roam
Enraptured through the vast illimitable Dome.

Meantime, hail warblings sweet! released from Night,
A thousand throats welcome the morning rays
With songs of gratitude, and sweet delight.
O Father of the Universe, these lays
Are Nature's hymns to Thee — Thy creatures' grateful
praise!

Then hail! increasing choir: sweet to mine ear
Your morning hymns of praise. O all I see,
And all beyond surveyance; all I hear —
All Nature, Mighty Father, praises Thee,
All lovely scenes and sounds, all varied harmony!'

His love and wonder at the creation of the universe complemented his thirst for knowledge of archaeology and geology. With Llewellynn Jewitt and other eminent friends, he regularly went on field club excursions and digs the results of which were written up in papers and essays of historical value. His paper on *Arbor Low* which was published in the *Reliquary* in eight chapters, was a study of sunworship by early Britons, the origins of Stonehenge and other vast monuments, astronomy and also the Celtic priests of Ancient Britain.

Another of his important essays was *Cloud Hill near Congleton*. It dealt with the origin of millstone grit, clay and ironstone, the geology of the Cheshire Plain, and the deposition of the flora of the Carboniferous Period in the coal measures.

Most of the essays he sent to the *Staffordshire Sentinel* newspaper were printed. He was obsessed with certain subjects, and at one time wrote repeatedly about frogs and toads in rocks. At the time his views caused much consternation, and provoked other naturalists to write on the same subject, leading to reports of their findings in other newspapers in other parts of England.

'British Perils: Past, Present and Future' was first printed in 1878; in this William outlined Napoleon's views of Russian ambitions, The Spanish Threat and Queen Elizabeth's speech to the British army.

For some time during the 1880's William anonymously edited the 'Fragments' page of the *Pottery Gazette* signing himself "Ceramicus". This page was crammed with little amusing incidents in the Pottery world, and typical were any incidents which caught his imagination or coincided with any of his own interests, such as the following which appeared in the *Pottery Gazette* dated 2 April 1883:

'MR. S. C. HALL, who for forty-two years edited the *Art Journal*, and with whom I have the pleasure of a personal acquaintance, has been engaged for several years in preparing "Retrospect of a Long Life, from 1815 to 1883," which is published in two volumes, by Messrs. Bentley & Son, 8, New Burlington Street, W. It consists of recollections of "things he has seen and people he has known" — authors, artists, actors, and the "giants in both Houses" — during the earlier half of the century; a review of the art history and that of art manufactures, as they were in 1840, and as they are in 1883; with many other matters of general interest. The volumes contain a memory of Mrs. S. C. Hall, and her works. Especially is reviewed the condition of Ireland, forty, fifty, sixty years ago, before England had adopted the "policy of justice," before the abrogation of all laws by which the one country had oppressed the other for centuries, showing that there is now no right or privilege to which the Englishman and Protestant is entitled from which the Irishman and Roman Catholic is excluded. That, consequently, the hatred sought to be engendered in Ireland against England is as groundless as it is impolitic and wicked — prejudicial to the one country, ruinous to the other. Mr. Hall has done much to educate the taste of the public in the purchase of works of ceramic art, and I trust that this useful and interesting work which he has just published will meet with a good sale.'

'A TEXAS correspondent gives the following snake story: "One night my wife and myself were awakened by a noise from the shelf which contained our small store of crockery, followed by a crash which showed that a great portion of our cups and plates had been flung to the floor. Springing up to discover the author of this 'attack upon China,' I found a large snake in a somewhat unpleasant 'fix'. He had crawled upon the shelf, attracted by a number of eggs which were scattered about. One of these he swallowed, and in order to get at the next he had put his head and a portion of his body through the handle of a jug which happened to stand between the coveted delicacies. The handle was just open enough to let his body, in its natural state, slip cleverly through, but not sufficient to let it pass when puffed out by the egg. In this position he had swallowed the second egg. His snakeship thus found himself unable to advance or retreat; and in floundering about to escape from this novel stock, had caused the accident which had aroused us. I, of course, proceeded at once to execute summary justice upon the interloper, but the eggs which he had swallowed were a dead loss.'

We doubt if the snake story interested many other readers but no doubt William enjoyed it. He would also take every opportunity to praise his friends in the columns.

One of his jokes appeared in the Fragments column 9 January, 1894: 'Bridget, why do my dishes disappear so rapidly?' 'Shure, ma'am, bekase they're break-fast dishes, I'm afther thinkin.'

He had also the gift of appearing to praise an artist/writer/etc in his criticisms, yet really exposing every fault and ridiculing them. The following letter in the *Pottery Gazette*, 1 February, 1881, is a good example of this. Fortunately perhaps, the identity of the poor victim is not known:

'Our "aesthetic friend" has been among us so short a time it is amazing how much he has done. Few men have been successful, few men deserve to be so happy. He has lived to see the years of fashion swept away in a few months, he has preached crusades, he has led them, he has returned from the war laden with trophies of conquest, blue china has been for him a revelation and has followed it as animals follow their instincts. Other men talk and are listened to. He has talked and others have done what he has said. It is he who has filled our drawing-rooms with these bilious greens and negative greys, who has covered our walls with plates 'till they look like a kitchen dresser, made our chairs so low that to sit down is to collapse, and to stand up is to grapple at one with a mental and muscular difficulty. He has familiarized us with symbols and marks. He has interposed between us and the objects we look at, the comforts we enjoy, the authors we like and composers we love, the artists we admire, the very chattels we possess — a pervasive foggy atmosphere which invests everything, distorts everything, magnifies trifles, puzzles, confuses, inverts and misleads and which he tells us (with a lisp) is "the aesthetic".

Ceramicus.'

William's most interesting and often amusing letters were those sent to newspapers about diverse subjects, more often than not defending the poor, the working classes whom he greatly respected, the sick and the blind. His ability to observe and recount details on paper provides an excellent description of life as it was then. Some of his letters were so outrageous that he preferred to remain anonymous to protect his peace, using noms de plume such as Ceramicus, The Cheil Amang Ye, the White Elephant letters, Minimus Lychnus and Electro-chemic. These pseudonyms were chosen very carefully. The Cheil Amang Ye appears to be the result of two famous quotations, one of them being taken from *Life of Scott Lockhart* by lawyer Lord Braxfield, to an eloquent young culprit at the bar: 'Ye're a vera clever cheil, man, but ye wad be nane the waur o' a hanging.' The other source is taken from Robert Burns '*Captain Grose's Peregrinations*'; 'A cheild's amang you taking notes, and, faith, he'll prent it.' Therefore, 'A child among you who sees all and repeats all.'

The White Elephant probably refers to the long memory of elephants and in particular their ability to never forget an injury, just like himself. Ceramicus is a reference to his pottery connections and Electro-chemic his chemistry.

William was a campaigner for better working conditions and for regular holidays. The local Wakes weeks were the holidays for the pottery towns and it gave him considerable pleasure to see others enjoying their hard earned time off.

It annoyed William intensely when he read adverse newpaper reports of life in the potteries. He thought that if outsiders wanted to judge workers in the pot banks, then they should do so during Stoke Wakes week, for when on holiday they could be themselves. Stories of constant drunkeness, poverty and infidelity could not be further from the truth; stories which, he noted, were only contrived during news famines for want of something to write about. Here is his account of the behaviour of the potters on holiday:

'The great holiday really commences on the afternoon of the Saturday preceding the first Sunday in August. The morning of that day is chiefly employed in the manufactories in thoroughly cleaning and setting to rights the workshops and their contents, and leaving everything straight and orderly before the vacation, while the home-tending members of the community are putting the house in holiday order, or making ready for the sea-side excursion; for in the afternoon thousands take trains to the sea-side; chiefly to North Wales and the Isle of Man, there to spend the forthcoming week; and on Monday many thousands more take their departure. So extensive is this exodus from the Potteries, that the lodging-house keepers and tradespeople of Rhyl, the Isle of Man, New Brighton, Southport, and other places, are quite accustomed to extra-crowdedness and extra business in the Stoke Wakes week, and know about that great holiday from this marked extra immigration. And these are the people described to all the world as so eternally condemned to sickly homes, desolation, and smoky darkness, that a charity organized visit to the sea-side would have been recommended, only for the fear that the unwonted change would utterly daze them, and amaze them out of their wits. The number who availed themselves of railway excursions during this last Wakes week, in excess of the usual traffic, is estimated at between 35 and 40 thousand. At home, for the amusement of those left behind, are to be seen and heard all the usual glare and bablecom of a great fair. If one were to search among the holiday-makers there for the man who is fond of his beer, the search would certainly be rewarded with success, even without the aid of a candle. But there is not, on the whole, any great feast in England more respectably and soberly celebrated. On Tuesday and Wednesday, Stoke becomes, without hyperbolism, the scene of the English Olympic games. This year is its eleventh Olympiad. From London, and from all parts of the kingdom the athletic flock to the Potteries on the

Wakes Tuesday and Wednesday, to compete for the prizes offered by the Stoke Victoria Athletic club, which this year amounted to £350 — something more substantial to struggle for than the olive wreath awarded to the victor at the famous Peloponnesian Games. And these sports are witnessed by a concourse of from twelve to fifteen thousand people, as respectable and well-conducted a concourse as could be got together in any industrial district in this land; while the spacious grand-stand is graced with almost as much of refinement, beauty, and wealth's representatives as if the fête had been held in Piccadilly. The day succeeding those of the sports is called Trentham Thursday, when those who have not yet gone off by the trains assemble in the beautiful park and woods of Trentham, which magnificent seat of the Duke of Sutherland is about three miles distant from Stoke, and the same from Longton. Here the potters and the Tubal-Cains with their wives, families, and friends assemble to stroll, play, pic-nic, and dance, and although they muster in many thousands — sometimes over thirty thousand — their conduct is so orderly that the Duke has never yet been induced to close his gates on Trentham Thursday. This last Wakes there were fewer at Trentham, because more than usual went further away by train. On Friday Trentham-Day was repeated on a smaller scale, while nearly six thousand availed themselves of the conservative trips to North Wales. On Saturday there were some excursions to the seaside, but in no great strength, for the holiday finances of the great mass of operatives had by this time got to a very low ebb, and on this last day of the Carnival there was, as usual on that day, a strong disposition to indulge in a quiet fish dinner at home. If the fishmongers are to be credited, they invariably dispose of more herrings on the last day of the Wakes week than in any other whole week during the year. If this Saturday's frugality of the poorer masses be necessitated by the freer expenditure of the preceding days, it has also to be recorded that the freer expenditure was made generally for sober, healthful, wise, and real enjoyment. And thus these people have kept their great carnival, and emerged from it with honour to themselves.

'The special correspondents to whom I have referred, pretended to have discovered in this district a land of darkness, and a community which civilization had left behind and lost sight of for a hundred years. It is something worse than a mistake. The people of the Potteries have kept even march with the progress of the times, although, as with all other communities, there is still plenty of room for improvement which is steadily going on and elevating mankind everywhere.'

William and his colleague W. Kirkham, a councillor of Stoke and owner of the factory next door to his own, were involved with the controversial erection of the Stoke cemetery chapels. In a series of letters they wrote to the *Sentinel* on the matter stating that their view represented a widespread wish of all classes and denominations that one chapel should be for the use of Church people and Nonconformists alike. Kirkham expressed his view that the extra expense of having two chapels would cost the ratepayers dearly and that this would bring offence to liberal-minded people to see fellow Christians and townspeople so divided. He urged readers to prove good feeling by abandoning the symbol of religious difference which is blatant in the use of dual chapels of Cemeteries. William wrote a letter in agreement but the suggestion was not adopted as two chapels can be seen today in the cemetery. William emphasised that the church had one foundation and did not like any division among its followers.

The mention of the name 'Josiah Wedgwood' in any lecture on pottery and ceramics would invariably provoke applause from any audience, so great a name was the father figure of the pottery industry. Yet his tomb was neglected and William wrote to *The Reliquary*:

'MY DEAR SIR,
The "Reliquary" is read by the influential of Stoke-on-Trent, Burslem, Hanley, and neighbouring towns, and I should like to suggest quietly through it, that before there comes another "cheild among us taking notes," something be done to the tomb of Josiah Wedgwood. The neglect of that tomb probably arises from general ignorance of its whereabouts. It is historical that "on the 3rd January, 1795, Josiah Wedgwood died, and on the 6th his remains were interred in the parish church of St. Peter, Stoke-on-Trent." His vault was beneath the pavement of the church porch, and for about thirty-five years all who entered the church passed over it. But at the end of that period, in 1830, was opened the new church, as it was called, which stands about one hundred paces northward of the site of the old one. The old St. Peters being removed, and Wedgwood's tomb left out in the open churchyard, the space was merely enclosed by strong iron railings, and has been left in that condition to this day. There is no monument over it, nor an inscription of any kind upon it, in fact the tomb of this great man has already become traditional. It was pointed out to me yesterday by an old inhabitant, who used to attend the old church, and said that the name "Josiah Wedgwood," and nothing else, was cut in the pavement over the tomb. There was, however, so thick a matting of grass, weeds, and land-cress, the growth of years from the chinks of the stone slabs, that no such inscription could be seen, if there. To-day I got over the iron fencing into the enclosure with spade and broom, and, with the aid of the sexton, cleared away all accumulated rubbish, and found no trace of an inscription. The name "Josiah Wedgwood" which my old friend remembers to have seen so often on the

pavement of the porch, has been worn away by the feet of the generation of worshippers who passed in and out of that old temple before their steps were diverted to the new edifice, and it has never been re-cut! My fellow-labourer, the sexton, while we were clearing away the rubbish said, "I do feel hurt at times; I've been working in this place eleven years, and all that time there's never been a bit of paint put to them rails. Many travellers come here to look at the tomb of Wedgwood, thinking to see a grand monument, and then I do feel hurt to show them this untidy spot." And every inhabitant of the Pottery towns has as much cause to "feel hurt" as my friend, the sexton, and ashamed too, in this matter. Surely the spot where the bones of Josiah Wedgwood rest should be indicated by a durable and striking monument. Ample funds might be readily raised, if a movement to do so were made, in the Pottery towns alone, to erect a noble granito obelisk over the now blank and neglected tomb of this great man.

I am, my dear Sir, yours faithfully,
WILLIAM H. GOSS.
Stoke-on-Trent

Now it is William's turn for his grave to become neglected!

Most of William's published volumes were written in his later years. His *Hebrew Captives of the Kings of Assyria* received this criticism from *The Week*:

'Any production from the learned and lucid pen of W.H.Goss, F.G.S. of Stoke-on-Trent, must be of no ordinary interest to the literary world. His studies of Art Pottery from the Ancient British, the Romano-British, and the Anglo-Saxon periods, down to Tudor times, place him in the foremost rank of antiquaries, and make him an indisputable authority on ceramics. It is a contribution to Oriental history that must have cost its author much research and considerable thought. It cannot be read without reflection. It is written in a fascinating manner, the style of the history romance, and contains much vivid description on both places and people, life and manners.'

The book was too erudite to be a good seller on bookstalls, but it was welcomed by historians, scripture students and the like as a record of Eastern life, so varied over the years. Other essays which were published included *British Perils: Past, Present and Future* and *The Messiah of the Jews* which was printed in the *Staffordshire Times* in 1878. The *Newcastle Guardian* had this to say of William's biography of Llewellynn Jewitt:

'But a perusal of the book shows that it must have been a labour of love with Mr. Goss thus to place on record something of the work and worth of his departed highly-valued friend.'

William was the best person to choose to write Jewitt's biography, as he had shared the same hobbies and pursuits; had all his letters still (and he had written to Goss several times a week), detailing his thoughts, wishes and actions, and also had a sound and personal knowledge of Jewitt's friends because they were also his own. These comprised contemporary artists and authors including William and Mary Howitt, Frederick Wm. Fairholt of the *Art Journal*, S.C. Hall and his celebrated wife Anna Marie, Charles Roach Smith the eminent antiquarian and Charles Dickens. William's work on Jewitt was an interesting scrapbook of memories, incidents and portraits. He wrote with vigour but modestly, undermining his own place in the life of Jewitt.

With the publication of *Review of Modern Science and Modern Thought*, press reviews appeared in force. The book was of additional interest as it was a collection of letters written by William to Mrs. Anderson, sister of General Gordon. The topics covered include astronomy, origin of man, the Bible, mythology and the wonders of the universe. One review read as follows:

'They are as a golden key to that vast and inexhaustable theme, the mystery and magic of the earth, and expression so simple, of insight so sympathetic, that the merest tyro in science, like myself, found them entrancing as a fairy tale. These letters were written originally to one woman, but yet they were meant for all men and women. Although William was a scientist he did not attempt to reason away from God. In his view everything grows towards God. The height of his argument is that all and everything, including insects like beetles, have their right and necessary place in the world, as in God's plan of life. God did not have waste in his world, nothing was superfluous. Decay and renewal, life and death was his plan and will always be.'

The *Liverpool Courier* received the book well and reprinted this quote:

'Decay and renewal — that is the order, from leaves to men, and from men to leaves. It is the law in creation.'

The last book William was to write *Primitive Man and His Work*, appeared in two thick volumes and was the second in a series of letters to Mrs. Anderson, dated September 1892 to September 1899. The basis of this work is a rejection of Darwin's Theory and the proposition that the human race descended from giants both physically and intellectually. To support his assertions he used as proof the remaining gigantic pre-historic monuments such as Stonehenge, which fascinated him, and animals of pre-historic periods which included enormous dinosaurs. The Goss factory produced a colour transfer of Stonehenge on some of its models.

## Reference

1.　*Jack Slow Boy* is shown on jacket front, bottom left open at the first page of the introduction.

# CHAPTER SEVEN

# Adolphus and Nellie

Posterity gives every man his true value.

Tacitus: 'Annals'

Adolphus's life revolved around Nellie, much in the same way that Godfrey adored Alice. Perhaps the lack of love in their parents' marriage made a good wife all the more necessary to them both.

In her diary dated 1877, Nellie recorded such illustrious guests to her father's home as 'Mr. William Goss, Georgie and Addie (Adeline), the Rev. Charlesworth, Miss Marshall, Edith, Victor and dear little Florry.' She also noted that the Gosses and the Dales all spent Christmas together, with Georgie and Adolphus building a 'huge snow monument.' She was a frequent visitor to the Rode and Stoke homes of the Gosses, and although never a conventional beauty, had a radiant personality. Her diary also recorded her constant ill health. Many a day she could not go out, and had to stay in bed. She described her home as 'draughty' which probably meant it was rather large, and when she was confined to bed she felt like a prisoner. Her own mother was an invalid and did not survive middle age.

She was a calming and relaxing influence on Adolphus and her favourite verse which she always wrote in the front of her books and diaries went as follows:

'What's the use of worrying,
Of hurrying,
And scurrying,
Everybody flurrying
And breaking up their rest.
When everyone is teaching us
Praying and beseeching us
To settle down and end the fuss
For quiet days are best.'

It was this poem that she contributed to Anie's* autograph album. Perhaps because she was rather lazy, for in any case she saw enough of Adolphus socially, she was not in a hurry to get married. When he began travelling in 1881 he was away weeks on end, and wrote to her every day, but he could not induce her to write as many letters in return although he always told her which Post Office

\* Anie Jewitt was Georgiana, only daughter of Georgiana Goss and Edwin Jewitt.

to address her next letter to. He called her his pretty blue eyes, a colour he liked very much, his own being grey.

A further reference to marriage was in another of his regular epistles to Nellie. This one, dated 6 September 1881, was posted from Barnsley, Yorkshire. It reads:

'What an awful old woman you are getting dear? Fancy this month you will enter your 30th year!! So you had better shorten your courtship as much as you can.'

*Adolphus's blue-eyed girl, Nellie, walking near Alsager*

Later on he stopped signing his letters Adolphus Goss but wrote 'Dolphus' instead, a name his family called him by. He finally persuaded Nellie to marry him in 1882 and in October that year the nuptials took place. Possibly it was her fear of such an occasion which led them to have a quiet wedding, so quiet it took us years to find out the date! Unlike Mrs. W.H. Goss's opinion of Huntley's future wife, Adolphus's choice greatly pleased the older lady. She wrote to Nellie on 1 June, 1881 from Rode Heath:

'My dear darling child,

I cannot express the great happiness I feel this morning on hearing the good news that you have promised yourself to my dear boy. There is no one on earth to whom I would so gladly give him up as your own dear self and I pray that The Father will bless you both and make you a blessing and comfort to each other the rest of your lives. I pray that you may help him on the way to the better life and that it will be a marriage not of earth only, but of heaven.
With fond love and many kisses
Believe me your ever loving

G. Goss.'

A letter from Adolphus to Nellie on one of his Goss tours dated 19 September 1881 in Birmingham, raises the issue of marriage:

'My own sweet Nellie,

I have, you see, made a fair start this time, if it can be called fair when the weather is the reverse of fair. I never saw the streets of Birmingham look so clean before, they are having a regular good wash. I told my father that I thought this journey would take me about three weeks and that I thought the next that I started on would be a honeymoon tour. He said — "Oh that's it is it? That's right I am glad to hear it" and he followed up with the usual high commendation of Miss Nell.'

The wedding was private, with no reception, but Georgiana and Adeline attended as bridesmaids. By this time Nellie's mother was dead and her father badly off financially, perhaps explaining the quiet wedding. Her two brothers were not in regular employment; one, Harry, tried Blackpool and then Kendal for work. Nellie and her father moved to a house next to Earnest Craig, the local Alsager M.P. in July 1881, with her other brother, Fred, living partly at Smallwood and partly with them. Adeline said of the impending marriage:

'I reckon Sarah Ellen will not make a very tidy wife but *guess* she'll do as she is *told* !'

For such a keen photographer, it is strange Adolphus should not have any photographs taken of the event; they also had a quiet honeymoon, with Nellie totally unaware of their destination. Adolphus organised it all himself; they travelled to Wales, then on to the Isle of Wight, staying at Marlow with his aunt at some stage. Our earliest photograph of them together was taken in Carnarvon in 1883 with Nellie looking remarkably slim. She wrote home about her honeymoon on 2 November 1882:

'Left home by the 12.40 train to Crewe under the impression that I was accompanying my husband to Shrewsbury, however we found ourselves alighting from the train at Chester. When I hinted that it must be a roundabout way to Shrewsbury, I got an evasive reply. By and by we reached Ruabin, where the guards enquired as to our destination, Adolphus replied Llangollen, to my great surprise, where we duly arrived after a run through the most interesting scenery.'

It was not all holiday, William would not have allowed Adolphus time off without doing any work. Nellie continued:

'We had a lovely walk tonight by the canal side after having first done justice to a substantial tea at the cosy little Temperance Hotel at which we have put up, besides sitting for about two hours in an easy chair, watching Adolphus display his samples of artistic ware and duly admiring the same — that over about eight, we took a charming stroll.'

Their stroll was up a hillside where, in the dusk, she mistook a canal for a river. 'Adolphus comments, "Fancy! expecting to find a river on a hillside!" in masculine superiority.' That particular walk turned out to be

*Adolphus and Nellie in Carnarvon on holiday in 1883*

notable in that they saw a meteor in the sky.

Adolphus was often critical of others who did not keep up with his enthusiasm for work, such as writing regularly everyday to Nellie when on a Goss tour. From Hastings on 8 July 1887, he told her:

'I have just been reading all your dear letters over again (each has already been read at least a dozen times) and numbering them. I find there are just 4 against 9 that I have sent you but I trust there are two or three awaiting me at various places. I carry them, not in my bag among commonplace business documents, but in a pocket inside my waistcoat on the left side mind.'

He had an eye for spotting an amusing situation, as described here in a note to Nellie from Hay, dated 4 May 1887:

'It is market day and I have just been much amused by some of the farmers wives who go and come on horseback. Fancy an old scraggy unclipped, ungroomed horse with an old patched saddle and a small dilapidated strap for a girth, a sack and two market baskets tied across its back and a great coarse woman in ordinary walking (and working) dress mounted on top of the sack and with a baby in her arms!!! That is what I have just seen take its departure to some out of the way farm house among the hills.'

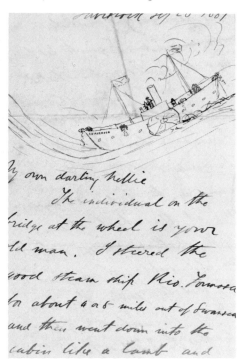

*A letter from 'Dolphus' to Nellie, this time from Tavistock. The last sentence finishes '. . .was gloriously sea sick. The sketch of the ship includes other seasick sufferers leaning over the side!*

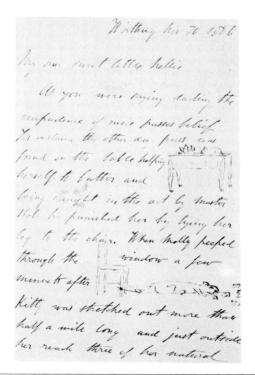

*Adolphus's way of illustrating a point in a letter from Worthing*

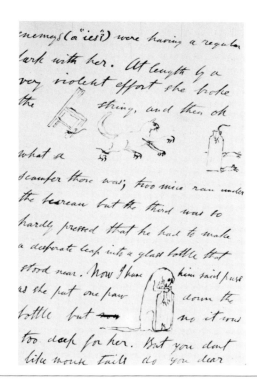

*A further page from the same letter dated 1886*

Another touch of good humour is shown in his letter to Nellie from Worcester, 26 April, 1887:

'Adeline, Edith and Mr. W.H.G. went to pay Mrs. Stewart a visit at Barford last night and came rolling home about half past eleven. You see sweet that they must just have waited till the pubs closed!'

A letter from a schoolfriend to Adolphus discussed their mutual love of birdwatching and fishing, and of country walks.

*The right half of this semi-detached building is 'Mere Leigh', Crewe Road, Alsager, the early home of Adolphus and Nellie, 1891. The top window on the far right is the room where many famous magic lantern slide shows were held by Adolphus and Huntley*

His clever use of the English language made his letters interesting to read and possibly this is why the family saved them. Those that were written during his expeditions to find agents to sell Goss wares are now over one hundred years old. His letter from Coventry, 26 October 1884, begins thus:

'My own darling Nell,

I made a small beginning in Birmingham this afternoon (Sir Stafford Northcote calls it the Dark Spot) and then got on here just in time to write a line to girlie mine who I left behind but keep in mind, and hope to find both well and kind, when home I turn, and not too stern. And now I tell, my darling belle, if she'd keep well, right down the dell, and up the fell, she must walk, not simply talk, and then sit still, but go with will, right up the hill, and cross the rill, and through the wood, T'will do her good, and make her eat, a lot of meat, and give her strength, perhaps even length; Though she's so short, yet me she caught, and that's not naught, if I know ought, with love and

smiles, sweet looks in piles and other wiles, she drew me miles, to her nice house, to be her spouse, though still I roam, yet still my home is where she is, with her sweet face, and eyes of blue, that look one through, and how one misses, those sweet kisses, that I give she, and she gives me, Write to P.O. Oxford, Your most affectionate

Dolphus'

Adolphus's first address before he was married was Betley Place, Alsager, later moving to a semi-detached house in the main Crewe Road, opposite the mere, called Mere Leigh, it was a large elegant new building, and he described it as:

'A very snug little house with 3 bedrooms, drawing room, sitting room and kitchen, I have gone in for old oak furniture: in the front room I have a splended oak cabinet 7 feet high, 5½ feet long and about 2½ feet deep carved all over, and beside it a large carved oak chair (now in the authors' possession). In the sitting room I have a carved oak cupboard, side-board and book case all in one which looks very fine. The only live stock we have except the servant is a white fox terrier who answers to the name of Caesar or Spot as he knows he has a large oval black spot on his bottom!'

*The same building in 1984, now a gunsmith's shop*

It was Mr. Dale who had given them the dog, which Adeline described as a 'regular blackguard of a dog', 'one of those white things with a black eye.' Adolphus had a boat called the *Cyrena* and with his good friend Dr. Kingston, the local practitioner, whose boat was called *The Senorita*, sailed regularly on the mere. In photographs of the two out in their boat, along with Dr. Kingston's dog Toby and members of their families, the doctor is always clearly discernible because he always wore a hat. Adolphus owned his own boathouse on the edge of the mere, as did all the local boat owners.

In September 1866 Nellie's father John, lost his Smallwood property. A builder most of his life, her brother Will Dale was on the verge of bankruptcy and out of work, with a wife and three children still at home to support. They moved to Manchester, and Adolphus dryly remarked in a letter to a friend that he had just lent Will Dale £80 knowing full well that he would never see it again. It must have distressed Nellie considerably to see her family in such difficult circumstances after a lifetime of prosperity even though her brother Harry sent Will what he could, from his work in Preston.

Although blessed with a good sense of humour, Adolphus was also capable of being firm, stubborn and hard. His pet hate was ties, which he only wore occasionally, most of his photographs showing him with an open-necked collar. Photography was the love of his life; he used to travel through Cheshire photographing with his friend the Rev. Charlesworth, a Methodist minister, with their tripod. The bulk of his surviving photographic plates are views of historic houses, country scenes and views of coastal resorts taken whilst on his trips about the country as the travelling salesman for the Goss firm. His father gave the following advice in the *Pottery Gazette* which was exactly what Adolphus did with his photographs:

*A snap by Adolphus of the Alsager mere, taken from his lantern slide show. His sense of humour needs no reminder*

HOW TO TRANSFER A PHOTOGRAPHIC PRINT ON GLASS. — Separate the paper print from the background by steaming it; dry thoroughly, and, having given the warmed glass an even coating of clean balsam or negative varnish, place the face of the print on the surface thus prepared, smooth it out, and let it stand in a cool place until the varnish has hardened. Then apply water, and, with a soft piece of gum-rubber, rub off the paper so as to leave the photographic image on the varnished glass.

Huntley and Adolphus held magic lantern shows for family and friends, using the slides and an early projector, and also for the public as a fund-raising activity, often earning about £2 a time. Florence Hammersley's diary for May 1897, reads, 'Went in the evening to a magic lantern entertainment that Adolphus and Huntley gave.' Later on in October of that year she wrote, 'Mother and father went to a lantern show given in a public room by Huntley and Adolphus in aid of a building fund. The room was very full and the show very good!'

'Mere Leigh' was where Adolphus held many of his famous lantern shows. The second floor window visible at the side is the room where many of them took place and some of his views of Alsager were photographed from this window, a good vantage point. The house has now changed drastically; what had been his sitting room and conservatory is now a gun and small arms shop with a hard forecourt for parking where there was once a large garden.

Adolphus bought Nellie a tricycle in 1886, a fairly new invention considering they had only been manufactured since 1876. In those days they had large wheels and were for adults who wanted sedate rides. The youth of the day would have ridden penny-farthings until 1884 when the

*John Dale of Smallwood, Nellie's father and close friend of William Henry Goss*

*Another slide show view. Adolphus liked to snap any scene of disaster. This sight of a steam engine on its side held attractions for others too at Penmaenbach, date unknown*

safety bicycle as we know it was invented.

After two miscarriages Nellie finally became pregnant for the third time and grew enormous. Adolphus used to joke about it, 'Dear Nell has got pretty plump and weighs about 13 stone', accompanying his remarks in a letter to Godfrey with a rude sketch of her. Godfrey once wrote and asked his mother if she was a granny yet. She replied, 'I am glad to say it is not likely at present for I can't think that Nellie would ever get on with a family.' But Nellie proved them all wrong and Ethel Maud Goss was born on 3 September 1885.

Adolphus was thrilled with his darling Effie, and was sad about being away on his travels so often. Ethel called her father 'Farvie', and in his letters home he would include a special message for her. Vernon William came along two years later, then Clarence Richard (Dick) in 1890, Hubert John in 1891 and George Raymond Henry, always known as Raymond, in 1893. Dorothy Muriel (Dolly) came last in March 1896 and was the only one to inherit her mother's plumpness. Adolphus was a very stern and strict father and beatings were a regular occurrence. Perhaps the children had a free and easy time when their father was away because of their mother's regular pregnancies and because she suffered from ill-health. Although they had a servant and a nurse, she was not completely a lady of

leisure in her early years, for she made her own butter and did some of the cooking. Because he was away so much when the children were small they decided 'to go to Australia.' When he came back from a tour and found the hole they had been digging in the garden, he beat them all soundly.

Adolphus often went for long walks, usually taking Ethel with him. Ethel and Dolly were close to William, and spent many hours with him in his garden. Adolphus believed that it was quite normal for close generations not to talk to each other, but that more distant generations could be very close.

Edith's unusual frankness in her letters leaves no uncertainty about her views on Nellie, for instance she wrote that:

> 'Nellie's baby is such a dear fat little thing, but she is such a dirty large thing herself.'

Adeline thought:

> 'It is most comical to see Adolphus talking to it (Ethel) and carrying it about, he is so proud of it and can do nothing but talk about it. I fancy Papa does not like the idea at all of being 'Grandfather' but he makes a great fuss about it. Florry has gone quite out of flavour. I think he will take to it instead of Florry. They are going to call it Ethel Maud.'

*Nellie on the tricycle given to her by her husband in 1886 in Christ Church Avenue (now Church Road), Alsager*

*Proud parents Nellie and Adolphus Goss about 1893. Nellie was to lose the will to live after losing her two youngest sons on the Somme. Left to right: Raymond, Vernon, Nellie, Dorothy, Adolphus, Dick, Ethel and Hubert*

As a young child Ethel quite won William's heart, and he showered her with toys when visiting with Adeline. Ever conscious of waste, he gave the family cot to Adolphus and Nellie. As she grew older, Ethel spent holidays at Rode and called Adeline 'Attylena'.

Very keen to become part of the local community, Nellie and Adolphus helped out at the Alsager Bazaar. They had their own stall selling donated bric-a-brac and made £56, a vast sum in 1889. He was dressed in a smocked frock with blue stockings, a tommy hat and hankerchief around his neck, and she was a country girl of the last century to match.

Adolphus wrote the lyrics for a school operetta entitled *Fairyland* in 1889 for which his friend, the Rev. W. Ding, composed the music. It was performed in early December at Arley, a small village five miles beyond Norwich, near Alsager. Victor and he rode over by bicycle and returned the same night. The show was such a great success, they had to give an extra performance and on the second day twice as many people turned up to see it. The script of this which was passed down through the Goss family contained a pencil sketch in the centre pages in Adolphus's familiar hand of a gentleman peeping out from behind the page with his thumb stuck out from his nose — his idea of a joke!

He enjoyed writing poetry and amusing stories with which to accompany his sketches drawn in ink on the photographic slides which he used in his magic lantern shows.

He used his favourite verses to decorate tea-pot stands, beakers and jugs in illuminated script.[1] Some of these verses he wrote by himself, including 'Goe not halfeway. . .'

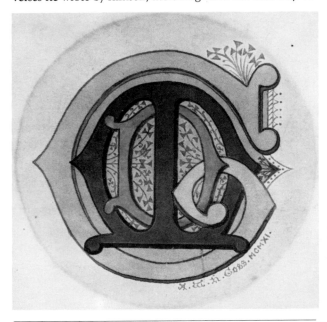

*The hand-painted illuminated initials of his daughter Dorothy Muriel Goss by Adolphus*

*The lovely Ethel, who called herself 'Gossie'*

which even appeared in postcard form much to Adolphus's amazement. On the back of one such card his daughter, Dolly, had written:

'This is a verse my father Adolphus Goss wrote to put on china and it was very popular. Someone sent us this P.C., we had no idea it had been done. Strangely enough the author John printed this in his 'Kings High Way' in 1916, and put an apology in the footnote explaining that he must have copied it into his rough notebook and later thought it was his own. Father was very flattered.'

Adolphus did not christen his children with family names as he believed it led to comparisons. After having her first child, Nellie began to grow very large in herself, and one friend remarked that she had become even bigger than her friend Mrs. Charlesworth, who was considered enormous. By 1886 Adeline thought that her brother Adolphus was a most tolerant husband but that:

'he lets Nell have all her own way and the consequence is she often makes herself very disagreeable to us. She is so lazy and so *awfully* fat and the baby is always dirty.'

By 1890 she had not changed her mind about Nellie:

'Nell is something truly frightful to behold now. She is the stoutest woman I think I ever saw and is expecting another baby in a month. She is always putting on the delicate invalid and hardly ever does a stroke of work but Adol seems to be satisfied so we must not complain. Adol's children are very pretty but the eldest and youngest are very coarsely built like the Dales.'

Edith shared her sister's views with Godfrey in America:

'You would not know Nellie now, she is something awful, her waist is about 40 inches or more. She is the fattest woman in Cheshire or Staffs. You may be very thankful Alice is one of the slim kind. I expect Alice keeps your children much nicer than Adolphus's are kept. Nellie stays in bed 'till nearly dinner time then reads 'till tea time, then rests on the sofa 'till supper, does an hour's sewing and goes to bed 'till dinner time the next day, so you may imagine how badly the children are all dressed.'

Their criticism does seem rather harsh because at that time Nellie was seven months pregnant, but the children certainly delighted their grandparents. Ethel called her Granny 'Ganmor', and was always mature for her age.

In June 1894, Nellie, feeling she was very near death, managed to write her husband a very moving letter, when she really believed she would not pull through:

'All the red corpuscles in her blood were killed and she lay like a wax image with no colour at all but dead white. However, she pulled round thanks to Murdocks Liquid Food,'

Adolphus informed his friends.

*Jim Burne, a good friend of Adolphus and William. His youngest son was to marry Ethel Goss*

*Dr. Kingston's boat 'The Senorita' on Alsager mere in 1901. He always wore a cap when sailing. In the boat also are Ethel, Vernon, Hubert, Raymond and Dick Goss*

*Alsager High School in 1904, was attended by the children of the local potters such as the Gosses, the Hammersleys, the Woods, the Fords, the Maddocks and the Leadbeaters*

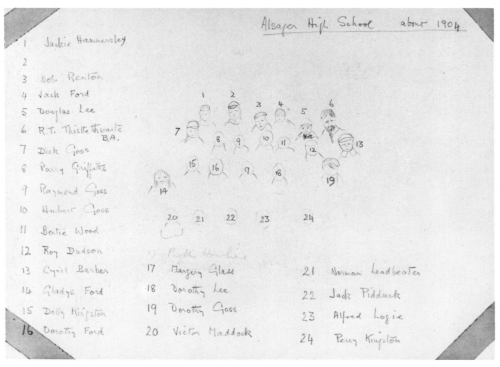

Alsager High School about 1904

1. Jackie Hammersley
2.
3. Bob Renton
4. Jack Ford
5. Douglas Lee
6. R.T. Thistlethwaite B.A.
7. Dick Goss
8. Parry Griffiths
9. Raymond Goss
10. Hubert Goss
11. Beatie Wood
12. Roy Dudson
13. Cyril Barber
14. Gladys Ford
15. Dolly Kinfston
16. Dorothy Ford
17. Margery Glass
18. Dorothy Lee
19. Dorothy Goss
20. Victor Maddock
21. Norman Leadbeater
22. Jack Pidduck
23. Alfred Logie
24. Percy Kinfston

*The key to the school group as drawn by Adolphus*

Although Nellie disliked sport, Adolphus was very active. Apart from his sailing, cycling and ice skating, at which he was adept, he 'took a bit to golf' and played on the links at Barthomley with the Rev. Skene, who had married another of his friends, Mrs. Lawson in 1885. He went on jaunts taking photographs with the Rev. Charlesworth, and evenings were often spent at whist drives with his two best chums, Dr. Kingston and Frank Ford. He added to his collection of bicycles, a 'decent pneumatic' costing £6.10s.0d in 1897.

His other close friends were the Burnes. Mrs. Burne was the former Annie Hilton, school friend of his sister Georgiana and Nellie. James Burne was the thirteenth child of a solicitor, originally from Dublin, who was a very good friend of William Goss. James had a good sense of humour and the two families enjoyed each others company, at weekends and on holidays especially to the Isle of Man. The Burnes lived for a time at Sale, Cheshire, having moved from Southport in 1885 when their child Harry was three years old.

Adeline was 29 years old when she recorded, in 1892, that Adolphus and Jim Burne had been over for tea that particular afternoon:

'Annie Burne looks the same as ever, just as nice looking, but Nellie — oh goodness she is like a great jelly fish or hippopotamus, something *awful*. Father says she is big enough to go in a show.'

Most of Adolphus's slides taken between 1885 and 1900 contain pictures of the Burne boys Harry, Leonard and Victor, taken on their long hikes with their father and Adolphus; their mother Ethel and Nellie, the younger Goss children presumably being left behind on the beach! Harry's youngest brother Victor was later killed in the Great War and Harry himself suffered plenty of leg pulling from Adolphus's sons because he was a young curate and not a soldier.

Adolphus was a devout Christian and regular worshipper. Despite his sparring with his father, the latter gave him a beautifully bound copy of the Bible, in which he had inscribed; 'To Adolphus Goss, with love from his father 29th July 1890.' When he first came to Alsager there was only one church in the parish, Christchurch, built by the Misses Alsager, ladies of the manor, in 1789 after a special Act of Parliament. As there was no parish attached, church-goers had to attend the neighbouring parish church of Barthomley — quite a walk! Mr. Skene the rector of Barthomley decided to convert the Linley mission room into the parish church of Alsager, dedicated to St. Mary Magdalene. Adolpus later spearheaded a committee who were organising the building of a new large church. The Rev. Moir wrote:

'Discussions took place as to the size of the church. The majority favoured a modest building, but Adolphus told me that he foresaw that Alsager would develop though it was only a village then. He advocated a fine church with a spacious chancel for a good choir and a large nave with aisles. His views were accepted and largely due to Adolphus an imposing church was started about the beginning of this century, to be completed gradually.'

He also raised money to build a porch in 1894 which was consecrated in 1898.

Adolphus's business travels took him all over England and Wales as well as abroad, and for twenty years he led an exciting life. He had his bag stolen at Stoke staion, 2 December 1883, the thieves being caught at Manchester, and on New Year's Day he had to go to Stafford to give evidence against them following which they were sentenced to three months hard labour.

Perhaps he tired of his constant travelling and wanted to spend more time with his large young family, and perhaps also he felt he did not want to continue working for his father who was difficult towards his own sons, although so very kind to his other employees. His last letter written on his travels was dated 16 August 1899, from Bolton and it appears he left the firm sometime between then and 1900.

### Reference

1. These are listed in *Goss Arms, Decorations and Their Values* by Nicholas Pine (Milestone Publications).

*The White Lion Inn at Barthomley, with Ethel, Annie Burne, Nellie Goss and Vernon in 1892*

# CHAPTER EIGHT

# The Children 1885-1900

Live as long as you may, the first twenty years are the longest half of your life.

Robert Southey: 'The Doctor'

It was in 1884 when Ted (Edwin Jewitt) rose from the position of bank clerk to manager, that he decided to ask William's daughter, Georgiana to be his wife. He had always liked her company; she was such a lovely person, with a sweet, kind and gentle nature, and very beautiful. Throughout her childhood she had two close girl friends — Nellie (Sarah Ellen Dale), who later married her brother Adolphus, and Annie Hilton (who married into the Burne family), all of whom were close to the Gosses. Georgie, as she was known, got on well with everyone she met. During the course of our research, we found no mention of any complaint or grievance against her, and she herself only spoke well of others. In appearance she resembled her mother, and her handwriting and style of letters were similar too. She wrote many letters but few have survived.

When Georgiana and Edwin's engagement was announced early in 1886, the marriage date was not decided due to Mrs. Jewitt's ill health. She died shortly afterwards and was buried on 9 March that year, followed soon after by Llewellynn himself. They then decided to get married at Stoke Church on 15 November. Beattie Jewitt and Adeline were bridesmaids, Huntley was best man and William gave her away. They honeymooned in the capital and Brighton, calling on S.C. Hall while in London. They received nearly forty wedding presents, the Goss works staff giving them a lovely clock. Beattie was to live with them at their new home 'Paxton Villa' in Matlock, which had five bedrooms, beautiful reception rooms, and a tennis court (Georgiana adored tennis). Surprisingly, William was critical about certain aspects of the marriage. Before the wedding Adeline said:

> 'Father is so nasty about it and wants her to be married at Lichfield. G says she will not and I don't know how it will be settled unless they make up a run-away affair.'

William eventually gave in to her wishes for a more simple ceremony, and to celebrate the marriage gave his work force a special 'tea'.

In 1888, Georgiana gave birth to a daughter, Georgiana Elizabeth, after having had one miscarriage. Adeline reckoned the baby was the image of Mrs. Jewitt, with not one feature of Georgie's. Later on that year, Georgiana and Ted, the baby 'Anie' as she was known, the nurse and Adolphus and Nellie, with their babies Ethel and Vernon, and their servant, journeyed to Rhyl for a long holiday.

*Parian bust made by William after the sudden death in 1889 of his eldest daughter, Georgiana. He gave her few privileges in her lifetime, although after he lost her he realised how much she meant to him*

William wrote to a friend:

'I was at his (Ted Jewitt's) home a few days ago and was delighted to witness his happiness, and that of my daughter, and their darling little daughter.'

It was tragic that Georgiana was to die only a year later on the 3 November, 1889, her second daughter Clara dying soon after on 21 February 1890, aged four months.

Young Anie was left at the tender age of two without a mother, and Ted was devastated. Adeline summed up the sad situation:

'The little baby whose birth caused so much sorrow has followed its poor mother, it was 4 months old and a lovely girl, with dark eyebrows just like poor Georgie. Poor Ted does not get over Georgie's death at all, he mourns *terribly* and writes *such* sad letters about his lost darling. There is no mistake about it that was a love match if there ever was in this world. Georgie was an exceptional wife and Ted appreciated her as she deserved. Poor Georgie told me the last time I saw her that she had more happiness in her three years with Ted than in all her life put together, and no doubt she had, poor girl, for father was shameful to her and never treated her well even when she was married.'

The whole family used black trimmed mourning writing paper and envelopes for nearly a year. William produced her bust in porcelain for family and friends. Adolphus said of Ted: 'There is no happiness in this world for him, and he only wished to join his darling as soon as possible.' Adeline regretted not being with her when her sister passed away:

'I saw her two days before she died and came home for she was considered to be going on well and she had two trained sick nurses so did not need any of us but if only we had known that the dear girl's hours were numbered of *course* we should have returned.'

William was immensely proud of his granddaughter Anie: 'Dear Georgie's little daughter is a precious little darling, and calls me Bandper.' Godfrey had thought that his father would have hated to be known as a grandfather because he worried about his age, but William quickly came to like the idea. In 1890 he went to stay with Ted at Christmas. Anie asked on Christmas Day, 'Where *is* dear pretty mammy? Let's go find her Daddy.' When the little girl used to see her mother's photograph in the album she would to kiss it, pat it with her tiny hands and beg her father to 'fetch mammy.' By the age of two she spoke beautifully and correctly and there was little of the baby about her.

Anie often came over to Rode to stay with her grandmother and the Gosses considered her a charming child and very forward. Ted continually mourned the loss of his wife over the years and made an idol of little Anie, with the result that she grew up to be somewhat spoilt, and rather a handful!

The Gosses did not approve of Ted's relationship with a Miss Arnold, nine years after Georgiana had gone. The father of Ted's new love was a country gentleman who had squandered his assets, lost all of his estate and was too idle to work for more, according to Adolphus, who did not approve of anyone who did not put in a fair day's work six days a week. Future relationships with the Jewitts were to be strained with the presence of the new Mrs. Jewitt. Correspondence failed to mention her except to complain about her. 'Ted Jewitt married again last summer,' wrote Adeline in 1900, 'She is very nasty to poor Georgie's only child.'

Anie and her father were wonderful friends until he re-married, but she could never get on with her step-mother. No doubt she gave her aunts and uncles the impression her step-mother was treating her badly. However, she became devoted to her new step-sister and step-brother Arnold, who was born with a slightly deformed back. They were now living at the old Jewitt home, Winster Hall near Matlock.

Anie once went to stay with her Uncle Adolphus and his family. He kept a cane over the dining room door and often used it when his children stepped out of line. When Anie first saw the cane and promptly announced in her upper class high pitched voice that *she* had never been beaten, he took her aside after the meal, put her over his knee and thrashed her with it!

* * * * * * * * * * * * *

*Anie (Georgiana Goss Jewitt), only daughter of Georgiana and Edwin, who went to stay with Adolphus and family, only to be undeservedly thrashed with a cane because she announced loudly that she had never been spanked!*

*The photograph Godfrey finally sent to his mother from America, several years after emigrating*

Godfrey found a job quickly enough when he first arrived in Trenton, New Jersey, which was the American 'Potteries' centre at that time. He became foreman at 'Edges' but unfortunately the firm went bankrupt, owing him 100 dollars in unpaid wages and, regrettably jobless. Godfrey took with him a reference from George Ash of the 'Ornamental China and Parian Manufactory' of Hanley, Staffs, to Ash's brother Mr. L. Ash of Trenton:

> 'Dear brother, the bearer is Mr. Godfrey Goss, the young man I wish you to get good and respectable lodgings for, I want you to be kind to him and serve him to the best of your power.'

So he had at least one person to go to for help and contacts for work.

He was only out of work one week when he obtained a job elsewhere. He earned enough to commence renting his dream farmhouse in January 1884 at the rate of 17 dollars per month. He was 25 years old that January, and felt it was about time he began his own business making colours. Meanwhile, he worked long hours at Hendricksen and Co., decorators and glass dealers. He fired all the kilns, supervised the staff, and had the keys in his care. He was the best paid member of staff and the most trusted.

His request to his father for the recipes of the famous Goss enamels was turned down in 1883 because William did not care for Godfrey's business partner at that time, a certain Mr. Rivers with whom he emigrated from Stoke. William warned him against that dangerous character and believed that if he sent him his recipes, Rivers would copy them and send them to his own father in England to use in competition with Goss's. Rivers' father was a traveller for another colours manufacturer, but as no-one could rival the quality of Goss, he would have been delighted to obtain William's recipes. Also, William planned to write a book called *The Formulae of British Potting* in which he intended to outline the history of the pottery industry and publish his receipts (recipes), the research for which he thought stood him at a cost of at least £1,000. It was to be a limited edition publication and very expensive, but he never got around to writing it. Godfrey who would not end his partnership, and indeed let Rivers move in and share half his farmhouse, bought enamel recipes from France, at great expense, and used these to start with in his own business of making colours.

Godfrey was proud and it really upset him to have to write and ask his father for his recipes, but to be turned down made him very bitter. A rare letter to a brother mentioned this episode:

> 'It cost me a lot of money to bye some receipts from France with W.H.G. refusing to send his to me thats the only thing I ever asked him to do for me and it will be the last he never paid me the money that he owed me and he never will.'

We think the last remark refers to wages unpaid when Godfrey emigrated without telling his father or even handing in his notice.

In February 1884, he left his job and went full time into colour making, determined to make a success of it despite his father. He disassociated himself from the untrustworthy Rivers and employed labour to work on his farm, meantime spending his own days building up the colours business. His own hours were 5 a.m. to 10 p.m. and he was, in his own words 'working himself to death.' He found out that the workers he hired for his farm were stealing half the grain, eggs and fruit (mainly cherries). His housekeeper was also taking his goods until he caught and dismissed her. As he told Alice, without a wife to keep an eye on things at home, he could not cope properly.

Adolphus contacted him in January 1885 and ticked him off:

> 'You see your old dad is not so bad as you thought. As soon as I asked him again to send receipts when I heard Rivers had gone he made no objection at all. Have you heard of anything more of Rivers? I hear he is doing well!'

Adeline laboriously wrote out in longhand all her father's recipes for her absent brother and they did indeed help his business. Godfrey never thought to thank Adeline for her part, but did reply to his father:

'I keep on making colours and shall soon have a large stock for my pans are working all the time I shall advertise in all the papers I am the first Colourmaker in this country all that are used in this country come from England.'

William sent him a £5 note every time he wrote, insisting that as soon as he acknowledged its receipt, he would send him another one. Godfrey was hard up but unwilling to be blackmailed into writing.

Adolphus, like the rest of the Gosses, learned more about his brother's movements through the relations of other emigrants in New Jersey, than from Godfrey himself. He asked his brother:

'They tell me you do not mean to write to your dad. If you do not you will be very, very foolish. If you have not written to him before you get this, by all means do so at once.'

But Godfrey only had thoughts for Alice; he continued to pine for her, and had she not promised to come over he would have tried his luck in the wild west and not attempted to save. He refused to even look at the local girls thinking that they 'paint and powder to a fretful extent and most of them have false teeth.' He also thought Americans wicked because they did not keep Sundays as a holy day. He couldn't find a church he liked locally so he tried to be good without going to church. Various untruths and misunderstandings were reaching William about Godfrey, so the latter wrote to his sister, Georgiana, who surmised that these misleading reports were coming via Rivers' father who met their father regularly through business.

When Godfrey gave up work for a while through ill health, Adeline begged her brother to write to William:

'You must let father help you and he is most willing to do it, but you know dear how odd he is and unless you acknowledge in your own hand every letter he sends he will not do it. Pray, do gratify him in that little trifle for I do so want you to have some money, and it is your right too for you have always been such a good son to him and as I told him today, he has never done *anything* for you.'

Throughout this bad time for the lonely Godfrey, his father continued to write regularly and send him the *Sentinel* each week. 'Remember that it is when you have bad news that you should write to me.' warned William. Adeline told him 'Father keeps saying 'I wish Godfrey would write, he *ought* to apply to me for anything he wants.' But Godfrey wanted Alice Buckley.

What was rather off-putting for Alice's confused parents, was the knowledge that many young people from the area had emigrated to Trenton and had returned, not liking it nor finding work. However, Emily Nicklin, a girl friend of Alice and former paintress at Goss's, had gone out and was still there.

February 1884 saw Alice secretly agreeing to go out to Godfrey despite not having her parents' permission. He warned her:

'Do not let anyone know you are coming soon not even your sisters or it will go to the Ashleys and then to my father and I do not want them to know you are on the way for if my father knew he would go to your mother and try to get her to stop you for he dose not like you darling and thats the reason I never write to him so be *verry* careful and keep things to yourself.'

Alice, meanwhile, was preparing to leave England and was waiting for a signal from Godfrey. Even William was expecting him to come home any day to fetch her. He wrote and told him he had a great regard for her and that he would be glad to recognise her as his daughter. 'I always said she was quite as good as my daughters' he said.

In January of that year he wrote to his family to announce that he was to be married, without disclosing the name of his intended. He told Alice that all the family had written and asked who it was, but they all knew.

When the signal to come did not materialise, an embarassed Godfrey eventually explained to Alice that he had loaned his money to a man called Leek to help him get a patent on a spinning ring he had invented. The gullible Godfrey had loaned him all he had, plus more, since it took a year for the patent to be granted and it was to be sold for 30,000 dollars and the sale was due to be going through any day. Their partnership had begun in early 1886 but months later Godfrey still had not been repaid. All promises and deadlines had fallen through and it looked as if he would have to sell his livestock in order to raise the money to pay for Alice's ticket, but not be able to afford to pay for himself to go over and collect her. She would have to make the journey on her own!

It was then all speed ahead and both sets of parents were informed about Alice's departure. Her brother and sisters had grown up and were in employment. Her brother-in-law, Edwin, was in casting, Emmie had married Joe, a fireman, Frank was a tile fixer and her mother worked at Cauldon Place. Godfrey purchased Alice's ticket and posted it to her and Victor took her to Liverpool and saw her on to the ship. As soon as she landed they were married in a nearby registry office and moved straight to his farm. Everything that Godfrey had worked for had begun to fall into place; all that was lacking was the capital, and it grieved him to see his young wife tackling so much work.

To celebrate their wedding back home in Hanley, Alice's father organised a firework display, with himself as Master of Ceremonies. It was held on 5 November 1886 at 8pm, in a yard in Cannon Street, complete with printed programmes, admission 6d.

Alice's father was in the 'doctoring' business, and that year took on a young assistant who had been Alice's girlfriend, to make out the bills and attend to the collecting of accounts.

Within four years, Godfrey's eyesight was beginning to fail. Victor told him: 'Mother thinks that it is because you went out of doors too soon when you had the measles.' But the cause was probably due to unhealthy contact with the chemicals with which he worked.

Godfrey had to weather other setbacks. He seemed to be a rather simple, trusting character who judged others by his own high standards. In 1891 he was 'taken in' with the purchasing of horses; Adeline wondered why he was not sharper with his experience of the world. The previous year he had stopped making colours, probably through a combination of the illness it caused and lack of commercial success, and concentrated on his farm. A year later someone shot his cow. His friend in Trenton, Fred L. Mathey, thought the culprit was 'one of them black niggers up the road. I would like to have seen him doing it, I would give him all the shooting he would wanted.' Apparently the cow pulled through with Godfrey's round the clock care.

But his ambition to use his pottery skills was still unfulfilled and he went to Indiana on his own, leaving his wife and family at the farm, and secured a short term job with 'Burns and Cole', manufacturers in glass, carbon, porcelain and metal in Peru, Indiana. He wrote to his wife daily whilst staying at the Tremont Hotel — for one dollar a day! He planned to rent a house in the main street of Peru, and began organising his own factory, looking for a suitable site and machinery. By April he had got his works operational and fired the first kiln. He recruited his staff and then began teaching them from scratch, which he admitted was quite a task.

He told Alice to sell the cow and pigs, pack up their belongings and join him in Peru, from where they eventually moved to Kokomo, Indiana. The following year he was considering taking a partner in his pottery, a Mr. Van Sickle, but this did not materialise. Two emigrants from the Staffordshire potteries who did join Godfrey were Albert Armisson who was experienced at firing and Theo Whitehead who was a clay presser.

Since his gift of the enamels recipes, relations between Godfrey and his father improved and they corresponded regularly, with the latter generously sending gifts of money and chemical compounds, and advising him on business matters. Godfrey was particularly selfish in not replying to the rest of the family at all, with the exception of the odd letter to Victor and Adolphus. Alice did not write either; possibly she did not encourage Godfrey to, as she could not stand the competition of his mother, Georgiana, Adeline, Edith and Florence all regularly sending him loving letters. It cost £20 for a return ticket to Trenton from Liverpool and they all considered undertaking the journey, but none ever did, possibly because their brother did not respond to their suggestions and invite them to visit him. He appeared to want to be independent of his family and manage on his own.

For the rest of their lives Godfrey's brothers and sisters, with the exception of Florry, wrote regularly to their beloved brother, and despaired at his lack of replies. They were left to wonder why he kept in contact with Florry and their father and it would appear that their secret was to address their letters to both Godfrey and Alice. The others continued to address their letters only to Godfrey, blissfully unaware how much this infuriated him.

Adeline really pined for her 'lost' brother whom she loved dearly, and in 1892 tried to explain the family's point of view:

> 'You might not bear us any grudge about Alice, I am quite sure we have never been unkind to her and I do not think you right to expect us to love her you know like you do, because you see we don't know anything about her and she was not even a friend before she left England. Suppose I were to write and tell you that I had married one of my father's workmen? Would *you* love him just because I had married him? No, of course you would not, you would probably swear and you certainly would *never* write to him and it would be strange if you did and it is just the case with us and Alice, so I do not think you right to let her be the means of estranging you from our family and she might not wish to widen the breach by persuading you not to write.'

This missive undoubtedly did more harm than good!

\* \* \* \* \* \* \* \* \* \* \* \* \* \*

Adeline was by far the most prolific letter writer in the family and she kept up her weekly letters to Godfrey, although he rarely replied to her, and kept him informed of anything of interest she felt he ought to know. She wanted him to keep in contact with their father so that he, Godfrey would not have to work so hard to earn a living.

> 'You may just as well have some money from Pa as he flings it away shamefully, I wish we could have sent you a nice present dearest but we get scarcely any pocket money.'

She looked after the gardens and greenhouse which Godfrey built at Rode, with one gardener to help her. 'I do a good bit of gardening and our front is said always to look better than any other on the terrace or heath.'

She was aware of all the local young men and hoped one day to be married, especially as her sisters had gone to the altar one by one. Adolphus was always amused by his sisters' antics, and once joked that Adeline was chasing doctor McAldowe and the local curates, Edith was trying to catch Gwynn Kirkham and that Georgie was still for Ted.

Adeline was seriously ill in 1884, with Dr. Greatex attending her for six weeks, resulting in him handing her father a hefty bill. Eventually she was taken to Penmaenmawr where she recuperated. It was the only time she was ever seriously ill.

Poor Adeline was attacked, the locals assuming it was rape, on an evening train which left Alsager for Stoke. This news was a sensation in the local press, headlined 'A Thrilling Story' and a 'Terrible Struggle With a Lunatic'. Apparently the train was pulling away from Harecastle station when she was terrified to see a man hiding on the footboard just outside her door. The news article read:

'Having in quite a rational manner explained that he had nearly missed his train, Miss Goss pointed out the risk he had run by entering the train while in motion. The man, who is stated to be about thirty years of age, clean shaven, and fair complexion, pulled the window up, and so conducted himself that the lady scented trouble. She at once made a dash for the communication cord, but the man knocked her down, and in the tunnel, which is about a mile long A TERRIBLE STRUGGLE ensued. Miss Goss is a fine, powerfully built lady, accustomed to an active life, and she made valiant efforts to free herself from the clutches of her assailant. She was successful in getting hold of the communication cord twice, but her hand was dragged down. She endeavoured to get out of the train, but was prevented, and the man threatened to throw her on to the line. Finding herself being over powered she appealed to the ruffian to have mercy on her and offered him all her possessions. He however, continued to behave like a madman and struck her several times over the temple in a most brutal manner, and seizing a handkerchief which the man had round his neck she tried to throttle him. The man asked for her purse, and seeing a little satchel suspended from her side pulled it savagely from her. He next opened the door of the carriage, and while the train was still in motion, disappeared. When the train stopped Miss Goss told of her TERRIBLE EXPERIENCE. Her appearance showed that she had been shockingly ill-used; her clothes were torn, and she was in a state of collapse. At Stoke a cab was obtained, and she was taken home where she was attended by Dr. Petgrave Johnson. She was found to be in a most prostrate condition. Her cheek bone was badly injured, and she had an ugly black eye. It is reported that Miss Goss's assailant was a man named Thomas Flynn, a dangerous lunatic who is stated to have escaped from Cheddleton Assylum about four o'clock on Tuesday afternoon. The statement of Miss Goss shows that the man displayed great coolness in carrying out the attack upon her, and it is not deemed likely that a lunatic, immediately he became possessed of her purse, which by the way contained £1 in gold in addition to some silver, would not have at once made off. The father of Miss Goss is a magistrate, and the lady is highly cultured, and a close student of scientific works.'

The incident caused great embarrassment and was never discussed outside the family. Adeline certainly did not want the affair to disturb her marriage prospects.

Although, like the rest of her family, Adeline complained of her father's ways, she agreed with many of them. She believed in not wasting anything and in rewarding honesty, as this tale illustrates. Adeline had been walking down a crowded street in Hanley one lunchtime when she came across an underfed scruffy little eight year old girl gazing wistfully at some tuppenny pork pies in a butcher's window. Putting two pence in the girl's hand and instructing her to get one, she walked off but about a quarter of a mile further on was surprised by the little girl chasing after her with the pie wrapped in paper. 'Oh Missus, yer pie' she gasped and held it up to Adeline. She saw the honesty in the little girl's eyes (which her father had taught her to look for), noticed her puny body, told the child that the pie was for her and let her run off eating it. William loved to hear about incidents like this and was quite upset when he could not trace the girl to reward her.

On another occasion Adeline and her brother Godfrey were staying at a friend's house in Wales in the early 1870's. Their servant at the cottage was an old Welsh widow who was finding it hard to make ends meet. She had several other houses to char for besides this particular one, so she generally worked very hard and did not appear to have much to smile about. One day the woman appeared absolutely radiant, going beaming about her chores and finally she blurted out to Adeline that she had been given a present that had really made her happy. She led Adeline to the kitchen where an old faded and worn black silk skirt lay, with a pair of villainous-looking black buttoned boots, rather down at heel. The servant said:

'Look 'um, did you ever see such a present as I've 'ad? This skirt will make me a best for a long time, and this beautiful pair of boots keep my feet dry all winter and just my fit.'

One of her employers had given her these cast-offs and Adeline rejoiced with the woman at her obvious pleasure with them. When she returned to her room she pondered upon the matter and wondered just how many wealthy ladies with plenty of clothes just let unused outfits lie in their wardrobes for years end untouched and useless to them, and what garments were tossed away surplus to requirements. What wasted blessings they were, she thought, when each unused item could be as successful as the black skirt and the black boots in the right place. She knew Mrs. Llewellynn Jewitt had a conviction that, if a thought flashed through her mind that certain persons would like or look good in some item of clothing of hers, she would go ahead and give it to them, as she believed these were not merely chance thoughts but God given commands.

The Goss family originally lived in one half of Ashfield Cottage, but in later years William purchased it and the other half, formerly occupied by a Mr. Bates. Adeline wrote to Godfrey and described what was happening, date unknown:

'Our old house at Stoke and Bates with some more additions is made into one house. The large room that we had upstairs is now the drawing room and a splendid one it is. Father has spared no expense in fitting it up, we girls have nothing to do but superintend the household arrangements. We have a servant. The two offices are shut off from the house and are now in the possession of Victor and Huntley who do all the writing etc. The dining room is Bates' front room downstairs, that is also handsomely furnished. Jewitts have been made to visit us and we have lots of nobby people for friends. *But dear Godfrey you must please not say anything about this in your letters to Rode Heath.* Mother knows nothing of it. If she did she would go up to Stoke and make a scene and Father says he should have a separation from her at once and sell up the whole thing. You see it would only make her unhappy to know that we receive friends at Stoke as she cannot figure as Mistress but then this house (Rode Heath) is very nicely furnished now and she can have here what friends she likes, so it is not very hard lines, though I wish Mother could live with Father but perhaps it is all for the best.'

Adeline, taking charge in her sister Georgiana's absence, became responsible for managing the household arrangements and acting as a go-between for both her parents, all in all a difficult and tiring burden which she carried out well.

\* \* \* \* \* \* \* \* \* \* \* \* \*

Edith was Victor's twin and lived with her mother and the rest of the family at Rode Heath. She was attractive, had her father's red hair, was outspoken and liked to catch the eye of eligible bachelors.

Albert Loring Murdock of Boston, Massachusetts, inventor of the famous Murdocks Liquid Food, and a business acquaintance and friend of William's, never failed to admire the Goss daughters, in particular the two youngest, Edith and Florence. His last unfulfilled ambition was to have a daughter, and on one of his regular visits to the Gosses he attempted to persuade her father to let him take Edith back with him to the States for six months, which request was promptly refused. In April 1884, she informed Godfrey of the possibility of Murdock visiting him:

'Has Mr Murdock called on you? He was here about a month ago (he lives at Boston) and said he should go out to Trenton to see you, he is such a nice man and is coming over again in July, so is sure to call on you before then. He has asked us to go and stay with him for Easter but Papa will not let us.'

*Edith in the garden at Rode Heath, June 1893*

As Murdock was a millionaire, it was possible William was concerned he might spoil them and even entice them to live in America. Having already 'lost' Godfrey, he was not willing to lose any more of his children to the Colonies and this thought was probably uppermost in his mind.

In 1893, Edith became engaged to James Mountford who used to work for Dr. Crapper, the dentist. He became a partner with a Mr. Cave at Birmingham and as a qualified dental surgeon he earned about £700 a year, considered then to be a very good wage and as his practice grew he expected to increase his earnings. Florry, the youngest sister, felt happy for them because they were obviously right for each other but was sorry to lose Edith because:

'we are great chums. Edith and I get on together far better than Adeline and I, for Adeline always wants to be 'master' over everyone. So I shall feel very lonely after the marriage.'

They were married in April 1894.

\* \* \* \* \* \* \* \* \* \* \* \* \*

Victor, Edith's twin, did not think there was much chance of his marrying for financial reasons, for in 1890 he came to the conclusion: 'after working for my father for over ten years, I am getting the magnificent sum of a pound a week.' That year he had been away travelling more weeks than he had spent at home, six or seven week trips at a time — but on his July trip to Ireland he made sure he had time for some trout fishing on the River Erne. He also visited Belleek, staying with Pat Cleary, an old friend of Godfrey's, and previously a Goss employee. He told Godfrey:

> 'He has not altered a bit since he left Stoke and I knew him at once, but of course he did not know me as I was only a little boy when he last saw me. Everyone remembered you going there and asked me how you were. Montgomery is still there and asked after you and so did Henshall.'

In 1889 Victor became a Freemason:

> 'but father jeered at it and said it was all nonsense, just as if *he* could know anything at all about it. He gets more conceited every day and I really believe that he thinks himself the greatest man in England and fancies himself perfect.'

It is quite possible that William, whose closest friends included Freemasons of high rank, was just teasing and merely trying to provoke conversation or some sort of reaction.

Victor fell off his bicycle in Wales during the Christmas holidays and his doctor advised his arm would never be strong again, which hampered his other great love of riding horses. He had a reputation for taking out difficult steeds, and it was perhaps his weak arm which led to the riding accident which killed him in later life.

Soon after, Victor again went to sea, leaving behind an anxious family. It was October and he had left Liverpool

*Pat Cleary, Goss employee who left to work for Belleek, in 1877*

on a steamer to go to the Mediterranean and Italy and he expected to be home by December. He thought he would go because there was not much 'travelling' for him to do for the firm until Christmas, and Adolphus was covering for him. In 1893 he was off again to sea, this time heading for South America. Whilst he was away, the family scanned the newspapers to check on his ship's progress because of the wars in that part of the world. When he returned, he announced that he had finally had enough of the sea.

The following year he was in London and called on his cousin Ted Goldswain for the first time. He was the second officer on the Castle liner *Dunrobin Castle* which sailed between London and the Cape. Victor found him a 'jolly fellow' and felt he got on well with him. He also went to Great Marlow to see his Aunt Maria, Ted's mother.

Victor held marvellous children's Christmas parties and would always provide a huge, decorated tree. These parties, which were regular occurrences during the time the Gosses rented a house in Barthomley, were held in the coach-house and Victor presented each child with a porcelain mug of half-pint size with blue handle, decorated with animals on the sides and so thin you could see your fingers through it.[1] Victor belonged to the Territorials and was known to bring his volunteer regiment to Radway Green station and march them to Barthomley for a mock battle on his land adjoining Mr. Hollinshead's farm. They used the fence to hide behind and also an old ditch for the 'enemy'. Mr. Hollinshead has since, over the years, ploughed up spent dummy cartridge shells which were used. When Victor had his volunteers down for the day, often numbering well over a hundred, they would dine in the school hall before their sham fight, which was held either on the farm land or the links and the selections played by the band were afterwards enjoyed by people all over the parish.

By 1900 Victor was an officer in the Staffordshire volunteers in which he was a great favourite with soldiers. He volunteered to go to the war in South Africa, nine men from his Company having already been sent out there, but he was not eligible because he had had less than a year's training. Adeline bemoaned:

> 'The war fills everybodys minds, everything else falls into the background. The send offs have been tremendous, nothing has been equal to it before.'

By 1901 Victor had got his own way and off he went, causing his family great sadness. Victor's youngest sister Florence, followed him out to South Africa to nurse the wounded.

In 1902 the Potteries staged a tremendous reception to welcome the Boer War veterans home:

> 'We have been having great rejoicing here during the last few days owing to peace having been proclaimed in S.A. — Bands of music have been parading the streets, flags and banners have been flying from every

*The front garden at Rode. Standing: Victor, Florence, Adolphus. Seated: Annie Burne, Edith, Mrs. Georgiana Goss and Nellie*

shop and almost every house, illuminations at night and altogether a very lively time. We are now preparing for a great bust up and rejoicing at the Coronation of our Most Gracious King Edward VII which takes place in London on 26th and 27th of this month, and we have also several Colonial Premiers of Canada.'*

One of the oldest residents in Alsager, Mr. Sam Shaw, can recall an evening in 1902 at Alsager station when there was a terrible commotion. A train came in and Victor stepped from it to a tremendous civic reception. He mounted a specially-made platform to make a speech to the crowd, after which he was taken home by a horse-drawn cab. Mr. Shaw was publican at the Lodge Inn in Alsager at the time, and remembered that Victor's homecoming from the Boer War was a major event in such a quiet village.

It is generally believed that Victor could have gone far in the army but he was required to partake in the active running of the firm. Victor served in the 1st Volunteer Battalion and then in the 5th T.A. Battalion of the North Staffordshire Regiment from 1899-1912 but during the Boer War was with the 2nd North Staffordshires.

As Lieutenant, Victor practically had command of the company in the camp at Stoke, because his Major (a Major Knight) held field rank in another company. Victor finally took over command in January, 1903.

Victor's friends, in recognition of his service in South Africa, presented him with a magnificent sword of honour.

The guard was of silver and gold, with the monogram VHG in enamels, and the badge of his regiment below. The scabbard was of silver, with gold mounts and rings, being decorated with the arms of the recipient in enamels and embossed with battle honours. The steel blade was elaborately etched and inscribed thus:

> 'Presented to Lieutenant Victor H. Goss by 181 of his friends and admirers as a memento of their congratulations on his safe return after serving with the 2nd North Staffordshire Regiment in South Africa, 1901-2.'

The sword is now on display at the Staffordshire Regimental Museum, Lichfield, alongside a large three-handled loving cup which was presented by Lieutenant V.H.Goss to Pte. T. Fradley, the winner of the 1st Volunteer Battalion's Recruits' Shooting Prize in 1900.

* Letter from 'Edwin' of 7 Kensington Road, Oakhill, Stoke-on-Trent to Godfrey Goss dated 5 June 1902.

\* \* \* \* \* \* \* \* \* \* \* \* \*

After a year living with his father, in 1885 Huntley moved back to Rode, travelling to Stoke by train and back each day to the Goss works. In 1895 when a new station was built between Alsager and Harecastle for the Audley line, called 'Alsager Road,' he got home an hour earlier

*Florence Hammersley who married Huntley Goss in 1899. Adeline did not think her pretty enough for her brother*

each day. In 1896 he began to court the young Florence Hammersley, whose brother Gilbert ran the Hammersley Pottery. She shared his interests in cycling and playing cards but his sisters, especially Adeline, and also his mother made it quite clear they did not think her pretty enough for their Huntley and she was never invited to Rode.

The earliest record of Huntley and Florence's friendship was in 1896, the year of the big freeze. They went skating, according to her diary, on a frozen lake at Rode where Huntley lived with his mother. Ethel, eldest daughter of Adolphus, acted as chaperone of both homes in the absence of Mrs. Hammersley. The couple attended progressive whist drive parties held at the Kingston's house and on one such occasion in 1897 Florence wrote, 'It was very jolly indeed and to my great delight I won the Lady's First Prize!' She learned to ride a bicycle and often joined Huntley in his trips into the country on long cycle rides. When William Henry Goss died, Huntley blackened the handlebars and chrome parts of his cycle which he used to cycle to Alsager station each day to catch the train to Stoke and from the station to the factory, a typically eccentric way for Huntley to show he was in mourning for his father.

Florence had swatches of material pinned in her diary as records of the garments local dressmakers made up for her. No 'off the peg' clothes then, for ladies would visit

material shops and have dresses made up to their own design. Florence and Florry Goss, Huntley's younger sister, used to go to Hanley to buy their material, and also to Extons, the tailors in Stoke, who would make up garments on the premises.

Huntley visited Florence almost every day except when she was ill, which seemed to be often. Huntley, Victor and Adolphus liked taking photographs of the family and friends and often caught them unawares. Florence never liked seeing her own photograph, especially shots of herself unprepared. Once, when buying a hat for her niece's wedding, her somewhat tactless friend said, 'Florence, you have a peculiar face and you need a peculiar hat'. Florence came home with a magnificent creation and never forgot her friend's advice.

Florence's best friend was Marian Alsager Craig, known as Ailsa, whose father Ernest was nominated in preference to Adolphus to be the local parliamentary candidate and was eventually successful in 1911. Quite possibly, if it had not been for Ernest Craig, Adolphus could have become the M.P., for he had the time and the resources and excelled at political speeches. Ailsa married F.W. Harris, a Burslem solicitor in 1897, and was possibly one of the two friends Florence took to see William Henry Goss at Stoke one May day that year. William accepted Florence Hammersley as a prospective daughter-in-law as she had the singular honour of being invited into his study!

Mrs. Goss however, did not approve of the match. Possibly she did not take kindly to her youngest son leaving home to get married, or perhaps Florence had offended her in some way. In any event Mrs. Goss, Adeline, Florry, Huntley and Florence all went on holiday together to Buxton on Saturday 1 August, 1896. The following year in 1897 they all went on holiday together again, this time to Whitby. There was a strange silence between Florence, Mrs. Goss and Adeline since the previous holiday which made this sojourn somewhat awkward. They had never really approved of her as being a suitable wife for Huntley, and in all probability the announcement of their engagement was not well received. In 1897 the engaged couple began buying furniture piece by piece for their future home. Florence used to travel to Stoke by train where Huntley would meet her and take her to the furniture shop. Purchases made included a 'bedroom suite comprising a dressing table with wash stand to match and a towel rail, all in the same pretty wood, then a hat stand made of oak and a nice old grandfather clock with a moon that works around with a changing date.'

The saga between Florence and her future mother-in-law continued. She wrote in her diary on 28 September 1898: 'After more than a year's coldness, Adeline called,' no doubt a duty visit due to the impending marriage. Florence was surprised to receive an invitation to tea at Rode in October of that year. To calm her nerves she walked there and was relieved to see a third person present, Mrs. Thistlewaite a friend of Mrs. Goss, 'so it was rather more pleasant.' Mrs. Goss seemed 'amiable enough,' and Florry came in later and walked home part of the way with her. Usually the Goss children went everywhere on horseback, the girls riding side saddle. Florence herself had the use of a pony and trap; often she used it to visit Huntley, but he usually preferred to walk or cycle rather than ride. He did not take to sport and disliked the tennis afternoons that Florence so much enjoyed. He was quite a romantic, and liked to turn up with a bunch of wild flowers picked on his way from Rode to Alsager, and in season he would pick violets, her favourite. He also liked giving her practical gifts, such as the cyclometer, he gave her at Easter, 1898. They went regularly to see Adolphus and 'Mrs. Adolphus' as they both called Nellie, and Huntley often dined at the Hammersley's home.

During the summer of 1898 they bought their future home, which was on the edge of Alsager mere, next door to Dr. Kingston's house, called 'The Lodge'. In October, a few months later, 'H, Ethel and I went up to the house and unpacked some of the kitchen things.' They began to arrange the furniture and possessions in their house, which was spacious and included a dining room with discarded panels from Christchurch (the local chapel), billiard room, gun room, and a drawing room and breakfast room each opening on to a conservatory. There was also an extensive garden with lawns and orchard which met the mere where their boathouse was situated.

They received some magnificent wedding presents;

*The entrance gates of 'The Lodge' in Church Road, Alsager, home of Huntley and Florence Goss from 1899 to 1929. Now two homes, this half 'West Mere Lodge' is where Aline Moir and Ethel Goss lived in the 1960's*

*Huntley's wedding day, 18 April 1899. Standing: Victor, Gertrude Walton, Huntley and Florence, eldest brother George Hammersley and Adeline. Seated: niece Vera von Berg and Vida Hammersley*

*Florence (Hammersley) Goss in her own garden, about 1900. She was great friends with Florence Goss who shared her married name*

*The lovely Florence Goss, or Florry as she was known, in the garden of Mere Leigh during the 1890's*

*The wall pocket William Goss modelled after his youngest daughter Florence*

Victor gave them a very large silver tray, 'E.P. of course,' and Florry sent a pretty pair of pictures. The wedding presents were ferried across the mere in Dr. Kingston's boat to 'The Lodge'. The entry in Florence's diary for 29 March 1899 reads: 'H brought Adeline's picture, it is her present to him.' It seems quite unkind that she did not address her wedding gift to both of them, but perhaps she relented because a few weeks later she sent another picture. Mrs. Goss also addressed her present to Huntley only. Their wedding day was the 18 April, 1899. A full report of the wedding in the local newspaper failed to include William in the guest list, neither was his wedding present recorded along with the rest. Probably the relevant details were omitted at his request for it was about this time that he was turning into a recluse. He was a naturally reserved person and liked all his personal affairs kept private and confidential. However, his dog Paddy was listed in the wedding report as giving the newly weds a gilt jam spoon! Florence's brother George gave her away as her father had long since died and they took their honeymoon in the Lake District, staying at 'The Old England Hotel,' Bowness on Windermere. They went by charabanc to see the Forth Bridge and enjoyed long walks on their own. Her diaries petered out after her marriage, like those of Nellie, no doubt due to the sudden increase in workload.

**Reference**

1.    See *Goss China Arms, Decorations and Their Values*. Flora and Fauna. Animals, Birds and Butterflies for illustrations and details of these decorations.

# CHAPTER NINE

# The Twilight Years

Art is a jealous mistress, and if a man have a genius for painting, poetry,
music, architecture, or philosophy, he makes a bad husband and an ill provider.

Ralph Waldo Emerson (1803-1882): Conduct of Life: Wealth

Between 1880 and 1890 William Henry Goss lived alone
with one servant and at least one daughter, the sisters
taking it in turn to be his housekeeper and companion.
Outwardly the family pretended all was well, but among
themselves they discussed the growing problems they were
having with him:

'Father gets very faddy. He cannot bear to meet anyone
in the street and never goes with the Field Naturalists
now. I expect he will be very trying when he is old'
(Adeline 1888).

A year later she complained to Godfrey:

'The older father gets the worse it is to live with him.
You may be thankful that you are spared the daily trial
of his temper. He has no favourites among us girls now.
Florry was the last and he tired of her in six weeks.
Now he tries to punish us all our lives for nothing,
we *never* please him, but I do not care as I do my duty,
as well as I am able, so do the other girls.'

By 1890, when Victor wrote to Godfrey to congratulate
him on the birth of his second son, the situation was
worse:

'But I hope they will not take after their *grandfather*,
for *one* like him is quite enough to be in the world
at one time. He is as tyrannical and underhanded as
he was when you left home and if anything, *worse*. Ted
Jewitt is his favourite now, and he thinks there is no
one like him, but as far as I can judge, he is no more
or less than a darn *sneak*. I have not seen Ted for over
three years and I am not particularly anxious to, but
I should like to see dear Georgie's little girl again.'

That year Victor and Huntley took their mother to the
Channel Isles during Wakes week. Victor, now 25 years
of age, wrote:

'She did enjoy it, but you may bet the old man was
not pleased at it. He never so much as gave us a cent
for a wakes tip, although I believe he is going to pay

Jewitt's expenses for a fortnight at the seaside. He
would have given us something if we had gone alone
and not taken mother, but I am not going to leave her
out in the cold, and I will take good care of her,
whether it pleases him or vexes him. Yes, she has always
been a good mother to us, while he has just been the
worst father anyone could have.'

Edith held similar views. 'Poor father gets very trying
as he cannot see any more or bear noises. But he is quite
unchanged in appearance and seems no older.'

William's old friend Mr. W. Kirkham was Mayor of Stoke
in 1890, and staged a glittering ball for over 400 people.
He invited all the Gosses, but, as usual, William did not
tell his children about it and just refused the invitation
without saying why. The Goss children noted with regret
that everybody else in Stoke appeared to be going
including all the curates, the attentions of whom Adeline
and Florry were desperate to attract. Even the Bishop went,
and Sir Lovelace and Lady Stamer would have attended
but he had a confirmation to take on that day. Later that
year the girls managed to be invited to tea at the Rectory,
and met such visitors as the Bishop of Ontario.

Their mother arranged for them to be invited to tea at
Lawton Hall and they were driven there by a Miss Ashton
of Boden Hall. Adeline wrote in 1891:

'We never tell Father anything about it for he would
stop it, he is horrid that way, does not like us to have
nice friends as you know and the best thing is to leave
him in ignorance.'

William's health was deteriorating; when writing to
Godfrey in February 1892, he admitted:

'Last October I had three weeks of influenza; and last
month I had another attack, and have been kept in
the house already five weeks, and as the influenza has
developed to rheumatism in foot and knee, I cannot
yet get on my shoe and am still kept in. I tried last

Friday evening to get out in a slipper, after dark, with Adeline, but 10 yards found me too lame and too weak, and we had to turn back. I seem to want the fresh air; but today we have a continuous heavy snow-storm.'

Edith did not seem to think he had rheumatism:

'Since father has had the gout he has been so bad tempered. He tells people it is rheumatism but the doctor says it is gout proper. He had it dreadfully at Christmas time and I never came home for six weeks. I was at Stoke all that time looking after him.'

Even Florry felt the same, writing in 1893:

'He seems to get more irritable every day. He cannot bear the boys outside to whistle even, and gets in such tempers, but he is very generous to outsiders as he always used to be.'

*Adeline with her mother at Rode. Her time 1900 to 1905 was divided between caring for her mother at Rode, and later at Barthomley, and for her father at Stoke*

William was regularly adding to his museum of curiosities at great expense. As Florry wrote:

'Father is getting on well but keeps his expenditure up high too. He has a perfect craze for buying books, curiosities, pictures etc., and is adding to his lot every day almost and is very difficult to keep clear. It worries me dreadfully and shall be thankful when I am out of it for ever. We have one servant but Father spoils her and allows her more privileges than his own daughters. He insists on supplying her with novels to read all afternoon when he would be extremely angry were *we* to take one up, but I never want to waste my time over such trash when I have little leisure.'

William indicated that he was not intending to leave his children any money or any part of the factory. In a message to his brother Godfrey, Victor confided that Huntley was copying down all his father's recipes for enamels. 'He does all the color work now you know and every receipt the old man gives him to make he copies down, and keeps for bye and bye.'

Victor also thought that:

'perhaps dear Georgie's death would have softened him a little and made him kinder to dear Mother but he is not a bit better and I have no respect for him whatsoever. I get along smoothly enough with him of course I see very little of him, as I am away from home so much. He shoved me out of the works clean enough, and if it had not been for Mother and the girls I would have left him altogether and gone to sea again!'

William never really took much interest in the factory after 1901 and did not agree with the expansion of the business and workshop extensions. He was sixty-nine when he began to live like a recluse in his Ashfield Cottage home, with Huntley sitting at his office desk and doing his old job. William ceased his daily visit to his office when Victor went off to fight in the South African war in 1901, because he insisted he could not bear the sight of Victor's empty seat. It so distressed him he said he preferred to stay at home. We doubt if Victor would have agreed with this! During Victor's absence his family lived on edge, grateful to receive any letters that their absent soldier could send. He wrote during his time allocated for sleeping, usually in awkward conditions in lonely blockhouses, and sometimes enclosing a little floral memento from the battle scene which he knew would please his father. When peace was finally declared on 1 June 1902, there was much rejoicing in the Goss family and William recommenced visiting his office, although on an irregular basis and a Boer War commemorative was issued by the firm.

Huntley was now in charge of the day-to-day running of the business, together with his older brother Victor, but their father still controlled everything from home. Although he only went in one or two mornings a week, William kept up his daily task of opening the firm's post which he had brought up to him each morning. After he had opened the letters and orders, written various instructions on some and taken the monies, he would then allow his sons to have the post.

Many collectors have long believed, incorrectly, that it was William who produced so many busts of himself because he was so self-opinionated. Adeline related the truth of the matter which was quite the opposite:

'For many years during his working life there has been demands for his bust in porcelain but he was a modest and retiring sort of person who was horrified at such an idea. Finally, one day, one of his sons hired a skilled modeller Mr. E. Chambers of Stoke, and took him into his father's study, clay, tools and all, taking William by surprise. He was so shocked he did not run off but just sat there and passively allowed the artist to get on with the job. The strategy worked, Father consented to the excellent portrait created by Mr. Chambers and from this original the factory produced the W.H. Goss busts which sold well to dedicated collectors nationwide.'[1]

Although now a popular and saleable bust, it cannot be said to be scarce, yet it commands a good price. William confided in his daughters that 'he had enough vanity to be pleased with it, and to wish all his daughters to have a copy.' Quite possibly *only* Victor could have got his own way with his father; no-one else could have managed it. The modelling of the bust took place in late 1905, three months before William's demise and was introduced upon his death.

When William ceased visiting the Goss works daily, he also stopped going on holiday; he still went for day trips but would come home each evening. He stopped visiting Barthomley where his wife now resided, having left Rode. He stopped inviting friends to visit him, and whilst frequently enquiring after those he knew, he did not feel the need to see any of them, not feeling any less love for them, but preferring instead a more secluded life, like that of a hermit. One particularly close friend of his ever since he started up his factory was Mr. W. Kirkham, who William often asked after. He would be delighted to hear if any members of the family had met him in the street and was keen to hear his news. The only visitors he would receive were his own family. By this time, Adolphus was married with six children, who together with his wife Nellie, regularly called. William's favourite granddaughter was now Dolly, the youngest, who apparently always knew when to chatter away quite happily to her grandfather, and when to be quiet when he wanted tranquillity. Huntley and his wife Florence were also frequent visitors with their young brood and the hapless Adeline spent alternate weeks at Barthomley with her mother, and Ashfield Cottage with her father. Edith and her family lived in Birmingham but visited often, and Florry had moved away and lived alone in Tewkesbury.

All his life, true to Goss tradition, William had benefited from good health. Now in his old age he still looked healthy and radiant with smooth unwrinkled skin, soft hair which had not receded, a fine moustache and tall manly physique. He rose earlier than he used to and slept rather less well, pottering around his home and garden, with even his ageing faithful friend Paddy the dog acquiescing to life in Stoke. In his 73rd year he had a little bower made in the elder trees, and there he sat for many an hour in the summer. He enjoyed good weather during what was to be his last summer, which was fortunate as he gained most pleasure out of doors, and did so enjoy the sun.

Towards the end of October 1905 William had a heart attack; it was about three in the morning; he was in much pain for several hours but it receded and he was well enough to come downstairs before 10 o'clock to open his post. After this attack, however, his eyesight became poor and Adeline had to read the *Daily Telegraph* and all his other magazines and journals to him. A detailed history of Trentham appeared in the *Staffordshire Sentinel* which she read to him several times and which he enjoyed as it awakened memories of old Stoke in the early days. During the night of 15 November he suffered a second heart attack, and two days later another. They were not as painful as the first and William insisted that his physician, Dr. Petgrave Johnson, who he greatly liked and admired must not be called out from his bed.

It was following his first attack that William asked Adeline to write his biography after his death. Some two months before his demise her father told her there was something he wished her to promise to undertake when he passed away, namely to collect all his unpublished manuscripts and have them published, and also to write a short memoir of his life. She felt herself incapable of writing the latter and was horrified to be presented with the task. She told her father she felt ignorant of literary work, although judging by the eventual result she was far from that, and proved to be an accomplished authoress. She asked if she could write the book under his guidance whilst he was still alive, and so get it right, but in that gentle but firm way of his, a way that brooked no argument, he asked for her word of promise, adding that he would prefer her to write his memoir to anyone else, and she could best please him by doing it entirely in her own way, without interference or help from anyone after his death. She eventually consented, being the dedicated and dutiful daughter she was. William refused to discuss the matter again and only once more referred to it, reminding Adeline of her promise. She felt she had only one qualification for the task; that she was a devoted daughter who loved and adored her father, despite his faults.

Shortly after she sent word to Godfrey:

'I should have written before this, but have had a lot of worry for Father was taken with a very bad attack on his heart early one morning, the shock was great to me for I thought he was dying. I had to get a doctor but he got over it and is about as usual, though I don't like to be very long away at a time and this makes it very awkward as Mother too was worse at the time. So I had to rush about between them more than usual. If only the two houses were nearer together how much easier it would be for me.'

In November Adeline urged Godfrey: 'It is simply your duty to come and see Dad. He sends his love; he seems quite touched with your words and I am sure he loves you deeply.' By mid December she was pleading with him to visit his father before it was too late. Godfrey had originally planned a visit back to England in 1905, but failed to make it. She explained their father was so ill she had to be with him every night: 'All I get of Mother and Barthomley is

*The parian bust of W.H. Goss produced by Victor and Huntley after their father's death. It sold well locally and nationally*

a few hours in the day when I can leave him.'

From the time of his third attack he could no longer get into bed and lie down so he slept in a chair, fitfully and at short intervals, but until the day he died he never admitted tiredness. His old dog Paddy passed away in late November aged 16 years, and William instructed Adeline to collect all his writings together which referred to Paddy and to read them out to him. He proposed she should collate these and publish them in the form of a booklet and give a copy to all those who knew and loved the dog. She spent so much time with her father during his last days that she could not fulfil that wish whilst he was alive but included a chapter on Paddy in her subsequent book.

That year William had his Christmas present list organised weeks earlier than was usual, and had his gifts handed round immediately. Some of these presents were newly minted silver coins ordered through his bank. He loved to give presents, especially at Christmas and his children were particularly pleased he managed to do this once more as it so obviously made him happy. William passed his time quietly and peacefully throughout December, but continually thinking of others and organising little gifts. He had overheard Adeline admiring a carved Florentine chair so he asked Victor to order one for her whilst he wrote a loving gift note which was tagged to the chair.

Joseph Myatt who had worked for William since childhood, and was his longest serving and most trusted employee, walked daily up to Ashfield Cottage from the factory, collected the cheques from William and then went to the bank. William used to sit in his study window and watch him go back down the drive until out of sight. He adored Joseph and they were great friends, liking each other's company and both holding similar views about hard work and honesty. Since his second heart attack William had allowed the post and cheques to be opened by his sons, and so Joseph had no reason to come up to the house. One day he requested that Joseph should come up again from the factory and walk past his study window as though to collect the bank cheques, just to bring back memories. Joseph duly obliged.

On 23 December 1905 William seemed to change for the worse and was very quiet all morning, as though rehearsing what he was to say to his family that afternoon. When they were all together he gazed at them and said gently:

'My work is finished, and the closing scene is not far off now. I beg you to be brave and not grieve, for it is but destiny, and no man can evade it, and things have happened as I wished, for I always hoped that I might go as soon as my work was finished, and my day of usefulness over, and I am so thankful to be spared the infirmity of age or painful illness.'

Shortly after this speech he closed his eyes and after some loving words to those seated around him, slept for a while, until his pulse became so weak they all thought he had gone. Soon after he awoke and appeared a little better, relieved even that he had got over the speech and could now talk freely about his impending death. He improved so much that he could use the stairs, but he did not sleep properly, taking only short naps. Even in his last few days he had a radiant complexion and looked very healthy for someone about to die. In her book Adeline painted a beautiful indelible memory of one of William's last scenes:

'A large and quaint armchair, occupied by one, upon whose features there shone more of the 'Light of Life, than of the Shadow of Death.' Soft hair, only slightly faded, rippled around a smooth brow, fully expanded by the development of mental faculties and framed a face which still bore the rose-tints of health, and temperance, and enhanced the brightness of eyes so soft and blue. Eyes now radiant with a new-born light which spoke of earthly things put away, and Heaven at hand. Standing over the chair, was a dark haired son, whose stalwart limbs spoke of full manhood and life-work still before him, and who now looked down on that one with sad eyes, and expression divinely sweet, for he had just spoken of the parting at hand. Firelight played on the two figures, the one whose work was all done, and the other with so much yet to do (Victor) and lit up a background of harmony composed of multi-coloured books and a figure in ancient armour, and completed a picture so striking that no child could treasure up one more glorious than of a father who had passed 'Beyond the Veil'.'

His family noticed that William did not complain or criticise during the last few months, but took each day as it came as a marvellous gift to be enjoyed. He continually blessed all his family and those who came to pay him their last visit. What he had to say was exquisitely said for their ears only, and not for publication. He was delighted when his daughter Edith came, and took great interest in what her children, who he referred to as 'Little darlings', were up to.

William began to leave instructions with regard to certain matters; that his gardener, the good John Orpe, who wanted to stay on at Ashfield Cottage be allowed to do so in order to keep the garden in its fine shape, and for the same consideration to be extended to other household staff. He blessed Sara Smith, a long devoted servant to him and his family for fifteen years, and told her that she had achieved much good in her life sphere. He arranged for his favourite tom-cat to be looked after in its usual luxurious style. His sons were instructed to keep up his many charities and to use their own importance to do good to other people; they were told: 'The pleasure of doing good is the only real pleasure to be sought after.' He explained his feeling of inner peace and described the brightness he saw in his mind as that of a sunset glowing.

He insisted he felt no physical pain and was pleased to be spared the torment of a lingering old age spent helpless in bed, being relieved to depart this life whilst still capable of normal active movement. He wanted, last of all, to be buried in his usual daywear, and directed Victor and Huntley to make sure that this happened, and not to let any funeral director dress him in burial robes. He was relieved when they promised to ensure his last wish.

On new year's eve a close friend, Mrs. J.C. Marshall, brought a bunch of Christmas roses which gave a great deal of pleasure during his last week of life. He rearranged them several times, moved them about his room and finally found the right position for them in front of his mirror, duplicating them visually. Although his family had not discussed the fact that it was new year's eve he knew well enough because when the Stoke bells rang at midnight he hugged Adeline and blessed her.

He spent the first few days of January in his favourite armchair, day and night, in a state of repose. At one o'clock in the morning on 4 January he awoke, had a sip of water, and fell supposedly asleep. He had a son or daughter sitting with him at all times, Victor, Huntley and Adeline all taking turns. It was Adeline who was with him at this particular moment and she asked him if he knew who was sitting with him. He replied whilst still asleep "Why yes dear" and went to kiss her but never managed it and he passed away shortly afterwards:

> 'A swift shadow fell upon those noble features which had passed away before one could realize it had come, and was succeeded by an expression of serene calm and then — not death — but LIFE, and a glimpse of Glory mirrored on that face, and shining wondrously in those radiant eyes as the Soul passed out to its ETERNAL REST.'[1]

William was buried in Hartshill cemetery on 6 January 1906, the service being conducted by the Rev. W.G. Skene, his rector at Barthomley. His grave is marked with a monument of grey stone in the shape of a gigantic replica of St Martin's cross, Iona. The date of birth on the stone cross was recorded inaccurately as July 31 instead of July 30, and one can only presume this to be a mason's error, for the family were very particular about such details.

The personal coat of arms of W.H. Goss was engraved in relief on the cross. The relevant entry in the cemetery records book is number 7807, which records William's age, the fees paid (19/9d), his career as a porcelain manufacturer and his place of death as Ashfield Cottage, Stoke-on-Trent. The grave is situated in consecrated ground in an important position near the main gates, but the cross is now surrounded by rhododendrons and encrusted with lichens, making it all but impossible to read the inscriptions.

Picture postcards of the monument were soon on sale throughout the Potteries and even at Cadmans, the small shop in Barthomley. The Goss family had no part in

*Adolphus's view of the floral tributes at the funeral of his father in 1906*

*The same St. Martin's Iona Cross memorial eighty years later*

arranging the publication of these cards, and none of them appeared to even suspect that a photographer was making a profitable sales line out of Goss's death. They believed the cards to be a great compliment to their father's memory, and bought copies themselves.

The *Daily Telegraph* recorded an obituary on 7 January saying that he died on Thursday, the previous day. William must have been among the famous at the time for such an important national newspaper to have prepared his obituary before his death, which read:

'The death occurred on Thursday of the famous potter. Mr. William Henry Goss of Stoke-on-Trent, and Barthomley, near Crewe. He was the inventor of the heraldic ware known throughout the world. He learned potting many years ago under the late Alderman Copeland, at one time Lord Mayor of London. At the International Exhibition of 1862 he won the much coveted award for the manufacture of articles in ivory porcelain.'

A couple of months later Adeline sadly surveyed the carefully prepared beds of blooming spring flowers, all arranged to be within sight of William's old study window. But spring had come and there was nobody there to appreciate their beauty.

Such was the mystery of William's strange seclusion for the last five years of his life that many rumours began circulating around the Potteries, including the tale of how he had hanged himself in his own factory and that his

In Memoriam
WILLIAM HENRY GOSS,
F.G.S., F.R.M.S.

Photo by W. W. Winter, Derby.
THE LATE MR. W. H. GOSS.

Born July 30th, 1833.    Died January 4th, 1906.

*This tribute to the late W.H. Goss appeared in the sixth edition of the Goss Record*

children took over the firm, pretending he was still alive and at home. This story certainly appeared true to some, partly because of their inability to believe he could be housebound for so long, and also because the tale was related to us in 1984 by villagers living in Stoke.

After William's death Adeline and Victor decided to move out of Ashfield Cottage. His huge collections were donated to the Hanley Museum, who welcomed them with open arms, the report of the donation being mentioned in the *Staffordshire Sentinel* dated 30 January 1908, the ancient pottery, tiles, coins, relics and fossils were appreciated far more than the Goss china, which even nowadays is barely given shelf space in the museum. It is possible that some pieces have been disposed of by the museum, as Goss china is of much less importance in the pottery centre than some of the better known factories like Wedgwood, Copeland Spode and Doulton.

The trusted Myatt family were installed in the former treasure house of Ashfield Cottage, where they could also look after the factory in and out of working hours.

William's will was most interesting. Victor and Huntley were left the factory, contents and land, in equal shares. His wife was to be paid £50 per annum by them and Adolphus to be paid 5% commission on all cash receipts from agencies which he started up. Victor and Huntley were also given £1,000 to share in forming a business capital. Adolphus was to be given £4,000, to compensate him for the pottery going to his brothers to the exclusion of himself, on the condition he did not try to set up business in competition with them. To Adeline he left his shares in the North Staffordshire and North British Railway Companies, and his house contents of furniture, plate, linen, china, glass, books, pictures, prints and other effects both at Ashfield Cottage, Stoke and Church House, Barthomley. Florence, Edith and Adeline were to each receive £1,000 cash. His two old oak 'Good Shepherd' chairs and two large old oak cabinets were for the Mayor, Aldermen and Burgesses of Stoke, and his entire museum of curios to be displayed as an extended museum for the literati to be organised by the Mayor and Aldermen of Hanley.

It would seem that William did not think his wife deserved any more than £50 per annum. On hearing the news of the bequest she said, 'That's good. Now he's forgiven me.' We wonder if that was a somewhat sarcastic response, in view of his wealth. If William had been difficult in his old age at least their mother Georgiana was somewhat easier. After years of being firm and dominant over her family, Adeline in particular described her mother in 1888, as becoming sweeter and more adorable with each year that passed. She was devoted to her grandchildren, especially Ethel. 'Grandmother Goss is quite a young woman yet and passes for eighteen in the dusk of twilight when she is on the tricycle' joked Victor. Although hampered throughout her life with one weak leg, she was spirited, persevered with her tricycle, and even in June 1907 was getting out locally and using the machine in the lanes. Her hair was jet black until the day she died.

Alice Goss came over from America with her youngest boy in 1905 and Georgiana was very grateful to see the boy, and delighted when her own long lost boy Godfrey also visited England a year later. After William's death, Georgiana felt perhaps she had to take over as head of the household and take care of the family. She certainly became more assertive and exerted her power over those nearest her. Adeline reckoned her mother had become 'very strong willed, ruling Victor and me with iron rods, I just buckle in to her as I don't want anything to regret.'

When Georgiana died two and a half years after her husband on 2 July, 1908, also of heart failure, her remains were interred at Hartshill cemetery under the great Iona cross, reunited with her husband, no doubt to William's chagrin had he known.

### Reference

1.  *Fragments from the Life and Writings of W H Goss* by Eva Adeline Goss 1907. Hill & Ainsworth

*Georgiana Goss, Anie's mother, wall pocket*

*Georgiana with grandchild at Barthomley*

# CHAPTER TEN

# Life Without Father

Every man's life is a fairy-tale written by God's fingers.

Hans Christian Anderson

Just before the turn of the century, Victor had moved into 'Oulton Rocks' a magnificent house at Stone which he rented, although he still kept his pigs and cows up at Barthomley, his former home.

After their father's death, Victor and Adeline took a cruise on the RMS 'Ortona' to the Bay of Biscay and Marseilles, Gibraltar, Naples, Pompeii, Rome, Nice, Pisa, Genoa, Florence, San Remo, Monte Carlo and by mail steamer back to London. Whilst crossing the Bay of Biscay they sailed into a terrific gale and poor Adeline was sick. It was a large vessel, but water poured down below and cabins were flooded, crockery smashed and even the settees which were screwed to the floor in the drawing room were wrenched from their fastenings and 'went waltzing about the place to the danger of everybody and everything.' The poor third class passengers lost all their goods. A collection was taken amongst the first class passengers to give those who lost the most the means to replace their clothing at Marseilles. Victor gashed his forehead when he was pitched against the bulkhead while helping to get everyone down below. He was bandaged up and his fellow passengers called him 'the Absent Minded Beggar' because they thought he looked like Kipling's famous picture of the Soldier in the Boer War.

He had a good sense of fun. In Anie Goss Jewitt's autograph book we found the following amusing ditty in Victor's hand, signed and dated 13.1.08:

'A *little* bald Parson most gritty
Fell in love with a *tall* girl named Kitty
He tried for a kiss, couldn't reach,
'twas a miss,
And he said, "Oh Good Lord, What a pity" '

Victor was a member of both the Highways and Plans and Public Libraries Committees of Stoke Council. In 1910 he was elected to the Potteries Federated Council as a representative for Stoke, and continued until his death in 1913. He was also a Freemason, being a member of the Menturia Lodge, No. 418. No wonder he never married, he did not have the time!

In May 1912 he was reported in the *Staffordshire Sentinel* as presiding over the annual dinner of the North Midland Telegraph Company of the Royal Engineers of Shelton. By now he was Captain Goss, and although no longer a member of the Company, he was interested in its welfare having been one of its founders and was pleased it was kept at its full war strength, especially as some critics had prophesied the breaking up of the Territorial Force.

It was a terrible shock for the whole town when Victor died from a fall from his horse one morning in March, 1913. A witness said he believed Victor was a brilliant horseman, but that his horse had trodden on a wasps nest which it knocked from a hedge, and Victor was thrown off, landing on his head. A full report appeared in the *Staffordshire Sentinel* on Thursday, 27 March 1913. There was a further report of the massive procession at his military funeral in the same newspaper four days later. The funeral was a very important affair, far more so than that of his father. Among the mourners were Goss employees such as Alfred and William Mollart, Joseph Myatt, D. Bradley, Joe Ashley and W. Watkin. His gardener H.W. Ratcliffe and chauffeur H. Perkins offered their services as bearers, but this duty was undertaken by Victor's brother officers. The route the procession took commenced at Oulton Rocks, his home, to Edward Street and then on to Hartshill Cemetery where he was buried at the foot of his father's Iona cross monument.

The *Pottery Gazette* (1 May 1913), gave its own detailed account of his death, but differed as to the place of death, recording it as Strongford, near Trentham. The accompanying photograph was of Victor in his twenties, sporting a fine moustache.

In the *Guardian*, 5 June 1914, details of his will included property left valued gross at £20,723 and net £18,163. He left £1,000 and his share in Ashfield Cottage to his sister Adeline, £1,000 to his niece Mildred Mountford (daughter of Edith) and £1,000 and his gold ring to Gladys Johnson, who we can only suggest was the woman he was to have married, although he had been courting Amelia Ash, head paintress at his factory. To his nephew Dick (Adolphus's

*'Oulton Rocks', Stone, which Victor rented after the death of his father. His lady friend is seated on the lawn*

son) he left shipping shares and a position in the factory as well as his motor tricar and motor bicycle. To his twin sister Edith, railway shares and his two houses adjacent to the Goss factory. His land at Alsager he left to his nephew Vernon (son of Adolphus) and to his brother Huntley his share in the factory and land (but not in the business), and his motorcar. He requested that the business be under the management of Huntley, and that the residue of his property be left to his niece Anie (Georgiana) Jewitt (daughter of his late sister Georgiana), and to his nephews and nieces the children of his brother Adolphus and sister Edith. He left £100 each (a fortune in those days) to the following employees of the Goss factory: Joseph Myatt, Alfred Mollart, William Mollart, Frederick Perkins, Laura Schofield, Sarah Smith, William Ratcliffe and Elizabeth Cartright. With hindsight, Victor's death a year before the beginning of the Great War may have been only a year or so before he surely would have fallen on the Western Front, an alternative which he would have definitely preferred.

\* \* \* \* \* \* \* \* \* \* \* \* \*

Florry managed to become engaged three times. The first was in 1901 to a young lawyer from Stafford who she met in Stafford rectory and as he was a stranger, William had to give his consent 'in the dark'. Discovering he was no good after embezzling £500, and after realising

what a rogue he was, she broke off the engagement. Two years later her second beau was a local curate from Rode and liked by her sisters. His name was Langham Muriel, and Adeline thought him 'a dear fellow though fearfully poor', his position being minor Canon of Lichfield Cathedral. She loved him intensely but he was a devout high church man who believed in confession and Rome and constantly tried to convert her. She did not wish to be converted so they parted amicably. She felt miserable during the time leading up to this parting and she was quiet and moody at home, leaving her mother and sister to discuss behind her back what could be the matter with her. The parting made her decide to leave the area and get away. 'I felt I should have died if I had lived in the place he had been accustomed to be in, or had been in.' She joined the hospital at Tewkesbury for one year after running away. Adeline was most put out:

'Florry has been very troublesome and discontented at home and without consulting anyone went off for a Hospital nurse last July. She was unhappy about her second engagement but would not tell anyone whether it was broken off or not. We think *it is* but she has refused to state anything definitely. We trust she will give up nursing at the end of her first year and settle down at home. She is wanted here and at Rode as I cannot be at both houses at once and both Father and Mother need me. We used to take each a week at Stoke and Rode before she left.'

The funeral of Captain Goss, who died from injuries received through being thrown from his horse while riding from his residence at Oulton to Stoke last week, took place at Hartshill Cemetery, Stoke-on-Trent, on Monday afternoon. Our photographs show: 1. The procession leaving Stoke. 2. Arrival at Hartshill Cemetery. 3. Rev. H. Moore, Vicar of Acton, Cheshire (on reader's left) and Rev. T. L. Palmer, Vicar of Oulton (officiating clergy), leading the procession. 4. Scene at the graveside.

*Newspaper report of Victor's magnificent funeral procession at which 'half the residents of Stoke paid their respects'*

*The dining room at Barthomley with Victor's silver and gold sword on the table*

Whilst Florry was working at the hospital she became friendly with the vicar who was kindly and so she began helping him in his missionary work.

By 1905 she became engaged to Albert Loring Murdock. None of her family was pleased but somehow she obtained her father's permission:

'There is trouble in the house just now for Florence came over a for a few days and wants such a big fuss over this wedding, which everyone thinks is such bad taste under the circumstances and it ought to be at a Registry Office, or at least a quiet one if she must take such a marriage into the Church,'

continued Adeline:

'I shall not go and hear it, or ever meet that man again, for if he had not met F she would have been a different girl and not the trouble she has been, but of course we are all glad for her to marry him for then we shall have no more responsibility. Dear Victor went abroad for his holiday and was away nearly a month; it was so desolate without him but he wrote me from every port, and I sent him the daily happenings.'

Florry had to sell her house and contents when arranging to get married and just before she sold 'Barton House' at Tewkesbury, Godfrey's wife Alice with her little son Percy, came to stay with her. She was much amused when Percy was taken by strangers to be her boy, because of his red curls.

Florry had corresponded with Murdock during her teens and throughout her relationships with her younger boyfriends. Murdock's wife died around the turn of the century and a year later he thought he would look up his 'little protegé' whilst in England, and found her to be a beautiful, mature and reserved lady of about 30 years of age. At this time he was in his 70's, and was immediately attracted to her, soon falling in love. When he first proposed she refused but eventually agreed to marry him. They were due to have a grand wedding at Lawton Hall on St. Valentine's Day 1906, but her father died on 4 January so they decided to have a quiet wedding instead, and were married at St. Bertoline's Church, Barthomley on 14 February 1906. Albert Murdock was three years older than their late father, looked positively older, and was extremely wealthy. The wedding was well reported, with a long article appearing in *The Gentlewoman*. Victor gave the bride away, but there were no bridesmaids. One of her school friends, a Miss R.C. Hodgson of Blundellsands House, Blundellsands, Liverpool gave her a Persian table-cloth and she received over a hundred gifts in all. Murdock's wedding present was gold jewellery and their honeymoon was a six month tour of Paris, Japan, New York and California. While in America they had a ride in Buffalo Bill's stagecoach.

*Florence Goss who married Albert Murdock in 1906 on St. Valentine's Day*

*Murdock on his wedding day only a month after William Goss passed away. He took Florence on a six month world tour for a honeymoon*

*Murdock at home at Maple Hall. Weeks after their marriage, Florence wrote to her mother. 'How long should a bride go before giving in to her husband?' Back came the reply, 'You had better give in right away or he will be dead!'*

*Maple Hall, South Hingham, Massachusetts, U.S.A., once the home of Florence and Albert Loring Murdock*

Florry took her servant, April Farmer, from Britain in order to maintain her English standards but after paying for a first class fare out for her, the 'ungrateful and dishonourable girl' left Florence and her £1 per week wages, to go and look after an invalid nearby for double the pay.

Some time after beginning her luxurious lifestyle, she wrote and asked her mother, 'How long should a bride go before giving in to her husband?' Her mother replied, 'You had better give in right away or he will be dead!'

Eleven and half months later, Mr. Murdock had his heart's desire — a baby daughter who was named Flora Valentine Murdock, in honour of their wedding day. During her pregnancy Florry and Murdock were very excited. 'We are looking forward to the event with great joy. To feel I have someone to love me as I love dear mother will be a great joy,' she said.

At first she enjoyed attending to baby Valentine. Later on she found it hard to cope despite having an English nurse, and Edith, who was a natural mother, offered to look after the baby in England, along with her own brood. The offer was not taken up!

Florry was always at her best socially, and at home in her large mansion miles from anywhere in Massachusetts, she began to feel restless and lonely. She eventually began to get used to her new life, but felt she didn't get out and about enough and wished for a companion.

When Vallie, as her parents called her, was one-and-a-half years old they went back to England to visit the Gosses and also for business reasons. Grandmother Georgiana adored her 'Yankee grandchild,' and Vallie can still remember crawling on her hands and knees up along the winding stairs at Barthomley to see black-haired Grandma who was in a four-poster bed in a high necked, long sleeved

*Florence with Flora Valentine in 1907*

lace trimmed nightgown and cap, molasses humbugs to hand. Georgiana died aged 79 before they returned to England again. It was in her honour, because she was of French origin, that Valentine's name was pronounced in the French way. Vallie was again taken to England when she was three years old. She can remember having toothache, and was unable to explain her discomfort to her uncle Victor and Aunt Adeline who both thought her a rather disagreeable little girl. Vallie remembers Victor and his antics, in particular pulling faces, trying to make her stop crying. When her problem was finally diagnosed, Jim Mountford, her uncle and a dentist, attended to her. He was abrupt and distant and she felt he was rather cold.

Albert Murdock was a doctor, who, together with another doctor, discovered around 1860 that liver, then only given to animals, was the life saving treatment for pernicious anaemia. Murdock bought out his partner and perfected his potion which he called 'Murdock's Liquid Food'. Sales boomed and the products sold successfully in drug stores all over America, throughout the continent and in parts of the Orient. Every two years Murdock went to Europe, and every five to the Orient, to keep up his agencies. Whilst in England in the 1860's, he wanted an advertising statuette of a bullock and sheep modelled in porcelain to use for shop window displays. He was told that William Henry Goss's china was the finest so he instructed William to design a suitable model. Possibly

*Florence at Maple Hall, always prettily dressed, but with little social life*

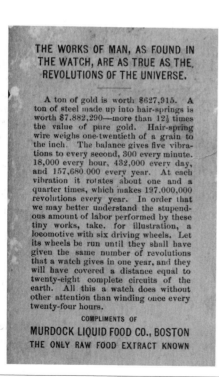

*Example of literature distributed by the eccentric Albert Murdock, advertising Murdock's Liquid Food*

they became acquainted at the Boston exhibition where William had displayed his wares. The result was acceptable, an order was placed, and the model of a bullock and two sheep on an oval plinth with Murdock's advertising slogan printed on the side — 'MURDOCK'S LIQUID FOOD IS CONDENSED BEEF, MUTTON & FRUITS' was produced for Murdock to give to his agents in 1868.

It is surprising that William undertook the order which was for advertising purposes, considering his own negative views on that subject.

Publicly, Murdock was a very generous and charitable man. He built and ran a free 175 bed hospital for the poor women and children of Boston and also sent free cases of his Murdock's Liquid Food to the Civil War wounded. Yet a member of his family can recall him as 'stingy', perhaps it was because he had started life as a poor boy. He founded the Boston Boys West End Lodging House on Causeway Street, and the Murdock Free Surgical Hospital on Washington Avenue and Gainsborough Street, and assisted girls in receiving a college education. He was also instrumental in founding the John Hancock Life Insurance Company, one of the earliest, and now one of the largest in the U.S.A.

Murdock was never able to learn from his new wife what sum her father had bequeathed her. 'Not that I want it as I am willing she should burn the whole of it before I would allow her to spend it on her own person.' Florry did not wish to burn it and used it to maintain what little independence she could. She told her brother Godfrey that she had a vault in the State Bank at Boston which cost her 10 dollars a year.

She was lucky to have a tennis court, croquet lawn, golf course, lake etc in the grounds of her home. She wanted a boat for the pool so she gave Albert one for his birthday. She even had a horse called 'Maple' and wished she knew how to ride it.

Although money was no problem, it seemed to divide the marriage. Florry wrote to her brothers asking for their advice on the matter of her husband selling some property, including the Bartoll Hotel on the corner of Huntingdon Avenue and Gainsborough Street in Boston, in secret without her knowledge.

Adeline was very worried about poor Florry and was concerned that Murdock had tried to cause trouble between his wife and Godfrey. Adeline told Godfrey:

> 'She was so firmly convinced you had backed up her old man and encouraged him in his wrong doing but I feel sure you would not and knew the old man had told lies in saying you had told him all sorts of things which were obviously absurd and untrue, yet which he used as a weapon against Florry. Poor girl, she had had to pay a bitter price for all she did.'

Her mother's death during these troubles affected her very badly.

*The Murdock family memorial stone at South Hingham. Florence chose to be buried at Marshfield, in the first settlers' graveyard alongside one of the original Pilgrim Fathers*

*An uncomfortable Alice Goss on a compulsory week's trip to visit Florence Murdock. Alice could not be persuaded to stay one day longer*

Murdock himself died when he was 82 years old. Before he passed away he asked to see his beloved Flora Valentine, who was then only five years old, and he told her:

'Flora, I want you to remember this. Your mother was the purest woman I have ever known and I want you to take care of her.'

After Murdock died, Florry was not able to continue her luxurious lifestyle and she had to give up their home and servants, for Murdock had bequeathed most of his wealth elsewhere. On her next trip to England 12 years later, Florry met Sir John Fagge on the ship, on his way home to claim his title. Mrs. Murdock and Sir John (a year older than she), fell in love and married a year later in 1932. The Stoke papers were published with large three inch headlines, 'Former belle of Stoke marries Baronet.' When she married her baronet, she told her daughter, 'If it doesn't work out it will be your fault.' With her new stepfather and mother, Vallie travelled around the world for 13 months, through 20 European countries, the States, Cuba, Canada and the Caribbean. Sir John had one daughter, Lucy, from his first marriage who was born about 1910, but she distanced herself from her father's new family. His title was dropped by his family after his death.

Harold and Georgiana Peavey, (Georgiana is the granddaughter of Sophia, who was the sister of W.H. Goss) visited Sir John and Lady Fagge once, and thought Sir John delightful. Georgiana recalled he was pleased to talk to another man, and fancied he was rather 'hen-pecked'.

Florence certainly held the purse strings. Georgiana first saw her as a beautiful bride in June 1906 at Arthur's (Hurlin) Harvard Class Day and remembered how all eyes followed her.

\* \* \* \* \* \* \* \* \* \* \* \* \* \*

After her father's death, Adeline began the dreaded task of his biography. He knew she would be discreet and maintain a strict silence over any of their family's differences and by October of the following year she had nearly finished:

'I have been very busy with my poor book for a long time and now it is being printed there is a terrible lot of work to do in correcting the proofs. It won't be out for 6 months they say and it does seem so long. But the Publishers tell me that no 'Life' of anyone ever comes out under 2 years after the death of the person as it is impossible to get hold of the matter necessary. I wrote it up under that period of time. This gave me a scrap of comfort.'

The resulting book contained little of the family's personal life and virtually nothing about the factory, because she insisted that her brother Adolphus was better qualified than herself on this aspect of her father's life. She did, however, record his beliefs, idiosyncrasies and various

*Adeline's sitting room at Barthomley, with the Alhambra Vase, bust of Goss and Aberdeen bronze pot on mantelpiece, the two terracotta Keystones of the Kingdom suspended from the wall and giant two-handled Loving Cup with flag decoration on the small table*

THE CLOUGHS, N! NEWCASTLE

'The Cloughs', Keele Road, a magnificent residence which Adeline rented, was famous for the monkeys kept by the previous owners

The entrance hall of Adeline's home. The origin of the large bust of Sir Walter Scott is not known

incidents which have helped us to understand him and the way he lived.

When the book was published in 1908, it was favourably reviewed in the Staffordshire press. The newspapers also mentioned the promise of a second volume *Antiquities of the Staffordshire Potteries* that William had compiled chiefly from manuscript memoranda written by Enoch Wood, the potter, and his contemporaries.

Adolphus told Godfrey that his refusal to write to his family was particularly upsetting for Adeline, who lived for her family, and was making her ill. She never failed to write regularly to Godfrey, keeping him up to date with their affairs. She was a 'loving and faithful sister' who had become 'very bitter'. She was by now in her early thirties and it did not appear as if she was going to get married. She was overjoyed when Godfrey finally did visit England.

She lived at Barthomley with her mother after her father's death, and continued living there for a while after her mother had died. She had weekend runs in the country with Victor, and paired up with him to have foursomes with married acquaintances such as Captain and Mrs. Giffard.

When she divided up her late mother's belongings, Adeline put Godfrey's in a drawer and locked them up. Adolphus said he would consult the American Consul to see if the possessions could be sent out free of duty. However, he was rather tardy in domestic matters not important enough to be in the nature of business, and did nothing, even leaving Godfrey's inheritance in the bank waiting for him to take the trouble of writing out the cheques, which Adeline thought a shame because it was only earning trifling interest. Eventually Godfrey, Florry and Adeline gave Adolphus instructions to give their share of their mother's money to their aunt in Marlow. Adolphus

eventually got around to sending the money including his share, and accompanying messages, a year after being asked. Adeline was disgusted with him.

Villagers can still recall a scandal in the village centred on the rectory which caused Adeline to move away from Barthomley. She rented 'The Cloughs' at Newcastle on the Keele Road, a huge house which was well known for the monkeys kept there by the previous owners. Adeline had a picture postcard printed of her seated in the walled vegetable garden with her staff and gardeners. She certainly lived well. She was intelligent and had a good business brain, but unfortunately never had the opportunity to use it. In those days it was unseemly for young ladies to have a job let alone 'in trade' and their only work was in raising money for charitable causes. She was quite wealthy in her middle age, having used her inheritance wisely in various investments and stocks and shares, and was thus able to afford a large staff to keep up her home and garden to a good standard.

Having studied this good woman, we can only feel she never married because she did not want to lose the name 'Goss', and because every man she met did not measure up to her feelings for her father. As she grew older she lost her looks although always remaining slim, with long hair piled up on her head in a typically Edwardian style, favouring white frilly blouses and long dark skirts. She regularly visited friends and family, her male companion being one Edgar Brunt, a name which also appears in her will. She died at the comparatively early age of 51 on 5 July, 1916, and failed to leave anything to 'Dick', one of Adolphus and Nellie's sons, although his brothers and sisters were all favourably dealt with. Obviously she disapproved of him, probably because he ran away from home in his youth.

*Adeline and her staff in her kitchen garden at 'The Cloughs'. Some of her servants used to work for her late father including Sarah Smith, far left of the three housemaids*

*Mrs. Alice Goss with son Frank at their farm in Eldorado, Oklahoma*

*An ageing Godfrey and Alice in Eldorado, 1925*

She had much expensive jewellery, including an old pearl and hair ring given to her by Mrs. Crapper, the wife of her father's old friend. Among her bequeathed treasured possessions was a silver gilt dessert service presented by Birmingham manufacturers to Samuel Carter Hall. Many of her porcelain treasures which had been her father's, were donated to the Hanley museum, with the exception of some choice pieces. One of these was the Alhambra vase, a huge winged vase of terracotta and turquoise blue in the style of the Alhambra Palace at Granada, Spain, which had been kept on the mantlepiece in her sitting room and is possibly the most important piece of Goss ever made.

To Edgar Brunt she gave £1,000 worth of shares; to Huntley, Hubert and Vernon all her furniture and household effects, each of them choosing in turn according to seniority until all the items were divided up. Vallie Murdock was left her Queen Anne silver teapot, two cream jugs and basins with armorial bearings, her Cloisonné ware and her collection of mother-of-pearl and tortoisehell card cases. Ethel and Dolly shared her Bonds and jewellery. Anie (Georgiana Goss Jewitt) was given various shares in Railway Companies. Edith received William's single stone diamond ring whilst her share in Ashfield Cottage went to Huntley and Grace and Peggy were left jewellery. The full list of bequests was enormous.

Although her cause of death was kidney failure, we cannot help feeling that Victor's death three years earlier took much of the light out of her life and she never quite overcame the shock.

\* \* \* \* \* \* \* \* \* \* \* \* \*

Edith and James Mountford, by now living happily at 'Mon Bijou' in Pinner, were bringing up Mildred, Grace and James, born 1901, 1903 and 1905 respectively. Eric, who followed four years later, died young. Ethel was a regular visitor and in 1916 they moved to Barnt Green in Worcestershire. Mildred and James both married and emigrated to New Zealand, whilst Grace remained single and taught at Cheltenham Ladies College before also emigrating to New Zealand and joining them in Gisbourne.

\* \* \* \* \* \* \* \* \* \* \* \* \*

Since Alice's departure to America in 1886 and her immediate marriage to Godfrey, very few letters arrived from the pair, apart from a couple to her parents. A friend, Albert, from 64, Cannon Street, Hanley, who worked for William, told them 'Your dear father-in-law Mr. Goss says it is very strange and can not understand it at all. All the work people keep asking me if we have *heard* from you.'

*The isolated Eldorado, Oklahoma farm, eventually run by the sons of Alice and Godfrey*

*A closer view with their sons and wives on the verandah*

*Godfrey's orange grove which he created on barren land at Raymondville, Texas, 1929*

The newlyweds were hopeless at letter writing, being so wrapped up in each other and with work and setting up home. At Christmas 1888 the whole Buckley family were in tears because there was neither news nor seasonal good wishes from Alice and Godfrey. It was as though they had lost her for good. They knew Alice was continually unwell, but had given birth to Godfrey Victor the year before. Their family was to grow and grow, Archibald Buckley came along three years later, Adolphus William in 1891, Frank Thomas, and a daughter who was lost in 1900, and finally Percy Edwin, who was notable for his long, brilliant red curls which people in the street stopped to admire. Godfrey Victor, the eldest boy, like Adolphus's children and Anie Jewitt — all had blue eyes and golden hair. Adeline supposed their hair would eventually change when they got older to that of her and her brother Godfrey's colour, a dark auburn. Godfrey had brown eyes. It appeared that Alice and Godfrey took it in turns to name their children after loved ones in their past lives.

Several of Alice's fellow workers at Goss's emigrated to Trenton, New Jersey including Emily Nicklin, Anne Jovett and H. Dooley, but they all ended up leaving Trenton through shortage of work for their husbands and returned to England. Alice's younger brother Frank went out to be a potter's apprentice in 1892. He had been errand running since he was 12 years old and was no doubt attracted by promises of the good life. Alice's sister Emmie and husband Joe had seven children, one of whom lived with Edwin

*The sons of Godfrey and Alice: Archibald, Godfrey Victor, Adolphus, Percy and Frank in Eldorado. The only daughter died at birth*

(Ted) and her sister Annie in Macclesfield. Her niece wrote to her in 1899 from 12, Foley Place, Longton to tell her that at the age of 15 years she had just got a job as an apprentice gilder.

Alice and Godfrey's children had little opportunity of

learning to spell properly. In 1906 Archibald Buckley Goss wrote home to Kokomo when he ran away to Parkin, Arkansas and managed to misspell mother and even father. He was 16 years old at the time! We wonder what Adolphus thought of him!

Despite Adeline pleading with Godfrey to hurriedly return home to visit their ailing father, or even write to him, by the time he did it was too late. He eventually came over in April 1906 and it was while he was away in England that his second son Archie ran away to Arkansas. Not only was Godfrey too late to see William Henry, but when he called on Alice's mother, a neighbour, Mrs. Wadkim, had to go over to him and tell him Mrs. Buckley had died just a few days earlier. He did go and see his own mother who for many years had to contend with hearing news about him third hand. No doubt she received him with open arms but he reported back to Alice that she was incapable of leaving the house at Barthomley, and didn't think she would ever get out again. Most of his month in England he spent with her although he did go to see Edith and her family whom he thought were doing very well.

He discovered from his father's will that he would have about £7,000 when all was settled, but that it would be a long time before he received it. When he did it would have to be invested in order to earn income and he would after be able to live without working, but until then he had to keep up his job.

By March 1907 Victor was sending out drafts to Godfrey for £1,000 at a time for security reasons. Victor advised him to buy the land that he had talked about on his visit to England, because he believed property was sure to go up in value.

Godfrey still ran his pottery business in Kokomo, Indiana, his main line being the production of electrical insulators; a photograph shows him travelling by wagon with his samples conspicuously displayed for sale, but although he entered this embryo industry early, he did not appear to have prospered.

Godfrey's pottery was never viable and although several plates, pierced fruit baskets, comports and floral crosses were produced, none were for commercial sale.

The only items we now know that were made for sale by Godfrey in Kokomo, and not by his father in Stoke-on-Trent, were a range of multi-coloured hand painted duck posy holders in two sizes and a derringer pistol designed for wall hanging. These pieces are of a similar, if not the same heavy porcelain as the fruit baskets we know Godfrey produced, and are marked UNDERGLAZE PORCELAIN BY GOSS. The porcelain used was based on his father's parian and he obviously developed the body from the local materials available and from what he had been taught by his father. These models appear in America with increasing regularity and were definitely retailed there.

When the bulk of his inheritance came through, a sum not unadjacent to $50,000, a fortune in those days, Godfrey closed or sold the pottery and moved to Eldorado,

Oklahoma in 1907 where he bought barren land upon which virtually nothing grew and turned it into a moderately successful farm.

Godfrey was not a good businessman and not a particularly good farmer, but he was adventurous enough to be in the front line of the opening up of the West and his land purchase at Eldorado proved a good investment.

Godfrey put up $85,000 to help found the First State Bank of Eldorado and then moved to Raymondville, Texas, near the Rio Grande river on the Mexican border, whilst retaining the Eldorado farm later run by his sons. Godfrey became a gentleman farmer who, like his own father, loved nature. He kept horses, fish and peacocks and appreciated his surroundings.

Although not particularly successful at business, he had a good understanding of chemistry and a practical turn of mind. Whilst in Indiana, he invented the drycell battery and had almost patented it when the idea was stolen by an employee and exploited. He also improved the carbon transmitters in telephones and even developed a chemical cure for cancer, the composition of which he steadfastly refused to disclose.

Alice died in 1936 and Godfrey in 1939 in Raymondville and both are buried at nearby Lasara.

* * * * * * * * * * * * * *

Huntley commuted to Stoke from Alsager on week days. His house afforded fine views over the mere and local countryside and his four youngsters had a large exciting garden to explore which encouraged Huntley's love of farming began as a child when he helped with his father's cattle in Barthomley. He began farming modestly in 1907 when he bought a red heifer and her calf for £16, which Victor believed would make a good milker. He became an active supporter of the Crewe and District Agricultural Society and was voted president one year, beating Mr. Ernest Craig on the strength of popular vote. Huntley and Florence used to keep a few hens, cows and pigs and every so often the old gardener used to come to the house and say, 'Morning, Ma'am — it's time us pigs went to market again.' And Florence would agree.

Huntley was a Justice of the Peace for the County and once, in court, a witness stood up and said, 'Yer worship, I wants all the ladies to leave the court for what I have to tell yer is VERY RUDE. . .' Huntley was amused to recount that all the ladies sat tight and didn't budge! Those who knew him agreed he was a man of rare integrity with a good sense of humour, who enjoyed practical jokes (the reader will recall his father's prank in the snow at Barthomley) and was a gentle, kind person. He was generous, affectionate, courageous, interested in local affairs, becoming a local councillor like Victor and a member of the B'Hoys, a local society together with his eldest brother, Adolphus.

*Taken in 1936, the children of Adolphus, son of Godfrey: Joyce, Berniece, Cora, Ruby, Bill, Adolphus himself, Eva and Betty*

*Godfrey the commercial traveller offering his porcelain electrical fittings for sale*

*Porcelain electrical conductor 40mm high, 40mm wide, invented, manufactured and sold by Godfrey in Kokomo, Indiana*

*Multi-coloured floral plate decorated by Alice (Buckley) Goss*

*Pierced cake basket, 220mm dia., made by Godfrey in Trenton, New Jersey*

*Reverse showing Alice's signature*

*Hand painted duck made by Godfrey in America*

*Comport modelled by Godfrey, height 110mm, width 220mm, with bird decoration in bas-relief*

*Adolphus (left) and Frank Goss (right) with mechanic Egbert Carlson and 1941 Chrysler at the Goss Motor Co. run by the two Goss brothers*

*Florence and Huntley with Margaret, John, Noel and Godfrey*

Huntley was very interested in old books and discovered several old first editions which he bought for a few pence from junk shops etc. and brought back to his youngest son John who shared his passion for reading. Huntley also had a passion for collecting stamps, and at one time had a valuable collection.

After the war, which Huntley took in his stride, and which affected him far less than Victor's accidental death in 1913 which had left him devastated, Dick Goss did not return to his job as travelling salesman, and so Huntley took on a female representative even though many said he would have done far better with a man. Although Huntley and Florence had four children, Huntley Noel William (Noel) born in 1899, Geoffrey Kingston in 1901, Margaret Winifred Elizabeth (Peggy) in 1903, and Richard John (John) in 1905, they were to have no grandchildren and so that particular line of Gosses has ended.

By the time Huntley had to sell the Falcon works to Harold Taylor Robinson in 1929, Huntley and Florence's wealth had all gone. They sold 'The Lodge' in 1936 and went to live in Hartshill, Stoke. The purchasers of their old house divided the massive building into two halves, Gwendoline Moir, daughter of the Rev. Moir, vicar of Alsager, who was later to share her home with Ethel (Goss) Burne, acquiring the larger half. One of the reasons Huntley had to sell up was because he dipped into his own pocket to pay the wages of his staff right up until the sale of the firm. No employees lost any wages, and he paid all the bills. In spite of the difficult times and having to subsidize a loss-making factory, he did not go bankrupt but remained solvent until the firm was sold to Harold Taylor Robinson, who owned Arcadian, Cauldon and eventually most other heraldic pottery firms.

Noel was a beautiful child, with fair hair and his father's looks. Like his brothers, was too young to enlist to fight in the Great War. All three boys went straight from school to work in the Goss factory, but Noel soon earned a pilot's licence and volunteered for the Air Force towards the end of the war when he was just old enough to do so. He had the necessary injections but developed a fever and was in hospital for months. By the time he recovered the war was over, so he had missed the opportunity of serving his country which distressed him. When he reached his twenties he occupied his spare time with amateur dramatics, belonging to the same club as his younger brother John, cousins Dolly, Ethel and Mary (Kingston) and members of the Hammersley family.

Huntley's son Geoffrey was appointed by the Rev. Moir to be Scoutmaster of the newly formed Alsager group of Scouts, which became famous for winning three life-saving medals. During the years following the Great War, when Ethel led the Primrose League Buds and Peggy was with the Brownies, Geoffrey worked hard with his Scouts. Even in 1931 they were still in charge of their respective clubs.

Margaret (Peggy) loved needlework and handiwork like her mother Florence. She once embroidered the Goss family coat of arms, which was perfect, accurate and pleasing even though it was a sizeable undertaking. She was also very keen on bowls, and Louise Goss recalls how in her youth Peggy liked to play day and night. She loved children, and was disappointed not to have had any of her own. Peggy was marvellous at writing children's stories and wanted to become a children's nurse, but Huntley would not allow her to work, refusing her permission even to earn a living. He took all his views and rules from his father even though they were no longer living in the Victorian age. She did, however, help out in the works' design department, and some plate and mug decorations designed by her, bear her initials, M.G., and the date 1922.

The youngest, Richard John, was always known as John, Jack or Rufus as a child. He and his mother were very close, and he soon showed evidence of having a lively and interesting mind which his father once told him he envied. John would spend hours reading books in the boathouse at the bottom of the garden, he painted well and was a good croquet player. He was artistic as well as good with his hands and used to make dolls houses complete with tennis courts, the nets made from human hair and also miniature boats. He became an amateur portrait painter, and his paintings were hung in a Paris portrait gallery where he obtained a silver medal.

John was a gadget enthusiast, and was always inventing things. He did not get the chance to work for his father's firm for more than a few years, but during his time there as designer he modelled the highly prized series of Goss animals, several choice models, and some cottages. John could remember an earthenware plate in his home as a child, impressed W.H. Goss, with the initials GG on the top. He thought perhaps it could have been a trial piece but what became of it he did not know. The initials could have stood for Georgiana Goss.

* * * * * * * * * * * * * *

*Adolphus in the grounds of 'The Old Villa', Alsager*

*'The Old Villa' today, minus its once glamorous grounds which have now been built on*

After 'Mere Leigh' Adolphus and his family moved to 'Lyndhurst', Church Road, still in Alsager, during 1901-2. After being left £4,000 in his father's will in 1906. Victor thought it:

'A splendid chance to buy that house on the Alsager Mere which Herbert Godwin built. The house and nine acres of land were offered to Adolphus for £2,500 but he has not enough go in him to buy it although he can *easily* afford to do so. The house alone without any land cost Herbert Godwin £3,000 to build. Adolphus has had nothing to do for the last seven years and might have built a house on his own land years ago but he is too sleepy and I do not think he will ever do it.'

But do it he did, and by August 1907 he had completed his transactions with the executors of a Mr. Gibbons who was the son-in-law of Thomas Walker, the previous owner who had been an earthenware manufacturer.

He immediately re-named Alsager Villa 'The Old Villa' because it sounded less pretentious. The house was a handsome and pleasantly situated brick building, erected about 1854, and was at that time surrounded by well laid out pleasure grounds. Adolphus described its views of the mere and wood from the front bedrooms, and views of Mellors Hill from the back bedroom windows. The Rev. A.L. Moir described the house as being 'set back from the street in an old-world garden stretching to Sandbach Road, not far from the impressive Milton House, the home of Sir Ernest and Lady Craig.'

Alsager had changed since the Gosses had first known it. In 1893 Florry had told Godfrey that he would not now know the place, as it was getting to be quite like a small town, and even some public rooms had been built where concerts and balls were held. One of the female employees at the Works regularly recited at these concerts, and when she did so she stayed the night with Adolphus and Nellie.

Alsager in Cheshire is about six miles north west of the Potteries, with Crewe approximately the same distance to the west. The community sprang up around a mere fed by natural springs, with a straight road dissecting the village. In 1925 the population was about 3,000 and in 1974 this had risen to 10,000. It evolved as a fashionable dormitory town for pottery manufacturers such as the Hammersleys, the Johnsons and the Maddocks. It was the ideal place then for Adolphus and his brother Huntley to live.

The earlier history of Alsager is summed up in a paragraph written by a native, Mrs. McEwen, in 1906, whilst Adolphus was there:

'Alsager 40 years ago must have been a rural spot indeed, a little hamlet set round with scattered farms and wild moss-lands. Instead of the shady, good roads of today, there were sandy lanes — improvements themselves on the dangerous bridlepaths through swampy 'moss' (morass) of only a few years before. So

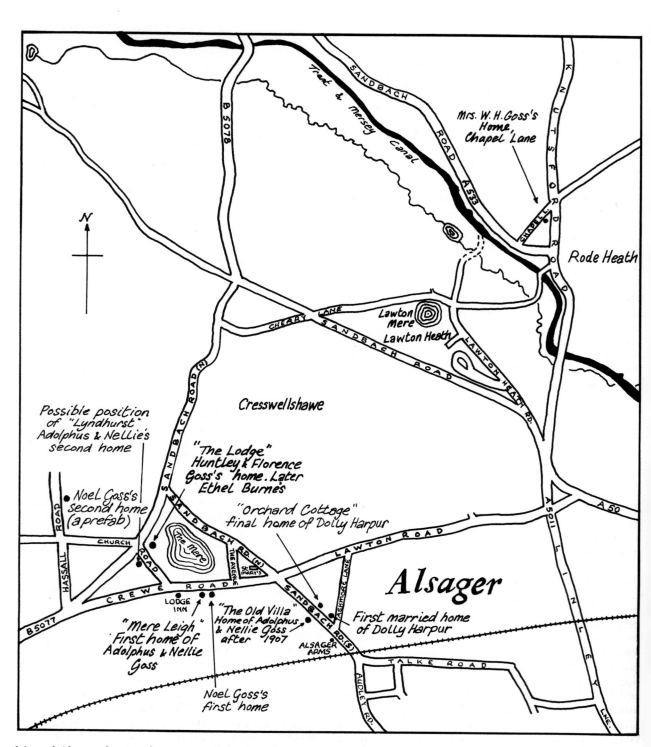

*Map of Alsager showing the position of the Goss homes*

bad was their reputation that Miss Wilbraham — who died last year (1905) at the age of 90 — told me that as a child living at Rode, she was only allowed to ride to Alsager on condition that the groom led her pony along the narrow paths that intersected the place. These bridle paths have since become the excellent roads of which we are so justly proud. Forty years ago, instead of the handsome houses and well-kept gardens, numerous shops and many villas of our day, there was here and there a house newly erected, a few old cottages, and three small and primitive shops, and one inn, 'The Alsager Arms'. One old house there was occupied by Mr. J. Mayer (still an Alsager name), since transformed by Mr. Frank Rigby into his pretty residence, and now in the possession of Mr. Huntley Goss.'[1]

Adolphus liked golf, and several of his photographs show his friends on the golf course at Barthomley. There was an extraordinary club meeting in 1909 to decide the question of Sunday golf, held at the Royal Hotel, Crewe. *The Guardian*, 6 March devoted space to the event. Apparently there were 32 members present, but strangely enough, not one of the seven clergymen, who were members of the club, attended. There was a motion for Sunday golf on behalf of those who worked the rest of the week, maintaining that golf was not a religious association. Adolphus, speaking against the motion, said that he did not think that the playing of golf on a Sunday was in the best interests of the club:

> 'Sunday football, Sunday cricket, and even Sunday horseracing, would eventually follow the example set by golfers, and Sunday would become more and more a day of pleasure for one part of the people, and of increased labour for another part, and thus would recede farther and farther from the ideal of a day of rest and worship for all.'

The final vote was 19 for Sunday golf, and two against. The course was to be open the following Sunday. Adolphus promptly announced his resignation from the committee and requested that the vacancy be filled at that meeting, which it was!

Adolphus's politics began as early as 1900 when he left the Goss Works. At the 1906 gathering of the Conservative workers appreciation of the election fights (which they lost), Adolphus stood on the platform on behalf of the Alsager district. It is not known when he first became a member of the local constitutional association but by 1909 he was regularly discussing political matters at the meetings, praising Conservatism, criticising Socialism and theorising on the Welsh Disestablishment and Irish Home Rule questions. He argued with the member for Newcastle, Staffs, Mr.J.C. Wedgwood, over the taxation of land values. By 1910 he was President of his village association and put forward Ernest Craig's name as the local candidate at the next election. He and Craig

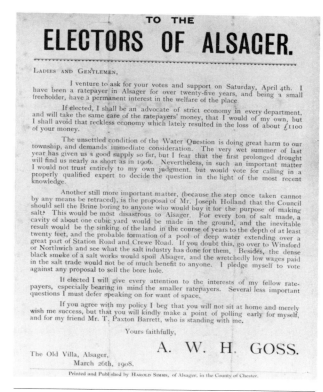

*Adolphus's election poster*

had been at school together and now lived near one another. The General Election of January 1910 proved unsuccessful for Craig, but the by-election of July 1912 caused by the death of the Liberal MP allowed him the chance to become a Member of Parliament. Adolphus was very active in the constituency and no doubt paved the way for Craig's success. The *Crewe and Nantwich Observer* of Saturday 10 February 1912, reported the Unionist meeting of the Crewe Division. Adolphus Goss was the President, with Home Rule again the issue. He quoted John Bright's well known speech denouncing Home Rule as a 'stupendous and injustive blunder.'

In 1914 at the outbreak of war he was elected by the Executive Committee to be Deputy Chairman of Crewe Division Constitutional Association, and was at that time also Vice-President, 'being one of the keenest and the most active members of the Executive Committee.' He had a deep interest in the welfare of the community and was rewarded with the chief duty of recruiting. Because his own sons had enlisted within two days he was able to appeal by force of example more powerfully than by words to those who were still holding back, and by February 1915, 90 men had enlisted from Alsager. He had been Chairman of the Alsager Junior Unionist Association since its foundation, and in March 1914 was the subject of an illustrated article which appeared in *The Lancashire and Cheshire Junior Unionist* magazine, which revealed that he regarded himself as something of a martinet but that it was real affection and respect with which he won the unswerving support of his juniors.

Adolphus and Ethel helped organise *café chantants* to raise money for the comfort of the soldiers of the 5th North Staffs. Regiment and the Belgian Red Cross Society. He assisted the Town Working Party with their sales of work throughout the war, organised by his daughter Ethel and his wife Nellie; organised garden fetes in various large houses, often Milton House, home of the Craigs, and Rode Hall, which was used as a hospital for wounded soldiers, raising money for the war effort yet at the same time providing entertainment for the soldiers and a chance for the local people to enjoy themselves. Nellie often used to present the competition prizes at these fêtes. Additional entertainment was often in the form of the 'Jingle Johnnies' Troupe from the potteries.

Adolphus was a member of the Ancient Order of Foresters, a Friendly Society, the arms of which were used as a Goss decoration, where members paid in subscriptions, and the society paid out when a subscriber was ill. There was an annual Foresters procession which used to finish at Dr. Critchley's house in Sandbach Road, opposite the Old Villa. Eventually Adolphus's daughter Dolly and her husband Dr. Harpur moved to that house when he took over the practice.

Adolphus was also one of the earliest Presidents of the B'Hoys, formed as a charitable society in Alsager to do

*Alsager B'Hoys meeting with Sam Shaw, a friend of Ethel (Goss) Burne, third from right, and Huntley Goss seated far left next to another potter, Billy Bloor. Note the china Willow Art baby saluting model on the table far right. It is inscribed, 'One of the B'Hoys'*

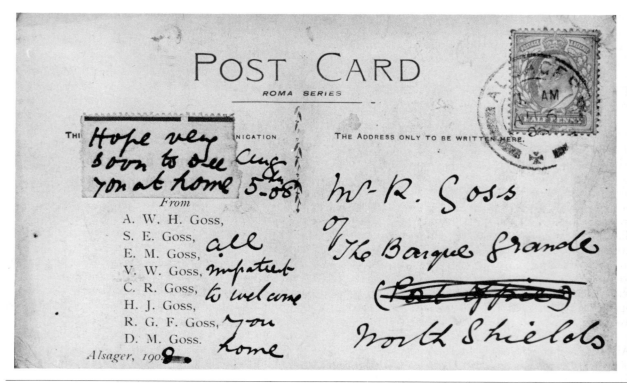

*A postcard designed by Adolphus, to save having to write out all the names of his children when sending greetings*

good deeds. They met in the lounge of the Alsager Arms on the second Thursday of each month from October to March — six meetings a year. The membership was exclusive and limited to 50. The *Crewe and Nantwich Observer* printed on 10 March 1928:

'It is of interest to record that one of the founders of the B'Hoys and one of its first presidents is now the honoured and beloved President of the Alsager Legion Branch, namely Mr. Adolphus Goss.'

A former member and past president Mr. Sam Shaw, a lifelong resident of Alsager, remembered his B'Hoys meetings, with the notched shillelagh on the table. He recalled a photograph of a group of men including himself at this top table, and Huntley Goss, a past president, and what should also be on the table but a crested Willow Art china model of a baby saluting with 'One of the B'Hoys' inscribed on its base. We wonder what Huntley thought of a rival firm's product sitting in pride of place at his table!

This Society made its mark in Alsager, providing gifts as diverse as the archway gates down to the mere, and fridges and electrical equipment for old peoples' homes. It bought the first ambulance for the area, donated the village clock and provided ornamental railings around the mere to name but a few examples of its earlier deeds. All members were pledged to remain 'boyish'.

Adolphus and Nellie's eldest child Ethel Maud was blonde haired and blue eyed and grew up to be the beauty of the family. Even so, she stayed single most of her life, becoming her father's companion after the death of her mother in 1916. She devoted herself to supporting her father's various committees and organisations, particularly the Alsager Primrose League Buds, of which for most of her time she was both Dame Warden and Hon. secretary. This group met the first Wednesday in each month at the local infants' school, and enjoyed a membership in excess of one hundred.

She was a member of the local philharmonic society, sharing her father's musical interests. As a child she sang when her mother played the piano, and her pony would come alongside the window and dance as her mother played. Ethel had a fine rich contralto voice and sang solo at many important events. She joined the society at its inception in 1909, and the *Staffordshire Sentinel*, on Tuesday 27 April of that year reviewed their concert and criticised poor Ethel, whose voice apparently vibrated due to nerves at facing a large audience for the first time. She was about 23 years old then and later, with experience, she became a controlled and expert soloist. Her public appearances were often at the close of the local Unionist meetings.

At various village events, especially garden parties in Alsager, she met up with her cousins who were in charge of other local activities; she would attend with her Primrose Buds, Peggy Goss with her Brownie pack and Geoffrey Goss with his Scouts. A keen amateur actress,

she often appeared in plays whose casts included her sister Dolly (who usually took the leading female role) and Noel Goss as well as Mary Kingston, who was later to marry Vernon Goss.

Adolphus was adept at hand painting illuminated letters, which often formed the first letter of the verses which adorned Goss china. He drew and coloured illuminated initials of both his daughters, each letter over laid on the others monogrammatically, such as one would find with school badges. Ethel had such a wooden framed initial picture which was rescued from an Alsager church jumble sale several years ago.

Ethel was proposed to by Harry Burne, who she had grown up with. She turned him down, and he later married a Miss Mary Housen in 1917, who was a governess and coached Quentin Hogg in mathematics at one time. Huntley Goss gave them a beautiful Goss china coffee service with the initial 'B' in forget-me-nots on the cups as a wedding present, Harry's daughter Rosemary still has two of these cups. Rosemary remembers her parents telling her how in their younger days, when her father used to accompany Ethel on the piano when she sang, they always had to have a chaperone!

During the Great War there were continual appeals for more nurses, trained or partly trained, and for nursing members of Voluntary Aid Detachments, who were required for the home hospitals. By 1916 there were between 5,000 and 6,000 members at work in the military hospitals. Ethel joined the Red Cross and became a V.A.D member in June 1915, eventually being awarded chevrons for long service, as was her sister Dolly. They served at Rode Hall, a local mansion converted into a military hospital, the First Southern General Hospital, Birmingham and the Queen Alexandra's Hospital in London. Dolly also went to nurse the wounded at Royallment, France and at the Scottish Women's Hospital.

*Dolly in front of the monkey tree at 'The Old Villa'*

Dorothy Muriel was the baby of the family and inherited her mother's lovely personality and plumpness; she really was jolly Dolly, for everyone who knew her loved her. She attended school in Abbots Bromley and adored Dick (Clarence Richard), her second oldest brother, and was desperately upset when he ran away — no doubt he had suffered most from Adolphus's cane!

Prior to the outbreak of war in 1914, they all went to church as a family. Ethel fainted and Vernon carried her out. As Dick did not care for long sermons, he whispered to Dolly, 'Look faint too', so she collapsed and he carried her out! It was through her pining for him when he ran away in 1906 that she was sent to boarding school, leaving at the age of 17 to take up nursing alongside Ethel. From nursing she progressed to taking an active part in the village, as her family had, not having to worry about earning a living. One day a week she spent nursing at the home for crippled children in Hartshill. On 2 September 1922, she married Dr. Henry Percy Harpur, M.D., the event arousing considerable local interest, but because of Dr. Kingston's sudden death earlier in the month the wedding reception was cancelled.

Dr. Harpur had graduated from Dublin University, and when the war broke out, had joined the R.A.M.C. holding the rank of Captain and serving for five years in France and in the East, being wounded in the Battle of the Somme in 1916. Dolly herself possessed the Victory and Allied medals and was a councillor for many years, becoming quite well known in Cheshire. She became Chairman of Alsager Town Council more times than anyone else, and was awarded the M.B.E.

Adolphus and Nellie had four sons in between the births of their two daughters; Vernon in 1888, Clarence Richard in 1889, Hubert Victor John in 1891, and George Raymond Henry in 1893.

With so many boys close together, it was no wonder Adolphus was such a strict father. All four boys attended Newcastle High School and were members of the North Staffordshire Rugby Football Club. They went straight from school to the Junior Division of an officers' training camp at Wolsely Park, Colwich, Cannock Chase, Staffordshire.

Clarence, or Dick, as he was always known, was the most adventurous and had the best sense of humour, and his brothers and sisters adored him. As a small boy he wore leg irons through an illness, and early on Adolphus forbade him to participate in any sport, which he loved, so he was somewhat miserable at being forced to spend his spare time studying instead. He felt his father was intolerant and impossible to live with so he ran away on 18 September 1906 at 16 years of age with only half-a-crown in his pocket. His brothers denied all knowledge of his destination, but it was believed that there was some collusion with Vernon. Dick stowed away on a three-masted barque and when the Captain discovered him, he arranged to send him ashore with the pilot cutter, but Dick persuaded him to let him remain on board. The ship was

en route for Australia, and he had no contact with his family for over a year.

His mother and sisters fretted over his absence. The year 1906 was bad for Adolphus; his father William had died and excluded him from a share in the factory in his will and was no doubt difficult to live with at that time. Dick eventually wrote to his uncle Victor, letting him know he was on board a 24 ton trading cutter in Spencer Gulf, South Australia. Adolphus was relieved he was safe, but expostulated 'He is of course wasting his time entirely but I dare say he enjoys it as it must be something like yachting.' Poor Adolphus — he had only been on a few long journeys since ceasing to be the firm's traveller — once when he saw Godfrey off to his ship on his return to America in 1907, and once to Liverpool looking for Dick when he first ran away. Dick had gone out on the *Andromeda* and had sailed on another ship as well. He had given Victor an address, not saying anything about returning and asking after everyone at home including the dog. His father immediately wrote to Dick, sent him money and told him he would be pleased to have him back if he would come home. It does seem remarkable that yet again it was the second son leaving home for the third consecutive generation.

Dick stayed away for 18 months before finally returning to the 'Old Villa'. His father was so shocked and ashamed of his scruffy appearance and his use of slang and swear

*Dr. Percy Harpur who married Dorothy (Dolly) Goss in 1922*

*Dolly's wedding, 30 August 1933. Back row: Noel, Geoffrey, John, Vernon (all Gosses). Front row: Patty (Martha) and Dick, Mr. and Mrs. Wheeler of Belfast, Rev. Hugh Harpur, Ethel, Dr. Percy Harpur and Dolly Goss, Adolphus, Rev. H. Moore of Acton, Wm. Harpur of Strabane, Georgie Wilmott of Coleshill, Margaret, Huntley and Florence Goss. Seated: Dick and Patty's son Richard John Victor Goss*

words in his everyday language that he made him sleep in the stables. Dick put up with this for only two days and then disappeared again.

On one occasion he appeared at the back door of Anie (Georgiana) Jewitt's house, with his coat collar up, very scruffy and with a dirty face. He asked to speak to her and when she appeared, said 'Got any odd jobs ma'am?' 'No I haven't' she squeaked in her high pitched voice. When he revealed his true identity she thought it was a tremendous joke.

He returned to his family in 1909 and Adolphus sent him to the Goss firm where Victor welcomed him and trained him to do his father's old job of travelling salesman, which no doubt suited him well as he was not keen to work in an office. Dick got on well working for his favourite uncle.

A few years after Dick went to work at the factory, his uncle Victor met his sudden death. Victor's will left the firm to Huntley, and although in the few previous years Victor had often spoken of leaving a share of the factory to his hardworking nephew, he died without altering his will. He probably did not intend dying quite so soon! Huntley however, saw to it that his nephew did not go without.

Raymond joined the Newcastle Cadet Corps and became a mining engineer at Birchenwood Colliery, Hubert who began training as a solicitor was articled to

Mr. Feltham, Town Clerk of Crewe and was approaching his final examinations when the war broke out. Vernon, known as 'Very' to those closest to him, passed his junior Oxford Locals, then joined the North Staffordshire Railway in July 1905, beginning as an articled pupil in the electrical shops, repairing and making telegraph, telephone and railway signalling instruments. Vernon had always been clever with his hands and had a practical mind. A year later he spent twelve months in the drawing office, gaining experience in estimating and surveying for telegraph lines. He then progressed to the maintenance and construction of telegraphs and then to electric train lighting in 1908. After gaining his City and Guilds Certificate he joined the North Midland Divisional Telegraph Company of the Royal Engineers as a subaltern, commanding the company within three years of joining. He rose to the rank of Captain, a commission which he resigned in 1914 when he went to Ceylon to take up a post as an assistant telegraph engineer for the Government.

When the war broke out in 1914 Vernon successfully appealed to the Government in Ceylon to release him. Dick and Raymond went to train with the 5th North Staffordshire Regiment at Luton and Raymond was promoted to the rank of lance corporal. Dick was rapidly promoted to corporal, then sergeant, soon after joining the North Staffs. Regiment but turned down the offer of a commission on several occasions because he knew that

*At 'The Old Villa' in 1913, just before the boys enlisted. Left to right: Vernon, Hubert, Nellie, Dolly, Adolphus, Ethel, Dick and Raymond, with Rap the dog*

*Tea in the garden in 1914 at 'The Old Villa', with Mary Elizabeth Kingston and Adeline*

if he accepted it would mean his departure to the front would be delayed. At the completion of their training they wrote home saying that they were 'ready for anything.'

The first tragedy to strike the Gosses was the death of Raymond, their youngest boy. Dick and Raymond were in Flanders and on the fateful occasion were together in a railway dugout near Ypres, along with Captain Ridgway (only son of the owner of the Bedford Works, Hanley), when a German shell dropped between them. Poor Raymond died instantly, and a chaplain who was on hand could do nothing to save him. Dick was wounded in one shoulder by the same shell; Captain Ridgway escaped with only scratches but he was to lose his life within a matter of weeks. At this time both Raymond and Dick were Second Lieutenants. Dick spent some time recovering at the Duchess of Westminster's Hospital in Etaples but was left with a weak arm and shoulder. Nevertheless, he was eager to 'do his bit' and returned to the front where the action was as soon as possible.

Raymond had earlier sent home a brass shell case to his father as a souvenir. It is now inscribed:

'French "75" Shell Case sent home by Sec. Lt. Raymond G.G. Goss 1/5th N. Staffs. Reg. 1915 (killed near Hill 60 in Flanders August 1915)'.*

Hubert enlisted in the 10th Royal Fusiliers as a private and within a year he was promoted to lance corporal and fighting in Flanders. Subsequently commissioned as a temporary Second Lieutenant in the Cheshire Regiment, he was awarded the Military Cross for bravery, the citation reading:

'for conspicuous gallantry in action. He made a bold reconnaissance of a point, and later seized it with 15 men, hanging on till his company arrived. Two days later he did fine work in an attack after his two senior officers had been killed. He was himself wounded.'†

He took part in the third Battle of The Somme in July 1916 and was reported missing on 15 July although the ground he had helped to win for the British remained in allied hands, his body was never found. Nellie was never to recover from losing her two boys; at St Mary's Church, Alsager, memorial services were held for the fallen, including the two Goss Brothers and other local soldiers, whose battle cry had been, 'Potters for ever.'

Hubert's name is recorded on the massive Lutyens Thiepval Memorial to the missing, on the Somme. The following inscription is recorded in the cemetery register:

'Goss 2nd Lt. Hubert John, M.C. 10th Bn. Cheshire Regt. formerly 10th Bn. Royal Fusiliers, 15th July, 1916, aged 25. Son of A.W.H. and Sarah Ellen Goss of the Old Villa, Alsager, Cheshire. Enlisted Aug. 1914.'

* Raymond was buried near Ypres, Belgium, in Railway Dugout Ground Cemetery, Plot 1, Row D, Grave 7.
†The Times, Friday, 12 January 1917.

*Dick who was injured in Flanders, 1915*

Vernon enjoyed a successful military career. Soon after obtaining a Government appointment in Ceylon in 1913, he enlisted as a rifleman in the Ceylon Volunteer Rifle Corps and after the declaration of war, he proceeded with that regiment to Egypt.

He was fond of writing beautifully descriptive letters, several of which were published in newspapers, such as those written during his early war days in Cairo where he spent five months service at the time when the Turks made their attack on the Suez Canal. In April 1915 he was commissioned as a second lieutenant in the Royal Field Artillery and transferred to the Western Front.

*The Guardian*, 10 March 1916, mentioned Vernon who had written home giving particulars of his first brush with the Germans in France, and who had received a card from his commanding officer stating that he had distinguished himself by his conduct in the field, and by his excellent shooting. The *Crewe and Nantwich Observer* published the very next day 'An Alsager Soldier's First Brush with the Huns:'

'An Alsager officer writing to his parents states:- I had my first brush with the Huns in the early morning of the 22nd. A patrol of three of us went out in front of our wire entanglements, and had not got very far before we were fired upon from a point close in front of our wire, and about one hundred yards distant from us. Fortunately, the Huns missed us, in spite of the fact that we must have presented a very good target against the brightness of the moon behind us. We dropped flat, and opened fire upon the flash and upon a vague, shadowy blotch which we could just see. Our shots told, and awful moans from the wounded Huns rent the frosty air. A party of ours, thinking that the groans proceeded from us, went out, as they thought, to our rescue, and brought in two wounded Huns, one of whom was so badly wounded in three or four places that he died almost immediately and the other died after a few hours. The fellows evidently had come out to bomb one of our saps, when we came along and spoiled their plans.'

November 1917 saw the acting Captain Vernon gazetted Acting Major, and in May 1918, he was listed in the Roll of Honour in the *Daily Mail*. The *Morning Post* of 4 June reported that he had been awarded the Military Cross in the Birthday Honours. Although he had been wounded — not mentioned in his letters home, he recovered and returned to the front. By December of that year he had been awarded the French Croix de Guerre with gold star after serving in the last great offensive in France.

All his life Adolphus was considered an expert on heraldry. He wrote to the *Morning Post* in 1917 about the words Ich Dien (I serve) on the coat of arms of the Black Prince, and in 1930 about Charles Dickens having a coat of arms. So his interest in the subject continued even after he left the Goss factory. After his two youngest sons died in the First World War he designed his own coat of arms. The official description of the arms is:

> 'Sable four swords interlaced fretwise argent, the hilts and pommels on a chief of the second two crosses gules. Mantling sable and argent. Crest on wreath of the colours and goshawk rising proper charged on the breast with a bomb fired.'

The motto was 'For King and Old England.' The four swords represented his four sons in the army, the two red crosses his two daughters working as V.A.D. nurses with the Red Cross. The bomb fired at the goshawk signifies the doom brought to the Falcon Works with its goshawk emblem. This design, typically Victorian, was very complex, compared to the marked simplicity of older coats of arms.

### Reference
1.     *Alsager 1789-1906* by Mrs. McEwan of Alsager.

*Vernon, who was awarded the Military Cross and the French Croix de Guerre*

*Book plate designed by Adolphus Goss*

# CHAPTER ELEVEN

# After 1920

Sed fugit interea, fugit inreparabile tempus.
(Time meanwhile flies, flies never to return).

Publius V. Maro Virgil Georgics 70-19 B.C.

Adolphus held many church offices including Sidesman. Parochial Church Councillor, Diocesan and Ruridecanal Representative, as well as being on the Finance Committee which built the church of St. Mary Magdalene, Alsager.

At the instigation of Ernest Craig in 1925 it was decided to put a stained glass east window in the new church 'in memory of all our loved ones.' The Parochial Church Council thought the window should be of the best contemporary glass, such as was found in Liverpool Cathedral. A small deputation including Adolphus organised the assembling of this window and the Rev. Moir dedicated it on 24 July, 1927. He later wrote, 'We recognised that Adolphus was really the only expert among us in making our choice.'

Another achievement, within the local church, was his gift of another stained glass east window in the south aisle in memory of his wife and two sons in 1926. It was when the Rev. Moir first moved to Alsager that he found Adolphus absorbed in this very task. In discussing it with him he told the new incumbent that his main problem was finding a craftsman competent enough to make glass sufficiently translucent as he disliked 'muddy' glass. He had searched through innumerable churches for examples before deciding on Karl Parsons of Northwood, Middlesex to carry out the work. The window was fitted in 1926, seven years after the death of his wife. The dedication service was in December, and Vernon Goss unveiled the window. The south aisle is now called the Lady Chapel and the distinctive coloured window stands out among all the other windows for its brilliancy. The vivid colours are mainly blue, violet and purple. Children now call it the 'Red Indian' window because the two figures of St. Michael the Archangel of War and Justice carrying his sword of flame and his scales, and St. Gabriel the Archangel of Peace and Purity, bearing a lily, from a distance look like two red indians. Beneath the figures are the arms of Cheshire and those of Adolphus Goss. In the tracery above are the Military Cross, the badges of the Cheshire and North Staffordshire Regiments and the 1914-15 Star. The brass plaque beneath the window reads

in embossed Gothic lettering:

'To the glory of God, and to the sacred memory of Sec. Lt. Raymond G.F Goss, 5th N. Staffs., killed near Ypres, August 13th, 1915, Sec. Lt. Hubert J. Goss, M.C., 10th Cheshires, killed at the Somme, 15 July 1916, their beloved mother, Sarah Ellen Goss who died July 14th, 1919, and all their gallant friends and neighbours who laid down their lives in the Great War.'

Adolphus wrote an account of the dedication service of the window, beautifully illustrated, and had some presentation copies printed and bound. He gave an autographed copy to the Rev. Moir, who predicted that the window would always be a memorial to the man who gave it as well as those it commemorated.

Adolphus was always very proud that his four sons had all signed up as soon as war broke out in 1914. He used to tell everyone he met that his two eldest sons were wounded and his youngest two killed long before Uncle Sam gave up singing 'I did not rear my son to be soldier.'

June 1920 saw the official unveiling of the Alsager War Memorial. The names of those soldiers who fell in the Great War are inscribed on the sides and include Raymond and Hubert Goss and Florence Hammersley's brother. On the rear of the memorial is a representation of the Alsager coat of arms. Dr. Critchley, the previous owner of Dr. Harpur's house, had donated the land used for the memorial, known as Critchley's corner.

Nellie died 14 July, 1919, on the third anniversary of Hubert's death. She never recovered from the shock of losing two of her sons, and just lost the will to live; Adolphus missed her dreadfully.

Adolphus lost his friend Dr. Kingston in 1922. A keen yachtsman, he was on holiday sailing the Menai Straits when he became stranded at sea. He caught a cold which developed into double pneumonia from which he never recovered. He died in early August, and his daughter had to move in with Dolly whose marriage had been arranged on the 30th of the same month.

Adolphus was Chairman of the Congleton Old Age

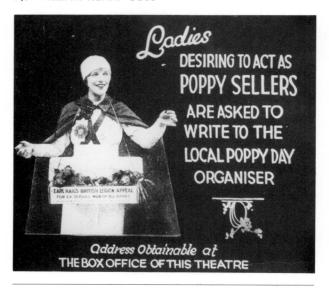

*Earl Haig's Poppy Appeal, organised in the Alsager district by Adolphus. This picture is taken from his slide show*

*Dedication of the Alsager British Legion Standard, 6 May 1928, at the War Memorial. Left: Fred Edwards, president of the B'Hoys. Right: Adolphus Goss, president of Alsager British Legion*

Pensions Committee 1908-1929, only retiring due to his advancing old age. He was also Life President of the local branch of the British Legion from its formation in 1924, an appropriate appointment as he had lost two sons in the war. It was a special day for him when the B'Hoys presented a standard to the British Legion, and indeed an important gift because to own a banner was a necessary requirement in order for the local Legion to compete in the Earl Haig Cup. The presentation took place at the War Memorial and Adolphus officially accepted it. His photograph in the newspapers following this event showed him to be a remarkably good looking and youthful man considering he was then in his 75th year.

As local President of the Earl Haig Fund. Adolphus organised the appeal for the area, his daughters taking care of their own village with the aid of some forty collectors. It was to their credit that they collected £55 for example in November, 1925, when compared with other local villages who averaged about £8 each. In the late twenties and during the thirties, Ethel and Dolly took charge of the Alsager Poppy Appeal. Empire Day was also celebrated every May, with all the various clubs and societies taking part, Ethel being in sole charge of organising the day and divine service for many years.

She played a part in the choir practice of the local branch of the Girls' Friendly Society and was reported in the *Staffordshire Sentinel*, Tuesday 13 May 1924, as having accompanied the choir to Chester for the final of the Diocesan Choral contest, which they won, having been successful for three years in succession. Busy Ethel was also a Bishop's messenger and visited the sick, as well as at one stage running the local Girls' Brigade.

True to Adeline's predictions, her eldest brother eventually opened up and sorted out his late mother's belongings in his final years. In 1932 he wrote and suggested to Godfrey that he collected them when he next visited England, but frail old Godfrey was by then not really in a position to travel anywhere. Adolphus's only contact with his brother was through Godfrey's children and, more particularly, his grandchildren. He had not had a letter from Godfrey since about 1910 and did not even send postcards to thank him for the Staffordshire newspapers he regularly sent over to America. Adolphus particularly liked to correspond with Godfrey's son, Percy, and niece Mary Alice Goss of Oklahoma. whose neat writing and many interesting letters brought great pleasure to the ageing Adolphus, whose own hand by now was rather shaky. January 1928 saw deep snow and terrific floods in southern England, seventeen people being reported drowned in their beds in London alone. Adolphus was rather fond of recording statistics of disasters, and also travelling to the scene to photograph such things. One of his slides depicts a complete passenger train derailed and on its side. Mary Alice also told her Uncle about the crisis in the U.S. banking system. He replied and explained about the five great banks over here with their branches all over the country, as well as smaller banks.

Adolphus himself was interested in his family's roots, and passed on to Mary Alice information he had collected: one of the earliest Gosses was a Stephen Goss, citizen of Exeter, born 1304; William of Wykeham, Bishop of Winchester, was reputed to have left 66 shillings and 8 pence to Charles Goss in 1404; one of the old streets in Chester was Goss Street and that a William Goss was the Mayor of Lincoln in 1592. In a letter dated 1929 Adolphus wrote:

'There is no family more certainly English than the Gosses though we have been a wandering race and have emigrated to most parts of the world.'

On one occasion he even met a dark little Japanese gentleman who said his name was Goss.

In February 1934 Adolphus became ill and on Shrove Tuesday on the 13th of that month he died peacefully with his family around him. The funeral took place the following Saturday with the Rev. Moir taking prayers with the family at the Old Villa prior to the service at St. Mary's Church and the burial at Christchurch. The British Legion provided the bearers, with representatives of many other public and political organisations present. A memorial service was held the next day at St. Mary's, Alsager.

No books were written about Adolphus but one person who realised his importance was the Rev. A.L. Moir, his vicar in Alsager from 1925 to 1934 when he buried him. When the Rev. Moir retired he found himself:

'at the age of eighty-six the only person living with an intimate knowledge of this man whose aims and achievements, I feel, are insufficiently recognised. It was suggested to me that I ought to write down my memories and impressions of him, 'lest we forget! My memories of Adolphus going back forty or fifty years may be defective but I have been able to supplement them with the help of a clerical diary, newspaper cuttings, parish records and talks I used to have with his two daughters.'[1]

His reminiscences, whilst occasionally incorrect, nevertheless made interesting reading and confirmed some of our suspicions. Perhaps through his interest in Adolphus, the Vicar began collecting Goss china, for when his collection came up for sale in a London Auction House in 1986, some of his old card indexes, written in the thirties, detailing his pieces, their coats of arms and even the paintresses marks, accompanied them. Ethel had given him her father's Goss elephant bearing a pink cushion and howdah, and a brown-washed model of the Sandbach Crosses.

The question of who really invented Goss heraldic porcelain is an important one, and one which can really only be answered by this quote from the will of W.H. Goss:

'I give and bequeath to my eldest son Adolphus William Henry Goss the sum of four thousand pounds which in my opinion will fairly compensate him for having devised and bequeathed my said Manufactory.'

In our opinion one would not have invented it without the other. Goss heraldic china evolved through their joint efforts. It is sad their business relationship ended abruptly, but it was still Adolphus who inherited his father's precious books, his gold watch and gold signet ring with crest, which he in turn was to leave to his eldest son.

* * * * * * * * * * * * * *

Ethel kept up her work with the Red Cross long after the war, and was presented with a medal in November, 1922 at Stoke Town Hall, for having accomplished 1,000 hours work during the war itself. She had been attached to V.A.D. 32. It appeared to be a strange coincidence that in 1935 the Rev. Harry Burne met Ethel again while she was staying with her brother Dick when he was secretary and manager of a hotel in Sidmouth. Harry was living in Lyme Regis and Dick (unbeknown to Ethel) invited him to Sidmouth for the day while Ethel was there. Dick must have known that Harry had proposed to her in her youth, and now that he was a widower, he brought them together again, and by the next year they were married, which was for the good of Harry's children, Rosemary and Peter, who gained a step-mother, and beneficial for Ethel who

*Adolphus, Nellie and Dick's gravestone at Christchurch, Alsager*

*Ethel and Harry Burne in the early forties*

acquired her very own family instead of becoming a lonely spinster. Her nephews Randle and Raymond used to come and stay with them at Rousdon Rectory in Devon before Harry became Rector at Eaton Vicarage in Congleton, then finally Rector of Rode Heath where they lived in a pretty vicarage only a few doors away from old Mrs. Goss's former house. Strangely enough we attended a house contents auction there in 1983, because of the auction catalogue listing the Sandbach Crosses. We had hoped that the model had once been Ethel's and that possibly she had left it for the next vicar when they left. However, the crosses were an additional item included in the sale from a different source, but the auction had drawn us to the house and enabled us to walk through every room, with its sloping floors and tiny windows and one could imagine what it looked like when Ethel was mistress of the house, with some of her father's furniture around her.

The Gosses loved their trees. Ashfield Cottage possessed a small orchard, and the Rode Heath house has its fruit trees still, as well as twelve poplars planted in a neat row down Chapel Lane outside Ethel's house, known locally as the twelve apostles. Godfrey had originally planted these and they have since been replaced. The abundance of trees in the garden is not now a blessing however, as a close chestnut has roots which extend under the house causing structural damage to the foundations and walls.

In 1961, the Rev. H. Burne died, and a local magazine reported as follows:

'Members who attended the M.C.D.G.A. Reunion at Buxton last year will remember with pleasure Ethel Goss's husband the Rev. H. Burne who joined the party for tea. We regret to say that he died suddenly on November 25th, 1961. He will be sadly missed in Rode Heath. The Bishops of Stockport and many other clergy were at the service. An unaccompanied and very moving farewell hymm was sung by his brother Masons.'

All we have to remind us of Harry are some of his fossils, including a sea urchin similar to the Goss model of a Steyning Sea Urchin.

It seemed a pity that Ethel did not marry during her father's lifetime. Harry's father had been Adolphus's lifelong friend, and would no doubt have been pleased at the liaison, just as William had been with his Georgie marrying Edwin Jewitt. Had Ethel not married she would probably have continued with her plans to open the Old Villa as a rest home for retired gentlemen. In 1924 she was nominated to a seat on the Pensions Sub-committee as well as being honorary organiser of the Poppy Day Fund. The special function of the Pensions fund was to find employment for out-of-work ex-servicemen and to find accommodation for 25,000 old soldiers. It was this background of interests that probably gave her the idea of using the spacious 'Old Villa' to help pensioners and disabled ex-servicemen. But by marrying Harry, whose first wife had died and left him with two young children Rosemary and Peter, she found the family life previously denied her through caring for her father in his closing years.

After her husband's death, Ethel moved in with the Rev. Moir's sister Gwendoline at her house in Church Road, Alsager. This house had come up for sale some years before, having once been the home of Florence and Huntley Goss during his time running the Falcon Works. When the business was sold in 1929, their home 'The Lodge' was divided into two and the half nearest Church Road, called 'West Mere Lodge' was purchased by Gwendoline Moir on the advice of her brother and his wife Aline. Ethel loved to visit various members of the family and relate tales about her father and grandfather; she was described as a great talker by several of her descendants. We have her to thank for ensuring the remaining Gosses are so well informed about their ancestors.

Ethel had a collection of Goss china but lost interest in it, possibly because of her father's disassociation with the firm. She certainly had a brown model of the Iona Cross, her grandfather's gravestone (perhaps all William's children had one originally and hers had been Adolphus's) but she gave it to friends. The blue handled mug Adolphus especially designed for her with three transfers of a cat being bothered by a fly, labelled CONTEMPLATION, INVESTIGATION, EXASPERATION, she had given away many years before. In the end she was pleased to part with all her pieces for as little as sixpence each. The last few years the two old ladies lived at West Mere Lodge were spent in squalid conditions, with their energies gone and no-one to look after them properly. Local residents and friends helped them as best they could and Ethel finally went to an old people's home that her sister Dolly had started, passing away in 1973 at the age of 87. She had earlier donated her father's slides to the local church. These contained views of the British countryside, foreign countries, family and friends, especially the Burne children who were slightly older than herself, and one of whom she had eventually married. But after they had lain untouched in the vaults for years, she had them retrieved and given to a good friend who immediately rewarded her by giving the locals a slide show. 'Introduce them as the Goss slides' she would insist. Her friend now holds slide shows with two projectors showing Adolphus's photographs of the locality in one, and his own taken of the same places in the 1960's. He now feels he needs a third projector to show the same views in the 1980's, so much has Alsager changed!

\* \* \* \* \* \* \* \* \* \* \* \* \*

After her marriage Dolly and Dr. Harpur lived in Sandbach Road South, opposite the Working Men's Club. Dr. Harpur took over Dr. Critchley's practice and they moved to the house opposite the 'Old Villa' in Sandbach Road, called 'Holmcroft'. Following her father's death when his house was sold, Dolly still felt for years afterwards she just wanted to run into her old home and find her father in his cosy den, reading *The Times* like he always used to do.

Dolly's daughter Doreen attended boarding school after 1938. At that time her parents insisted they were not well off as Dr. Harpur had no wealthy customers on his list. He was too kind to charge his many patients the correct fee as he felt they couldn't afford it.

Doreen liked country life, was devoted to animals, and inherited her mother's interest in the community. She became a Welfare Officer after earlier training as a nurse at the Queen Elizabeth Hospital, Birmingham. Dolly devoted her life to Alsager Parish Council, and was in charge of many committees. Her influence is still visible there for she helped name many of the new roads, and apart from Harpur Crescent and Percy James Close, there are roads named after trees.

She was Mayoress of Alsager one year, and started an Alsager teacher training college as well as the old people's hostel in which Ethel spent her last years. Dolly also used council money to crush old cars as a way of earning a profit for the village out of scrap metal. As Chairman of Alsager Urban District Council she had donated her father's large oak and leather chair, which had been in the family for some time, to be used as the Chairman's chair. When the Alsager U.D.C. ceased to exist in 1974, due to the

reorganisation of local government, the chair, no longer required, was stored in a cupboard. Alex Shaw, an Alsager schoolteacher, learned of the disused chair and suggested the Mayor present it to the authors for the benefit of Goss collectors. The then Mayor, Jeremy Smith, and his Councillors agreed and there was a formal presentation ceremony in the summer of 1983.

After her husband's death, Dolly had a bungalow built on part of an orchard which she had inherited from her father and called it 'Orchard Cottage'. She had also inherited his boathouse on the mere but had sold it years before.

Although Dolly had looked fit and well throughout her life, she became ill and aged quite suddenly. Before she died she showed Aline Moir her Goss collection which consisted entirely of the earlier choice pieces belonging to her grandfather William. Although Goss heraldic china had been on sale all her life, she had always resisted the temptation of buying any, preferring the rare vases and urns which her grandfather had made. The majority of her collection was photographed and published in a book entitled A *Pictorial Encyclopaedia of Goss China* by Marjorie Cawley and Diana Rees, now out of print. Mrs. Cawley visited the house to photograph the china and the book is the only record of the prized collection, which was stolen shortly afterwards. The sad story was told by the Rev. Moir as he prepared to attend Dolly's funeral in May 1972, announced in the newspaper only days before:

> 'Aline and I were staying with Gwen at West Mere Lodge. Just as we were about to set out for the funeral the telephone rang. A nephew of Dolly rang up to say that he had just been to Dolly's house and found that a thief, or thieves, had broken in through a back window and stolen all the china. The choicest objects were a terra cotta vase with winged handles marked W.H. Goss, a bust of William Henry Goss, a bust of Georgiana Goss and some parian ware.'

The pieces were never recovered, but most have since surfaced in collections about the country. The police believed that an authority on Goss china must have sometime visited the house and arranged the robbery, for although they thought they knew who was responsible, they were unable to prefer charges.

The funeral service in a full church was a tribute to the self-sacrificing life of Dolly Harpur, regardless of cost or pain. Meanwhile the thief insulted her memory by making off with her family heirlooms.

\* \* \* \* \* \* \* \* \* \* \* \* \*

Adolphus's son Clarence Richard (Dick) transferred from the 5th North Staffordshire Regiment in which he had been made Lieutenant two years before, to the Grenadier Guards in August, 1918 and in November 1924, was

*Orchard Cottage, Sandbach Road South, Alsager, which Dolly had designed and built for herself. It was from here that burglars stole her Goss china collection whilst she was being buried*

promoted to the rank of Captain, retiring in 1930 as a Major. Dick married Martha Letière Sheldon (Patty) on the 29 June, 1916, whilst on leave. On 26 March 1918, they had a son, Victor John, who was born during a war and was to die in a war. Patty, a very attractive girl, was not devoted to Dick; she had an affair with Ned Guinness (of the brewing family) but Dick was not prepared to allow any scandal because of his connection with the Grenadier Guards. He finally let her divorce him in 1929 and she married Ned. Dick married Alfreda (June) Hewlett and in 1930, took his new wife to meet his father, his mother having died in 1919. Adolphus showed June around the 'Old Villa', warning her as he went, 'You'll never be married to my son', because he did not believe in divorce and remarriage. But she already was Mrs. Dick Goss! Her father-in-law never accepted her as a member of the family, a pity as she was such a lovely girl. Dick and June started a new life by attempting to sail and navigate to America from Plymouth but their 54ft. ketch *Hearts of Oak* was shipwrecked in Barbados. The voyage lasted four months, the vessel having no engine and depending entirely on sail. They eventually ended up at Vancouver Island where the only job he could get was as a stevedore. The work caused him great discomfort because ever since he was wounded twice in the Great War he had had difficulty with one arm and shoulder, which caused him great discomfort, especially when dressing. Before long, an acquaintance contacted the Canadian Government who

*Dick Goss, Captain of the Grenadier Guards, seated centrally in the front row, with Bob the mascot dog. Taken in 1925*

*Vernon, Dolly and Mary Kingston in 1912 outside 'The Old Villa'. Dolly was acting as chaperone for the day*

considered he had been badly treated by the British Government and he was offered a job in the Mounties, patrolling the Pacific coast north of Vancouver, well known as a tricky area.

One terrifying tale they related was how, when exploring in a remote part of Canada, they met a man who had been mauled by a bear and had one eye hanging out. June put the eye back in its socket and they put him in their boat and took him to hospital — he lived!

They eventually returned to England in 1939, Dick wishing to 'do his bit' on hearing war declared. He secured a position as head of Air Raids Precautions for Devon with the grand title of 'Chief Civilian Defence Officer', with 16 main offices under his jurisdiction, for which his efforts were rewarded with the M.B.E. It was believed that if it had not been for his permanent injuries he could have probably gone far in the army.

They did not see much of Dick's son through being in Canada, and because of the war when they returned. He had followed in his father's footsteps, becoming Capt. Victor Goss of the Grenadier Guards, and was killed in action in the Mawell Line in Tunisia in March 1943. There are memorial plaques in the Guards Chapel, Windsor, to both Dick and Victor. In the 1960's Dick and June lived in Sherfield English, near Romsey, having moved from Manor Farm, Farnborough, Hampshire.

* * * * * * * * * * * * * *

Major Vernon Goss married Mary Elizabeth Kingston in April 1922, in Alsager. Almost the whole village turned out to witness the event as both the Gosses and the Kingstons were such well known local families. Mary had served as a V.A.D. throughout the war at Rode Hall Hospital. Dolly was one of the bridesmaids and the best man was Major Ellis, who had lost four brothers in the war, all friends of the Goss brothers. Amongst those who attended the wedding were Adolphus, Ethel, Huntley and Florence Goss with Geoffrey and John their children, Mrs. Burne of Herne Bay (Ethel was to become her husband's second wife after her death), Miss Anie Jewitt of Crick, Northants (granddaughter of both W.H.Goss and L. Jewitt) and Dr. Harpur (Dolly's husband).

Vernon and Mary set up home in Manchester, and for most of their lives they lived at Little Croft, Station Road, Whalley, where they had two sons, Randle and William. Vernon died in 1968 aged 81. William (Bill), has the same sandy hair and similar looks as his grandfather and great-grandfather. In true Goss tradition he is rarely called by his christened name, with his mother knowing him as Raymond, his ex-wife calling him George (his army name), yet he signing his own name Bill! He attended Newcastle under Lyme High School with his brother, like the previous generation, and later went to Aberdeen University, before working for an electrical firm who supplied the power to nearly all the cotton mills in Lancashire. He joined the army and spent a year in India in 1946-7 retiring as Major, and now works for the Ministry of Defence. He met all the members of the Goss family at his wedding in 1953 when he married Jocelyn Truell of Wimborne. They have five sons and one daughter, all bearing traditional family names. George did not inherit any Goss china due to the theft during Dolly's funeral, but felt attracted to it and during the fifties when stationed in the Salisbury district, began buying odd pieces when he could afford them at around sixpence a piece at Salisbury Market.

* * * * * * * * * * * * * *

Edith's son had a farm in New Zealand where Mildred also lived. After a long career teaching young ladies at Cheltenham Ladies College, living with her mother and running her own car, quite an unusual thing to do for a single woman in those days, Grace eventually emigrated after her mother's death to join her brother and sister. Her other brother Eric died in 1927.

In her old age Edith became quite disenchanted with her family for not replying to her many letters over the years. When living at 41, St. Bernards Road, Otton, Godfrey wrote to her when he was dying, one of only half a dozen letters in about fifty years. She replied quite coldly that because of a nasty fall a few years before when she broke her wrist, she rarely wrote because it was such a labour to her and she felt quite alone although she had such a large family. What a difference the years had made to the vivacious young Edith who was capable of so much love, and who used to cry with worry about her absent brother. As Dolly Harpur remarked in a letter to John Willis, a Goss china collector, in the 1960's, 'For some reason we didn't keep in touch with the Mountfords.'

* * * * * * * * * * * * * *

Florry Goss had tried for years to persuade Godfrey and Alice to write to those left in England. She particularly liked Percy, the youngest child, and asked him to try to urge his parents to write, but Godfrey was finding farming hard work and Alice was permanently unwell. They moved to Lasara Park, Raymondville, Texas in 1926 and in 1927 Godfrey had a bad riding accident from which he took a long time to recover. Adolphus wrote to his 'special chum' in 1928 telling him about a letter he had just received from Pat Cleary of Clymore, Belleek, Co. Fermanagh, Northern Ireland. Adolphus was pleased Pat was still living at the same old place where Godfrey and he had spent a few days in 1877 and he reminded him how the the Irish girls were knocked backwards by Godfrey's good looks. Although Godfrey never replied to his letters, it did not deter Adolphus from writing and he

spoke warmly of Godfrey until his dying day. After Alice died, Percy and his wife Clara looked after Godfrey who only lived another two years after losing his beloved partner.

* * * * * * * * * * * * * *

Anie Jewitt never married, and her only real problem all her life was her eyesight. In 1906, shortly after her step-sister Sally was born on 25 May she had an important eye operation performed by the famous Dr. Snell in a Sheffield private hospital, where she stayed for three weeks. By this time her father and his second wife had moved to Melborne, still in Derbyshire. She adored her step-sister and step-brother Arnold. Sally was diabetic and later, when her health failed, Anie looked after her. In her youth Sally was a brilliant horse artist as well as being a good rider; she understood horses and could paint exquisitely with water colours. She had the skill to have become a famous artist but she was never allowed to paint professionally by her father, and few of her paintings are known to remain.

In their last few years, Anie's parents lived with her in a large house at Rugby and she nursed both of them until they died — both on the same day! Her faithful servant Laura Horner was favourably mentioned in her mistress's will. Louise and John Goss, who remained in regular contact with her until her death, remembered that when she died on 1 September, 1973, she still had the golden hair so typical of the Gosses, the same observation that was made about her grandfather William when he died.

* * * * * * * * * * * * * *

It would appear Florry married Albert Murdock for his money because her letters are full of her attentions to financial matters. After his death she reverted to her maiden name of Goss, was lonely and had few friends, not caring very much for her neighbours or for her nephews. Her second husband Sir John Fagge was often poorly and in the thirties their only contact with the outside world was the radio, which Vallie and Edith had given them for a wedding present. 'My husband is quite a hermit and doesn't like society at all and shuns everything he can', Florry sadly told a friend. It seems she was prevented all her life from leading the gay party style of living she really wanted. Instead she ended up living in the small rural village of Marshfield, Massachusetts. In the early thirties she had electric light installed:

'just two jets in a room downstairs and one in each bedroom. I don't like it too brilliantly lighted, it makes my forehead ache but I am so thankful I have no lamps to trim.'

There was a serious depression in America, as in England at that time, and many were in financial difficulties, as Florry once described:

'There are so many wicked things being done. Banks broken into, homes and places set on fire to obtain insurance. Ladies are unsafe to go out alone as bags are being stolen and people are being kidnapped. One man was kept in a beach house not far from here and gagged and strapped down and made to sign papers for thousands of dollars for a ransom. Two of my banks that I had savings in, had a rustle, and had to close up and now I see in this weeks paper I shall only get 20%. And two days ago my Trustees wrote that I should get three hundred less next year and may be even worse. My husband is poor, so I shall have to be careful. He wants me to sell and go to England, but I should hate to do so.'

*Vallie and Milton Taggart in the early years of their marriage (1937)*

In 1932 her husband John was eventually diagnosed as suffering from cancer of the eye. His stepdaughter, Vallie, used to tell him it was his heavy smoking that caused it, but he would not believe her and the cancer finally penetrated his brain.

Vallie meanwhile was growing up quickly, with childhood ambitions to become a doctor. She went on a tour of Europe with Gracie Mountford, 'The one who is such a blue stocking and passed through Oxford University', Florry was proud to say.

Vallie grew up to become a registered nurse, and later a civil service employee, then a social worker. Eventually she became a property broker, influenced perhaps by her hobby of moving house. She has moved some ten times following her divorce after an unhappy marriage, building two of her homes herself. Her children, Rohiah, David

and Jonathan were married in 1936, 1940 and 1942 respectively and all have children, seven between them, and grandchildren.

Valentine and her uncle Adolphus, kept in touch throughout their lives. However, Adolphus did not care for his young American niece's awful handwriting and numerals and imitated them in a letter to Mary Alice Goss, alongside a list of what her alphabet letters were meant to be.

As is often the case with mother and daughter relationships, problems arose between Florence and Vallie. Florence thought Vallie's husband Milton was wonderful and showered him with gifts but Vallie and Milton could not get on at all and had a fierce argument in front of Florence and John when visiting them one day. In the end John had to call in the police. Milton walked out and Florence consulted a fortune teller who said he would never come back and he didn't. Vallie had purchased their home with the arrangement that Milton would pay back his half-share. As Vallie had inherited more from her father than her mother she was able to support herself and her family.

After Milton's abrupt departure Vallie stayed on occasions with her mother with the latter protesting to her friends that she had not invited her. She had a weak heart in her old age, and complained that she could not stand the noise of Vallie's children, or seeing her precious furniture damaged by their horseplay, and that her daughter did not help with the housework. She believed

*Vallie Taggart, last surviving grandchild of W.H. Goss, beside the intended grave she has already reserved, next to her father Albert Murdock, taken March 1985*

her daughter had been gossiping in the village, telling locals that her mother was going out of her mind and that she would have to get someone to take care of her money for her, as she was giving too much away to worthless people! Florence died on 5 October, 1949, at the age of 79 in Massachusetts, with Vallie living with her and nursing her until the end. Valentine wrote this poem about her grandfather after listening to her mother's stories about life with William Henry Goss:

'My Grandfather Wm. Henry Goss'
by Val Taggart.

My grandfather was an Englishman
With golden hair and a beard of tan
When my mother was eight or nine
He'd take her for walks, when the day was fine.
They'd stop at a farm and buy 'high tea',
Toast and a salad of vegetable three,
Tomatoes, cheese and lettuce green,
With great dignity it would seem.
One pretty day as they ate formally,
My grandfather, as he ate his 'tea',
Gave a gulp, and putting down his mug,
With his fork, took off a 2-horned slug!!
And put it on the edge of his plate,
Ate his salad, so they wouldn't be late,
As he finished his lettuce and wiped his mouth,
Again he gulped and turned due south!
That cute little 2-horned slimy slug,
Was found chewed up well by that gentleman mug!!
And his face turned green and then bright red,
When he realised how he had been fed!!!
Shhh!!!
Not a word.'

Apart from writing poetry, Vallie used to play the violin, ukelele and mandolin and belongs to a Ceileah Gaelic gathering where members entertain one another.

Her nephew Bill remembers her as being very striking, full of fun, having brilliant red hair and she amused him on one occasion by eating an apple whole, pips, the lot!

* * * * * * * * * * * * * *

Huntley lost his wife Florence in 1930, after selling his factory the year before and then his beautiful house in Alsager. All his unmarried children were still living with him in Hartshill until at least 1938. Ethel described the three sons as 'just about keeping the home fires burning between them.' No doubt the treasures they had inherited from their grandfather and aunt Adeline were sold in order to keep their heads above water.

During the Second World War Noel had an Austin 7 which he ran on coal gas. The car had a huge bag on the roof which he connected to a gas pipe at night-time in order to refuel. He would drive to Radway Green, to the ammunitions factory, near Alsager where he worked for a while. He never married and grew to be a typical bachelor, owning a wireless-cum-motorcycle shop in Alsager for many years. The shop was always in a frightful muddle although Noel was very good at repairs and knowledgeable. His home was pulled down years ago and was approximately in the area where Lloyds Bank and the Alsager telephone exchange now stand. He then moved to a small prefab in Hassall Road, close to his old shop.

*Noel with gas balloon on his car which he used during the war when fuel was in short supply*

John, Huntley's youngest son, first met Louise his future wife when she was 10 and he was 16, through her brother. They married in 1942, went to Sunderland and rented their first house which was so large and cold they cycled around the bedroom to keep warm, as they could not afford to heat it. Huntley was a frequent visitor. In 1946, they began working in a china shop in Hertford, and were directors by 1953. Louise (christened Daisy Louise Adams) had been a V.A.D. nurse and then worked in a bank for 15 years before their move to Hertford. Her distant cousins were the Furnivals and the Adams, both potting families.

It was not unusual at that time for most inhabitants of the Stoke area to be connected in some way with the pot banks. Her uncle had a small pottery and his friend had a factory which ground down bones for china. Louise recalled that they once said one to the other. 'I couldn't sleep for the smell of smoke,' and the other replied, 'I couldn't sleep for the smell of bones.'

Both Louise and John shared a great-grandmother, Mrs. Thomas Hammersley, who emigrated to Philadelphia, and whilst they never managed to prove it was the same lady, it does seem likely that it was. They had only been married two years when Geoffrey, John's older brother, came to stay.

Huntley's fabulous home, 'The Lodge', which he had to sell in 1930

Pottery figure of a soldier standing to at dawn, privately modelled by John Goss

John Goss working on his designs in flint glass for Pyrex Glass

Louise noticed he was ill and he later died of tuberculosis, contracted after the war. She remembers him as yet another member of the Goss family who had both integrity and charm. and John had intelligence as well.

Some of John's last projects at the Goss firm were designing memorial statues for those lost in the Great War. He designed and modelled a 350mm pottery soldier standing to at dawn, decorated in blue and green. This was a statue commissioned for the Lady Chapel of a Stoke Church, but the church ran out of funds and the order was cancelled. At this time there were ex-infantrymen working at the factory. They praised John's model which captured the mood of a soldier who had the unenviable task of keeping guard at first light between 5 and 6 a.m. when a surprise raid was most likely. There were always one or two men on guard in each trench at this time of morning, and for most of the year it was a bitterly cold duty. John managed to portray cold, fear, and weariness in the stance and expression of the figure he modelled.

In the mid-thirties he worked as a designer for John Maddock and Sons, where he modelled an excellent figure of an Australian soldier. Later, Louise's brother Charles found him a post as designer in flint glass for Pyrex Glass. One always associates oven-to-table glass dishes with Pyrex,

it being such a household name, but in those earlier days the firm produced small quantities of exquisite, tasteful ornaments and centrepieces, which John designed and which had the look and feel of Lalique.

During the Second World War he was often fire watching on the roof of the Pyrex factory, keeping warm over a cauldron of molten glass and was certainly lucky on one occasion when, during a daylight raid, a bomb fell and split the buttons on his coat! One of Louise's amusing memories is of listening to Huntley and John having a conversation. To anyone who did not know them and their harsh voices it would appear they were having a row, but it was just their way of discussing things.

Florence died in 1930, eighteen years before Huntley. Peggy looked after her father until her marriage in 1938 to Ferris Allardice, when she went to live in West Wickham, Kent, and Huntley moved to Sunderland as a paying guest along with John. When John and Louise married, Huntley eventually moved in with them, and later all three moved to Hertford. Louise recalled that Huntley was very much a black and white person; there were no grey areas. Everything was either true or false, and he would argue until the cows came home with anyone who disagreed with him! He liked symmetry, and if he saw

*Margaret Goss's wedding day, 1938. Left to right: Huntley, Mrs Allardice, Ferris Allardice, Margaret (Peggy), Dr. Anthony Allardice, Miss Shelley and Dr. Allardice the surgeon (he certified Adeline Goss dead in 1916)*

a vase on a table which was not absolutely in the middle, he would always centre it. Louise, being artistic, often arranged her flowers so that the vase was placed to one side of a table for effect. But Huntley always waited until her back was turned and positioned it back in the centre of the table! These antics amused her no end.

Even in his eighties Huntley still took an interest in his stamp collection, and when Louise saw in the local paper that there was to be a meeting of stamp collectors in the town, she asked if he would like to be taken to see it. 'What', he replied, 'go to a meeting with a load of old fogies? No, thank you!'

Through looking after him in her own home Louise got to know her father-in-law really well and realised, that among all his good qualities, he had an amazing streak of obstinacy, so that when his mind was made up, nothing would alter it. It appears he was very much like Adolphus and of course William Henry Goss, although John recalled Adolphus as being 'a bit of a snob'.

Huntley smoked the most fearful tobacco. One day Louise gave him some expensive tobacco to try in his pipe and he told her firmly, 'I'm not going to smoke that damned puritannical stuff.' His own exceptionally strong brand of tobacco had quite ruined his taste buds. One year he became seriously ill and after he recovered, he wanted to prove he was still agile, so one afternoon he climbed up into the apple tree to try to get Louise to panic. When a doctor arrived, and could not get Huntley down, he asked her what she was going to do, to which she answered, 'Nothing'. The doctor said she was quite right. She waited a little while, then called out in the usual way, 'Tea's ready' and he came down like a shot! He was very fond of cats all his life, and always had a cat, unlike the rest of his family who preferred dogs. During the last two years of his life he grew a full beard, and was still a handsome man when he died. When certifying death, the doctor turned to Louise and said, 'Mrs. Goss, what a beautiful old man.' How true that was, she confirmed, 'for he had good bone structure and an excellent nose.'

Louise and John had her mother to stay the week after Huntley passed away, and also Anie Jewitt, and Noel Goss in the last months of their lives too.

Michael Willis-Fear who wrote his M.A. thesis about the Goss factory and products, met John and Noel in the 1960's and conducted extensive interviews with them. He traced Noel through Norman Emery, then Deputy Chief Librarian of the Staffordshire Library, who in 1959 had spotted a magazine article by Noel about Goss and pottery tanks entitled *Cracks and Crazes*. Norman Emery gave a copy of this to Michael Willis-Fear who through this lead traced Noel to Alsager. The impression Willis-Fear obtained of Noel was that of a scruffy, managerial bachelor. He had most definitely 'gone to seed', and his house looked in need of a woman's touch being knee-deep in dust and empty coffee cups, but despite this Noel was clean-shaven, had impeccable manners, an Oxford accent and that typical Goss courtesy. He passed on valuable information to his interviewer about the production of Goss china because he had supervised its manufacture during his years working for his father Huntley. He died in 1967 a few years after the interview.

Peggy died of cancer in 1972, just short of her 70th birthday, John being the only one who lived past 70 years.

## Reference

1.     Reminiscences of Adolphus W.H. Goss (paper) by Rev. A.L. Moir.

# CHAPTER TWELVE

# The Falklands Connection

If a man does not keep pace with his companions,
perhaps it is because he hears a different drummer.
Let him step to the music he hears,
however measured or far away.

Thoreau: 'Walden'

William's eldest brother Jacob Napoleon, and his wife Ann Elisabeth Pedrick emigrated to the Falklands in 1850 when William and Abner his younger brother were still students. Jacob had been working in the west country as a stonemason, where he met Ann.

Their parents followed him out there on his recommendation, claimed land as early settlers, and began building. The first building Jacob erected was Marmont Row, originally six terraced houses in local stone. The walls were 20 inches thick and for 130 years have weathered the South Atlantic gales and the Argentinians. Over the years it has changed and the interior altered considerably. The two cottages at one end became the Eagle Inn (named after the family arms) which was sold to the Falkland Islands Company and later to a private owner who converted it into a public house called 'The Ship Hotel'. Two other houses were converted into the Colony Club, for many decades a haunt for the upper classes. The other end of Marmont Row later became the 'Upland Goose Hotel' (again the Goss family crest) which opened in 1970. The whole building is still the largest in Stanley and the oldest. It overlooks Victory Green and became well-known during the 1982 Falkland War because its telephone line maintained a link with the outside world after British troops had liberated Port Stanley.

Richard and son Jacob increased their wealth rapidly and erected many houses in Stanley. Richard had named his eldest son Jacob Napoleon because of his involvement in the surrender of Napoleon I to the crew of HMS Bellerophon in 1815. Jacob Napoleon in turn named his son Richard William Napoleon. Jacob and Ann Pedrick raised six children, but Jacob died suddenly in 1868. The local residents thought it ominous when his father Richard died three days later, and predicted more bad luck, which materialised when Jacob's widow Ann was swindled out of everything she owned, houses, land, a schooner etc. Some of the family to this day suspect foul play, and the story is that the father and son had entrusted an Anglican

priest with their fortune, and that after their sudden deaths he disappeared on their schooner with the money and many other possessions including deeds to their property. It was said that traces of poison were found in the dead mens' bodies, and after that some of the Gosses became Catholics! Richard's wife died within four years, and William appeared to lose contact with his Falkland cousins after 1872.

Of Jacob and Ann's children, the largest families belong to Richard William Napoleon and William Henry.

One of Richard's sons, Richard Victor, his wife and their children came back to England in a sailing ship, the Galgorm Castle, in 1894. They all stayed in Great Britain except for one brother, Sidney, who went back to Port Stanley and died there in 1944, leaving a large family.

Ernest and Sidney's brothers William Henry and Richard William Napoleon and their sister Ada made their way from England to Belfast where the two men contracted tuberculosis and became quite lame. The two brothers were heavy drinkers and Ada's husband put them on a ship back to the Falklands where alcohol was not so freely available.

Ernest started a 21 year naval career by sailing round the Horn at the age of 14 years in 1903 and saw active service in the 10th Cruiser Squadron thoughout World War I. He became a Captain in Lamport and Holt Shipping Company for some years after the First World War and then set up an insurance business with his brother William who died in the late thirties. Ernest, by then an ardent Methodist, continued alone as an insurance broker in Reading. His youngest son, Brian Goss attended Reading University and obtained a Degree preparatory to entering the Church in which he is now a Methodist Minister.

Richard Victor of Port Stanley was the eldest brother of Ernest. He was a keen soldier and a member of the Local Defence Force, similar to the Territorial Army, since the age of 16. It was he who discovered his cousins in England, there being no prior contact since 1872. Richard wrote to these distant cousins in the early 1970's that the main threat to the Falklands was the Argentine fanatics such as those who landed there in 1966 in a D.C.4. aircraft. He commented that the total artillery consisted of two 1902 Hotchkiss 3 Pdrs! He earned his living as the General Secretary and Treasurer of the only local Trade Union and joked that he hoped he earned his living in a more rational manner than some of the British Trade Unions he read and heard about! He rose to become Lt. Col. Goss, O.B.E.,T.D. and a member of the Falklands Legislative and Executive Councils. He married Dot and had four children during the 1960's. Richard wrote to Bill and Jocelyn Goss in Surrey, England, in 1970, thanking them for the pieces of Goss china they had sent him, and apologised for not being able to buy any Falklands postcards to send them. He explained that the islanders imported just about everything and their only exports were raw wool and skins. With their own inter-island air service, it should have been possible to obtain aerial views of Stanley in his opinion, but the islands had no professional photographer as such.

Eric Goss, a farmer, is a descendant of Jacob's son William Henry. He rose to fame in the 1982 Falklands War by playing an instrumental part in the Argentinians' surrender at Goose Green and appeared on British television.

He is now Farm Manager of the Falkland Islands Company Ltd, Farm Darwin at Goose Green, with 100,000 sheep to care for. He was already aware of his distant connections to the Goss potters of Stoke, as his elder sister Greta Skene is a keen collector, now living in Scotland.

Arthur Hurlin of the United States, a grandson of Sophia, sister of William and Jacob, visited his Falklands relations before his death in 1926.

From the Falklands family tree of those descended from Jacob which we have compiled, the same names regularly appear, but there are several somewhat unusual names, especially Georgina Ellen's son (grandson of Jacob Napoleon), christened Abner Marentius Napoleon Cosmopolite Lars Berntsen. Major Dick Goss from England told a Falklands relation that the family motto was 'It is written in the stars.' He joked, 'All I can say is that there must have been a hell of a lot of stars out the night they named that boy!'

One wonders why William's parents and brother chose to go to the Falklands, such barren and severe islands cut off from civilisation as they were. To try to understand, we looked at the history of the islands. Two sightings were made in 1592 and 1594 by British navigators but the first landing was made by Captain Strong of HMS Welfare in 1690 who named them after Viscount Falkland. It was 74 years later before the first French settlers arrived at Port Louis in East Falkland. Two years later in 1766 the first British settlement of about 400 people was set up at Port Egmont in West Falkland. When the French sold their area to Spain, a Spanish expedition out of Buenos Aires forced the British to surrender Port Egmont and an Hispanic-British war was only averted when Spain failed to acknowledge the Buenos Aires group. By 1771 the British settlement was re-established. In 1820, the United Provinces of La Plata, governed from Buenos Aires and covering the countries now known as Argentina, Uruguay and Paraguay, hoisted their flag on East Falkland and appointed their own Governor for both islands. Britain protested officially in 1828. The South American 'governor' Louis Verner, erred when he arrested three American ships for alleged breaches of sealing regulations. The United States sent two warships to destroy Verner's artillery and declared the islands free of Government. Buenos Aires appointed a new governor, who was murdered by his own men, and reports of other outrageous acts of lawlessness reached London, which prompted Britain to send HMS Challenger out there and to install her first officer, a Lieutenant Smith, as Governor in 1834. Since then the Islands have stayed British and the Gosses were amongst the earliest pioneers to try their luck in that inhospitable land.

The Goss factory produced three different Falklands crests during the reign of three different sovereigns, and the magnificent model of a Falklands penguin in black and white, modelled by John Goss, no doubt all prompted by the family connections with the Islands.

*Book plate designed by Adolphus Goss for his father William, with the motto 'It is written in the stars'*

# CHAPTER THIRTEEN

# The Beginnings of a Career

And if the world had found some good in me,
The prompting and teaching came from thee!
God so guide both that so it ever be!

Samuel Carter Hall

Whilst a student in London in the 1840's, William Henry Goss formed one of the most important friendships of his life and one which would shape the path of his career. Through fellow student William Copeland Astbury, he met Astbury's cousin, Alderman William F.M. Copeland, a former Lord Mayor of London. This white haired and bearded intellectual came to look upon his teenaged protégé rather like a son. Under his guidance the keen student mastered the art of potting and the advanced skills of chemistry which were to prove invaluable.

In the biography of her father, Adeline maintained:

'To this knowledge of chemistry he doubtless owed his success in potting for later on when he started manufacturing on his own account, he not only invented all the enamels with which his ware was decorated, but also constructed from the older and original 'parian' body, the material he called 'ivory porcelain', which has never been quite successfully imitated, and which, decorated with emblazoned heraldic devices, has become well known all over the civilized world.'[1]

Alderman Copeland owned the famous Copeland Spode china works at Stoke-on-Trent, with a branch in London. In 1852 he offered William a job as a clerk in his London office where he learned the business side of the pottery industry. This establishment at Lincoln's Inn Fields was once the famous theatre in Portugal Street which was constructed by Rich, the celebrated manager who produced *The Beggars' Opera*, but became the Copeland warehouse. He continued to make contacts like William Savage of Winchester and these acquaintances were to prove useful to him when he started his own factory six years later. Savage was supplied by Copelands with utility shapes bearing Winchester motifs such as William of Wykeham and the Trusty Servant during the 1850's. A year after his marriage in 1853 William Goss was sent to the Copeland factory in Stoke to work with parian, which had been invented in 1847 by an employee of that pottery.

After a brief apprenticeship he became a designer and artist, working with jewelled parian vases, plates and figurines. In 1857 he became chief designer and artist, and his skill and mastery over a wide range of high quality artistic shapes was noted. One ornament which aroused much attention was 'Mr. Goss's new Medallion Vase of 1857', a revived shape from an 1820 Spode Pattern book.

William found the greatest pleasure in working with high quality decorative ware with which he could use his exquisite taste and innovative designs, such as a fantastic dessert service for Copeland purchased by the Shah of

*William Henry Goss at the beginning of his career*

*Alderman William Copeland, who personally directed William Goss's instruction in chemistry and potting at his own expense*

Persia for his personal use. The production costs alone were about a thousand pounds and the design incorporated glass jewels which were encrusted in the decorations. Each piece, which was made by William Henry Goss with his own hands, and probably his last major work at Copeland, had a hand painted Swiss landscape. This unique dessert service not unnaturally caused a considerable stir in the pottery world at the time.

This service which comprised 29 pieces, had a predominant ground colour of turquoise blue, the shade with which William loved to decorate porcelain. The floral borders to the landscapes are attributed to D. Lucas, the rims to each piece are white. Leonard Whiter, the definitive writer on Copeland Spode, who was a prominent works manager, visited Teheran to borrow a dozen pieces for a display of Copeland Spode in England in the 1960's.

Whiter took some beautiful colour photographs of Goss's work and made these observations:

'All pieces were modelled with embossed designs which allow for insertion of simulated gems of cut glass with mirrored backs in ruby, emerald and topaz colours. These were stuck into the modelled recesses when the rest of the decoration was complete. The invention was attributed to W.H. Goss who was Copeland's art director at the time and who subsequently made use of it in his own business, started in 1858. The design of the plate is still used at the Spode factory for production of jewel embossed shapes in earthenware.'

*William's student prize awarded at Somerset House, 1852 and a medal awarded at the Boston Exhibition 1883*

*William Savage of Winchester, taken at his own Wykeham Studio in 1880, with hand written message from Savage to William Goss on the reverse, 'With best respects, W.S.'*

*Examples of jewelled ware William Henry Goss helped produce at the Copeland factory in the 1850's*

*The sample room at Copelands about 1870. Note the parian figures on the top shelf. Copelands did not attempt to make heraldic china but specialised in quality dinner and tea services, parian busts and figures and beautiful ornamental ware*

*A jewelled plate from the Shah's Dessert Service encrusted with jewels and turquoise enamelling. The hand-painted Swiss landscapes were attributed to D. Lucas*

*The magnificent jewelled comport from the dessert service designed and made by W.H. Goss*

The comport and stand stood on models of three lions rampant, decorated with chased gold, bearing shields standing on a pedestal and supporting a separate comport of inverted dome shape containing a separate vase shaped top piece. One shield is decorated with the Royal Arms of England, the other two of Queen Victoria and Prince Albert. There is mention of this service in *The Reliquary* of 1857, and these were William's first heraldic decorations. The service was known to be still intact in 1965 when Willis-Fear succeeded after two years of correspondence with the British Ambassador in Iran and the then Shah's Golestan Palace, Teheran, in obtaining permission to photograph the pieces. Whether or not the Palace still possesses the service is unknown.

The *Pottery Gazette* reported in 1857:

'It is always gratifying to notice a spirit of honourable rivalry as it indicates improvement and progress. This laudable emulation, which has always shown itself in the Staffordshire Potteries, has been productive of the most important benefits, as by raising the standard of excellence, and continually urging on to improvement, the reputation of the district has become more firmly established, its prosperity placed on a broader base, and the disadvantage that might arise from foreign competition less likely to be experienced. These observations naturally lead me to a new item to be placed to the credit of this interesting district. At the extensive manufactory of Alderman Copeland, M.P., at Stoke, a new showroom has been prepared, which will be opened in the ensuing week. The room, which is upwards of 100′ in length, is approached by a noble flight of steps, and is enriched with an extensive collection of exquisite specimens from the manufactory, in porcelain, statuary, vases and numerous other works of art, including a variety of new productions of special interest, which, whilst they manifest the enterprise and spirit of the worthy proprietor, reflect much credit on the taste and skill of Mr. Goss, the chief artist.'

Most of William's work at Copeland Spode was in the relatively new medium of parian. Whilst still in London, he made contact with the inventor of parian, John Mountford, and later wrote the history of that discovery. In his *Encyclopaedia of Ceramics*, W.P. Jervis revealed that:

'Its origin has been disputed, both Minton's and Copeland claiming to have invented it. Mr. W.H. Goss, who, when all the experiments were being conducted, was a young boy, knew all the parties concerned and afterwards wrote the particulars of the discovery for a book published at The Hague in 1864, entitled *Verslag der Wereldtentoonstelling Te London in 1862*, which was an important work on the London Exhibition produced by order of the Government of Holland. Mr. Goss states that it was during the year 1845 that experiments were made at the manufactory of Mr. Alderman Copeland to obtain a ceramic material that should resemble marble.'

S.C. Hall, Editor of the *Art Journal*, suggested that reductions from stone sculptures of the modern masters be made in a material that could imitate the stone visually. These miniatures could be offered as prizes by the Art Union of London. Following this idea a reduced model of Gibson's Narcissus was despatched to Copeland's works for the potters to work from, until there was success with John Mountford's invention. These experiments were conducted by several experienced artistic potters at Copelands but the first parian was produced there from Mountford's recipe. He had served his apprenticeship at the old Derby China Works during its last days, and had progressed from there with many other Derby potters to the fast growing up-to-date pot banks of Staffordshire. After Mountford had created sufficient examples of parian which was then known as 'porcelain statuary', he made the first figurine on Christmas Day, 1845, copying the model of Gibson's Narcissus. This was then sent to Mr. Gibson himself for inspection and he decreed it to be the best material next to marble for the reproduction of sculpture. The new porcelain body was an instant success and it firmly established itself in the ceramic world. It was at about this time that Messrs. H. Minton & Co., started similar experiments for imitation marble and it was not long before they discovered their own version which they termed 'parian'. It was noticed that their parian was slightly tinted and approximated freshly chiselled parian marble,

but Copeland's efforts were those of marble toned down with age.

Inside a book which once belonged to Llewellynn Jewitt we found a portion of a letter from W.H. Goss stating his beliefs concerning parian:

'We believe the day will arrive when these cream-color wares shall again be chosen in preference to the bluish tint. For we certainly think that if the materials were thoroughly magnetted, well lawned, and finely ground so as to leave a clean pure tint, the prevalence of the cream or ivory color of the Dorsetshire ball clay would form a much more pleasing ground for decoration in colors and gold than that of the stained ware.'

The term for the new porcelain composition 'parian' was originally derived from Paros, an island in the Aegean Sea. The marble of Paros was thus known as parian marble, but it would not be correct to call the invention parian marble, only parian. W. P. Jervis concluded that basically parian was a non-plastic body composed of three parts china stone to two parts felspar.

William left Copeland in 1858 following disagreements over managerial decisions. In truth, he needed to be his own boss and he founded his own firm the same year in John Street (now non-existent), in very modest premises backing on to Ald. Copeland's works. His friendship with Copeland possibly became quite strained because we could find no evidence of further contact between the two after this date, or photographs of Copeland in William's albums.

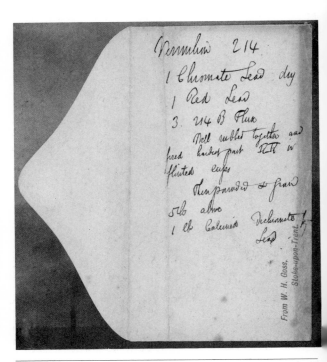

*A printed envelope from the Goss works with William's recipe for vermilion, which was unsurpassed*

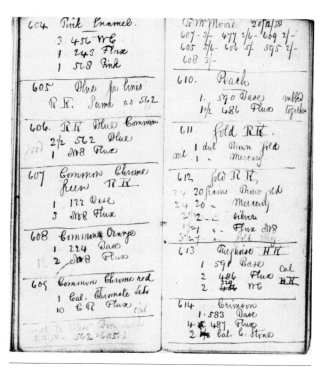

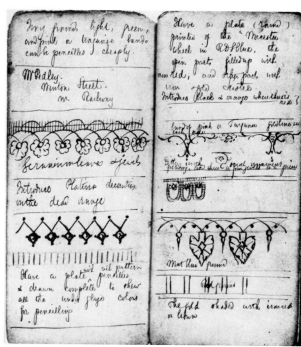

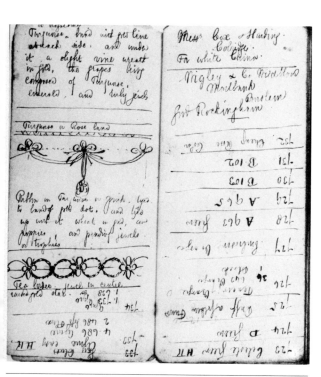

*Pages from W.H. Goss's hand-written ideas notebooks. He reused partly used books by turning them upside down and filling up the spaces*

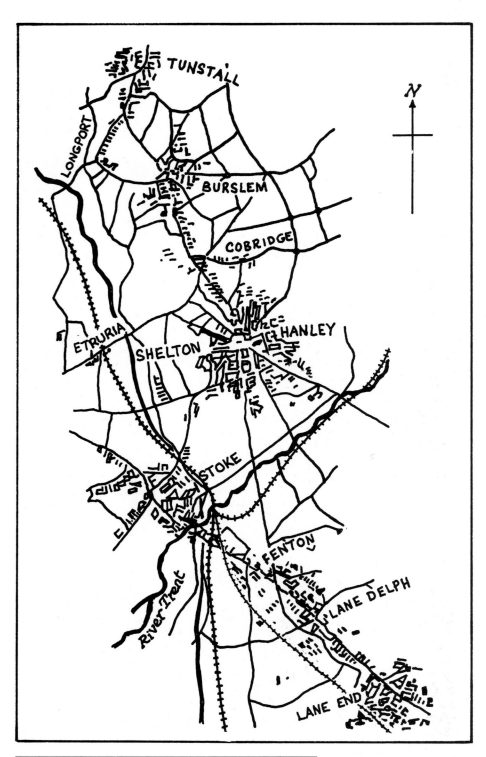

*Map of the Pottery towns in Staffordshire, 1850*

When running his own factory, William practised and experimented continually with both the parian body and the various types of decorations including gilding and enamelling. It was in the outbuildings and stables at his home that he experimented, recording all he did in a series of notebooks filled with beautifully neat handwriting, describing the recipes for all his shades of enamels and parian bodies. We did not realise there were so many shades of blue, for example! The recipes (or receipts as they were then known), look most impressive, and probably involved far more work than would be needed today. The enamels were made to last, and the way he perfected his turquoise blue, crimson, vermilion, sapphire blue and a few other favourites, to be used for decorating parian ware, makes fascinating reading. In particular, his vermilion was unequalled anywhere in the world until decades later a French chemist managed to emulate his success. Needless to say his enamels sold very well, and he earned more income from them than through his pottery sales.

### Reference

1. *Fragments from the Life and Writings of W.H. Goss* by Eva Adeline Goss 1907, Hill & Ainsworth.

# CHAPTER FOURTEEN

# The Factories

Stoke holds the pride of place as being the producer of all that is most artistic, ingenious and costly as well as utilitarian in the potter's art. Its environment is most attractive. As the traveller is sped towards it, with all the luxurious comfort of a North-Western express, he notices as he leaves grimy Crewe behind him the changed aspect of the country, the undulating 'smiling' plains and uplands, suggestive of 'the gentle shepherd' and his 'wanderings solitary'. And then he soon espies in the close embrace of the valley, Stoke with its cluster of conical 'ovens', for all the world like so many Brobdingnagian ninepins in a Gargantuan skittle alley!

'A Peep at the Potteries': *Morning Advertiser* 7 January 1902

After leaving his post as chief artist and designer at the Copeland Works, William Henry Goss set up his own firm in 1858 at the age of twenty five in John Street, off Liverpool Road, Stoke, a site which backed on to the works of his former employers Copeland. In his *Ceramic Art of Great Britain* , Llewellynn Jewitt mentions an earlier or extra site at neighbouring Eastwood Vale in Hanley. Possibly this was the Keys and Mountford works. Existing street directories from 1862 onwards record the Goss factory at the John Street site, known to locals as the 'Cock' works because it was next door to the Cock Inn.

There was a brief partnership with a Mr Peake, who was a specialist in terracotta ware, being a roofing tile manufacturer. It was earlier in 1856 that a valuable deposit of red clay had been found in this area giving rise to the clay tile industry. Norman Emery, F.L.A., then deputy librarian at Stoke library, discovered that a local Potteries' historian of the 1930's, the late Alfred Meigh, studied the voluminous old Rate Books for the area for the previous century and noted a reference to the partnership of Goss and Peake in 1868, described as parian manufacturers at the John Street, Liverpool Road site. These Victorian Rate Books were taken for salvage during the Second World War and Emery was unable to find any mention of the Goss and Peake firm in the remaining local trade directories for that time. A variety of terracotta items marked GOSS & PEAKE in black capital letters on the base were made by the Goss factory and two of these have been found dated 1867. Few of them are still perfect today as they were sold to be used. Pieces manufactured after the partnership dissolved were marked W H GOSS only, and decorations included transfers with Egyptian influence in black, red and green, or with amusing cartoons in black. Such terracotta ware is heavy; shapes made include tobacco jars, narrow-necked vases with stoppers (wine bottles) and base-plates and a variety of vases. Four

substantial figurines, each over 17 inches high, were modelled in parian ware during the Goss and Peake period. The Bride of Abydos and Ophelia were a magnificent pair as were Leda and the Swan and the Lady holding a Kid. Obviously William found it easier to be his own master. Mr Peake was thought to have had financial difficulties as a result of his other activities and the partnership was dissolved in 1868. The 1861 Census recorded W.H. Goss as a pottery manufacturer living at 10, Stoke Ville, with a staff of 15 men, 12 women and 35 boys. These included his unmarried younger brother, Abner Mitchener who lived with William and his family, and worked for him, and also the foreman William Bromley and W.W. Gallimore, the famous modeller. The factory site was described in the 1877 Ordnance Survey as being a very small pottery of 250 sq. ft. with a kiln at the end of John Street adjacent to the Cock Inn. Norman Emery and Michael Willis-Fear, leading authorities on the sites of the Goss works, both believe this to be Goss's first factory.

*Terracotta tobacco jars. These often contained a separate inner lid (damper) which kept the tobacco pressed down inside*

*Colin Minton Campbell, M.P. in 1875. He owned the tile works below the Goss factory site and sold the present factory site and Ashfield Cottage to William Goss*

Street directories proved that William had this factory until 1870 at least. These directories also revealed that William Bromley lived in nearby William Street, so he did not have far to walk to work! Joseph Myatt, another faithful employee, lived in London Road, and his father was the Town Crier. A grocer, Thomas Peake, lived in Stoke Road, and possibly was related to the Peake who once worked with the Goss firm. Other known Goss employees were John Astley, William Mollart, Mr. Ratcliffe and Thomas Boden whose home addresses were listed. Also, in *Keates and Fords 1867 Directory* we noted that Ald. William Copeland J.P., lived at Cliff Bank Lodge, and owned a further home in High Street, Stoke.

William's address was to influence the site of the more widely known existing Goss Works. His first home was listed in Kelly's Post Office Directory of 1860 as 'Ashfield Cottage, Stoke'. At this time it was set in unspoilt countryside with particularly beautiful views. From the house ran a drive bordered by giant trees which ended at London Road. He leased it from the owners of what became Campbell's Tile Works, until he and his family moved to 10, Stoke Ville during 1861. In 1867 the Annual Directories of Potteries in Newcastle records the Goss residence as Princes Street. The factory once adjacent to the present Goss site was built in 1862 by W. Kirkham

*Ashfield Cottage from the spoil heap, 1960*

*The Goss works in 1962 with the disused glost ovens on the left, one of which was used for the porcelain model. The buildings at the rear were the Goss factory from 1858 to 1905 and all the First Period Goss and much of the Second Period ware was made there. This area, rented from Kirkham's, was demolished about ten years ago but the surviving buildings which date from 1902-5 are the subject of a preservation order*

GOSS FACTORY, STOKE ON TRENT.

*Postcard with 1916 postmark depicting the Goss factory. Note the superb grounds*

*View of the works from the garden of Ashfield Cottage, taken in 1962. On the left is the ground floor warehouse, first floor enamel shop and second floor printing shop. On the right is the three-storey warehouse, offices and workshop. The original Goss factory is on the right*

*View even further to the right of the rear of the warehouses, also in 1962. This area was the original Goss factory 1858-1905*

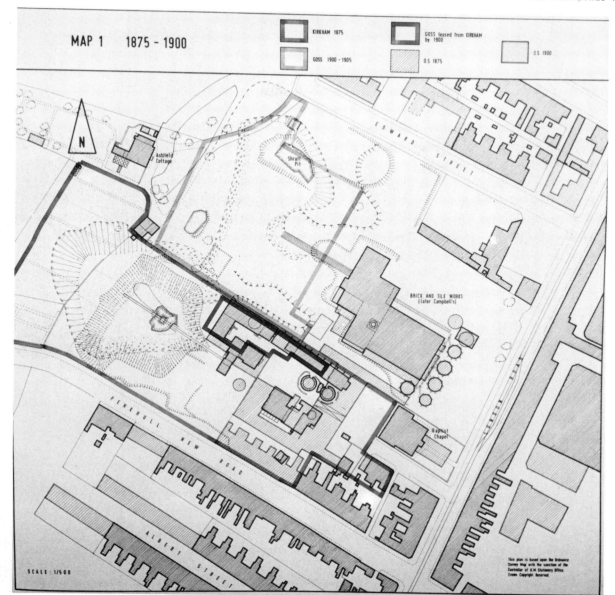

MAP 1    1875 - 1900

Map devised by Michael Willis-Fear, M.A. for his thesis. Date 1875-1900

as a factory to produce general earthenware and terracotta for both home and foreign markets. This has been demolished and the site is now the Portmeirion factory.

From the 1870's onwards William leased part of Kirkham's works as he needed more space for his steadily increasing business. Between 1870 and 1872 he moved his entire factory to Kirkham's site, which he both shared with and leased from his friend Mr. W.R. Kirkham. By 1885 he purchased it and had part of the works pulled down and rebuilt larger. This vastly improved production. Eventually this too became too small and the Goss factory as we know it was built next door between 1902 and 1905.

After Adolphus Goss, eldest son of William, joined the management, the main product was the heraldic china for which the firm is most remembered. Although earlier heraldic dinner services had been produced for the nobility bearing their particular family's coat of arms or more usually just their crests, by Dr. Wall at Worcester, Champion at Bristol, Josiah Wedgwood and the Leeds factory after 1755, for example, none had been produced as a souvenir before. However, fancy armorial services had been imported from China for general sale.

The manufacturing of heraldic china was the brainchild of Adolphus, using his father's original ideas he marketed

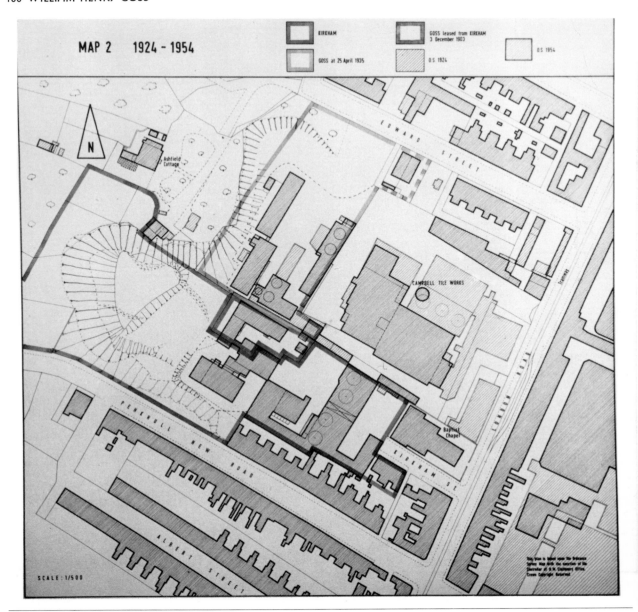

*Further map 1924-1954 by M. Willis-Fear*

it in a businesslike way. This led to the growing national hobby of collecting Goss heraldic porcelain, increased production and a demand which, it was obvious to William, the factory could not meet, so in 1880 he took on extra assistance in the form of Victor, his younger son, and additional staff. Willis-Fear noted:

'A comparison between the 25″ Ordnance Survey maps for the area dated 1875 and 1900 reveals that W.R. and H.G. Kirkham nearly trebled the size of their factory during this period, and whilst the original extent of W. H. Goss's leased rooms, etc., cannot now

be ascertained, certainly by 1900 he was occupying some 1323 sq. ft. of three-storeyed warehouse and manufacturing accommodation, including at least two ovens and was sharing Kirkham's grinding mill. By August 1900, W.H. Goss was granted permission to erect a further enamel kiln of some 105 sq. ft. in area by the local authority in order to deal with the increased flow of business.'[1]

In the Fifth Edition of the *Goss Record*, J.J. Jarvis informed unhappy subscribers who were having difficulty in obtaining the shapes they wanted:

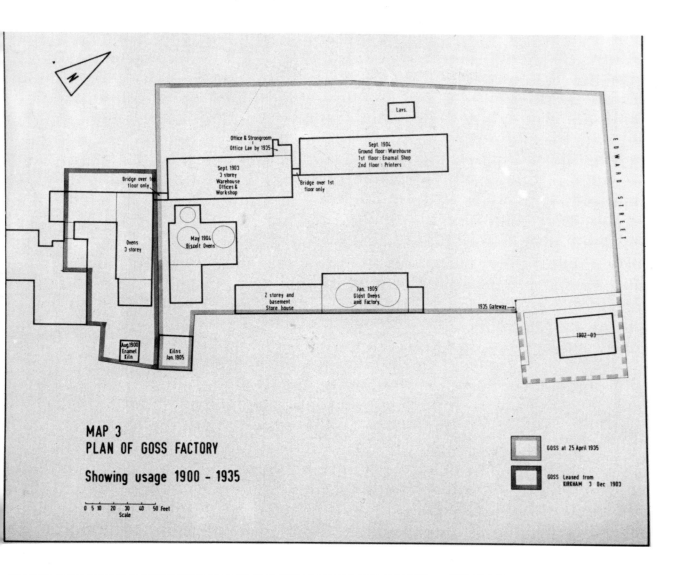

*Plan of usage 1900-1935 by M. Willis-Fear*

'It is a source of very great regret to me that year by year the demand for Mr. Goss's ware far exceeds the supply, and much of my correspondence is attributable to the complaints of collectors who find it difficult to obtain pieces at every town they visit. I am pleased, however, to be in a position to assure my readers that still further extensions of the works at Stoke-on-Trent are proceeding, and there is every reason to hope that if Agents will only order sufficiently early, all their requirements will be met more promptly in the future.'

The new land adjacent to Kirkham's works was purchased by Goss from Messrs. Campbell's Tile Works, and this was paid for in cash out of William's savings. Work started on the building in 1902 and completion finally took place in 1905. Willis-Fear investigated the plans and observed:

'The completed factory then comprised the original three-storey buildings and ovens, linked by a first-floor bridge to the first of the new three-storeyed warehouses, which also included offices, workshops and an office with a strongroom at the back, which was completed in September 1903. By September 1904, the second three storeyed warehouse, linked to its predecessor by a similar first-floor bridge was completed. This had an

*Stone Goshawk inset into the end wall of the last warehouse to be built, and still in existence*

*The Goss factory in 1975, already in decay*

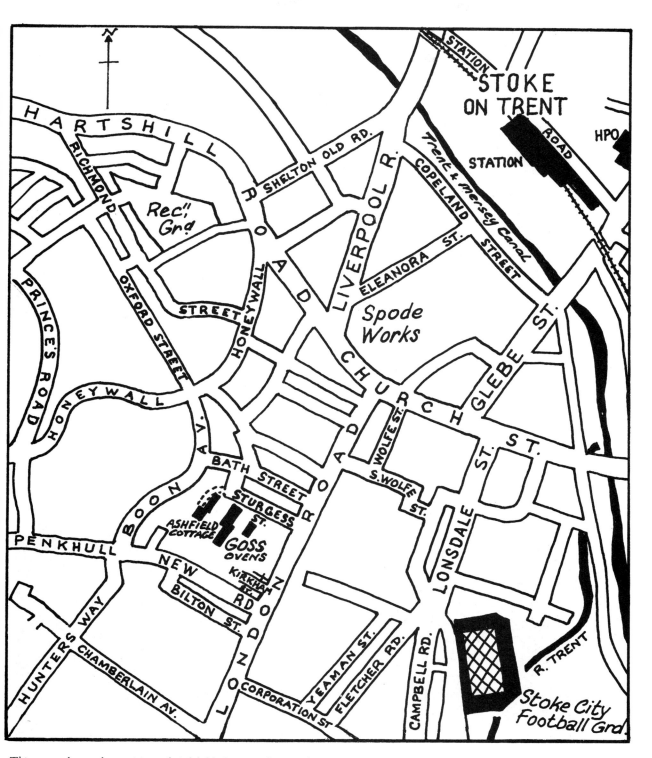

*This map shows the position of Ashfield Cottage, home of W.H. Goss and the Goss factory in Stoke-on-Trent*

Enamel Shop on the first floor and a Printers Shop on the second floor. In May 1904, three more biscuit ovens had been completed, and in January, 1905 the extensions were completed by further enamel kilns, a two-storey storehouse with a basement, and two large glost ovens for glazing the pieces, one of which the firm modelled for public sale to commemorate these extensions.'

On the gable end of the large warehouse there was an inset stone carving of the Goshawk trademark to indicate that this was the Falcon Pottery Works. Included in the programme were two houses completed in 1903 to provide homes for the senior staff at the factory's new entrance in Edward Street. The additional buildings covered an area of 84,000 sq. ft. These premises remained in use until the firm was sold by the Goss family in 1929 and were improved by 1935 whilst in the possession of subsequent owners. The trademark W.H. GOSS was not used on china after 1940 and the factory has not produced pottery since that date. It has in recent years been a warehouse for Slumberland bedding, an electrical factory, a clothing works, and is currently owned by the adjoining Portmeirion pottery.

Today, little remains of the original area as it was at the turn of the century except for the ovens and warehouses built 1902-5, and Ashfield Cottage. Portmeirion Potteries, owners of the adjoining factory on the original Kirkham's site have recently extended modern premises to within a few feet of the derelict, decayed ruins of the Goss ovens. The difference is startling. Electrically fired kilns means there are no large bottle oven chimneys, and no smoky coal fumes. Vast expanses of new corrugated metal walls and roofs overlook the shaky, crumbling brickwork and rotting woodwork of the once magnificent Falcon Works.

The old factory and kilns are now listed buildings and can be seen today from Sturgess Street, off London Road, Stoke, which was once the magnificent tree-lined drive for Ashfield Cottage.

**Reference**

1.   A History of the firm of W.H. Goss of Stoke-on-Trent, together with a survey of his wares M.A. Thesis Durham University, May 1970. M.J. Willis-Fear, M.A.

*Victor's two houses in Princes Street by the side entrance to the Goss works, taken in 1958, now demolished*

*1962 view of Ashfield Cottage looking down over the last warehouse to be built*

# CHAPTER FIFTEEN

# The First Period

As old as civilisation itself, the art of the potter represents a kaleidoscope of alluring charm.

H.W. Lewer

William Henry Goss's early introduction to parian blossomed into a lifelong respect for the medium, and was the basis of most of the factory's products. With the exception of the red-brown terracotta ware already described, he experimented and improved upon his earlier work at Spode, including the jewelled ware so sought after at the time. Indeed, he supplied exquisite jewelled scent bottles to Eugene Rimmel the Strand perfumier, for sale in Paris and London. Thousands of experiments were conducted in his workshops at home. His notebooks started on 18 November 1857, and included any ideas he had for decoration or possible shapes to manufacture, as well as the results of his tests on glaze, enamel and porcelain, all in his own hand. His improvements for securing the handles of cups, articles of jewellery, dress fastenings and smokeshades for lamps and gas burners, were patented by him on 23 October, 1872.

William's intense education and instruction in the arts influenced the type of product his factory was to make. His family had no previous connections with the china industry, and no ties with Staffordshire. He seemed to have a desire to create shapes of beauty, mostly relating to known subjects in order to teach the general public an appreciation of art, history and culture. He felt, as head of his firm, and of better education and intellect than most, that he had a responsibility to educate others. As a student he had studied art at Somerset House from the age of sixteen to nineteen, and had taken a keen interest in the subject ever since. The long reign of Queen Victoria had led to a peaceful and stable era in fashions and art, and made the nation feel secure in the permanency of its beliefs and tastes, and this was reflected in its choice of ornaments and porcelain and pottery as well as clothes and furniture. William was a typical Victorian gentleman.

He also produced superb classical statuesque figurines in the popular fashion at that time of draped mythical subjects in a variety of poses. A lady holding aloft an asp was 'Cleopatra', a woman deep in thought, with a dagger partly concealed in her dress, 'Tragedy' and a young woman praying, the 'Virgin Mary'. Not all the figurines were plain;

some were coloured or were trimmed with colours, particularly gold and turquoise — William's favourite combination. His forté was the portrait bust of white unglazed parian ware and with impressed factory mark and title. The first bust to have been made was Mr Punch in 1861; somewhat heavy and solid, it was sculpted by Goss and bore his impressed signature. The original still resides in the offices of *Punch* magazine in London. The first busts for retail sale were those of Lord Palmerston whose second term of office was 1859 to 1865. The earliest of these models were Copyright and signed W.H.Goss in his own hand.

Some busts are unnamed. The two children 'Grief' and 'Mirth' each with a cartouche depicting putti affixed to the front of their socle bases, have been described by Willis-Fear as being the style of Massimiliano Solidoni-Benzi's bronze version of the San Ilde-Fonso Greek marble fawn. A unique piece was the parian group including Venus, trimmed with gold and made between 1858 and 1862. This group was housed in the Victoria and Albert Museum, but was apparently destroyed by bombing during the Second World War. Another model, Pallas Athene, with armour and helmet completely gilded, and the face tinted with natural colours, still exists in a private collection. The busts which were mostly produced prior to 1900 covered a wide range of contemporary subjects, including political and literary figures, royalty, members of Willliam's family and friends, eminent musicians and members of the clergy, mainly from the Victorian era. Busts of those in the public eye had extra sales appeal. The main series of busts had either a square two-step plinth or a socle base, sometimes octagonal. The square base bust would carry the name of its subject impressed on to the lower step, or impressed into the back of the shoulder. Early busts had a round (or socle) plinth and tended to be of classical subjects.

The Beautiful Duchess was perhaps the most attractive bust produced by Goss but few examples now exist of Georgiana, the Duchess of Devonshire. She was a great beauty of her day, with Sir Joshua Reynolds painting her

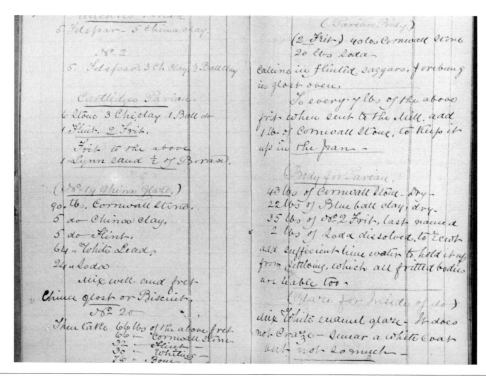

The Goss recipe for parian and glaze

William Henry Goss used this photograph of himself as a New Year's card to friends in 1885

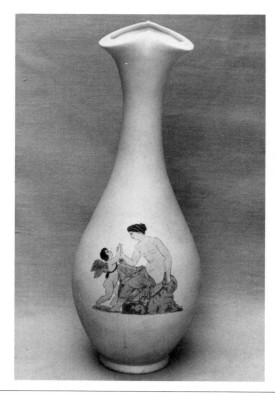

Early unglazed parian vase with classical decoration in colour

three times; as a child, as a young woman and finally as a beauty. William probably made his bust after the second picture which is 'curious in point of dress.'[1] The fair Duchess at that time originated the fashion of wearing high plumes as a headdress, a feature of the bust.

During the thirty years after the 1862 Great Exhibition the portrait busts were William's best line. They were still of an extremely high quality, being made individually from moulds from one original of each bust modelled by William Gallimore, William Goss himself and later Joseph Astley. Llewellynn Jewitt personally prepared the original bust of Samuel Carter Hall which was completed by Gallimore. Many of the busts have 'Published as the Act directs. . .' impressed on the back of the shoulder and the date. A few female busts were made, including several of Queen Victoria as early as 1876, with and without mob cap and crown, as well as a Diamond Jubilee commemorative example in 1896-7. William's dearest daughter Georgiana was immortalised in this way after her untimely death. The Keystones of the Kingdom were made in 1876 in both parian and terracotta of Lord Derby and Lord Beaconsfield (Disraeli). These were intended to be hung on a wall with their large gloomy heads looking down their noses at any observers! The mounting represented the keystone of an arch and William had a pair either side of his fireplace in his sitting room at his holiday home in Barthomley, Cheshire. In the centre of the mantlepiece stood the massive Alhambra Vase, a unique gigantic Moorish creation, with winged handles and intricately detailed body decorated in turquoise blue and reddish browns. The pattern was his own interpretation of the decorations in the Alhambra Palace in Granada, Spain. He also kept busts of Jewitt and Hall in his own collection.

When a Goss bust is compared with a photograph of the subject, the likeness is startling. They were all exceptionally well modelled, and the eyes look life-like, with pupils, unlike many other makes of bust which have the appearance of being blind. Reviews by Jewitt in *The Reliquary* were most complimentary. About 'Mr. Goss's Bust of Mr. Gladstone', we are told:

> 'It conveys to the eye a far more truthful speaking and eminently pleasing likeness of the great stateman, than has ever yet been produced either by painting, engraving or sculpture. It is a splendid and faultless work of art, and one that will well sustain Mr. Goss's reputation as the leading "portrait bust" producer of the age.'

Of Goss's bust of the poet, the late Charles Swain, *The Reliquary* revealed that the boss himself modelled it from life and who threw 'his whole heart and soul into the work' and produced 'not only a pleasing but a truthful and intellectual likeness — a likeness in which the genius and the brilliance of the poet combine with the genial and kindly disposition of the man.'[2]

*Two Goss classical figures*

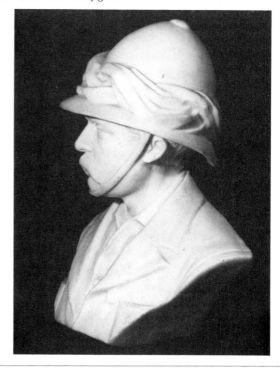

*Goss bust of H.M. Stanley, shown here without its socle plinth*

*Terracotta Keystone of the Kingdom, Lord Beaconsfield*

*The Alhambra Vase, a Moorish design after the Alhambra Palace, Granada, Spain. This fabulous creation was probably modelled by William whilst studying at Somerset House*

The Rev. Charles Swain was a well respected friend of William's, and his personal photograph album contains several of Swain's photographs.

Possibly the most important of William's inventions was jewelled ware. This was rarely made with real jewels, but with cut glass stones, the colours of which were intensified by the use of enamelling behind each stone, although he had, on rare occasions, used real jewels and real pearls. No jewelled ware was made after 1885 and only a few pieces of jewelled ware are currently known to exist. William's family thought as highly of his jewelled ware, which could not even be perfected by the famous French Sèvres factory, as he did himself. Adeline believed that:

'The jewelled vases are by far the most choice, indeed some are quite superb, being heavily encrusted with jewels and gold, and beautifully pierced. Others embellished with groups of exquisitely modelled flowers between rows of rubies and emeralds. There are scent bottles so delicate they are like lace, the entire surface cut in a trellised design, mounted in gold and jewelled, real pearls being used in some of them. In china, the choicest specimen of his ware is a cup and saucer of egg-shell, elaborately pierced and windowed (if that is the correct term!) but that is the effect for the glaze

is so ordered that it makes a window of every hole, appearing like an inset of opal glass.'

In 1862 William won the much desired award of a medal at the Great International Exhibition for his display of parian and figurines. Many laudatory articles and engravings of his exhibits appeared in journals such as the *Illustrated London News* and *Cassell's Illustrated Family Paper*. Cassells wrote on 15 November, 1862:

'On this page we introduce a group of statuettes etc, in parian and other ceramic materials, from the exhibit of Mr. W. H. Goss of Stoke. It is necessary to glance at our engraving to perceive with what exquisite taste this manufacturer has worked out the several designs he had produced in fictile wares. Here classic forms blend harmoniously with the more ordinary forms in use in our domestic life. But to comprehend fully the charm which belongs to these and like objects, they must be examined in the material in which they are composed. Wood-graving, after all, presents but a very faint and imperfect picture of articles like these, in which not only form and outline are to be admired, but which colour goes to produce the beautiful effect observable in all the efforts of the potter's art. Few displays of porcelain are to be seen in the Exhibition which excel those made by Mr. Goss. The great difficulty in producing statuettes in parian arises from the fact that the fictile material is apt to shrink unequally in baking. Thus it may happen that one portion of a vase, or figure, is perfect, while another is defective, which fact would render the whole object unfit for sale. But in the parian statuettes etc, under notice, the perfection of art manufacture seems certainly to have been reached.'

It was this particular award which first made his name well known and which founded the fortunes of his firm.

'Ivory porcelain' was the term used to describe William's invention of glazing his particular recipe of parian. He experimented with it until he could produce porcelain shapes, paper thin, but very strong. One can easily spot the difference between his earlier attempts and later, improved ones. Some of his earlier trial models were on taper vases with everted and inverted rims, bearing the coats of arms of schools and colleges. They are thick, pitted with firing dust, and yellower than the later ivory ware, and the gilding of a much poorer quality than normally associated with the factory.

*An important jewelled vase with over 600 inset stones*

*Leading collector and authority John Galpin with his enormous bust of Charles Dickens, the Beautiful Duchess and part of his superb collection*

Over the years some of these early efforts have become antique, i.e. over 100 years old and in the authors' opinion highly desirable. The gilding on the early heraldic ware usually wore off easily, often without trace, giving the impression that the plain rims have always been plain, although it is possible some were plain when they left the factory. Although earlier, cruder attempts at heraldic ware are scarce, it is the later, more common armorial ware, fine, perfect and regular that is currently in demand from collectors. After 1880, William's techniques had improved so much that the firm could produce ware of an even quality.

A similar plate with arms of Winchester College, owned by the same family

Winchester bread plate depicting the arms of St. Cross Hospital which was once owned by Godfrey Goss, still in the possession of the Goss family in America

The firm demonstrated its superior skills in the production of eggshell ware, which was manufactured in small quantities under the guidance of master craftsman Thomas Boden. Llewellynn Jewitt waxed lyrical over his friend's best egg-shell, hailing it as yet another achievement in the plastic art in which W. H. Goss stood pre-eminent:

'The pieces produced in this almost ethereal and very difficult ware are so light as to be almost devoid of gravity, and yet the body is of such extreme hardness and firmness as to be strong as thicker and more massive wares of a finer and purer body than the Sèvres, thinner and far more translucent than the Belleek, more delicate in tone than the Worcester, and more dainty to the touch than any other, the 'egg-shell' produced by Mr. Goss is an achievement in ceramics of which he may be justly proud. Lighter and more delicate than even the shell itself, and of perfect form down to the minutest detail, nature has in this instance been outdone by imitative art. The specimens of Mr. Goss's egg-shell porcelain are worthy of places in the choicest cabinets.'[3]

According to Willis-Fear who interviewed the late Noel Goss, a cup was once made in the normal eggshell ware, but on removal from its mould, it was accidentally splashed with acid, which destroyed some of the outer layers of the cup, leaving an outline 1mm thick. This piece was fired in the normal way in an effort to preserve for posterity the thinnest piece of eggshell ware ever produced, but it crumbled later into dust from its own unsupported weight on removal from the biscuit oven. William's experiments led to some exquisite eggshell miniatures, with a variety of sizes of jugs and matching bowls and tea sets less than half an inch high with tiny butterfly handles on the cups. Yet they are so very strong, indeed it is unusual to find a broken miniature. More desirable still are the jugs produced in the shape of leaves with the veins picked out in gold, and the smaller size pink-tinted Nautilus Shell which is so transparent one can see right through the porcelain sides! With some eggshell it is possible to read a newspaper through the porcelain.

During the 1870's William experimented with pieces of china decorated with jet and cane, as well as jasper ware, and some shades of lustre. These earlier shapes and the figurines, busts and groups were marked 'W.H. GOSS' by impressing the wet clay before it was baked. The Patent Office's Register for 26 April, 1909, for item 312559, records that this mark and the printed Goshawk had been used continuously for thirteen years before 13 August, 1875, the date on which trade marks had to be registered in order to be valid. Because of the nature of the body, it could not be economically produced with any form of mass production, and the casting or coulage process had to be used, whereby the wet clay or 'slip' was poured into moulds, a costly business.

In 1863 the foreman William Bromley, chief artist

W.W. Gallimore and some ten other workers strategic in the manufacture of the Goss eggshell porcelain, were induced to leave W.H. Goss and go to Ireland to the Belleek factory, taking their knowledge of Goss's methods with them. The Belleek factory, run by Messrs. David McBirney and Robert Armstrong, had been unsuccessful in its earlier attempts in the manufacture of china. It was situated in the village of Belleek, from which its production took its name, in County Fermanagh. It was Robert William Armstrong who persuaded William Bromley of the Goss factory to organise the group's sudden defection to Belleek to produce high quality eggshell there. The Belleek ware which has been produced ever since has become traditionally associated with the translucent ivory coloured paper thin material. Barber in his history of *The Pottery and Porcelain of the U.S.* admits that the Belleek factory obtained their earlier secrets from the employees of W.H. Goss, and that this type of china 'has since become world famous, being characterised by extreme lightness of body, and a beautiful lustrous glaze.' A difference with Belleek and Goss is that the Irish felspar used for Belleek was much purer than that used in Goss manufacture.

The white Fermanagh felspar was used for centuries to whitewash the local cottages, and lay near the surface of the soil. When used in the manufacturing of porcelain, the resulting effect was of a more yellow parian, strangely enough. The china clay used by the Belleek factory was conveniently situated under the local fields, with a water wheel on the River Erne as a source of power. It is notable that William Henry accepted his runaway staff back a few years later in 1866 with the exception of William Bromley who stayed until 1883 when he went to America to assist Mr. J. Hart in his development of Belleek type ware. After having given all the manufacturing secrets away to their Irish rival, the guilty parties, including Gallimore, all went back with their 'tails between their legs' to William. It is to his credit that he bore them no malice and was still fond of Gallimore who continued as his chief modeller for many years. Adeline Goss often accompanied her father when visiting Gallimore in his own home where he carried on working all hours during the 1870's. She was fascinated to see him at work and recorded in her notes:

'I was charmed to see things of beauty grow under his magic touch. He never appeared to take any care, but a lovely form, or perfect portrait would appear to grow out of a series of hurried and apparently careless dabs with various tools at the wet clay.'

Whilst he was in Ireland, Gallimore lost his right arm in a shooting accident. As he was right handed it was feared that without his right arm he would never model again, but he surprised all who knew him by returning to potting with his left hand, and working so hard that he became just as good, if not better, than before. Huntley, William's youngest son, confirmed this. It was as though

*A selection of eggshell miniatures*

*Gigantic bust of the Prince of Wales, later Edward VII, wearing the Masonic Collar of Grand Master of the Grand Lodge of England, 520mm*

the artistic skill he had before was magically transferred to his other arm. An example of William Henry Goss's humour was the joke he used to relate for long afterwards explaining the tale of Gallimore's arm:

'Poor Gallimore was out shooting when it occurred, and his arm was so fearfully shattered by the bursting of a gun, so much so that it literally 'hung by a thread'. He was a man of great pluck and iron nerve, and he did not lose heart, but simply relieved his feelings by emphatic words. First one doctor came, and then another to look at the wreckage, but nobody seemed anxious to finish the severance, till at last Gallimore, losing all patience, cried out: 'If one of you don't get to work and cut it off sharp, I'll get a knife and fork and cut if off myself!' '

It was W.W. Gallimore who sculpted the bust of Llewellynn Jewitt which was commissioned in 1875. One of the three busts made was inscribed:

'This bust of Llewellynn Jewitt F.S.A. is made expressly for presentation to his son Mr Edwin Augustus George Jewitt on the occasion of his 21st birthday the 13th October, 1879, as a mark of the highest esteem for both by their devoted friend Will. Henry Goss.'

Gallimore also modelled the gigantic bust of H.R.H. The Prince of Wales wearing the Masonic Collar of Grand Master of the Grand Lodge of England. There is no Goss factory mark but impressed on the back are details of Bro.J.S. Crapper and Bro.C.Marsh, both friends of William, and dated 1875.

After Gallimore retired in 1881 and emigrated to America, Joseph Astley became Goss's chief modeller and designer, carrying on where Gallimore left off with the creation of parian busts, with his boss often putting the finishing touches to his work. William valued his work highly and respected his talent. The two men worked well together for twenty-one years, with Astley religiously carrying out William's every instruction. It was as though William had two pairs of hands. It was Astley who modelled the bust of Georgiana Jewitt, William's daughter, who met a tragic early death, and that of the Princess of Wales, as well as the range of oval wall plaques, with busts in bas-relief and also the only known lithophane.

When Astley died in 1902 William's interest in the pottery seemed to die with him.

### References

1. *Homely scenes from great painters* by Godfrey Wordsworth Turner; Cassell, Petter and Galpin.
2. *'The Reliquary'*, Vol. XX. Edited by Llewellynn Jewitt
3. *The Ceramic Art of Great Britain* by Llewellynn Jewitt 1878.

# CHAPTER SIXTEEN

# The Second Period

The heights by great men reached and kept
Were not attained by sudden flight;
But they, while their companions slept,
Were toiling in the night.

**Longfellow**

After his uncle, Abner Mitchener Goss, the firm's foreman, left in 1880, Adolphus joined his father in the management of the growing pottery. They shared a keen interest in history, archaeology and heraldry, the vital ingredients of the products they were to produce together, and a joint achievement was the Gold Medal they won at the 1883 Boston Exhibition in America. When in management, Adolphus began assessing the factory and was critical of its products. A clever young man in his mid-twenties, he was full of ideas, but found it very difficult to work with his father. He was a natural businessman who put profit before aesthetic appreciation, and could see that the firm was making a few expensive and costly high quality items and would see a better return with a larger number of cheaper, less costly goods. With the institution of the Bank Holiday in 1871, he was looking to the future, with the ever increasing number of day-trippers journeying by train and by boat to all parts of the British Isles, he thought that a souvenir of the holiday or journey would be a saleable commodity.

He persuaded his father to let him decorate cheaper, smaller ornaments in a way which would be easier to produce in larger quantities. William finally agreed and Adolphus's first designs to be applied to his ivory porcelain vases were seaweeds, moths and seagulls. The choice of these decorations reflected his love of nature and the Victorian hobby of collecting seaweeds and making them into pictures.

About this time he explored the possibilities of copying original ancient artefacts and decorating these in the same manner. He produced a few specimen shapes such as the large Gloucester Jug, Seaford Urn and Elizabethan Jug and some of his early designs appear on those models.

Although the invention is widely attributed to William it appears to have been Adolphus who suggested the brilliant idea of using miniature historic porcelain models to be decorated with local coats of arms of the towns or villages nearest to their origins.

His obituary in the *Pottery Gazette* was later to state he was 'the founder of the noted Goss Heraldic Porcelain', but other sources give the credit for the invention to his father. Adeline Goss emphatically stated that credit was due to William. 'It is so well known that my father was the originator and inventor of heraldic pottery that it

*Adolphus in 1882, the young businessman at the Goss works who styled himself 'Goss Boss'*

PLEASE RETURN THIS CARD with photos

Prices quoted are for ordinary arms, those with supporters &c. are extra

NOT LESS than ½ dozens under 12/- do

In ordering please quote distinguishing letters of photograph, size, & price, thus

(A77) 2 dg 3 inch Bass arms of —— 6/-
  1 " Ball box        Do    7/-
  1 " Fairy Way vase   Do    6/-

Please do not make any mark on photos.

It is earnestly requested that you will return photos & card at ONCE as they are urgently required elsewhere. If detained they will be charged for

Photos. must not on any account be lent to others.

*Handwritten card by Adolphus sent to agents to assist ordering together with a set of photographs of models*

needs no repetition here.' She wrote in her biography of her father:

> 'He produced heraldic ware in his early days, but these examples were restricted to the universities and some of the more noted public schools, for in those days the public knew very little about heraldry, and understood probably less. It occurred to him that so interesting a subject should be better known, and only required introducing to the public to obtain a thorough appreciation. He was right in this conjecture as events proved. With the help of my eldest brother Adolphus, whose artistic talent enabled him to make sketches of all the antique pottery to be found in various parts of the Kingdom from the originals, he conceived the idea of producing the arms of every town, etc., in Great Britain, and publishing the same on some antique model from an original in that town, the sale of which was to be reserved for that particular town through one agent only. The idea became popular, and heraldry is now well-known and appreciated.'

Llewellynn Jewitt also supports William in his report in *The Reliquary*:

> 'We have on several previous occasions taken opportunity and that always with extreme pleasure, of calling attention to the Art-productions in ceramics of Mr. W.H. Goss, of Stoke-upon-Trent, and we again venture to put on record a word or two as to a new

*Illustrated ordering card sent to agents*

*Early models without the coloured enamelling inside the outlines of the coats of arms*

*Three early domestic shapes, the first two with butterfly decorations*

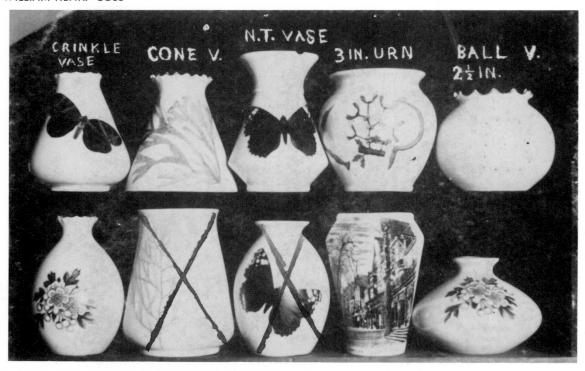

*Domestic ware — note the emergent wide range of decorations*

*Six larger models for agents to choose from*

departure in decoration, for which the world is indebted to him. This consists of the introduction of the arms of cities and towns, universities and colleges, founders and families, carefully emblazoned in their proper heraldic colours on a number of exquisitely beautiful articles, for use or for ornament, which he produces in endless and choice variety, in his delicately-beautiful ivory-body porcelain. The effect of the rich heraldic colours on the soft, creamy tint of the body itself is charming in the extreme, and when, as in some instances, they are accompanied by or heightened with gold, they become treasures of art that it is highly desirable to obtain. Of the body itself, of which these various choice and delicate elegancies are formed, it is needless to add to what we have already written — that it is simply perfection in purity of colour, in hardness, in fineness of grain, in transparency, and in every other respect and the enamelling and other decorations which Mr. Goss, with the utmost good taste, introduces upon it is always rich, pure, and harmonious in effect. We feel that we are doing good service to our readers in thus briefly directing their attention to the heraldic jardinieres and endless other useful articles, upon which armorial bearings are made the prominent feature, which are now so well and so extensively made by their introducer, Mr. Goss.'[1]

Having studied many facts and opinions on the subject, we have come to the conclusion that whilst William invented it, heraldic ware would never have been marketed with the success with which it was, if it had not been for Adolphus. One needed the other!

As a true artist, William was not pleased to have cheaper, mass produced ornaments, however well made, connected with his good name and reputation, for it suited him to be associated with the upper end of the market rather than the lower. Also, it meant an end to his factory producing each piece individually. From now on, moulds would be made to accommodate several pieces at a time.

The first registered design was granted in 1884, No. 25547 for a hair tidy with floral decoration on the lid. Other designs which appeared in 1885-6 included Robin Hood's Last Shot, Classical Armour, the Scottish Regalia and the Man of War of Henry VIII's reign.

Trade was very poor in the potting industry in the early 1880's, and by 1883 nearby firms such as Dimmocks of Hanley, James Berington and Furnivals had gone bankrupt. Adolphus wrote to his brother Godfrey in America, 'We are still so busy that I cannot go out after orders as we could not execute any more'. A year later he wrote to him again that 'trade is pretty bad all over England but we make some lovely things now and·they take well.'

One of the books William gave Adolphus to assist with the heraldry was *Heraldrie* by John Guillim, dated 1660. A letter written in 1934 by Vernon Goss, eldest son of Adolphus, kept in the flyleaf, states that this book was given to A.W.H. Goss in 1885 by his father W.H. Goss.

*The original Glastonbury Roman ewer*

*The Goss model Roman Ewer found at Glastonbury, Somerset*

*Prototypes of the Kendal Jug and Southwold Jar, complete with Adolphus's doodlings*

By 1885, William said himself 'Business is very good, and although it is so early in the year I am as busy as in the season.' He admitted he had more orders for his heraldic wares than he could possibly send off.

At Christmas, 1886, he wrote to Godfrey:

> 'You will be glad to hear that I am still very busy. You would be rather surprised if you were to come among us now and see what we are doing. I am making some very beautiful porcelain for the Jubilee Commemoration. The Earl and Countess of Iddesleigh are delighted with it. They call my porcelain 'magnificent', 'lovely' and 'beautiful' and everybody seems to admire it. It is immensely better in every way than it used to be.'

It is likely that the Queen Victoria Golden Jubilee designs in 1887, and used again for 1888, 1889 and 1890 were a trial to test the market for royal souvenirs. They were very successful, and were later used again for the Queen's Diamond Jubilee in 1896-7. The Garter Star design, a very intricate and colourful device, was originally issued for the Queen's Golden Jubilee in 1887, but was withdrawn after official protests over its illegal use, and a design called 'Liberty, Loyalty, Legality' issued instead. Such beautifully made royal souvenirs could hardly be attractive solely to the lower end of the market, (i.e. for the middle classes, the working classes having a problem earning enough money to buy food, let alone ornaments). Indeed, Queen Victoria owned examples of all Goss designs connected with her or her family. It is thought that she was given them by the Goss factory. Later commemoratives were for the Silver Wedding of the Prince and Princess of Wales 1888, and the 1893 may blossom design for the wedding of the Duke and Duchess of York,

*The Garter Star design copied on Goss porcelain to commemorate the Queen's Jubilee in 1887. The factory was ordered to withdraw it by the Palace*

1.                    2.

3.                    4.

1. *Large York Roman ewer bearing the arms of the Silver Wedding of the Prince and Princess of Wales 1888*

2. *Jar with Edward the Peacemaker's death commemorative*

3. *The Garter Star design was replaced with 'Liberty, Loyalty, Legality'*

4. *Folkestone Roman ewer depicting George and Mary 1911*

considered very appropriate because Princess Mary was also known as Princess May of Teck. The tremendous response from the public and the orders placed set the factory firmly on the trend of concentrating almost solely on heraldic and decorated ware, and only four busts were produced after 1906. One commemorative which had personal connections with Adolphus was the Primrose League produced in 1884. The League was founded in memory of Lord Beaconsfield who died 19 April 1881, and Adolphus's wife, Nellie, and himself organised the Primrose Buds in Alsager and their daughter Ethel became Dame Warden in later life. Adolphus's design on Goss china consists of the letters P L in monogram form surrounded by primroses and surmounted by the Imperial crown. The inscription 'Peace with Honour' appears below, said to have been spoken by Benjamin Disraeli, later Lord Beaconsfield, on his return from the Berlin Congress in 1878. Primroses were his favourite flower.

It was on long travels at home and abroad that Adolphus collected orders from established agencies, organised new stockists in fresh areas, at the same time drawing relevant coats of arms for his firm to reproduce, and both sketching and photographing scenes to be made into transfers and artefacts for new shapes. He never failed in his task of appointing only one agent per town, and instructed that his agents could only sell Goss, not the other makes of heraldic ware. In this way each agent would not have a rival to undercut him in the same area, because only he would have the coat of arms of his own town. The Goss family felt that by making collectors buy the crests from the correct towns, Goss china models would be genuine souvenirs.

*Slide of Moreton Old Hall, Cheshire, taken by Adolphus in 1891*

*Adolphus's sketch of 'Old Moreton Hall' as it was then known, to use as a transfer on Goss china*

Much research and hard work went into the preparation and organisation of the heraldic devices. Adolphus and his father were already both experts on heraldry, and insisted on every detail in their coats of arms being correct. There was much skill and craftsmanship in the drawing of the applied transfers which were placed on the ware, first fired, then painted in by hand with the correct coloured enamels, then fired again. Meticulous care was taken with the exact wording of mottoes and Latin inscriptions, and with applying the devices squarely and centrally on each piece. The coats of arms were produced in various sizes, smaller ones being used on smaller models. The public did not understand heraldry and William felt

*Hand tinted paper transfer prints with Adolphus's instructions for the colouring*

that by producing the heraldic ware he would be educating all who came into contact with it, and that they would gain an appreciation of it.

Originally Adolphus intended only reproducing models with their historic inscriptions printed on their bases and the correct arms; for example, a Reading Jug would carry the Arms of Reading, or University College of Reading, which could be obtained from the official appointed agent in Reading. If a model was required by a collector, with a different coat of arms, it could only be obtained from Messrs. Ritchie Ltd., the main central agents in Stoke-on-Trent, and only then by special order. Soon after the venture was commenced, the agents found it too limiting to stock only a few shapes, and after 1883 were allowed to order any shape they wished, in any quantity, as long as the coats of arms were the correct ones for the area for each agent, with the exception of decorated pieces. It was in William's nature to endeavour to make a seasoned traveller out of a novice collector by causing him to travel to Land's End for a Land's End crest, and to Edinburgh for an Edinburgh crest.

Indeed there was no alternative until after the turn of the century when groups of collectors were formed who swapped and sold pieces second-hand.

It was Adolphus who, as he toured each part of the country, visited museums and places of interest, and selected a few objects in each area for reproduction in the form of porcelain models by his factory, in miniature. He sketched, photographed and measured ancient pottery,

buildings, fonts and the like, with Victor assisting after 1885. Eventually most areas of Great Britain were represented in some form.

There was a persistent tradition that about 1887, Adolphus Goss, with parental approval, circulated a letter to the Town Clerks of all the towns, cities and boroughs in the United Kingdom, asking for permission to reproduce their respective town and city coats of arms on his ware. This letter aroused such enthusiastic support that a conference of all interested parties was called at the Stoke factory to discuss the means by which this idea could be implemented. Unfortunately, the exact date of this meeting is unknown, if indeed it ever materialised. The intention was to exhibit specimens of their heraldic ware in the form of menu-holders with gilt edgings, at the opening banquet.

In that year Adolphus told a friend, 'I am still very busy at the Works, but am ready to do more, so Victor is now my second traveller and is doing well.' He considered he was earning a good rate of commission and believed Victor would too. Adolphus earned about £250 a year in the early 1880's. He covered England, Wales and the Isle of Man and Victor Ireland, Scotland, Cornwall and the Channel Islands.

The same year William himself noted that he was 'Very busy at the Works and I have had to put down more enamellers, and the ware I am making is more and more beautiful. It is as famous now throughout the country as the production of Mintons and Copelands.' The following

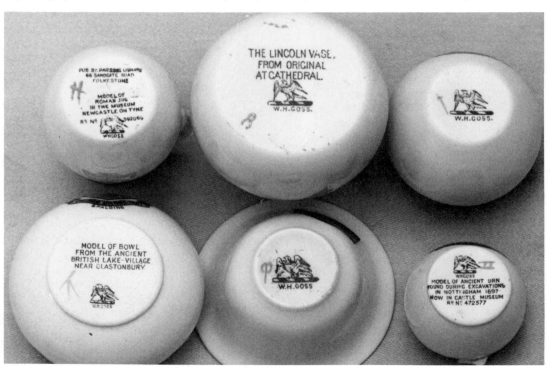

*The bases of six small Goss models showing the Goshawk, description (if on the base) and paintresses mark*

*Adolphus's sketch of Burnham*

year, 1888, was their best ever year for business.

Huntley joined the management in the mid 1880's and by the age of 21 years was in charge of the books. He had spent his previous years since leaving school learning how to prepare and mix enamels as well as various other aspects of the trade. Adolphus was proud to tell his friends how good a traveller Victor was and that 'Huntley sticks to the works and gets on very well.'

In the 1880's and 1890's Adolphus and Victor were away on their travels for weeks on end, and rarely at home. It was not always plain sailing when arranging a new agency. When they could not obtain a local authority's permission to use its coat of arms on Goss china, or if a town did not possess arms, it became necessary to design some. These home-made arms were designed as seal patterns within a consistent circular design, using some local symbol for the centre; that for Newquay, for instance incorporated a fish to represent a fishing port. Each seal was registered to prevent the numerous other local factories from copying them as they had attempted to copy most of the Goss innovations. The registration number was 77966 and this was printed on the base of each item bearing one of these specially designed circular seals. Patents began in 1883, and ran for four years but could be renewed with a maximum life of 15 years.

As travelling sales director, Adolphus began to lose touch with much of the day-to-day running of the factory. During his years away on the road, the continuing success of heraldic ware consolidated and it became hard to satisfy demand. Agents kept a standard stock of Goss and would accept orders for customers' special requirements; such pieces would have the Agent's name and address stamped on the base. As trade rapidly increased, delays for ordered items became the norm and production levels rose as did the number of staff employed.

Victor and Adolphus were so thorough in their field work that they ceased to have anything more to do with the daily running of the firm. By 1900 they had secured 481 agencies inland. Adolphus considered he was the mainstay of the business and called himself 'Goss Boss', a name which irritated his father intensely. Victor was also too good as a manager and William felt his power threatened, as he did not wish to relinquish a single business decision. He preferred to be completely in charge on his own, so he made sure that his two clever sons were out on the road as much as possible. In late 1889, Victor wrote to his brother Godfrey:

'I came back from Ireland a few days ago and shall not go another journey until after Christmas, so I shall have a good spell at home. I wanted to go to Stoke and give Huntley a hand at the books, but the old man would not let me, although the Day book is about four months behind hand and needs much posting up. I suppose he thinks that if I once get in again he won't be able to push me out!'

*The young Victor as a traveller for the Goss firm. He was to prove excellent in this position*

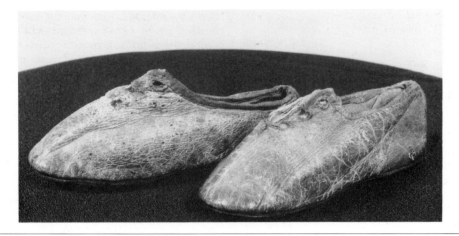

*The original Queen Victoria's first slippers*

*A page of Masonic decorations from a Goss pattern book*

Among the first models was Queen Victoria's First Shoe. A folded advertising leaflet based upon a newspaper review which explained the original story, was sold inside each shoe. The inscriptions underneath earlier models of the shoe refer to 'Queen Victoria', but later versions after 1901 refer to her as 'the late Queen'. William was rather pleased with this particular shape and kept a supply without coats of arms to use as gifts for friends. The story behind the shoe is fascinating; the Queen's father, the Duke of Kent,

went to live in Sidmouth in 1819 to get the benefit of the Devonshire climate. Whilst there, a local shoemaker, John Taylor, received an order for a first pair of shoes for the infant Princess Victoria. He made an identical pair of shoes on the same last for his own daughter. This pair was kept by the child and later, as Mrs E. Selleck, she owned a china business, and became the Goss agent for Sidmouth in Fore Street. She loaned one shoe to William Goss and he copied it in china. The actual shoes were four inches long, daintily made with white satin upper, brown leather sole, laced and tied in front with a light blue silk ribbon and bound around the edge with the same ribbon down to the back of the heel. In 1820 the shoemaker received the Royal Warrant which was preserved alongside the little shoes. It read as follows:

> 'His Royal Highness the Duke of Kent has been pleased to appoint Mr. Taylor to be bootmaker to his Royal Highness at Sidmouth. Given at Sidmouth this fourth day of January 1820. Signed O.M. Conroy.'

A second warrant was also received from the Duchess of Kent. Their Highnesses regularly stayed in Sidmouth at a house called Woolbrook Cottage, now the Royal Glen Hotel.

The china shoe, owned by the shoemaker's great, great, great, grandaughter, is inscribed:

> 'Model exact size of first shoes worn by Princess Victoria, the late Queen, who died 1901. Made in Sidmouth 10th January 1819. Signed W.H. Goss.'

The Goss porcelain copy was faithfully coloured like the original, complete with little stitch marks and creases such as a soft shoe would have. The crest was placed on the toe, Sidmouth being the matching arms where the cobbler lived.

The public adored these china shoes, despite some bad press reviews. The Queen herself was given a pair by Mrs. Anderson, sister of General Gordon and a good friend of William himself.

We found a reference to this gift in a letter written by William on 2 January 1893 to Mr. Lymington of Langside, Glasgow, author of *Porcelain art manufacturer*:

'That you may understand Miss Gordon's reference to the Queen (in an enclosed letter), I have taken the liberty of sending you a pair of the latter by parcel post, which kindly accept. The Queen will be all the more interested in the shoes on account of their coming from Miss Gordon as they are on very affectionate terms. Sir John Cowell is an old friend of the Gordon family. Mrs Anderson wrote to me that he had saved her husband's life in one of the Crimean battles. My review letters are sometimes sent to him by Mrs Anderson, and thus, like the spiders, are sometimes found in the Queen's palaces. There will be lots of fun at Osborne over these shoes. I wonder if anybody will be calling the Queen a Royal Cinderella. Lady Cowell will be carrying them with her to each of the palaces, as she and her husband always accompany the Queen, so the fun will extend.'

The Queen was said to be thrilled with the shoes and obtained further models directly from the factory to use as gifts for the younger members of her own family. Six years after the Queen's death in 1901, the King of Spain visited Windsor Castle and a London newspaper reported that when the King was viewing some of the late Queen's possessions he was attracted to the same pair of china shoes which came from Mrs. Anderson.

In the 1890's members of the Royal family took an interest in the craze for collecting Goss china and were known to have made several purchases. Queen Victoria possessed a Goss bust of herself and an assortment of shapes bearing her own royal arms which, it is believed, William Henry Goss had given to her. The only remaining evidence of Queen Victoria's crested china collecting is a Shelley late Foley tea service with the Royal arms, on display amongst her other collections of fossils, shells, stuffed birds and animals at the Swiss Cottage museum in the grounds of Osborne House, East Cowes, Isle of Wight.

Another royal collector was Alexandra, Princess of Wales. *The Pottery Gazette* reported in 1894 that 'in 'Princess' magazine, there was an article about the Princess of Wales and her huge collection of tiny china animals, as can be bought at any bazaar or toyshop.' This collection was carried about with her baggage and needed packing on every journey and entailed no end of trouble for her attendants as she would never allow her rooms to be dismantled until the last minute. 'The packing of these fragile pets has caused losing more than one train and a good deal of irritability on the part of the Princess's immediate circle.'[2] The Princess, whose collection included no Goss as they did not make animal novelties, used to decorate her rooms with them when paying overnight visits and on holidays so as to make the rooms more like home.

In 1893 Adolphus introduced a new range of coloured cottages. His first models were the famous Shakespeare's Birthplace and Ann Hathaway's Cottage at Stratford-on-Avon and Burns' Cottage, Ayr. This new line proved immediately popular, and the range was gradually extended to 42 buildings, with miniature and half-size versions and large night-light burners, the first six cottages produced being night-lights. Those surviving today can sometimes be found with candlewax still inside, or with heat cracks. Most cottages produced during the 1893-1929 period of manufacture were unglazed, but in the latter half of the firm's life some cottages were glazed and this intensified the colouring.

Other changes in the moulds occurred when the original buildings that the models were reproduced from were altered in any significant way. For example, at Charles Dickens house at Gad's Hill, Rochester, when the ivy was cut down from around the porch, the Goss artists discovered that there were two small windows, one each side of the front door, and so future moulds of this cottage included these windows. There were slight differences in colours used over the years, not surprisingly with a succession of paintresses decorating the cottages, but generally the colours and moulds used were consistent. The coloured houses were not crested, although the First & Last House in England can be found with a glass badge containing Cornish arms affixed to one side wall.

Until 1890 trade was brisk for the Goss family firm and in 1891 they obtained the highest honours, a gold medal and diploma at the Boston Exhibition, Massachusetts. But the firm did not persevere with the American trade, and William wrote to Godfrey in New Jersey that he was 'not exhibiting at Chicago. It is such a lot of trouble.' Neither could he afford the expense, 'We have not got the gas wells here, nor the petroleum.'

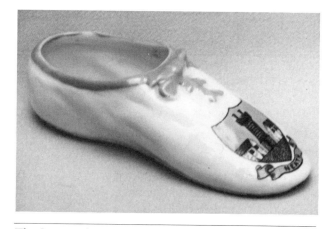

*The Goss Model of Queen Victoria's First Shoe complete with blue trim, arms of Neath*

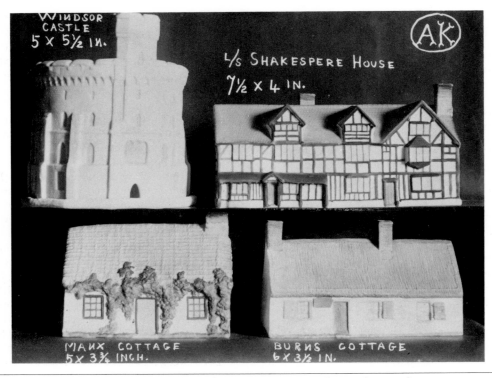

*The night-lights Adolphus introduced in 1893 shown here on an agents' ordering photograph*

By 1892, business had rapidly slowed down:

'Three successive wet seasons here have injured trade very much, and for the first time during the 34 years that I have been manufacturing, I have had to put the work people on short time. The bad trade is quite general, and I never knew so many failures among potters as has happened lately. Other people are much worse off than I am. If we could have now about 3 weeks of fine weather to let people get out and buy my porcelain I believe it would set us right. But it rains nearly every day and this is the third year of it, so customers don't get rid of their stocks so rapidly as usual.'*

The miners' strikes from mid-March onwards in 1892 involved over half a million colliers calling for higher wages. In 1893 they came out on strike and knocked the potting industry for six again. It was reported that Copelands and many other firms would have to close in consequence. Even Joseph Astley (Alice Goss's brother-in-law) left the firm briefly. Alice's mother, Mrs. Buckley, wrote and told her, 'Joe left Goss's to get a better place, they got very short of work there before he left and he had this place offered to him at Longton, so he took it.'

Various members of the family reported to Godfrey in America how bad business was. Florry mentioned that:

'Trade seems bad everywhere, the coal strike has done a great deal of damage to trade, put thousands out of work but we are glad to say men are going in again. All the big potters have had to stop.'

In August, 1893, his father told him how upsetting the riots were and how the coal strike had had terrible effects on business all over the kingdom, but added that he felt it could not last long. Huntley also reported that trade was bad all over England, 'For some months we scarcely got any orders.'

By 1897 Adolphus was writing to friends, 'Trade has been pretty good this last year but before that it was very bad so that I went back a good deal.' From then on business was booming, right up until the First World War.

Adolphus was a prolific letter writer and had the thoughtful habit of writing a letter each day to his wife whilst on his travels. Some of the letters still exist and we can see from these just how well or badly he fared in the various resorts. He measured his success on each trip by the amount of orders he took. In Eastbourne in 1887, he wrote, 'This journey has not as yet been a very prosperous one. I have sold £80 worth since I started.' He travelled by steamship, four-horse coaches, trains, on foot and even in rowing boats up the smaller rivers. He would carry a briefcase of traveller's samples, plain models with no coats of arms, and when walking would loop the handle of his umbrella in the handle of the case and carry the umbrella over his shoulder with the weight of his case

* Letter from William H. Goss to Godfrey Goss, 17/9/1892

behind him. His letter from Winchester in 1898 read:

'I went to Henley-on-Thames yesterday and got on to Basingstoke where my customer would not order so I opened with a new man this morning then I went to an out of the way old place called Andover and took a very nice order there and came back through Basingstoke here where I have just arrived. I am going to the Guildhall (Portsmouth) tonight. . .'

His was a busy life indeed!

Adolphus's missive to his wife in May 1887 read:

'Here I am in the middle of Dorset (Lyme Regis). . . I started from Seaton which is a very pretty place. . . then I went on to Colyton as I could get no further and getting caught in the rain took shelter in the village smithy. Then I called at a pub and ordered some chops and cyder and Devon cream and went to look at the church to see if I could find some arms. Then I got on to Axminster and took a £5 line which was the second that day (the first was at Seaton) and took the coach to the Royal town of Lyme-Regis. I found that the china dealer here knew all about my ware and was glad to have the chance of buying it so I took a good order for so quiet a place.'

From Tavistock, the same year, he reported:

'I am glad to say that this journey has been fairly successful, total up to this £287.9s.10d. I ought to have told you darling in my last that I cannot possibly get home this week but mean to next.'

Whilst touring with Victor in 1887 he went by steamer from Bowness to Ambleside, then by charabanc to Grasmere:

'where we had several hours to wait after business was finished so we took a boat on the lake and spreading our umbrellas to the breeze, we sailed across the lake and then re-crossed it, tacking cleverly, then we ran down to the bottom of the lake before the wind and rowed back. At 5 we started by the 'four hoss coach' to Keswick passing Thirlmere.'

Adolphus and Victor certainly enjoyed their work, but no doubt they failed to mention their sailing to their father! Judging by Adolphus's poor spelling in his letters, something which his father excelled at, we are not surprised at the occasional spelling mistakes which occur in mottoes under Goss arms, especially the long Welsh towns.

His earlier letters are marked by comments about the difficulties of starting up agencies and persuading the agents to stock up. Letters dated early 1880's show how hard Adolphus had to work, but in the later 1880's and 1890's he found it easy. From Aberystwyth in 1883 he remarked:

'I am thankful to say that I have done fairly well on this journey so far and that is more than I could ever say before, for I have usually done very little. You must excuse short letter as I have been writing for the last 3 hours and am tired. Please write on Monday to Shrewsbury.'

In February 1884 he wrote, 'Today I have not done very much. I have been in Whitby which never affords anything brilliant and often nothing at all.' Southern resorts were a representative's dream and, for example, in 1885, he landed a £75 order at Bath for Bath arms in just one visit.

There were often problems, which meant Adolphus had to change or adapt his route. In a letter addressed from 'on the sea' 4 June 1886, he confided to Nellie his wife:

'I thought that by this time I should be a good stage on the way to my own magnet but alas I am en route for South Wales. The Steamship Co's bill said that a boat left Ilfracombe for Bristol today at 5.30 but when I got with my luggage down to the harbour I found that they had considerably altered their arrangements and that she sailed not for Bristol but for Swansea. So as my South Wales journey is so much overdue, and as the week after next is Whitsuntide, and as Swansea is only 2¼ hours sail from Ilfracombe I very reluctantly made up my mind to go over and work South Wales next week. By doing so I shall save in time 2 days and in railway fare about 30/- or 40/- besides giving me a better chance of keeping out the German competition.'

When he went to Germany he had little success in securing agencies and orders, but spent much of his time on German soil designing a commemorative in memory of Emperor Frederick who died a few weeks before his visit in 1888. He had to make several copies of this commemorative. 'One first in ink to show one customer. Another then in colours to send to my father. A third with the flag on a larger scale to engrave from and a fourth to show other customers and a fifth (in the letter) to show to my beloved old Nellie.'

When Adolphus had difficulty organising an agency in a place where he wanted one, he had his own methods. From Plymouth, in June 1886, he wrote:

'Last year I could not sell aught here and the best shop would not see me at home so on Sunday finding that Mr. Dutton was going to Plymouth on Monday I asked him to put a spoke in my wheel. I said 'When you next see Jarvis (the shopkeeper), ask him if he sells my goods, and when he says no, express your unbounded astonishment and tell him how much it sells in other towns.' This worked nicely and when I called this morning, I took an order for £18 which I hope will lead to a lot.'

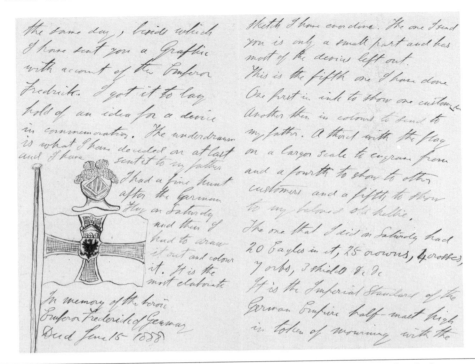

*Adolphus's letter to Nellie revealing his excitement at sketching the death of Emperor Frederick flag commemorative for his father, an idea he had shortly after the Emperor's death in 1888*

He finished that particular missive with:

'My father keeps saying he wants orders though I have sold £496 since I started.' To get an idea of just how hard he worked, in July 1887 he wrote to his wife from Watford, 'I have got so far on my journey and am waiting for the train to St. Albans. Write to PO Eastbourne where I hope to get by tomorrow night. Then to Lewes Seaford Brighton Worthing Littlehampton Chichester Bognor Portsmouth Ryde Sandown Shanklin Ventnor Newport Cowes and Southampton. Besides 2 or 3 new towns that I mean to take in such as Shoreham Horsham Petersfield etc.'

He even spent his honeymoon in 1882 touring England getting Goss orders — which was the only way Adolphus could get permission from his father to get some time off to get married!

During 1887 Adolphus was selling photograph frames according to his letter to his wife from Barnstaple in May of that year: 'I stick the photo of my little beauty into the photo holder when I am showing it and it makes it look so very pretty that I have sold twelve times as many as I used to before I had your likeness to set if off.' We have no knowledge of any porcelain photograph frames ever being produced by Goss and so have no idea what these could be.

The agent for Winchester, William Savage, was an old friend of William's. Adolphus, when visiting Shanklin in

1884, told his wife, 'I saw old Savage of Winchester yesterday and I got a very good line out of him.' No doubt when he wrote to his father he chose his words more carefully!

Sometimes he mentioned the shapes he sketched in museums which the factory was later to model. From Leamington in 1884 his letter to Nellie read:

'I could not write last night as I had such a big order for Oxford Arms to write out amounting to one hundred and nineteen pounds, besides finishing two sketches of old pots in the Ashmolean Museum at Oxford for which I have taken orders. Today I went to Banbury where the sight of Banbury cakes made me somehow think of you darling, I don't know why. I got a nice little order for Banbury arms near the celebrated Banbury Cross.' (Nellie was an extremely plump young lady!).

He did not want to spend too much time away from his growing family and expressed his aims in a note to Nellie dated 1886. 'What I like is to sell as much in a week as we can make in a month so that I can spend the other 3 weeks with you dearest.'

He was very honest when describing the places he visited. If he found a town beautiful he waxed lyrical about it. If he didn't, he could be quite blunt. We do not know his description of Hartlepool, but Nellie replied to him when he was touring up north in 1881 that she did not 'think the good people of Hartlepool would enjoy reading your description of their grimy port.'

During the 1890's there was also great demand for transfer printed pictorial views, with the more popular sepia, black and red colours being favoured. A few specimens were made with blue or green transfers, particularly for the Crystal Palace exhibition, but these were not made in any great numbers. Full colour views were also popular. These transfers increased the range of agents' stock and in all over a thousand different views were produced. Transfers were the forerunner of picture postcards. After the British Postal Authorities reforms of 1 November 1898, collecting postcards became the most important national hobby, and up until World War I sending postcards depicting views led to a decline in sales of Goss transfer pieces until their production ceased altogether.

With heraldic ware attracting attention from all over Britain, collecting Goss china became one of the nation's fastest growing hobbies. Goss was not the first firm to produce china bearing coats of arms, as it was normal practice for the nobility and gentry to have their table-ware decorated with their family crests, usually made by the more important firms of Spode, Minton and Wedgwood. The Gosses and the Jewitts had their family crests decorating their flat ware as well as dinner services.

Llewellynn Jewitt had brass buttons on all his coats with his arms in bas-relief. From 1881, heraldic china production really grew apace until the course of the firm had changed and most of its previous lines were discontinued.

The crest, which is the part of an heraldic device surmounting the shield was incorrectly used by heraldic china manufacturers to mean an entire coat of arms. Although a misnomer, the word crest now has this double meaning, at least in heraldic circles.

Victor left to fight in the Boer War in 1901 as an officer in the 5th North Staffordshire Regiment and the youngest son Huntley was left in charge alone. Adolphus had ceased to be employed by the firm after 1900 for reasons unknown although he still continued to earn a percentage on sales of models he himself designed. Their father had begun to live like a recluse and took two years off and stayed at home apparently because he could not bear to see Victor's empty chair. It does appear that Victor had ceased to travel and had become resident in the office, some time after 1900. Whilst his father took care of the finances and opened and answered the post from home, Huntley bore most of the managerial workload. He was no youngster at 34, but felt a tremendous obligation to assist his father. He was not a businessman, disliked commerce and had never intended to work in an office.

The far-sighted Adolphus organised the expansion of the Goss works and his father unwillingly agreed to pay for these works.

*Transfers sketched by Adolphus for reproduction by the factory*

*Lieut. Victor Goss in the uniform of the North Staffordshire Regiment, 1901*

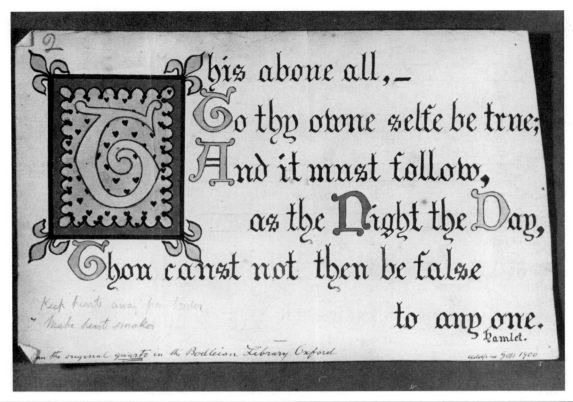

This aboue all,—
To thy owne selfe be true;
And it must follow,
as the Night the Day,
Thou canst not then be false
to any one.
Hamlet.

*Adolphus's original coloured illuminated verse on parchment, mainly used on tea pot stands*

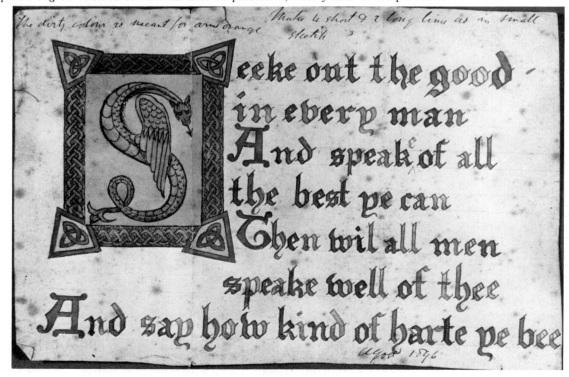

Seeke out the good
in every man
And speake of all
the best ye can
Then wil all men
speake well of thee
And say how kind of harte ye bee

*Hand painted verse by Adolphus drawn in 1896*

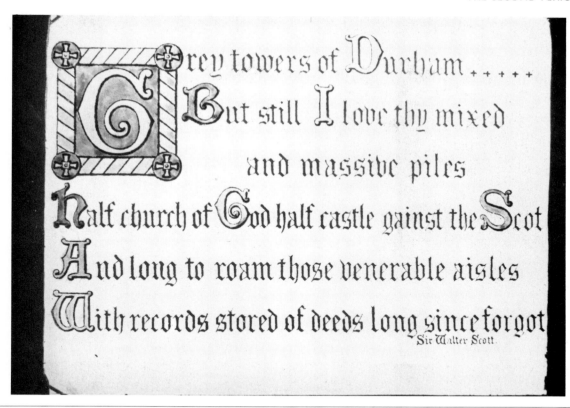

*Glass slide from Adolphus's film show. This verse appeared on tea pot stands*

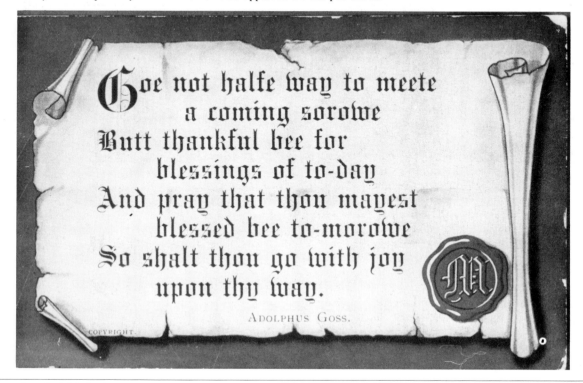

*Postcard with Adolphus's own verse*

Whatever his methods, Adolphus's hard work over two decades left its mark and the whole nation knew of Goss china. The pottery, often mentioned in newspapers, received an excellent review in *The Daily Mail* in Birmingham, Saturday, 16 September, 1905, when the firm was at the pinnacle of its success.

*An assortment of Goss League models*

\* \* \* \* \* \* \* \* \* \* \* \* \* \*

It became obvious to the many avid collectors all over Britain that some sort of cataloguing of agents names' and addresses was required to enable enthusiasts to plan their excursions. It could prove daunting to make a long, difficult trip to search for a Goss agency that did not exist as yet, or could not be found (no Yellow Pages in those days!). Also, the Goss agent for each area could be anyone — from the owner of the local fancy store, restaurant, hotel, bazaar or pharmacist, to a private house, station bookstall or local library.

J.J. Jarvis, an enterprising collector, approached William Henry Goss and put forward his idea of producing such a listing. William told him that he had been asked many times before, but he was a busy man, and thought it would be too time-consuming, the thought of constant revision also deterred him. Eventually, after some manoeuvring, Jarvis won William's confidence and he was granted the

vital permission required to publish the first *Goss Record* which appeared towards the end of 1900 price one shilling per copy. Mr. Jarvis, who lived at 'Riversdale', Enfield, Middlesex, did not have any financial interest in the Record's production, and the proceeds were donated entirely to a fund promoted by the Misses Evans of 58, Holly Road, Handsworth, Birmingham, for giving a Christmas tea and entertainment to some of the poor slum children in their area. Possibly this helped William change his mind and allow Jarvis to go ahead! William was always very much in favour of helping the poor and needy, but Huntley Goss also smoothed the way and helped persuade his father to accede to Jarvis's requests.

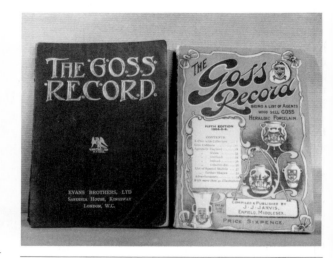

*The sixth and fifth editions of the* Goss Record

The first Record was a hand duplicated sheet, not even bound or stapled. It listed the authorised agent in each town, the address, the models, the coats of arms stocked and the agents' opening hours. Jarvis was limited in the number he could produce by duplication and those printed sold out immediately. He was by now receiving letters from all over the country requesting further copies and he became determined to edit an improved edition with the latest information on new models. By having it printed and stapled professionally he could have a large quantity made. Huntley Goss checked the rough draft, making any necessary corrections and additions. Jarvis wrote to every known agent and asked them to write back confirming their particulars. Most of the agents complied with this request, but some were too lazy or too busy to reply and so providing he thought their addresses were correct, Jarvis kept them in his listing but printed their entries in italics. He was quite happy to send collectors a free updated list upon receipt of the stamps for postage. Certain statements had to be made in the *Goss Record* in order to satisfy the Goss factory management.

One was:

> 'I am not personally acquainted with Mr. Goss, or in any way financially interested in his business, but I take this opportunity of thanking him most sincerely for trouble he has taken and the assistance he has given me in compiling this book. — J.J. Jarvis.'

Another was:

> 'Mr. Goss will not supply any of his porcelain except through individual agents; arms of one town where an agency exists cannot be obtained off an agent in another town.' Also, 'Collectors are warned against many inferior imitations of Goss porcelain, mostly of foreign manufacture, that are being sold.'

The agents themselves were very pleased with Jarvis as he increased their trade. In April, 1902, he published an eight page supplement giving the latest corrections and amendments and in August of that same year he produced the second Goss Record, very similar to the previous edition in format and layout. In 1900 the number of British agents was 481, and there were then no overseas agencies. The first of these was Hamilton in Bermuda in August 1902 and by then there were 601 British agents. By the time the third Goss Record appeared there were interesting advertisements from the larger agents, including Henry Jones & Co., of St. Paul's Churchyard, London, who sold the little fairy mugs and beakers bearing forget-me-nots and verses — in addition to the City of London and London borough arms, hospitals, colleges and masonic emblems as well as a range of brown crosses. An important new line was 'The Empire Plate' which displayed the arms of the United Kingdom and eight of the Colonies. By now the Record was not just a list of agencies but contained snippets and hints to help collectors, details of the latest shapes being made and historical background information about the models. In the third edition there were asterisks against certain agencies in the list to indicate which shopkeepers were prepared to open after closing hours to sell Goss to those collectors unfortunate to arrive too late for shop opening hours, and photographs of the latest Goss models. Certain models listed were numbered, for example the Salisbury Gill was No. 127, this was to facilitate ordering by post from agents. Jarvis, in his 'Hints to Collectors' column, made it clear that his own favoured method was to buy matching or local arms on the correct models. Prices would vary from agent to agent, but had to be reasonably fair otherwise Mr. Goss would have withdrawn the franchise. It was usual to expect that smaller agencies in less accessible places were more expensive than those in large cities with higher turnovers. William's books were also advertised as being available from Jarvis, price 7/6d each. Ingenious inventions were also included in the advertising such as the 'Doylesava' which was a circular glass pane for protecting lace cake doilies. The 'Dursley Pederson' cycles illustrated for sale looked the most uncomfortable ever made and were supposed to be the 'featherweight of featherweights' in cycling.

The fourth edition was a supplement to the third. The fifth edition had a varnished grey cover decorated with artistic sketches of various matching Goss models. Jarvis admitted that the reason he finally obtained permission to go ahead with the first Goss Record was as follows:

> 'And then, as Mr. Rider Haggard would say, a strange thing happened. A map of the United Kingdom was ruled into small squares, and after a discreet interval, Mr. Goss's office at Stoke-on-Trent was bombarded with letters from all over the country each one athirst for information as to the Agents' whereabouts in the towns mentioned in the short lists they enclosed. Will it surprise my readers that by a remarkable coincidence all the replies ultimately found their way to Enfield, and that each one embraced the towns on one of the ruled squares of the map so that by piecing them together, after the manner of a child's puzzle a true and authentic list became an accomplished fact even if it were not quite complete? As this will be the first intimation Mr. Goss has had as to the method adopted; its progress and development, some acknowledgement is clearly due to him and to his overworked clerical staff of that period for the trouble they must have been put to.'

The cost of printing the covers for the second edition amounted to 3/- but by the time the fifth edition was printed in 1904, the numbers were so much greater that Jarvis was thinking in terms of pounds, not shillings. His postage bill was £50 a year alone, a terrific sum in those days considering that small Goss models were retailing for 9d each. The Record could be ordered direct from the editor or through most of the Goss agents.

The first major innovation by Jarvis was announced in the fifth edition. He had formed the National League of Goss collectors in 1904 and advertised for subscribers; all readers were eligible for membership. He had started a small exclusive club for himself and a few friends a few years earlier, but decided to make it national as its usefulness might be extended if it had a wider following. Leaflets were enclosed in the 5th Edition showing the specially designed coat of arms of the club, together with a form for joining.

The subscription was 2/6d for two years in the beginning, and for this the subscriber was entitled to a free Goss Portland Vase emblazoned with the special arms of the 'League of Goss Collectors.' These arms could not be bought elsewhere but only obtained in this way. New members were also given a copy of the Goss Record and a Certificate of Membership. Members of two years' standing received the Ancient Costril with the same League arms.

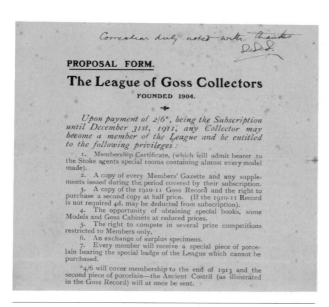

PROPOSAL FORM.

## The League of Goss Collectors

FOUNDED 1904.

*Upon payment of 2/6\*, being the Subscription until December 31st, 1911, any Collector may become a member of the League and be entitled to the following privileges :*

1. Membership Certificate, (which will admit bearer to the Stoke agents special rooms containing almost every model made).

2. A copy of every Members' Gazette and any supplements issued during the period covered by their subscription.

3. A copy of the 1910-11 Goss Record and the right to purchase a second copy at half price. (If the 1910-11 Record is not required 4d. may be deducted from subscription).

4. The opportunity of obtaining special books, some Models and Goss Cabinets at reduced prices.

5. The right to compete in several prize competitions restricted to Members only.

6. An exchange of surplus specimens.

7. Every member will receive a special piece of porcelain bearing the special badge of the League which cannot be purchased.

\*4/6 will cover membership to the end of 1913 and the second piece of porcelain—the Ancient Costril (as illustrated in the Goss Record) will at once be sent.

*Top half of a proposal form for the League of Goss Collectors with the initials J.J. Jarvis at the top*

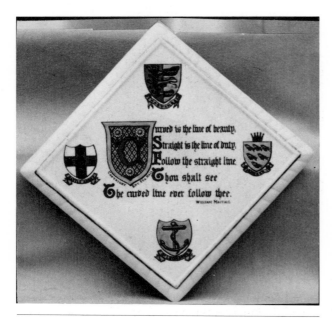

*Goss tea pot stand with verse in illuminated lettering and four crests*

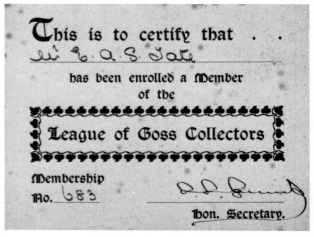

*League of Goss Collectors membership card*

The aims of the club included helping to spread a correct knowledge of heraldry amongst members, recommending suitable books on the subject, and organising meetings where groups could meet one another, the holding of display competitions and swapping and selling duplicates or unwanted pieces. The judges at these display competitions would award merits to the better entries, and the winners would have a photograph of their display published in the next *Goss Record*.

The models given free to each League member were as follows:

Portland Vase — upon joining
Ancient Costril — membership of 2 years
Staffordshire Tyg — membership of 4 years
Kings Newton Anglo-Saxon Cinerary Urn — membership of 6 years
Cirencester Roman Ewer — 1918
Contact Mine — 1919
Gnossus Vase — 1920
Greek Amphora Vase — 1921
Italian Krater — 1922
Egyptian Lotus Vase — 1923
Wilderspool Roman Tetinae — 1924
Cyprus Mycenaean Vase — 1925
Staffordshire Drinking Cup — 1926
Colchester Roman Lamp — 1927
Fimber Cinerary Urn — 1928
Irish Cruisken — 1929
Northwich Sepulchral Urn — 1930
Chester Roman Altar — 1931
Cheshire Roman Urn — 1932

Towards the end of the First World War, 'The League of Goss Collectors' became 'The International League of

Goss Collectors', and this was announced in the War Edition supplement. With the exception of the Portland Vase, the league models were reissued with the distinctive green International League arms instead of the former red National League decoration.

It is thought that the last few models were made in the late 1920's in advance of their being required in the light of the uncertain future of the factory at that time.

There are 136 models listed in the first Edition of the *Goss Record*, and 400 in the ninth and final edition. These numbers do not include earlier discontinued shapes or later pieces, but the Records were not completely accurate in listing all the current models. During the publication of the Records we can see just how quickly the agencies were growing. In 1902 there were 601 British agents, and by 1921 a total of 1,378 agents in Britain, and 186 agents overseas in 24 countries. By 1914, the task had become too great for the ageing Jarvis and the eighth and ninth editions, much expanded and improved, were published by Evans Bros. of London.

The *Goss Records* were not produced in a regular or systematic way, and only the fifth, sixth and seventh bear publication dates which are approximately as follows:

| | |
|---|---|
| 1900 | 1st edition duplicated leaflet, with four subsequent pamphlets |
| 1901 | 1st edition printed booklet |
| 1902-3 | 2nd edition (supplement to 1st) |
| 1903 | 3rd edition |
| 1903 | 4th edition (supplement to 3rd) |
| 1904-5-6 | 5th edition |
| 1906-7 | 6th edition issued in two forms, with a red binding before W.H. Goss's death on 4 January 1906, and with a purple binding after his death, with obituary. |
| 1910-11 | 7th edition |
| 1911 | (supplement to 7th) |
| 1913-14 | 8th edition. Published by Evans Bros. |
| 1916-18 | War edition (supplement to 8th). Published by Evans Bros. |
| 1921 | 9th edition. Published by Evans Bros. |

The War Edition was a concise booklet due to the shortage of paper at the time, and sold for only 3d. Earlier Records cost 6d each, and the 9th edition was a shilling.

In the fifth edition, Goss Cabinets were advertised, being designed and made under the supervision of Jarvis himself. They were made by one of the leading wholesale cabinet makers in the country with a finish of Chippendale or fumed oak. These were available from Jarvis or through any Goss agent. The same cabinet-makers were selected by *The Times* to make revolving bookcases for their *Encyclopaedia Britannica*. The Goss cabinets included two revolving types (designs A and C), two wall hung varieties (designs B and D) and two floor standing (designs E and F). Inside each cabinet was a shaped

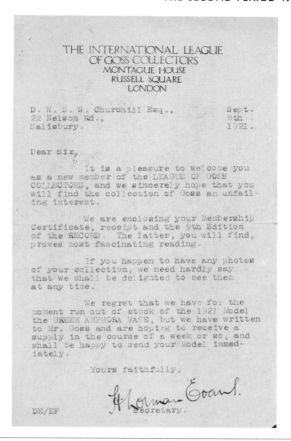

*Reply from the International League after J.J. Jarvis handed over the reins to Evans Bros*

*Goss cabinet design D containing a good collection*

porcelain plaque bearing the Goss personal arms.

The cabinets were advertised in the fifth, sixth and seventh editions as being available on *The Times* system of monthly instalments (hire purchase). This indicated that the working classes had now joined the middle classes in the pursuit of collecting Goss china, as in 1904 hire purchase was only associated with the more impoverished sections of the community! In the ninth edition of the *Goss Record* J.J. Jarvis advised his readers:

'In consequence of furniture trade difficulties and the heavy demand for essential articles of furniture, Goss Cabinets are no longer available.'

The *Goss Records* are the only means of dating the first appearance of a model, with the help of any registration marks. In the first edition pamphlet are listed Dorothy Vernon's Porridge Pot, the Elizabethan Jug, the Brading Ewer to name but a few of the popular models, and other shapes included the Inverary Cross of the Nobles, Winchester Bushel and Haddon Hall Font. The second edition records the new Welsh Leek, Walmer Roman Vase, Salisbury Kettle and the bust of Peeping Tom of Coventry. The third edition shows new additions such as the St. Ives Cross, Manx Peel Pot, Canterbury Pilgrim Bottle and Tewkesbury Saxon Urn. Each edition listed new designs, the production of each one being possible until the firm was sold in 1929, so no piece can be dated exactly except for Commemorative ware, unless the original buyer pencilled on the base the date and occasion of the purchase, which sometimes happened.

Huntley Goss was a chivalrous and likeable young gentleman, and it was with him that Jarvis communicated when updating the *Goss Records*. Huntley told Jarvis several stories which he though worthy of publication, none more strange than that concerning the King of Siam.

An Agent was appointed at Bangkok in Siam (now Thailand), probably arranged by post rather than a personal visit by the Goss salesman. The agent was sent a delightful assortment of pieces all carrying the Siamese arms, designed to appeal to far eastern tastes. Fairly soon after the porcelain was put on sale, the King of Siam paid the agent a visit and purchased every single item for himself. In order to prevent similar pieces being sold in the future he passed a law immediately prohibiting the importation of Goss porcelain within the limits of his kingdom!

Jarvis also recalled the curious tale of the Goss tea set with the Royal Arms of Japan. Huntley made a special tea-set for a small girl (a great favourite of his brother's) to present to a friend of hers, one of the Japanese Ambassadors. The cups and saucers only carried the arms of the Ambassador, but the teapot and sugar basin had space for two arms so Huntley naturally added the Royal Arms of Japan. Quite some time later he discovered that when the Ambassador returned to his country he had to smash the tea pot and sugar basin before stepping on to Japanese soil, otherwise he would have faced a serious risk of forfeiting his life, because the Royal Arms were not allowed upon anything other than the property of the Emperor himself. Huntley found this out when the Ambassador wrote to his little friend.

Jarvis personally replied to the hundreds of letters he received from keen collectors, a typical example being dated 8 September 1912, in reply to a query from a collector. He now gave his address as Sunnybank, The Uplands, Enfield, telephone Enfield 247. The query was whether or not a Bath Urn, bearing the arms of the Duke of Norfolk and Sussex was genuine. Jarvis's short reply was that the piece was genuine and was 'one of the very oldest pieces'.

Jarvis played a major part in popularising Goss china. He ignored the negative response from William and persevered independently to tirelessly promote Goss heraldic porcelain.

Eventually, the fruits of Jarvis's efforts became too important for the Goss Pottery to continue to ignore and William grudgingly acknowledged the value of the *Goss Records* in dramatically improving sales.

Jarvis was never approved of by William, no doubt much to the former's chagrin, but Huntley and Victor saw the commercial merit in his work and encouraged Jarvis's diligent and unpaid labour of love.

The editor of the *Goss Record* eventually became Sir Joseph John Jarvis and he died on the 3 October 1950 at his last home in Godalming.

*Brass pipe rack with inset Queen Victoria commemorative plaque in porcelain*

William disliked advertising and thought that if a product was good it would sell itself and not require any gimmicks such as advertising. Therefore, the monthly *Pottery Gazette*, the trade magazine for pottery and glass manufacturers, did not carry Goss advertisements until February 1906 — a month after his death! Even so, the advertisement, which was to remain the same for the next two decades, was rather modest and staid, giving no address and presuming the reader to know who made Goss china and where. Each month the magazine printed this same rather plain advertisement, which took up space on a third

A letter from William to Adolphus showing something of their relationship and business ethics.

*Writing an afterthought vertically down the margin was commonplace*

of a page. We have seen a copy of the *Pottery Gazette* dated as late as 1919 with the same Goss advertisement within which boldy states 'original heraldic ivory porcelain'. William had little respect for other potters who cheapened themselves and their wares and felt there was no advantage to be gained in 'the enormous amount of puffing which some effect.' He considered that a plain, sober, well written announcement carried more weight than an elaborate one. In a letter to the *Pottery Gazette* in 1884 he remembered with distaste a go-ahead transatlantic editor who said, 'He who would in business rise, must either bust or advertise.' His answer was that in any case customers would soon 'winnow the chaff from the wheat.' He thought that this vulgar practice also led to the dubious methods used by some 'honest(?) gentry', who went around buying up bankrupt stock at less than 20% of its value, simply by advertising in cheap evening papers all over Great Britain. The Goss agents often bought space in the *Goss Record*, and probably elsewhere with good results.There is no doubt that William was much too conservative ever to be in 'big business', and it was not surprising that so many others competed with him — he left the field so wide open! Towards the end of his life he did accept that china dealers solely engaged in legitimate trade needed to advertise in order to bring their wares prominently before their potential customers. There is a possibility that the format of the Goss advertisement was shown to and accepted by him before his death, for he relented towards the end and agreed to previously impossible requests, such as allowing a bust of himself to be modelled.

Although William always insisted he was flattered rather than angry, it was much regretted by the Goss family that other factories jumped on the bandwagon and manufactured similar heraldic ware, thus capitalizing on their father's success. Some hundred factories, mainly in and around Stoke, imitated the Goss shapes and crests, but they all failed to match the Goss standard of perfection and quality. The market was flooded with heraldic ware after 1900 and many other factories, in particular Arcadian

*Envelope containing the set of six. Two further postcards were added later*

1. Abbot's Cup, Fountain's Abbey
2. Aberdeen Bronze Pot
3. Ancient Welsh Crochon
4. Roman Ewer from York
5. Loving Cup
6. Roman Vase from Chester
7. Bronze Ewer from Bath
8. Irish Mather

Teaspoons were produced under licence from 1905 to 1915 by the firm of Arbuckle in Birmingham. The spoons were made from silver-plated brass and the end of the shank was fashioned into the shape of a Portland Vase. They too were advertised in the *Goss Records* but were not a great success.

### References

1.  *The Reliquary* Vol. 25 1884-5
2.  *Pottery Gazette*, 1st December 1894
3.  Other manufacturers can be found listed, together with their histories, products and manufacturers' marks in *Crested China* by Sandy Andrews, Milestone Publications 1980

*Goss postcard No. 3 featuring the Welsh Bronze Crochon, arms of Chesterfield*

headed by the businessman Harold Taylor Robinson, went on to develop the idea further to include comic themes, novelties, animals, figurines and a vast array of First World War militaria, as well as vases, jugs and urns of little apparent historic interest.[3]

William considered that these imitations lowered the tone of the whole market, and rigidly kept to the straight and serious path of quality, perfection and aesthetic value. Even after his death his sons Victor and Huntley dutifully continued in the same manner as though their father were still there directing them. The output of other firms in total far exceeded that of the Goss pottery and appealed to a wider audience, even royalty, but 'Collect Goss, and only Goss' was the message spread by the *Goss Record* booklets to their eager readers.

Between 1905 and 1912 a series of six picture postcards was issued, each illustrating a Goss model. The arms were over printed on the illustrated shape as ordered by the agents. Cards No. 7 and 8 were added to the range a few years later, and are now scarcer. They were produced with the permission of W.H. Goss by S.A. Oates and Co., of Halifax who printed on them, 'None genuine without the name 'Goss'. ' These postcards were only sold for a few years so presumably they must have rivalled china sales. The card numbers were as follows:

# CHAPTER SEVENTEEN

# Victor and Huntley at the Helm

'The art of the potter has always exercised, no less for the craftsman than for the man in the street, a charm and fascination of which no other craft can boast'.

H. Woolliscroft Rhead

Although William had long since retired from the day-to-day running of the factory, his death on 4 January, 1906 had its impact on the family and the firm. It was said that he departed this world without having spoken to his wife for about twenty years, and that relations with Adolphus had been strained. When he felt others were in the wrong he punished them with cold silence, even to the extent of destroying relationships. His name means Helmet of Resolution, and he certainly lived up to it. His descendants feel it was due to the manner in which he treated his wife that divided Adolphus and him, and so Adolphus was excluded from the firm in his will, which he had rewritten in 1904. The firm, its land, buildings, stock and equipment, and good will he left to Victor and Huntley, and £4,000 in cash to Adolphus to be paid by the two younger sons, on condition that Adolphus did not start up in business in opposition to them. William believed that the four thousand pounds for Adolphus would 'fairly compensate him for having devised and bequeathed my said manufactory', but it did leave Adolphus in middle age with wasted energies and talents. At the age of 53 it was cruel to cut off his career in his prime and he was too old to train for another. Who knows what the firm would have produced if he had been allowed to remain in it. Perhaps their critical father had not thought it possible for all three sons to work and get along together without arguments and disagreements, but it was still the 'Goss Boss' who was left out. The £4,000 was unexpectedly demanded by Adolphus at once, thus causing financial problems for the firm, but somehow the two new partners managed to pay him out of the firm's current account, leaving their new responsibility with little or no capital, a precarious situation for a large business with many wages to pay each week. Despite their mature years of 43 and 41 respectively, it was a difficult and worrying time for Victor and Huntley, with the change of ownership, loss of their experienced

father and his advice and guidance, and the irreplaceable loss of their innovative and energetic travelling salesman-cum-artist and photographer brother. It was ironic that it should be Adolphus's second son Clarence Richard (Dick) who took over the position, and remained there until the outbreak of war in 1914, when he enlisted.

Trade was still very good and eventually, under Victor's guidance, the firm was in a favourable financial position. Describing the Goss market in 1906, Mr. Charles Martin, a large china dealer in Manchester who was to be manager of the new branch of Messrs. Stephenson and Co. Ltd. to be opened in London that year, when asked what the prospects of success were likely to be, he replied 'We shall meet our expenses here with Goss alone.'[1] When W.H.Goss's traveller came along in those days Mr. Martin never gave him an order for less than £100. He remembered on one occasion when there was an important football cup tie replay in Manchester on a Monday, they sold £30 worth of Goss ware between 7 p.m. and 9 p.m. in the evening, and the most expensive piece was a half-a-crown and the majority not more than one shilling.

The years when Victor was in charge were the factory's best. He had inherited his father's business acumen, and led the firm with a strong arm, increasing the range of heraldic models, adding to the coats of arms, transfers and decorations, and appointing even more agents both at home and abroad. In 1910 they exhibited in the British section of the Brussels Universal Exhibition.

The period of 1910-15 was one of intense activity, including fifteen new cottage models. A new line of special interest was the brown and white crosses and stones. Trade was booming and there were 1,299 agents in Britain, and 140 foreign agents in 34 countries listed in the eighth edition of the *Goss Record* (1913).

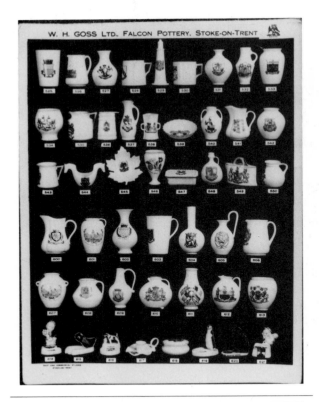

This favourable review appeared in the *Pottery Gazette*, 1 May 1912.

'Mr William H. Goss, Stoke-on-Trent, is the well-known manufacturer of original heraldic ivory porcelain. I had the pleasure of a short interview with Mr. Goss, who was able to say, what few other potters could say just then, that his workpeople were all busy. But then, he is a manufacturer of specialities — and artistic ones at that. 'Goss's Heraldic China' is known to every one in the trade, and to thousands who have no connection with it. There is probably no other description of ceramics of which there are so many systematic collectors. This is easily explained. All his productions are suitable for presents; they are all artistic and are easily portable, so that friends — even ladies — can carry to the recipients the pleasing mementos they wish them to accept. There are many occasions — birthdays, wedding days, Christmas, and the New Year — of which most of us like to present our intimate friends with some appropriate souvenir. Goss has been something like a national benefactor in providing a number of acceptable, artistic, and not too expensive presents for all these occasions. When a lady has had a few pieces of 'Goss' presented to her, she wishes for more, and buys an attractive piece now and then to add to her store. She is proud to show her possessions to her friends and when, in turn, they wish to make her a present, they say 'We will give her a pretty piece of Goss'. That is how 'collectors' are made. I know

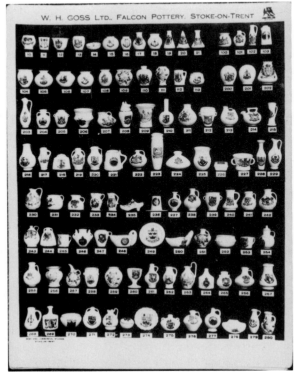

*Photographs sent to agents for ordering*

*Four white unglazed parian crosses placed in front of William's oak sideboard. Left to right: Bakewell, Eyam, St. Martins Iona and Campbeltown*

a lady who never visits a place of interest for the first time without inquiring from local dealers for a piece of 'Goss' china, with the arms of the city, county borough, or town, enamelled in colours upon it. She has a wonderful collection, and as it is known I am connected with the china trade I fancy it is expected that whenever I visit her I shall take her a new shape in 'Goss' china. Those of us who cannot afford to make a collection of 'Old Wedgwood,' 'Old Bow,' 'Chelsea,' or 'Derby,' can gratify our hobby for artistic china by securing a great variety of Mr. Goss's beautiful ware. The business was founded more than half a century ago by the father of the present proprietor, and the popularity of the ware has increased year by year. Foreign makers were quick to appreciate the saleable value of miniatures as souvenirs, but though they have imitated the style they cannot supply the beautiful body of the ivory-like porcelain made in such perfection by Mr. Goss. His great forté is in china miniatures in classical and quaint forms, with coats of arms in correct heraldic colours; but he also supplies figures and landscapes with floral and conventional accessories of great artistic merit. I do not know of a city, borough, county or university that is not represented on Goss china. He selects his forms from classical, historical, and artistic sources generally, and amongst his quaint pieces are many representations of the antique.'

The Mr. Goss referred to in the interview was William Huntley Goss, who conveniently possessed the same initials as his father and was often mistaken for him as the inventor of heraldic porcelain.

Between 1906 and 1910, collectors could add to their growing collections items such as the Musselburgh Kirkpark Urn, Stirling Pint Measure, Louth Ewer, London Wine Flagon, Kettering Urn, Nottingham Ewer and Urn, Boulogne Milk Can, Shoe and Sedan Chair, and many more, especially foreign models.

This was the most prolific period of production, with the factory space doubled, better equipment and more staff. There was a promising trade with Canada starting up and prospects were good right up until the tragic death of Captain Victor Henry Goss on 27 March 1913, when he was thrown from his horse as he rode to work one morning and instantly killed. He owned a new motorcar, but was an expert horseman who usually rode when travelling to work, having been a Captain in the Staffordshire Territorials.

A trade note appeared in the *Pottery Gazette* on 1 May 1913:

> 'It should be pointed out for the benefit of those interested in this firm's original heraldic wares that the regrettable and untimely death of the Senior Partner, Captain Victor Henry Goss, will not affect the business being carried on as heretofore.'

*Victor, who met death in his prime. He was thrown from this horse near his Oulton Rocks home in 1913*

*Mr. W.H. Goss's Exhibit in the King's Hall, Stoke-on-Trent, 22 April 1913, on the occasion of their Majesties' visit to the Potteries*

To Huntley in particular this was a terrible blow, having lost his father seven years before, and without the help of Adolphus. Now suddenly the responsiblity was all his, and he responded to the challenge with great effort, with the impending royal visit to the potteries by their Majesties King George V and Queen Mary on 22 April 1913, to prepare for. The exhibition in the King's Hall, Stoke comprised a stand from each pottery, and Huntley's display of Goss was very tasteful, including The Trusty Servant, William of Wykeham, Shakespeare leaning on a lectern, a large 'Think, Thank and Thrive' bread plate, two pierced plates and a wide range of heraldic ware, mainly domestic. The day was a big success for the potteries, affording them world wide notice, and certain products were paid particular attention to by their Majesties, but their comments, if any, regarding Goss were not mentioned in the report in the *Pottery Gazette* on 2 June of that year. The small paragraph concerning Goss was as follows:

> 'Mr. W.H. Goss had a stand showing a typical selection of his popular productions, and both antique and modern shapes in his famous heraldic china. The display was principally concerned with the crest china, as might have been expected, but other specialities were shown nevertheless.'

After the display at the Kings Hall, Stoke in April, and at Brompton Road, London in May, Harrods removals took the exhibits first to Harrods in London then to the Liverpool Trades Exhibition where they remained until the end of the season. The Benevolent Institution placed collecting boxes around the room, and the King became a patron upon his visit to the Potteries. Her Majesty said at Harrods that:

> 'It afforded her great pleasure to see the display and re-inspect the exhibits in such pleasant surroundings and considered it a great accomplishment to have removed the goods so successfully.'

The total value of goods in the exhibition was £16,000, a small fortune in those days.

Until July, 1914, the firm registered its products with the Patent Office because of the numerous potteries copying and imitating the Goss shapes and designs. From its earlier days up until October 1901, patents granted were for designs and decorations of unspecified models and pieces. After 1901 patents were awarded with registration numbers until July 1914. After that date the registration design number was no longer printed on the base of each piece but 'COPYRIGHT' was printed instead.

Despite the good trade and sizeable business, Huntley was never one to keep pace with progress. For years he refused to install a telephone but used the telegraph system as his father had done, although the telephone had been invented in 1876. When his sons finally persuaded him to have a telephone installed in 1921, their number was Stoke-on-Trent 839.

*Flying the flag for Goss china in St. Leonards-on-Sea. This card is postmarked 1929*

*Huntley and Florence Goss, owners of the factory*

After publication of the eighth edition of the *Goss Record* in 1913, there was not another full edition for eight years, due to the outbreak of the First World War in August, 1914. The war had a profound effect on the Goss firm, taking its young male employees for war service and many members of the female staff to the munitions factories, or for nursing at home and abroad. Collectors did not pursue their hobbies with their previous enthusiasm during the hostilities. There was little money for leisure, travelling or holidays, and no doubt most people's prized possessions were wrapped up and stowed away. So the firm lost not only its employees but its customers. The war changed many lives and careers, and not all the staff returned after the Armistice had been signed.

Apart from the war making it exceedingly difficult for output to be maintained, it nearly bankrupted the firm because foreign agents found it impossible to forward their remittances for the stock they had been sent before July, 1914. It was unfortunate that vast quantities of foreign armorial ware had been exported that summer, under the firms's normal three months' credit terms, allowing time for the goods to arrive and often sold before payment was due. Remittances which would normally have been received by Christmas 1914 just did not materialise, and not much of what was owing was sent after the war ended. The loss of stock and income seriously altered the firm's financial position and its reserve funds were used.

In order to improve sales with topical products, Huntley was quick to launch a series of both Great War models and military decorations with the 'Flags of the Allies' design on sale within two weeks of the country going to war. This particular badge was redesigned as more countries joined the allies, and appeared with four, six, seven and eight flags.

Blue patriotic ware depicting the Arms of England, St. George, and Tudor roses made in 1915 was experimental, and all existing examples have been found marked 'DEFECTIVE' or 'SECONDS' due to the failure to stop the blue running into the glaze in the final firing.

The 1918 War Edition of the *Goss Record*, a slim booklet produced as an update to the eighth edition and to be used in conjunction with it, recorded all the new models introduced after 1913. These included the British Six Inch Incendiary Shell, Russian Shrapnel Shell, Bury St. Edmunds Bomb, which was modelled on a bomb dropped from a zeppelin on 30 April 1915, and the Maldon German Incendiary Bomb, also dropped from a zeppelin fourteen days before the Bury St. Edmunds bomb. Other war models, such as the British Tank Mark II were produced between 1916 and 1917.

The moulds of the war models were intended to be destroyed after one year's use in order to make these models scarcer. Thus the limited production period would help these pieces to become quickly sought after, the early beginnings of the 'limited edition' market perhaps. The tank was not listed in the 1918 War Edition because it was no longer on the production line!

The firm received a good write up in the *Pottery Gazette*, 2 April, 1917, with illustrations of the Russian Shrapnel Shell, Malden Bomb and Bury St Edmunds Bomb, together with the Lion of Flanders plate commemorating the heroic stand of Belgium, and Flags of the Allies plate.

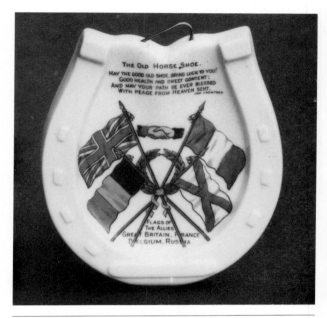

*The four flags of the Allies decoration on a horseshoe model*

*The Goss agency in Brussels between the wars*

*Bury St. Edmunds Bomb, Russian Shrapnel Shell and British Six Inch Incendiary Shell*

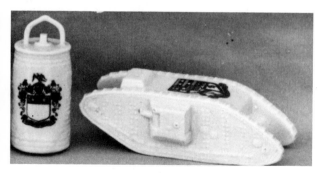

*Maldon (German) Bomb and British Tank Mark II*

As there had been a strong demand from our troops in France for heraldic ware decorated with the arms of the various places in which they were billeted, the firm had hoped, providing the Military Censor permitted it, that these, along with the arms of the towns in Belgium, and possibly even German towns, would tell of the story of the forceful progress of the 'Big Push' as the third Battle of The Somme in July 1916 was called.

All the war models were copyrighted, and the Goss range was surprisingly small when compared to the prolific Arcadian, Willow Art, Carlton and Savoy factories which channelled all their energies into soldiers, figures, tanks, guns, helmets, tents and a wealth of ammunition in crested china. They manufactured as much as would sell, getting their details from photographs of the men at war from newspapers.

In 1917 acting Major Vernon Goss (eldest son of Adolphus) was wounded in action and returned home briefly. One of his colleagues, Major Embleton, an Australian who was 6'7" tall, was an eminent ear, nose and throat specialist. During the war there was a severe epidemic of influenza at home and thousands of swabs were collected at the Royal Victoria Hospital, Netley, near Southampton where Majors Goss, Harvey and Embleton were engaged into research into the disease. These swabs were from all the military camps in the area extending as far north as Winchester. No doubt Major Vernon Goss thought he would have a little light-hearted fun and commissioned his cousin Margaret Goss (Peggy) to design a plate depicting Major Embleton in khaki with a theatre gown over his uniform, taking a swab. He was pictured as a towering figure over the patient. The owner of two of the four bagware plates made kept them in her possession for over 50 years, and died aged 90 in 1975. She was given one of the plates by Vernon Goss when she worked in the Pathology laboratory with Major Embleton. Before she passed away she told friends the story of the plates, and revealed how Majors Goss, Embleton and Harvey were all close friends who had worked at the same hospital in the Great War. The caricature was captioned 'SWABS', and she believed the patient was meant to be Vernon Goss. The four plates were identical, but only one was factory marked. When Major Dennis Harvey died he left his plate to the lady to make a pair with hers. She understood the remaining two were taken to Australia.

*The 'Swabs' plate designed by Margaret Goss*

*Huntley and Margaret photographed at the time of the British Empire Exhibition at which the factory displayed and sold B.E.E. arms in 1924 and 1925*

The Chapel Royal is all that now remains of the Royal Victoria Hospital which was demolished in the early 1970's and the area is now a country park. It was Queen Victoria's favourite hospital as she could look over to it at Netley from Osborne House, her home on the Isle of Wight.

During the war Huntley continued to introduce new historic models, and the Fenny Stratford Popper, Chesterfield Brampton Ware Mug, Lancashire clog, King Richard's Well Cover, London Stone, Fourshire Stone, Cuckfield Bellarmine, Whitby Pillion Stone, Queen Philippa's Record Chest, Gullane Smithy and Rhayader Capel Madoc Stoup were added to the firm's range.

The International League of Goss Collectors used a military original for their annual model for 1918 — the Contact Mine which bore the League's new international arms. Only seven military models were produced, culminating in a model of The Cenotaph after the war. Huntley left the opposition to specialise in militaria and he concentrated on what the firm was unequalled at — the perfect reproduction of coats of arms. A very wide but now scarce range of regimental and battleship badges were produced on the smaller sizes of the historic models, which were particularly popular with our troops abroad who wanted suitable souvenirs for their families. The standard of workmanship both in the china and the painting of the armorials was magnificent. It was to the credit of Huntley, and his three sons and daughter who had by now joined him in the firm, that in spite of the increased costs of raw materials, inflation and wage rises which had taken place during the war years, he did not skimp any of the processes. It was mainly through the many requests received for Goss to be made with Naval, Regimental and Air Force badges that Huntley branched out into that area,

for he was not one to make money from the misfortune of war. The special commemorative made for the Dutch market to mark the heroic stand of Belgium, was welcomed by the *Pottery Gazette* as being a small export order valuable in trying to balance the trade with Holland without importing their produce. Another WW1 plate with flags had a verse as follows:

'TO COOK A GERMAN SAUSAGE
Cook on a British Kitchener,
Use a Japan Enamelled Saucepan
Grease Well with Russian Tallow,
Flavour with a little Jellicoe,
Servia!! up with French Capers
and Brussels Sprouts.'

*The 'Lion of Flanders' plate*

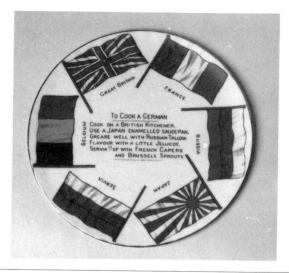

*'To Cook a German Sausage' plate*

Another plate, this time fan-shaped, designed especially for the Southport agent, immortalised the babies killed in the bombing of Scarborough, where a bomb passed completely through the lighthouse, leaving it standing with a gaping hole right through its sides.

During the war another attempt was made to revive the then ailing factory by making china dolls' heads, legs and arms, as the chief source of supply for high class quality china dolls. The German firms, who previously dominated this market, could no longer export their wares to Great Britain as trade with the enemy had been cut off since 1914.

It took much time and expense to buy the correct equipment, and make the moulds and organise the sales. Goss dolls had only just begun to capture the English toy market, despite their high price, when the war ended in November 1918 and in no time at all the German factories were flooding Britain with their much cheaper versions. This competition killed the Goss doll trade. Noel Goss said that the firm did not manage to break even on their costs, so their losses only added to their troubles. Another new line attempted was porcelain buttons but the few trial shapes were never sold.

In 1919 the pottery's special 'Peace' commemorative was issued, decorated in the familiar turquoise blue, together with the 'Peace Plate', a magnificent piece designed by Huntley. Both were favourably reviewed in the *Pottery Gazette and Glass Trades Review*, 1 October 1919. The Peace Plate, available in 8″, 9″ and 10″ diameters, was only on sale for twelve months.

*A Goss doll with porcelain head and arms, movable glass eyes and real hair*

CHERTSEY ROAD LOOKING EAST, WOKING

*The Woking Agency in the twenties*

The *Pottery Gazette* rarely published reviews of other heraldic manufacturers' work but it had long standing ties with the Goss firm since William Goss used to regularly write articles for the magazine.

Huntley's children joined their father in the firm as soon as their education was completed. Noel and Geoffrey were 18 years old when they became supervisors on the factory floor in 1918 and 1920 respectively. John joined as an artist in 1922 at the age of 17, and Peggy (Margaret Winifred Elizabeth) helped in the same department for five years. Her childrens' mugs decorated with illustrations of nursery rhyme and amimal characters, together with some plates and bowls, were signed M.G. and dated 1922.

Only Peggy and John inherited the Goss artistic talent, their mother Florence being a good needlewoman. John designed and made the Goss animals and some cottages, all of which were beautifully reproduced, and are now valuable.

Noel Goss, with help from foreman Alfred Mollart, measured up certain buildings for reproducing as cottages, such as John Knox's Edinburgh house in 1929. In 1925 they visited the Cat and Fiddle Inn near Buxton, Derbyshire, and measured it for production later that year. It was John who modelled these later cottages using Noel and Alfred's measurements and photographs. He also modelled Izaac Walton's cottage at Shallowford, near Stoke between 1925 and 1928 from photographs as the original building had burnt down completely long before. Apart from the cottages, John also modelled the animals

## William H. Goss,

### Manufacturer of the original Heraldic Porcelain,

**MARK**

**W. H. GOSS.**

### Falcon Pottery, Stoke-on-Trent.

*The trademark from the advertisement in the* North Staffs. Chamber of Commerce Year Book *for 1921*

including the lion, rhino, hippo and an alsation lying on a slab, as he himself called it. A special piece he designed was a paperweight of a cherub sitting on a cushion with gold tassels, tinted in natural colours and trimmed with turquoise blue, but his 4″ bust of Winston Churchill never went into production.

A much expanded ninth edition of the *Goss Record* was finally published in 1921. It listed more British agencies but overseas agencies covered only 24 countries as opposed to 34 in 1913.

Although the standards set by William Henry were maintained, there were certain changes in the supplies of raw materials. For example, the enamels used in William's day were his own preparations, but Noel revealed that in their day, the firm used enamels imported from various local specialists.

After the war the mood of the nation had changed, and the younger generation was not as keen on collecting souvenirs, by now a rapidly fading Victorian and Edwardian pastime. The Gosses tried to make some concessions in order to attract new customers as well as keep old ones interested. They introduced various pieces of brightly coloured hand painted pottery, especially floral decorations of crocuses, poppies and hollyhocks, and beige coloured 'Royal Buff' tea sets for everyday use. Some designs bordered on the Art Deco, although none were really quite so

*John Goss, youngest son of Huntley, and the firm's artist and designer in the twenties*

outrageous, but it was precisely these weird and angular shapes and designs which were the winning lines for other potters. The Goss factory never quite captured the flavour of what the market then wanted, although the garish jampots with matching saucers depicting different fruits, coloured brooches, and attractive Flower Girls were their best selling lines of the 1920's. These ladies were brightly multi coloured, mostly holding baskets of flowers and wearing crinolines and overskirts in a variety of sizes and colours. No two looked the same as each one was individually hand painted. Huntley also re-employed several former workers who used to specialise in brooch making in order to reintroduce this once popular line.

Heraldic ware was now becoming decidedly unpopular as tastes were rapidly changing. The 1926 coal strike, which left the works without the much needed fuel for about twelve weeks, finally made the closure of the firm imminent. They lacked the assets to survive the enormous loss of business and good will caused by the ovens being closed, and having no emergency funds, unlike some of their competitors and neighbours, they could not bounce back. The 'Churchill Toby Jug' registered in 1927, the coloured lifelike orange marmalade pot and the coloured Cornish Pasty were some of the last lines made together with the 'Royal Buff' beige coloured pottery, including the 'Little Brown Jug' designed by Peggy. By now lack of money forced the family to buy the cheaper inferior local clays instead of the expensive felspar china clays from Devon and Cornwall, but it was impossible to make the original heraldic ware with the heavier pottery clays so those lines were abandoned and sales were lost. The firm's raison d'être since 1885 was now no more. It took some experimenting to get the flints ground to the necessary level to suit the local clays, and there were many failures in the firing due to the flints having been ground too finely causing the china to crack in the ovens.

These firing difficulties, due to shortage of funds in the first place, now depleted the firm's finances still further and spelled the end for Huntley. In 1928 private talks were held with several interested businessmen for the sale of the factory, including site, premises, equipment and good will, in order to avoid bankruptcy. Huntley ensured that all bills and wages were paid before he sold up in 1930 and although he stayed on as manager for a while, it was the end of an era.

**Reference**

1.     *The Pottery Gazette*, 1 September 1938.

*Late advertising plaque made for agencies in the 1920's*

# CHAPTER EIGHTEEN

# The Third Period

'There's a divinity that shapes our ends,
Rough hew them how we will.

Hamlet V.2

Cauldon Potteries purchased the assets and business of W.H. Goss from Huntley in early 1930 for £2,000 but the bank retained the Goss premises as the main mortgagee. Harold T. Robinson bought the business from Cauldon for £2,500 a few months later, and then borrowed money to buy the factory and land for £4,000. Mr. Robinson also owned the Cauldon firm, having bought that ten years before! As owner of Cauldon he also owned Arcadian, Swan, the Crescent China Works, Coronet Ware, Robinson and Leadbeater, Ridgeways Ltd, Wedgwood of Tunstall, Hewitt Bros (who produced Willow crested china) and Royal Worcester Porcelain.

This adventurous businessman formed the new company of W.H. Goss Ltd in 1931, with himself as director, he recommended the production of models from original Goss moulds as well as from other factories, all with the Goss mark. Pieces made during this period tend to be glazed on the base making the black Goshawk darker. The production of heraldic ware during this third period was discontinued in 1934 as H.T. Robinson was declared

*The Royston 'Crow'*

bankrupt in 1932 and the report of his bankruptcy proceedings in the *Pottery Gazette*, 1 July 1932, makes colourful reading. He continued in pottery manufacture until 1939 and production finally ended in 1940.

Between 1920 and 1930, Robinson had become the largest employer in North Staffordshire. He dominated most of the china trade and was more concerned with the successful running of his business than with the quality and beauty of the products. He directed thirty-two companies at one point, and even bought companies which supplied his firms with fuel and clay in order to purchase more cheaply.

During his bankruptcy hearing he insisted that had not economic events been so desperately bad he would have been a millionaire by then, not a bankrupt. He had had to weather the 1914-18 World War, the coal strikes, the loss of foreign trade with unsettled international markets, Britain leaving the gold standard in 1924 and the world-wide depression. He said:

'When I saw the depression was developing to the extent it was, I left my country house and came to live practically next door to the works and I have been working fifty weeks out of fifty-two to try to circumvent the terrible effects of that depression. When you get down to the basic facts you will realise that as the largest potter in North Staffordshire, I have been the largest victim.'

The Goshawk mark was used during Robinson's ownership in preference to other factory names because the name 'Goss' stood for quality and perfection and it had always been the market leader. Some of his ware was marked 'Goss' and some 'Goss England'. Small white glazed buildings of excellent quality were made such as Big Ben, Banbury Cross and St. Paul's Cathedral, usually only with the correct matching arms. A large range of Flower Girls in two sizes including a miniature set of 'The Wedding Group' modelled from the original designs of the American artist C.H. Twelvetrees, appealed to the public, as did the brightly coloured Toby jugs. Tiny animals, usually comical

*The heading of a special circular issued by the Goss China Co. Ltd. to all the former agents stocking Goss china in 1934, announcing the creation of the new firm*

rather than realistic, a limited set of black boys and black cats and the Royston Crow probably did not sell well, or were not in production long, judging by their scarcity now.

Comical figures made include two partly coloured babies seated on an ash tray confiding in one another and titled 'That's the one Daddy told Nurse!'; an old and young lady seated at the side of a dish 'Gin and It', and father struggling to hold a yelling baby beside an open bag (match holder), named 'Married Bliss'. Some new transfer designs were issued between 1931 and 1934 including those using stylised flowers, mainly poppies and cornflowers in red, blue, yellow and green. During this period Huntsmen decorations 'A Present from Clovelly' — possibly a reference to the Clovelly Hunt, and stagecoach and horses transfers 'A Present from Dover' — perhaps a reference to the arrival of the Dover mails — were produced. The designs in the pattern books of the Goss China Co. Ltd. were registered in the name of Allied English Potteries Ltd., one of Robinson's companies. The 'Crocus' design with three red, blue and purple tulips with foliage, the 'Glendale' design which we have yet to see, 'Garden Scene' with yellow thatched cottage with large floral border and the distinctive 'Cottage Pottery' which had the picture of a thatched cottage on a cup with a brown handle and a raised border of flowers on a saucer, were recorded in the pattern books. The colours used on each design were recorded beside a sketch of each, such as 'Coral 271D, Green 874, Black 260B, Blue 2307, Orange 3282'. The Cottage tea set was immensely popular, with each teapot, milk jug, sugar bowl etc., formed as individual cottages.

Commemorative mugs, plates and beakers were issued for the Silver Jubilee of King George V and Queen Mary in 1935, the Coronation of Edward VIII and the

*The only known pair of 'Daisy' bookends. The idea was never marketed*

Coronation of King George VI and Queen Elizabeth in 1937. These were of beige pottery with brown trim and brown lettering. A series of circular ashtrays in bas-relief commemorating Edward VIII's coronation, 12 May 1937, were made in startling colours of purple, yellow, blue, green and pink. These were uncertain times for the nation and when Edward VIII abdicated before his coronation, many of these commemoratives were left unsold in the hands of the retailers and factory. The last commemoratives were for the 1938 Glasgow Exhibition, and had a distinctive green trim instead of the usual gold gilding. It was common for the majority of these later pieces to be crazed showing the poor quality of ware during these last years. Perhaps it was just as well that output ceased mid 1940. In 1939

*'Garden Scene' from the pattern book dated May, 1934*

*'Cottage Pottery' design from the same book*

production was situated in Hill Street, Stoke, and the old works closed. Derek Ashton of Stoke who was employed by W.H. Goss Ltd. in 1939 as a trainee works manager, can remember:

'The product at that time was mainly confined to the famous Goss flower girl series, bowls of china flowers and similar. Most of this went to the U.S.A. In 1940 the Hill Street factory was closed and the Goss work was transferred to Crescent Potteries (Geo. Jones & Sons) at South Wolfe Street, Stoke, which in turn was owned by the big potters Millers Harrisons (Hanley). In addition to the remnants of the Goss factory, this concern also controlled Coalport China and Cauldon Potteries. Soon after the war Crescent Potteries folded and Coalport eventually became part of the Wedgwood complex.

The Goss Works were used for a couple of years after 1940 by an electrical firm for their wartime wares. After nearly a year of disuse, the Crown Bedding Co. took it over in 1944 to pack parachutes. They purchased the premises in 1945 from Coalport, who by then had taken over Cauldon Potteries, owner of the works. After the war Crown Bedding used the factory for making upholstered car seats and mattresses. Mr. Angel of Hendon in London acquired the Goss premises in 1947 and found large quantities of moulds (later destroyed) and assorted colourful ornaments including Toby jugs, as well as a huge, un-opened post containing orders for Goss china. He sold

*75mm high, coloured porcelain flowers marked 'Goss England'*

*Flapper on ashtray cigarette box and Judy, Toby and Mr. Punch cruet, all coloured and without coats of arms*

the site in 1951 to Washington Potteries (China Craft) Ltd. Coalport still owned the Goss trademark, the Goss name, and what patterns, moulds, designs and cases remained, but finally let them go to Ridgeway Potteries Ltd., of Ash Hall, Stoke, in July 1954. In 1959 this firm then acquired all the other assets of the Coalport group. After 8 July 1964 the group was known as Allied English Potteries Ltd. and in 1971 A.E.P merged with the Doulton group. This rapidly expanding pottery had begun production of E.T.C. (English Translucent China) in the 1960's. This china was similar to bone china but produced without bone, and for half the cost. By now most of the smaller firms had been taken over by larger, more successful ones, and the potting industry changed from one based on crafts and skills to one supported by science and technology.

In recent years the factory was used by a clothing manufacturer but was sold in the mid 1980's to the adjoining Portmeirion pottery which has demolished what remained of the original Kirkhams' part of the factory and used the land for expansion of their works and for car parking.

All that now remains are the two 1902-5 buildings and the carved stone Goshawk in the gable of the later building and the two glost kilns. Both are 'listed' buildings and the bottle ovens are two of the few still standing in the Potteries. Perhaps one day they will be restored to their former glory. The factory spoil heap is situated behind the main buildings and has been excavated in the early 1980's. Amongst the shards and manufacturing rejects have been found fragments of new models which did not go into production and shapes with different colouring or decoration to those sold.[1]

Further up the hill behind the spoil heap stands Ashfield Cottage, now divided into two halves and let. Although the gardens are no longer maintained to William's standards, many of the original garden sheds in which he conducted his early experiments still remain.

*Early collector John Willis's snap of two Goss signs hanging outside the Wells, Somerset agency in 1958*

### Reference

1.    Details of these are given in *The Price Guide to Goss China* (3. Non-Production Ware) by Nicholas Pine Milestone Publications 1986.

# CHAPTER NINETEEN

# The Manufacture of Goss Porcelain

No Art With Potters Can Compare,
We Make our Pots of What we Potters are!

T. Locker 1770

Potting in the last century was truly an art, and unsurprisingly the manufacturing processes used in the Goss factory were not as sophisticated as those applied in most potteries nowadays. These earlier methods were used and modified over hundreds of years and remained virtually unchanged until the changeover to gas and electric kilns. The Clean Air Act 1960 caused the old bottle ovens to be rendered obsolete and quickly led to the majority being demolished to make way for new developments and roads.

The ingredients for Goss parian were selected according to William Henry Goss's own recipe, modified from the first parian produced at the Copeland factory in 1846 by John Mountford. William first modelled parian at the Copeland Works and the formula for this was forty parts felspar, thirty-six parts china clay, twenty-four parts frit. The frit comprised eleven parts Cornish stone, fifty-seven parts white sand and eight parts of potash.

The ingredients of Goss china, which William termed ivory porcelain, were Norwegian and Swedish felspar, white glass (obtained from grinding up old bottles made of clear glass only) flints and kaolin or china clay. Goss obtained the latter from Varcoes Sales Co. Ltd., High Cross Street, St. Austell, Cornwall, Cornish kaolin being necessary to bind the other ingredients together. The type of felspar used came from certain beds in Norway and Sweden which were just about worked out by the end of the Goss factory's life, and there was no similar alternative available. It is the felspar which influences the colour, texture and feel of the final result, making each factory's products so different from its rivals. The felspar William favoured produced the ivory translucency which was so distinctly his own. These materials had to be shipped by sea to Liverpool and from there to Runcorn, where they were transferred to the Middlewich branch of the Shropshire Union Canal and on to the Trent and Mersey Canal which

passed through Stoke.

It was the great Josiah Spode, the immediate predecessor of the Copeland Works, who originally began using felspar in the composition of the porcelain body, the results being finer than any previously obtained.

It is useful to define porcelain, as used by the Goss factory, as distinct from other types of china. Porcelain is a semi-vitrified compound, in which one portion remains infusible at the greatest heat to which it can be exposed, whilst the other portion vitrifies* at a certain heat. This ultimately combines with and envelopes the infusible part of vitrification producing a smooth, compact, shining and semi-transparent substance, well known as the characteristic of true porcelain. Porcelain is really a finer species of pottery, with ingredients selected in such a way that they act chemically upon each other. As the surface of porcelain, be it glazed or unglazed, is like a flint stone, it is not easily acted upon by acids. When free of colouring matter it is called china, of which there are two types, hard and soft. The hard type includes ingredients like kaolin or Cornish clay, felspar, sand and selenite. The soft variety is of a different composition and made from ground calcined bones, aluminous and silicious earths in such proportions that they will vitrify together. The methods of mixing and manufacturing are like those of earthenware.

Pottery includes the manufacture of the coarsest and commonest wares, and involves the use of clay only. It requires less careful processes although still skilful. Earthenware is generally used for tableware and can be white, blue and white or yellow ware. This encompasses many forms and recipes and is tough, durable and fine.

All the ingredients of porcelain were ground to powder in a mill. William was always short of space in his factory, so as many of the raw materials as possible were brought in

* Rendered non-porous.

*A group of employees from the Goss factory in the early twenties. Back row, left to right: Frederick Myatt, Harry Myatt, Mr. Hesketh. Front row: Joseph Myatt, Fred Charlesley, Don Bradley*

*The Goss factory cricket team, date unknown*

*Weighing raw materials*

*Grinding the ingredients for parian in the mill*

ground and ready for manufacture, a system which was continued long after William's death.

The materials brought in, which did require grinding, were ground in Kirkham's mill, in what resembled a large wooden vat with central shaft and revolving arms to which were attached large lumps of Derbyshire limestone. These ground the contents into the stone floor of the vat. The hardest stone for the grinding floor usually came from Wales and all materials were ground in water to prevent dust rising. After grinding, the powder was washed to sort out any lumps and then run into large arks. These ground ingredients plus ground flint were then ready to be transferred to the slip house of the Goss factory. Flints were ground in nearby water mills and were necessary to give whiteness and prevent excessive contraction in the firing. Today there are substantial remains of at least 50 water mills in Staffordshire, such as the Cheddleton Flint Mill. Great water wheels drove machinery which pushed the calcined flints around huge circular water filled tubs like giant food mixers. Rocks crushed the flints which were filtered, iron was removed by powerful magnets, and the resulting powder put in sacks and taken away by canal boat on the Cauldon canal to supply the potteries.

Flints were first introduced into recipes for earthenware in the 18th century, first as a whitener and later as an integral component of the clay body. Originally flints came to be added to clay by Astbury the famous potter who was travelling to London on horseback and whilst stopping at Dunstable, discovered there was something wrong with his horse's eyes. Astbury found some flints, burned them in the fire, pulverised them and applied them to the sore eyes of his horse. He noticed that the flints which were black had turned white after being burned so he filled his saddle bags with pieces of flint and took them back to his pottery where he experimented with the production of earthenware using flint as an ingredient. It was a success, with all other potters henceforth incorporating flint in their wares, providing a whiteness and durability which previously they did not possess.

In the sliphouse, the mixing of ground flint and kaolin was done by hand in open tanks, with a separate tank being used for the 'scraps' or broken pieces of clay ware, clay shavings and various bits and pieces of clay left over from the manufacturing processes. The men stirred or blunged the slip with long wooden sticks like rakes (blunge was an amalgamation of blend and plunge). No mechanical blungers were used in this factory. The ground ingredients were usually added in a certain order; first the kaolin, then the flint, followed by the ground glass, felspar and scraps. The resulting creamy liquid slip was passed through a series of boxes or sieves covered with silk or wire lawn screens, which sieved out all the dirt and lumps. This now fine liquid parian was known in the trade as 'frit', being a glassy compound of silica and alkali, white clay and lime.

Earlier traditional forms of potting were throwing, where a lump of clay was thrown on to the potters wheel and fashioned by hand on a revolving surface into the desired

*The creamy slip passing through a series of boxes covered with fine screens to sieve out the lumps. The resulting fine liquid parian was called 'frit'*

shape, and pressing. However, due to the absence of ball clay, there was no plasticity in the parian slip which resembled batter, and casting or pouring into absorbent Plaster of Paris moulds was the only method possible. The plaster moulds exerted their power of suction with a coating of clay adhering to the inner surface. The mould had to be filled up and left for a certain length of time and only when the desired thickness was obtained was the surplus slip tipped out and returned to the tub to be used again. The soda ash or sodium silicate added to the basic slip helped to reduce the drying time. This withdrawal of fluid was the method of making hollow pieces. Solid items, especially figurines, had the hollow refilled with thicker liquid and was left rather longer before being withdrawn.

It required a skilled craftsman to judge the correct amount of time for the slip to have formed the required thickness of porcelain to adhere to the walls of the mould. At this stage this thickness or cast should slightly contract back from the mould itself. If the original slip mixture contained too much water, the plaster of Paris moulds became very soggy and took too long for the cast to dry out. A good ratio the factory usually used was one gallon of water to 2 cwts. of clay. In correspondence dated 1884 William advised that the best consistency for white liquid in the slip state was 32 ounces to the pint or 20½ ounces of clay material. The required thickness of the parian ware varied from shape to shape, but for a tiny piece it was usually enough to allow 10 minutes for the slip to stay in the mould filled to the brim. For a small piece of terracotta it would take 20 to 30 minutes due to the main ingredient being heavy ball clay. It was possible to test whether enough slip had adhered to the mould walls by touching the spare slip around the hole in the top of the mould through which the slip had originally been poured. The mould's gradual absorption of water meant that by the sixth time it had been used, the mould would be rather soggy, so the time for setting would have been increased to 15-20 minutes for parian and 30-40 minutes for terracotta.

After the slip had been poured off back into the tub to be used again later, the casts had to stay inside the moulds for a further 20-30 minutes for parian and one hour for terracotta. This extra time spent drying before a stove ensured that the piece was satisfactorily set before it was removed from the mould. When the mould was opened, the piece was taken out as soft clay and potters then had to remove mould marks, and have the edges fettled or smoothed down.

The various casts were passed on to the repairer who worked in the 'greenhouse', whose job it was to join the halves together to make whole shapes. Composite pieces he built into a whole unit around a basic plaster prop. When assembling the shapes he trimmed the edges to make sure there was an exact fusion. This work was extremely skilled, requiring expert touch and years of experience. Any flaws or faults were covered up with dabs of liquid slip.

Surplus slip from the joins or seams was removed with a finger or a soft brush, which sometimes left fine lines across the pieces. These lines tend to confuse the inexperienced collector who might sometimes mistake them for damage cracks. Any warping or bending of figures or tall shapes had to be corrected whilst still 'green' (before the first firing). This was done with the aid of props made of the same material and dipped in ground flint to prevent sticking. A major problem in the making of a piece of many parts joined together was that the individual parts could shrink at different rates according to their size and thickness. Laurel wreaths which adorned the heads of the classical female figures, upper limbs and objects carried were all cast separately, thus complicated figure groups could have 20 or 30 different castings. It was at this stage that teapot spouts, pedestals for busts, handles and pieces not cast from the first moulds were added on by fusing them to the other parts with liquid slip. Handles, lids and spouts were made in bulk in either lead or fired clay master moulds. These moulds were more expensive to make but had a longer working life.

The completed pieces were known as 'green ware'. Although normally dry, with parian body it was necessary that pieces were thoroughly dry before being fettled or smoothed off, otherwise the seams would reappear during the biscuit firing when pieces could shrink up to as much as 25%. This could spoil busts and figures in particular

*For the manufacture of pottery vessels, the clay wedger kneads the clay to the right consistency and elasticity*

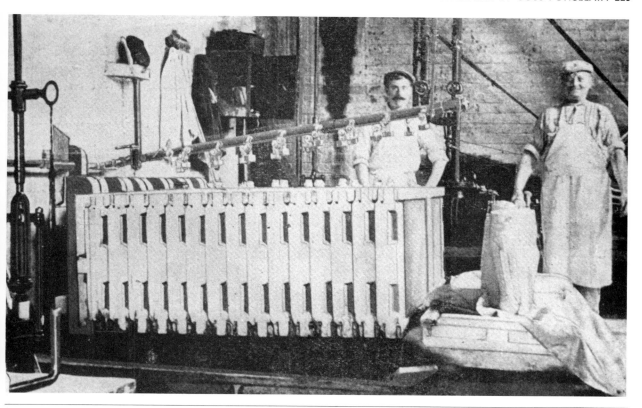

*Clay has moisture eliminated under high pressure in the clay presses*

*The potters wheel, on which vessels are shaped by hand from clay*

*Parian ware is not moulded by hand with clay, but poured in a liquid state into moulds*

*Casting cups from liquid parian*

*Putting handles on cups. These workers were known as 'handlers'*

and especially composite shapes. Casting was the main method of manufacture in the Goss factory after 1880. Most heraldic ware was made in two halves. Before being fired, whilst still damp, the bases of early models were impressed with the W.H. GOSS name, and the busts impressed on the back. Figures in particular had to be left for at least a week in a warm temperature where they could be kept an eye on by the repairer at work in the 'greenhouse' in case of any further warping or slipping. The hours spent on individual pieces in those days could not nowadays be expended without incurring considerable expense. If the green ware was fired too soon after being made it could crack or craze. Another cause of crazing was the over grinding of flints in the parian mixture.

The master clay or Plaster of Paris moulds had been made from the original model in the model maker's shop. To make the working plaster moulds, a bucket was filled with sufficient water for the size of the mould required. Plaster of Paris was then added, until the surface of the water was broken. After letting the mixture blend and settle for about 10 minutes, a thin creamy texture appeared. This was poured for two to three minutes over the master clay or plaster model. After trimming off excess plaster and smoothing the edges, the mould was left for about five minutes for the plaster to fully set. This would be the female or block mould from which the male or case mould would be made. The actual working moulds were made from these case moulds after the block moulds had been sized with soft soap. About ½1b. of soft soap to one pint

of water made a good mixture. This sizing or treating with soap was essential in order to prevent the two blocks of plaster of Paris from sticking to one another. The soap size was sponged down over the surface of the block mould and any excess material wiped off. This was continued for 10 minutes until a shiny surface remained on the plaster, making it slightly water repellent but with no coating left on top of the surface which would probably occur if other methods were used to prevent the surfaces from being sticky. When the case moulds were made, they were left for a week to allow enough time to dry out completely. It was important for them to dry thoroughly. Often the first cast from a new working mould was not good as it took all the rough edges off the inside surface.

The size of the piece was never the same as the model. Before the working moulds were obtained from the model, at least three casts had to be made, as with each casting the plaster swelled about 10%, so that the piece when made from it would be slightly larger than the model. In drying there would be a certain amount of contraction. In drying and firing together, parian contracted about 25% and earthenware 8%, so that the finished products were smaller than the original model. Pieces made to an exact size, such as bases and lids, had to be fired in a part of the oven where there would be the least variation in heat. The general rule in the Goss factory was to make pieces one sixth larger than finished size to allow for the necessary shrinkage.

*The flat presser who made plates and saucers*

*The hollow-ware presser who put together soup tureens and vegetable dishes from moulded parts*

A parian repairer at Copelands in 1899, putting the various moulded parts of a figure together

The greenhouse where shapes which have been formed from two or more moulds, are left to dry

Moulds were the most costly and cumbersome part of the potter's stock in trade. They were required in every size for every piece or part piece to be made. Plates being solid unlike hollow items were usually made in one piece from one mould with the moulding for the front and the back being fashioned by a tool or profile. Jiggling was the term for making plates or 'flatwares' as they were known, and jollying was that for cups.

All large moulds were made of plaster because of its facility in working and its great absorption of water. The only disadvantage was that constant wetting made them liable to rot and eventually perish. Moulds had to be thoroughly dried at moderate heat between each casting, the longer they took to dry the longer the mould would cast. If moulds were in more than one piece, the parts were keyed together by 'natches'. These were vital in the mould making as without them the different parts of the mould would not fit exactly together without movement.

'Natches' were called hump and hollow, with one half being hump the other being hollow. The hump was a round stud that fitted into the hollow without any lateral movement. The position of the natches in the moulds also required careful thought for if they were too near the edge they would break out in working and unless they were placed with care, the parts would not hold together properly.

*Carrying full saggars on their heads, these workmen load the bottle oven*

It was necessary for moulds to dislocate easily without pulling away any of the piece inside. If in several parts, they had to join closely or the seam would be too noticeable. The closer the parts of the mould fitted, so the closer the pieces cast inside them would fit.

When the improved greenware was ready for the first (or biscuit) firing, the pieces were placed in deep sided oval containers called saggars. The external dimensions of an oval saggar were 20″ by 15″ by 8″. Saggars were usually constructed of local marl or fire clay and broken biscuit, a crucible material able to withstand intense heat and flames. It was necessary that they were refractory enough to support the high temperatures without sinking out of shape. They also needed to be of a grain sufficiently coarse to endure rapid changes in temperature and regular firing without cracking. They had to be carefully made on the inside so as not to shower little particles of sand or clay on to the greenware inside. William Burton, F.C.S., a noted authority on the manufacture of earthenware and porcelain, wrote in 1906:

'In every county the problem of making clean and durable saggars is an important detail in the successful conduct of a manufactory; and every potter strives to obtain mixtures of fireclay and pounded pitcher which will answer his requirements.'[1]

*The interior of a biscuit oven, with the horse (ladder) used for stacking the saggars right up to the top*

The saggar maker made the saggars on wooden drums, after which they were placed in a steam-heated hothouse to dry, and afterwards fired at the top of the oven.

The placing of greenware in saggars required skill and care. The job took place in the small room next to the oven called the placing room or saggar house. In this state the ware was easily damaged or dented. The Placer was responsible for the ware being placed carefully without touching other pieces and the items were embedded in ground flint in layers, earthenware being placed in fine clean sand. This prevented the articles from fusing together during the extreme heat of the firing. When the Placer had finished his work he carried his full saggars to the ovens where they were piled one above the other in tall columns until the oven was full.

By placing these saggars, which resembled hat boxes, in tall single columns, each individual saggar covered the one beneath it, the bottom of each being the lid for the one below it. This protected the contents from the contact of smoke and flame. It was important the saggars were strong for if one gave way in the lower part of a bung or stack, the whole bung could come down knocking down other bungs at the same time, smashing the precious contents. Apart from the considerable loss in breakages the falling saggars could fill up the bags and flues, the bags being the small firebrick chimneys immediately above each firemouth on the inside of the oven. The bag directed flames from the fire below into the oven and protected the saggars. The flues were the channels beneath the oven floor which distributed the heat from the fires around the oven up into the centre of the floor.

The oven for the first firing was cylindrical in form, with walls made of the hardest firebrick, built two feet thick and pierced at regular intervals by the firemouths which opened into the interior. The floor of the kiln was hollow and over an opening in the centre a column of rings was placed, made out of saggars with their bottoms knocked out (a pipe bung), and these carried the flame right up the centre so that the whole oven would fill up with flame during the firing. The fireman could walk completely around the oven which was in an inner chamber of the bottle shaped building.

If there was any blockage of air the corresponding side of the oven would be short fired and spoiled. The fireman had to be able to draw his trials which were samples pulled out of the oven during the firing and examined so that he could judge the progress of the firing. If the fireman could not do this it meant that he had to fire the oven by guesswork.

The saggars were placed in this biscuit oven in a special way to ensure adequate firing. It was important to fill the kiln thoroughly because space was valuable. A full oven regularly fired kept the various workmen and paintresses in work for the later processes. The full saggars were usually carried into the oven on the men's heads or shoulders. To protect their heads they wore wads of material called rolls under their peaked caps. This was a necessary precaution considering that full saggars could weigh around 50 lbs. each. About 2,000 saggars would fill the average bottle oven. The men who carried them had to be strong, especially as greenware was so heavy. The stacks or bungs reached from the top of the oven to the floor, and the men had to climb up ladders or 'horses' to get to the top of the bungs with the least movement. Horses were of varying heights and very sturdy as the top of the horse had to support a full saggar, and was shaped in a circular manner so that it could rest securely against a bung of saggars. Any unevenness in the floor of bungs was corrected with pieces of broken saggar to keep the stacks upright. The contents of each saggar determined its position in

*External view of a typical Bottle Oven*

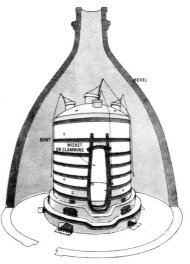

*Cross section showing position of oven inside Hovel*

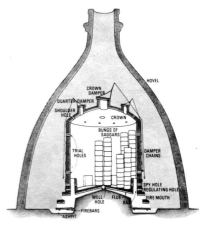

*Cross section of oven in detail*

*Preparing the coals for starting the fires under the ovens*

*Firing the oven*

the oven. The fireman and his men knew their own oven best, for no two ovens behaved exactly the same. Usually the hottest or hardest part of an oven was between the bags and just above them, and in the first ring just above the bags, the next hottest part was the top. The number of smoke holes could also affect the heat range within, with certain pieces more heat resistant than others, and some obviously more expensive and precious. Anything likely to warp under too intense a heat, or items with feet, centre pieces or composite wares were placed in the protected parts of the oven.

A certain length of time was required to gradually heat up the biscuit oven to the high temperatures for firing so the fires around the oven were usually lit up before the last saggars were carried in. Over the well hole in the centre the pipe bung (a stack of saggars with their bottoms knocked out) was placed to allow smoke to escape. When the oven was eventually full, the doorway, known as the 'clammins', was bricked up and plastered over. A coal fired oven usually had about eight fire mouths around its outer wall. The coal fires already lit in piles outside the oven were then shovelled into the fire mouths simultaneously. Initially the chimney smoked heavily but this did not last too long for when the fire had permeated the coal, the smoke was mostly consumed. These fires were baited or stoked at intervals of four hours.

Around each oven were placed eight trial holes, usually four at the top and four near the bottom of the kiln. These holes were blocked with a loose brick which could be removed by the fireman to draw a trial. This was a sample of ware which could be inspected in order to judge the progress of firing. There were no temperature gauges so the fireman would stay up all night if necessary in order to keep attendance at the firing. Methods of testing were by means of Bullers Rings, Seger Cones, Holdcroft Bars and Pyrometers. Bullers Rings were circular hoops of ceramic material which were measured during a trial on a scale for contraction. Seger Cones were used by many factories after 1886 and comprised several pyramids of different ceramic mixtures which were used to indicate when certain temperatures had been achieved. One cone was designed to collapse before the required heat, one at the exact heat, and one beyond the heat. The cones were placed in a spy hole so the firemen could look in and follow their progress. Holdcroft Bars worked on the same principle but were bars which sagged instead of cones that collapsed. The crucial period in biscuit firing was about 12 hours from the end. The Goss factory tested a series of Bullers Rings at regular intervals after the first 12 hours. The firemen withdrew these through the trial holes using special long bars with hooks on the end from thick saggars with holes cut in the sides, which had been especially placed adjacent to the trial holes. Rings were held up to the light for their translucency to be tested against a known series.

These trials were placed on two pegs on the inside of a rectangular box which had a moveable metal bar fixed to one end. This was then placed on top of the trial piece and the amount of contraction was shown by the other end of the metal bar on a special scale marked on the vertical side of the box. It was important to keep a close watch on the temperature inside the oven and to eliminate unwanted variations which could ruin several thousands of pounds worth of ware as well as damage the saggars. A large oven of 20 ft. in diameter took about 50 hours to fire plus another 3-4 days to cool. By allowing the contents to cool naturally no sudden changes in air temperature were experienced. Some 22 tons of coal would be used for one firing, but varied according to the quality of the fuel.

When the firm expanded between 1902 and 1905 adjacent to the Edward Street site, the Goss sons took the opportunity to build three biscuit ovens of the latest improved down-draught principle. These needed less fuel for the same length of firing time and it was easier to achieve a more regular temperature throughout the inside of the oven, as hot air had further to travel. A disadvantage was that this type of oven was more expensive to build and the repairs more costly. But these ovens, being 20 feet wide or less, were considered easier to manage as they took less time to set in and draw and less cooling time was required. This made it easier to 'get up' orders and kept the next stages of production in regular work. A temperature between 1000°C and 1,200°C was reached depending on whether terracotta or parian ware was being fired. The fireman saw a colour first appear after about 25 hours when the flues were beginning to get red hot about two feet from the bottom of the kiln. After 45 hours the interior reached a brilliant red, getting white-red at the end of the firing after 50-55 hours. The fireman never used a timescale on its own as a sole guide, as variations in the quality of coal, changes in wind direction, outside temperature and the type of products being fired could all vary the firing time.

Control of the heat was obtained by changing the position of the dampers on the crown or top of the oven. These were made of iron flaps and firebrick which could be opened or closed by a pulley system. By opening them the temperature could be raised and by closing them it could be lowered or steadied.

It was well known that William Henry used to take a personal interest in the firing, and actively helped in the process in the earlier days of the firm, training his firemen to his own high standards.

When the fires had been drawn and the ovens had cooled down, the clammins was broken down and the workers entered and removed the saggars, carrying them away on wareboards on one shoulder to the biscuit warehouse. There the ware was emptied out of the saggars and the ground flint brushed away by women. Then it was carefully examined to discover any defects which may have occurred during the firing. Cracked and crooked pieces were thrown away on the factory spoil heap, whilst the

*Firing up time in the early evening. The skyline was a mass of smoking chimneys and bottle ovens*

*Examining fired ware in the biscuit warehouse in order to reject defective pieces*

*Scouring rough edges to make smooth after the ware has been fired*

perfect pieces were cleaned, usually by hand, to remove any dirt or flint stuck to the surface, as any grit left on would be even more noticeable after glazing. This stage of the work involved a certain amount of dust harmful to the worker, which was eliminated by fans covered over with glass frames which drew the dust away from the women. After 1903 much of the cleaning was done by machinery but many older workers did not approve of this method and still preferred to rub by hand with sandpaper. The perfect biscuit ware was stored in the biscuit warehouse until required for dipping. It was at this stage that the transfers of the Goshawk factory mark and descriptions of named models were applied. The rubber stamp mark used on some of the lustre ware and coloured ware was applied by a rubber die first pressed on a charged flannel pad rolled and bound with twine. All pieces with lids were carefully matched in this warehouse to make sure the fit was good before being sent to be glazed. Other factories decorated some of their wares under the glaze. The Goss factory glazed their pieces first before decorating. Exceptions to this rule include the lustre and plain coloured pieces, such as domestic shapes, coloured bright yellow with a black trim instead of gilding. Lustre was used to decorate models as well as an assortment of vases, and shades used were mauve, green, rose pink, turquoise and a rather gaudy orange.

At the Dipping House the biscuit ware was dipped individually into vats of cold glaze which resembled thin cold cream. Each shape was inserted and quickly withdrawn, the dipper spreading the glaze evenly over the whole piece by an expert flick of the wrist in a circular motion, which prevented the glaze setting unequally. This process had been personally organised by William in the earlier days of the firm to ensure the glaze spread evenly over the parian body because there was very little absorption left in it. The 'dipper' wore a long iron crook attached to his thumb, with the help of which he was able to grasp each piece and not let his fingers touch the glaze. The coating had to cover the surface equally, otherwise the piece would be unmarketable.

Those pieces not requiring glaze such as the majority of the busts, cottages and figures, were not sent to the dipping house. Glazed ware was put on shelves near the stove to dry; bases of the shapes were not glazed for this reason although the earliest heraldic ware was glazed underneath but had slightly concave bases. Pieces produced after 1930 were also glazed underneath. The materials for glazing parian were similar to those used for glazing earthenware. These were flint, china clay or carbonate of lime, Cornish stone, boracic acid, tincal, borax, carbonate of lead or oxide of lead, carbonate of soda, potash and felspar, all finely ground and mixed with water. This frit was made in bulk, enough for six months' production at a time and was then heated in a small oven, probably Kirkham's, until all the constituents had fused together; it was then allowed to run off by unstopping and

channelled into tubs of cold water. Sudden cooling caused the frit, which resembled molten glass, to break up more easily so helping the next process of grinding the lumps, again carried out next door at Kirkham's grinding mill. Ground frit or glaze was taken to the dipping house for mixing to the required thickness for the ware concerned. After drying, the glazed ware was placed in saggars again for the glost firing. To prevent sticking together during the firing, pieces were kept apart by props or cones made out of fine silica sand. Props were shaped into triangular cockspurs, stilts, thimbles and pinpoints, striped in turquoise and red and used according to the shapes requiring support, and placed under and above each layer of Goss china. The average glost oven was an updraught one, similar in construction to a biscuit oven but smaller, capable of holding an average of about 500 saggars and taking about 18 hours to fire, although the Goss glost ovens took between 16 and 24 hours to fire. About 5 tons of coal were required for one firing in order to reach a temperature of 1000°C.

With this firing extra care had to be taken to protect the goods inside the oven. The saggars were brushed on the inside with a coating of infusible liquid made of a compound of glaze with lime and clay, so that nothing could attach to them. In addition, a layer of wad clay or local marl was placed on top of each saggar, as these were stacked in bungs. This meant that no flame or smoke was likely to penetrate them, but flames could play around the outside of them in all directions. After the firing a couple of days were required for the oven to cool down before removing the ware to prevent the surface of the china being crazed or warped which is what would have happened had it suffered a sudden change in temperature. It was not unknown for some unscrupulous pot bank owners to send the men in before the ovens had properly cooled down in order not to waste any valuable time getting orders out, and no amount of wet rags over their faces prevented them from suffering from the heat for some time after. However, this would never have happened at the Goss factory.

When drawn, the saggars were taken in baskets to the Sorting House. This was a large, light warehouse where saggars were first unpacked and the stilts and spurs put aside to be returned to the dipping room. The sorters, usually women, were supervised by a male foreman. Their sorting tools, pieces of iron about ⅛″ thick, 1″ wide, 10-12″ long and sharp at one end, had to be kept clean and dry and never allowed to go rusty. When the ware was first unpacked it was piled on the floor at one end according to shape. The women had to be careful how they handled the ware because any protruding bits of glaze could be as sharp as broken glass. The number of sorters employed depended on the timing of the ware coming in from the next firing. It was necessary to sort out each oven load and then clean up before the next load came. Sorting was the next step, in three piles — best, seconds and lump.

*Dippers glazing the ware*

*The inner chamber of the Goss bottle oven where glazed ware was fired. Taken 1975*

*Transporting the ware from one process to another on boards and in baskets*

*The sorting house where china was kept in piles awaiting orders from the gilding, transfer and enamelling rooms*

*View of the spoil heap behind the factory, 1959*

*The printer engraved the outlines of coats of arms and decorations on to tissue paper with ink*

Each piece was checked by a sorter as she cleaned it, but the foreman had the responsibility of examining every cleaned piece of best before it left the warehouse so there was little chance of any defective piece passing as best, although this occasionally happened.

All 'firsts' were put together according to shape. Similar pieces were placed 'in court' so that there were rows of equal number for counting. Each type of model was kept in separate bins to await orders. When there were enough models in the bins to fulfil orders the chosen pieces were taken to the printing shop. The 'seconds' pieces were slightly substandard and the 'lump' was cracked and damaged. What pieces could not be made good from the 'seconds' were dumped behind the factory along with the lump. It is quite easy to find these spoil heaps today as some pieces are visible from the surface of the ground.

The printer had the relevant designs for each order. He had 700 copper plates with up to 24 designs of coats of arms, mottos etc. engraved upon each. The engraving was not done in the factory as it was in the larger potbanks but by Henry Fennell of Hollart Street, Hanley. The printer put the relevant copper plate on top of the stove to heat and then put a flexible knife bearing the correct colour on — usually black but often sepia, and on rare occasions red, blue or green ink — on to the part of the plate being used. He then scraped off the excess ink (which was already mixed with a very thick oil) and polished the surface with a velvet or corduroy boss or pad, which left the colour only in the interstices of the pattern. He then put the copper plate in the printing press bed; took a sheet of prepared tissue paper, saturated it with a solution of soap and water, then carefully placed it upon the copper plate. The engraving was then pulled through the press by the rollers which were covered in felt. The tissue was pressed on the copper plate and on the bed of the press when the roller revolved, then the engraving was placed again on the stove and the impression carefully removed from the copper by lifting one corner and dried. The ink used in printing was made of linseed oil boiled with lithange, rosin, balsam of sulphur or Barbadoes tar, and tinted with any of the usual finely ground mineral colours — blue for example being formed from oxide of cobalt. It was then given to the cutter who cut off any excess paper around the transfer and passed to the transferer. The cutter and transferer were usually women. The transferer applied the transfer, usually of the outlines of a coat of arms, to the correct place on the ware by hand; it being important to place it level and consistently on similar models. The next woman used a bound flannel, or rubber lubricated with soap, to rub the print carefully yet firmly on to the piece of china. Although the heraldic ware was designed to carry a coat of arms, not all pieces had an even surface on which to apply the transfer. Most pieces were curved, but on some like the bushel measures, the transfer of the device was required to go on the inside of the piece. The whole of the device had to be rubbed into any cavities, and sometimes a stiff brush was used to do this. The transfer was left on for some time before being washed off, perhaps all day. This allowed the transfer to adhere and harden

*The transferers who applied the devices centrally and consistently level on similar models*

*The end result*

on the porcelain. To fix the transfer, the china was dipped in a large tub of water, and the transfer paper came away easily without disturbing the print left on the china. It was the thin film of soap size which protected the print. Transfers of scenes etc. required no enamelling but heraldic devices and other decorations requiring hand painting were sent on to the enamelling department. The ware already had printed outlines of the devices and the enamellers had to fill in the outlines with the appropriate colours in accordance with the chart of the devices hung on the wall in frames above the paintresses. Only one colour could be painted on each device per day to avoid smudging. The enamels were oil based and contained lead. After completing the colouring on each piece, a paintress would paint her own mark on the base, thus identifying her when the ware was inspected by the foreman later.

The onglaze enamels used meant it was easy to obtain a great variety of shades and tones which would have been altered or faded had they been used under the glaze or incorporated with it. The modern potter of the 19th century had many more chemical compounds at his disposal unknown to his predecessors of the 17th and 18th centuries, particularly chromium, uranium, platinum and iridium, many of which were only recognised and isolated by the labours of European chemists during the 19th century.

Some of the chemical ingredients of William Henry's own recipes included purple cassin, oxide of nickel, whiting, oxide of tin, black flux, carbonate and also oxide of cobalt (blue), red lead, borax, lynn sand, arsenic, prepared silver, oxide of copper, nitre, flint and flint glass, rose, oxide chrome, chromate of iron, boric acid, potash, litharge, antimony and many more as can be seen in his own notebooks. In the firing, the fluxed colours melted and fastened to the glazed surface of the pieces, forming coloured glasses.

The next process was gilding, which not every piece required, but those that did were sent to the gilding department. Here the gilder placed each item to be gilded upon a revolving wheel, set in motion by hand, and held a steady brush to the rim. Some of the earlier jewelled ware and parian vases and figurines had fine gilding applied freehand by an experienced gilder. The gilding applied was 90% brown oxide of gold and very expensive. Occasionally a gilder would also put her mark on the base of the pieces.

After gilding, the wares were fired in the enamel kilns which were considerably smaller ovens. According to size, firing could take five to nine hours, and the temperature required was 700°-800°C. The amount of coal to fire the oven could range from 12 cwt. to one ton. The heat could not be so hot as to melt the glaze, but it could soften certain colours due to the fluxes in them. Pieces had to be placed separately on iron slabs or bats which acted as shelves kept apart by supports, making sure no pieces were touching. The colours most likely to be affected by heat were flesh pink, light orange and coral red, so pieces with

these colours predominant were placed away from the fires. The stronger colours like brown, green and blue could sustain greater heat without spoiling. If placed on bats or shelves in the kiln, these would be less than one inch thick and quite strong enough to support most ware, except for the heavier items. Bats were perforated so that the heat could travel thoughout the kiln and were also lighter to lift when placing and drawing. They also required careful cleaning after each firing, with the iron material being ideal because it did not flake when subjected to frequent intense heat. If bats and props were well placed in a kiln there was little risk of damage. If a prop fell during firing it could cause considerable damage and loss. Saggars were not used as flames did not enter the firing chamber in this type of oven. After being painted and gilded the ware was brought from the dust free enamelling and gilding rooms to the oven and was not left anywhere between the two places to avoid dust sticking to the colours. If too much china was brought to the oven then those pieces left out had to be taken back to the enamelling room to be kept clean.

*Packers boxing wares into crates*

The enamel or muffle kiln fireman tried to arrange for fires to be drawn or put out at about 5 p.m., in order that the oven could be opened up about midday the following day, and the wares taken out. The cooler the oven was allowed to get before removing the ware, the better for the china and the more comfortable for the workmen. Tests were made with small pieces of broken porcelain with dabs of rose colour upon them, which changed in tint according to the heat in the oven.

After this firing the goods were taken back to the enamel warehouse where pieces were checked for warping and smudging of painted coats of arms or decorations. If they were perfect each piece was wrapped in tissue paper before being passed to packers who made up individual orders, packing them in specially made woodwool into wooden casks. Woodshavings were never used for packing. The casks were sent to the respective agents with the firm's name only on the label. If the agents did not return the casks to the factory they were charged 4/-, 6/- or 8/- according to the size of the cask supplied.

The Goss factory had its largest total of up to 120 staff between 1900 and 1914, with only 80 members of staff in the 1920's. Of these 60 were engaged in the various manufacturing and decorating processes, and the rest in accounting and office work. Gradually numbers were run down on the office side of the business, even at its peak the Goss factory could never really be said to be a big firm.

Today no coal or coke is used in potteries. The old bottle ovens have been replaced by tunnel kilns, automatically fired by gas, electricity or oil. These new methods do not require firemen and their skills, but instead depend on a scientifically controlled rate of firing and temperature control. In this way Britain has attempted to keep up with competition abroad, improve the quality and consistency of goods and keep the prices of the end products as low as possible.

**Reference**

1.     'Porcelain: A sketch of its nature and manufacture'. William Burton F.C.S. Cassell 1906

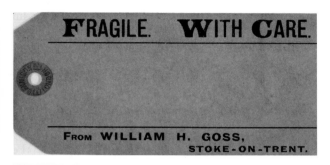

*An address label used on crates of china being despatched to agencies*

*The Goss factory today*

*Variations on a Winchester theme comprising First, Second and Third period Goss wares*

# Glossary of Potting Terms

**Bag:** The firebrick chimney over the inside of each firemouth around the oven. It directed the flames into the oven.

**Baiting:** Stoking the fires during the firing of an oven.

**Bats:** Portable perforated iron shelves used to support ware in the kiln.

**Biscuit:** Pottery that has been fired once but not yet glazed, under the hardest heat attainable.

**Body:** The clay mixture containing all the necessary ingredients.

**Bone China:** A hard, vitreous china made from bone ash, china clay and china stone, particularly white and translucent.

**Bonts:** Iron bands which encircle the oven at regular intervals of height to strengthen it during contraction and expansion.

**Blunge:** To mix clay ingredients with water.

**Bullers Rings:** A method of testing fired ware in the oven by means of circular ceramic hoops, measured during a trial for contraction on a scale.

**Bung:** An upright stack of saggars.

**Calcine:** To heat materials to a temperature (such as bones or flints) to make them easier to crush.

**Casting (or Coulage):** Pouring the slip into moulds which will absorb moisture and so form a cast on the inside of the mould.

**Ceramic:** Derived from the Greek 'Keramos' — clay that is first shaped and then hardened by firing.

**China:** Western imitation of porcelain from China.

**Clammins:** The large door of the oven which is bricked up and plastered for firing, and broken down for drawing.

**Dipping:** Briefly immersing china in a tub of glaze.

**Drawing:** Emptying the oven or fires.

**Drawing a trial:** Taking out a sample of ware or a mean test out of the oven during firing, with a long pole with a hook on the end.

**Earthenware:** Ceramic ware with a main ingredient of ball clay which makes it plastic and possible to fashion by hand before firing. When glazed it is impervious.

**Enamel:** A chemical colour which is painted on to the glaze and then fired in a muffle kiln.

**Fettling:** Smoothing down the rough edges of casts and seams in greenware, caused by joining parts together.

**Fireclay:** Heat resistant clay.

**Fireman:** The craftsman trained to organise and supervise the firings of his bottle oven.

**Firemouth:** There were usually about six of these openings around the base of an oven to contain the fires.

**Firing:** Heating to a certain temperature in an oven in order to turn moist clay into hard ware.

**Flatware:** Plates, saucers, bowls etc. (not hollow).

**Flues:** Channels below the oven floor which keep the heat moving up and around the oven.

**Frit:** Molten mixed materials for making pottery glazes.

**Gilding:** Edging with gold using a thin paintbrush.

**Glaze:** Hard thin glassy permanent film on the surface of the porcelain rendering it impervious.

**Glost Oven:** The oven used for firing freshly glazed ware.

**Greenware:** Unfired ware just out of the moulds.

**Hardest:** Highest.

**Holloware:** Hollow shapes.

**Holdcroft Bars:** A method of testing fired ware in the oven by means of bars of ceramic material which sagged when certain temperatures were reached.

**Horse:** Wooden ladder used for stacking the saggars.

**Hovel:** The brick bottle shaped outer walls which enclosed the actual oven, and protected it from the outside weather and sucked the smoke upwards out of the chimney.

**Hump and Hollow:** Moulds made of several parts were fitted together by means of natches, which were either hump or hollow. The hump is a round stud that fitted tightly into the hollow.

**Jiggling:** Manufacturing flatware (plates, saucers).

**Jollying:** Manufacturing cups.

**Kaolin:** Chemical formula = $Al_2 O_3 2S; O_2 2H_2O$ (39.77% of alumina, 46.33% of silica, 13.90% of water) white china clay.

**Kiln:** Oven for firing ceramic ware.

**Mould:** Casing, usually made of Plaster of Paris, for casting parian or pressing earthenware.

**Muffle Kiln:** Small oven for firing enamelled and gilded ware.

**Natches:** A key pattern to ensure moulds fitted together correctly. (*See* Hump and Hollow).

**Parian:** A type of porcelain, named after Paros, an island in the Aegean Sea, famed for its white marble quarries.

**Placing:** Positioning of ware in saggars and in the ovens ready for firing.

**Porcelain:** Fine earthenware, white or pale grey, thin, translucent and vitreous.

**Potbank:** Pottery factory.

**Pottery:** General term for clay wares.

**Props or Cones:** Supports made of fine silica sand to keep pieces apart during firing to prevent sticking. Shaped into triangular cockspurs, stilts, thimbles and pinpoints.

**Pressing:** Pushing clay into moulds.

**Print:** Transfer decoration on tissue made from an engraved copper plate spread with ink.

**Pyrometers:** A method of testing ware during firing.

**Run-Down:** Sufficient heat to melt the materials.

**Saggar:** Fireclay container for holding ware during the biscuit and glost firings.

**Segar Cones:** A method of testing fired ware in the oven by means of ceramic pyramids which collapsed when certain known temperatures were reached.

**Slip:** Liquid parian mixture.

**Soaking:** Continual maximum temperature during firing.

**Spyholes:** Holes in wall of an oven usually filled with loose bricks which could be removed by the fireman to examine the contents.

**Stoneware:** Strong, vitreous china.

**Throwing:** Age old traditional way of potting on a revolving wheel.

**Trial:** Sample of ware removed from the oven by the fireman to judge the progress of the firing.

**Vitreous:** Unglazed china which has been fired to render it non-porous without glazing.

**Wareboard:** Large wooden boards for carrying ware about the factory, usually on one shoulder.

*Margaret Latham, secretary of the Goss Collectors' Club and one of its founder members, with part of her magnificent collection*

# Bibliography

*Fragments from the Life and Writings of W.H. Goss* by Eva Adeline Goss, 1907, Hill & Ainsworth.

*Primitive Man and His Works Vols. I & II* by William Henry Goss, 1901 & 1902.

*The Life and Death of Llewellynn Jewitt* by William Henry Goss, 1889, Henry Gray, London.

*Review of Modern Science and Modern Thought* by William Henry Goss, 1882, Vyse and Hill.

*Hebrew Captives and the Kings of Assyria* by William Henry Goss, 1890.

*A History of the Firm by W.H. Goss of Stoke-on-Trent, together with a Survey of his Wares* (M.A. Thesis) by Michael J.W. Willis-Fear, May 1970 (University of Durham).

*The Illustrated Guide to Goss Porcelain* by Michael J.W. Willis-Fear, M.A. (unpublished).

*The Price Guide to Goss China* by Nicholas Pine, Milestone Publications, 1978, 1981, 1984, 1986.

*Goss China, Arms Decorations and Their Values* by Nicholas Pine, 1982, Milestone Publications.

*The Goss Records 1st, 2nd, 3rd, 4th, 5th, 6th, 7th editions, 1901, 1902-3, 1903, 1903-4, 1904-6, 1906-7, 1910-11,* edited by J.J. Jarvis.

*The Goss Record 8th & 9th editions 1913 — 1920* Evans Bros Ltd., reprinted 1973, Milestone Publications.

*The Goss Record, War Edition, 1917,* Evans Bros Ltd., reprinted Milestone Publications 1980.

*Goss for Collectors* by John Magee, 1973, Milestone Publications.

*Goss China* by John Galpin, 1972, Milestone Publications.

*Crested China, The History of Heraldic Souvenir Ware* by Sandy Andrews, 1980, Milestone Publications.

*William Henry Goss and Goss Heraldic China* by Norman Emery, F.L.A., 1969, Stoke-on-Trent Council.

*Goss and other Crested China* by Nicholas Pine, 1984, Shire Publications.

*The Art Union, An Illustrated Catalogue of the International Exhibition of 1862,* London, J.S. Virtue.

*The Transactions of the North Staffordshire Field Club 1905-6.*

*Handbooks to the Industries of Newcastle and District* by Andrew Reid, 1863 and 1889, London and Newcastle.

*Porcelain, A Sketch of its Nature, Art and Manufacture* by William Burton, F.C.S., 1906, Cassell & Co. Ltd.

*The Art of the Potter* by W.B. Honey (of the V. & A. Museum), 1944, Faber and Faber.

*The Art Journal,* edited by Samuel Carter Hall.

*The Ceramic Art of Great Britain,* by Llewellynn Jewitt, F.S.A. Vols. I & II, 1878, Virtue, London (2nd edition in one volume 1883, R. Worthington, New York).

*The Pottery & Glass Trade Gazettes.*

*The Reliquary.* Edited by Llewellynn Jewitt. Vols. XIV (1873-4) — XXV (1884-5).

*Cassell's Illustrated Family Paper,* 15 Nov. 1862 (Report of the International Exhibition, London 1862).

*The Illustrated Guide to Victorian Parian China* by Charles and Dorrie Shinn, 1971, Barrie & Jenkins Ltd., London.

*Copeland's (Late Spode) China,* 1900 Wood, Mitchell & Co., Hanley.

*Gazetteer & Directory of Cheshire* by Francis White & Co., Sheffield 1860.

*Fairbairn's Book of Crests of the Families of Great Britain and Ireland 4th Edition,* 1905, London.

*Staffordshire Leader 1908.*

*Who's Who in Staffordshire.*

*The Earthenware Collector, A Guide to Old English Earthenware* by G. Woolliscroft Rhead, Herbert Jenkins Ltd., London.

*Notes on the Manufacture of Earthenware* by E.A. Sandeman, 1901, H. Virtue & Co, London.

*The Development of Ceramic Colours and Decorating Techniques in the Staffordshire Potteries (leaflet)* by P. Freeman 1977, Gladstone Pottery Museum.

*Transport in the Potteries 1750-1950 (leaflet),* Gladstone Pottery Museum.

*Bottle Ovens (leaflet),* Gladstone Pottery Museum.

*Shelley Potteries, The History and Production of a Staffordshire Family of Potters* by Chris Watkins, William Harvey, Robert Senft, 1980, Barrie & Jenkins Ltd.

*Belleek Porcelain and Pottery* by G.M. Smith, 1979, Toucan Press, Guernsey.

*A Family Business, the Story of a Pottery* by Peter Brannam, 1982.

*The Register of the Patent Office,* Item No. 312559 (26 April 1909) for the Goss Trademark.

*Heraldic China Momentoes of the First World War* by Surg. Capt. P.D. Gordon-Pugh, OBE, RN., 1972, Ceramic Book Company, Newport.

*The Price Guide to Crested China* by Sandy Andrews and Nicholas Pine, Milestone Publications.

*Take Me Back To Dear Old Blighty. The First World War Through The Eyes of the Heraldic China Manufacturers,* Robert Southall, Milestone Publications.

*A Pictorial Encyclopaedia of Goss China* by Diana Rees and Marjorie Cawley, 1970, The Ceramic Book Company, Newport.

FAMILY TREE No. 1
# William Henry Goss (U.K.)

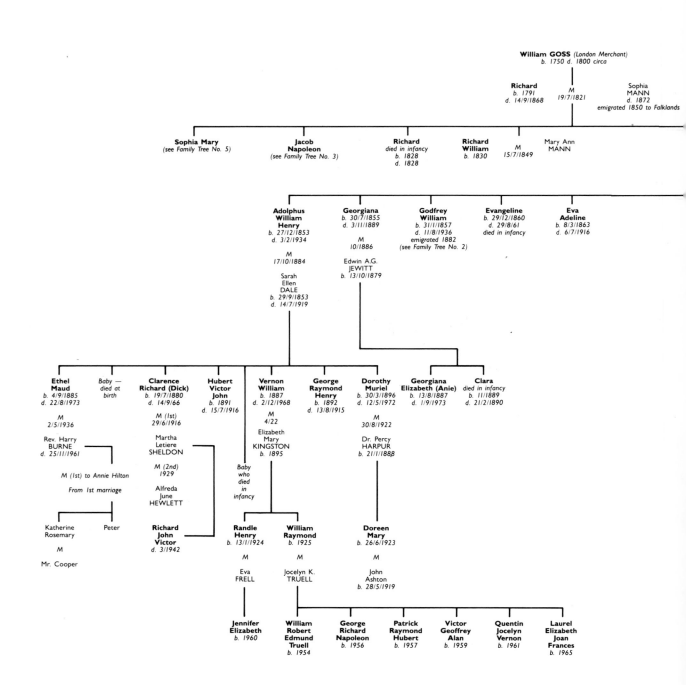

William **GOSS** (*London Merchant*)
*b. 1750 d. 1800 circa*

**Richard**
*b. 1791*
*d. 14/9/1868*

M
*19/7/1821*

Sophia
MANN
*d. 1872*
*emigrated 1850 to Falklands*

**Sophia Mary**
(*see Family Tree No. 5*)

**Jacob Napoleon**
(*see Family Tree No. 3*)

**Richard**
*died in infancy*
*b. 1828*
*d. 1828*

**Richard William**
*b. 1830*

M
*15/7/1849*

Mary Ann
MANN

**Adolphus William Henry**
*b. 27/12/1853*
*d. 3/2/1934*

M
*17/10/1884*

Sarah Ellen
DALE
*b. 29/9/1853*
*d. 14/7/1919*

**Georgiana**
*b. 30/7/1855*
*d. 3/11/1889*

M
*10/1886*

Edwin A.G.
JEWITT
*b. 13/10/1879*

**Godfrey William**
*b. 31/1/1857*
*d. 11/8/1936*
*emigrated 1882*
(*see Family Tree No. 2*)

**Evangeline**
*b. 29/12/1860*
*d. 29/8/61*
*died in infancy*

**Eva Adeline**
*b. 8/3/1863*
*d. 6/7/1916*

**Ethel Maud**
*b. 4/9/1885*
*d. 22/8/1973*

M
*2/5/1936*

Rev. Harry
BURNE
*d. 25/11/1961*

M (1st) to Annie Hilton

From 1st marriage

Katherine Rosemary

Peter

M

Mr. Cooper

Baby —
*died at birth*

**Clarence Richard (Dick)**
*b. 19/7/1880*
*d. 14/9/66*

M (1st)
*29/6/1916*

Martha Letiere
SHELDON

M (2nd)
*1929*

Alfreda June
HEWLETT

**Richard John Victor**
*d. 3/1942*

**Hubert Victor John**
*b. 1891*
*d. 15/7/1916*

Baby who died in infancy

**Vernon William**
*b. 1887*
*d. 2/12/1968*

M
*4/22*

Elizabeth Mary
KINGSTON
*b. 1895*

**Randle Henry**
*b. 13/1/1924*

M

Eva
FRELL

**Jennifer Elizabeth**
*b. 1960*

**William Raymond**
*b. 1925*

M

Jocelyn K.
TRUELL

**George Raymond Henry**
*b. 1892*
*d. 13/8/1915*

**Dorothy Muriel**
*b. 30/3/1896*
*d. 12/5/1972*

M
*30/8/1922*

Dr. Percy
HARPUR
*b. 21/1/1888*

**Doreen Mary**
*b. 26/6/1923*

M

John
Ashton
*b. 28/5/1919*

**Georgiana Elizabeth (Anie)**
*b. 13/8/1887*
*d. 1/9/1973*

**Clara**
*died in infancy*
*b. 11/1889*
*d. 21/2/1890*

**William Robert Edmund Truell**
*b. 1954*

**George Richard Napoleon**
*b. 1956*

**Patrick Raymond Hubert**
*b. 1957*

**Victor Geoffrey Alan**
*b. 1959*

**Quentin Jocelyn Vernon**
*b. 1961*

**Laurel Elizabeth Joan Frances**
*b. 1965*

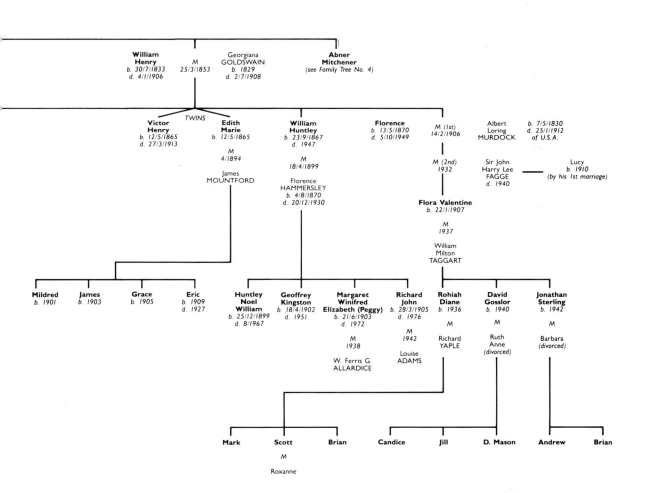

**William
Henry**
b. 30/7/1833
d. 4/1/1906

M
25/3/1853

Georgiana
GOLDSWAIN
b. 1829
d. 2/7/1908

**Abner
Mitchener**
*(see Family Tree No. 4)*

TWINS

**Victor
Henry**
b. 12/5/1865
d. 27/3/1913

**Edith
Marie**
b. 12/5/1865

M
4/1894

James
MOUNTFORD

**William
Huntley**
b. 23/9/1867
d. 1947

M
18/4/1899

Florence
HAMMERSLEY
b. 4/8/1870
d. 20/12/1930

**Florence**
b. 13/5/1870
d. 5/10/1949

M (1st)
14/2/1906

M (2nd)
1932

**Flora Valentine**
b. 22/1/1907

M
1937

William
Milton
TAGGART

Albert
Loring
MURDOCK

b. 7/5/1830
d. 25/1/1912
of U.S.A.

Sir John
Harry Lee
FAGGE
d. 1940

Lucy
b. 1910
*(by his 1st marriage)*

**Mildred**
b. 1901

**James**
b. 1903

**Grace**
b. 1905

**Eric**
b. 1909
d. 1927

**Huntley
Noel
William**
b. 25/12/1899
d. 8/1/1967

**Geoffrey
Kingston**
b. 18/4/1902
d. 1951

**Margaret
Winifred
Elizabeth (Peggy)**
b. 21/6/1903
d. 1972

M
1938

W. Ferris G.
ALLARDICE

**Richard
John**
b. 28/3/1905
d. 1976

M
1942

Louise
ADAMS

**Rohiah
Diane**
b. 1936

M

Richard
YAPLE

**David
Gosslor**
b. 1940

M

Ruth
Anne
*(divorced)*

**Jonathan
Sterling**
b. 1942

M

Barbara
*(divorced)*

**Mark**

**Scott**

M

Roxanne

**Brian**

**Candice**

**Jill**

**D. Mason**

**Andrew**

**Brian**

## FAMILY TREE No. 2
# Godfrey William Goss (U.S.A.)

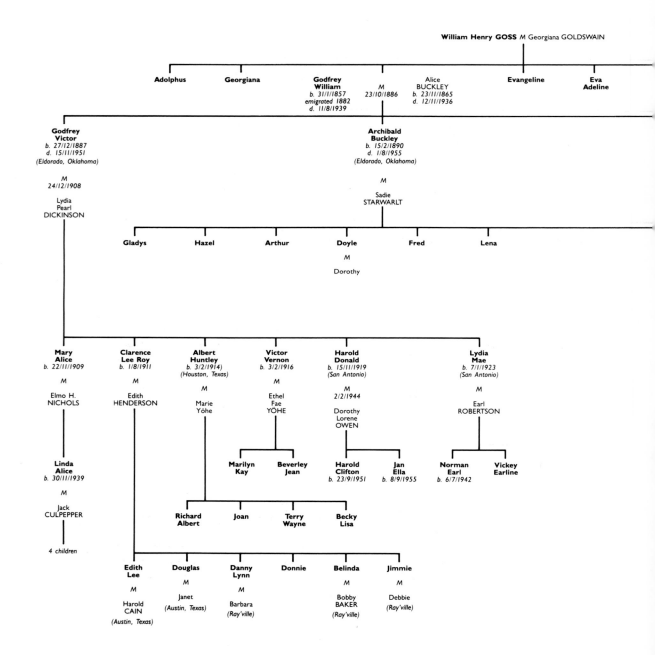

**William Henry GOSS** M Georgiana GOLDSWAIN

**Adolphus** — **Georgiana** — **Godfrey William** b. 31/1/1857 emigrated 1882 d. 11/8/1939 — M 23/10/1886 — **Alice BUCKLEY** b. 23/11/1865 d. 12/11/1936 — **Evangeline** — **Eva Adeline**

**Godfrey Victor** b. 27/12/1887 d. 15/11/1951 (Eldorado, Oklahoma)
M 24/12/1908
Lydia Pearl DICKINSON

**Archibald Buckley** b. 15/2/1890 d. 1/8/1955 (Eldorado, Oklahoma)
M
Sadie STARWARLT

**Gladys** — **Hazel** — **Arthur** — **Doyle** M Dorothy — **Fred** — **Lena**

**Mary Alice** b. 22/11/1909
M
Elmo H. NICHOLS

**Clarence Lee Roy** b. 1/8/1911
M
Edith HENDERSON

**Albert Huntley** b. 3/2/1914 (Houston, Texas)
M
Marie Yöhe

**Victor Vernon** b. 3/2/1916
M
Ethel Fae YÖHE

**Harold Donald** b. 15/11/1919 (San Antonio)
M 2/2/1944
Dorothy Lorene OWEN

**Lydia Mae** b. 7/1/1923 (San Antonio)
M
Earl ROBERTSON

**Linda Alice** b. 30/11/1939
M
Jack CULPEPPER

4 children

**Marilyn Kay** — **Beverley Jean**

**Harold Clifton** b. 23/9/1951 — **Jan Ella** b. 8/9/1955

**Norman Earl** b. 6/7/1942 — **Vickey Earline**

**Richard Albert** — **Joan** — **Terry Wayne** — **Becky Lisa**

**Edith Lee** M Harold CAIN (Austin, Texas) — **Douglas** M Janet (Austin, Texas) — **Danny Lynn** M Barbara (Ray'ville) — **Donnie** — **Belinda** M Bobby BAKER (Ray'ville) — **Jimmie** M Debbie (Ray'ville)

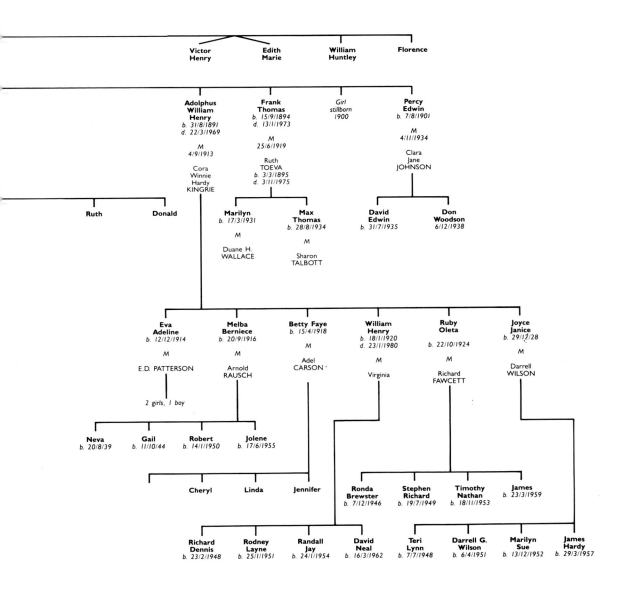

**Victor Henry** — **Edith Marie** — **William Huntley** — **Florence**

**Adolphus William Henry**
b. 31/8/1891
d. 22/3/1969

M
4/9/1913

Cora Winnie Hardy KINGRIE

**Frank Thomas**
b. 15/9/1894
d. 13/1/1973

M
25/6/1919

Ruth TOEVA
b. 3/3/1895
d. 3/11/1975

**Girl** stillborn 1900

**Percy Edwin**
b. 7/8/1901

M
4/11/1934

Clara Jane JOHNSON

**Ruth** — **Donald**

**Marilyn**
b. 17/3/1931

M

Duane H. WALLACE

**Max Thomas**
b. 28/8/1934

M

Sharon TALBOTT

**David Edwin**
b. 31/7/1935

**Don Woodson**
6/12/1938

**Eva Adeline**
b. 12/12/1914

M

E.D. PATTERSON

2 girls, 1 boy

**Melba Berniece**
b. 20/9/1916

M

Arnold RAUSCH

**Betty Faye**
b. 15/4/1918

M

Adel CARSON

**William Henry**
b. 18/1/1920
d. 23/1/1980

M

Virginia

**Ruby Oleta**
b. 22/10/1924

M

Richard FAWCETT

**Joyce Janice**
b. 29/12/28

M

Darrell WILSON

**Neva**
b. 20/8/39

**Gail**
b. 11/10/44

**Robert**
b. 14/1/1950

**Jolene**
b. 17/6/1955

**Cheryl** — **Linda** — **Jennifer**

**Ronda Brewster**
b. 7/12/1946

**Stephen Richard**
b. 19/7/1949

**Timothy Nathan**
b. 18/11/1953

**James**
b. 23/3/1959

**Richard Dennis**
b. 23/2/1948

**Rodney Layne**
b. 25/1/1951

**Randall Jay**
b. 24/1/1954

**David Neal**
b. 16/3/1962

**Teri Lynn**
b. 7/7/1948

**Darrell G. Wilson**
b. 6/4/1951

**Marilyn Sue**
b. 13/12/1952

**James Hardy**
b. 29/3/1957

FAMILY TREE No. 3
# Jacob Napoleon Goss (Falklands)

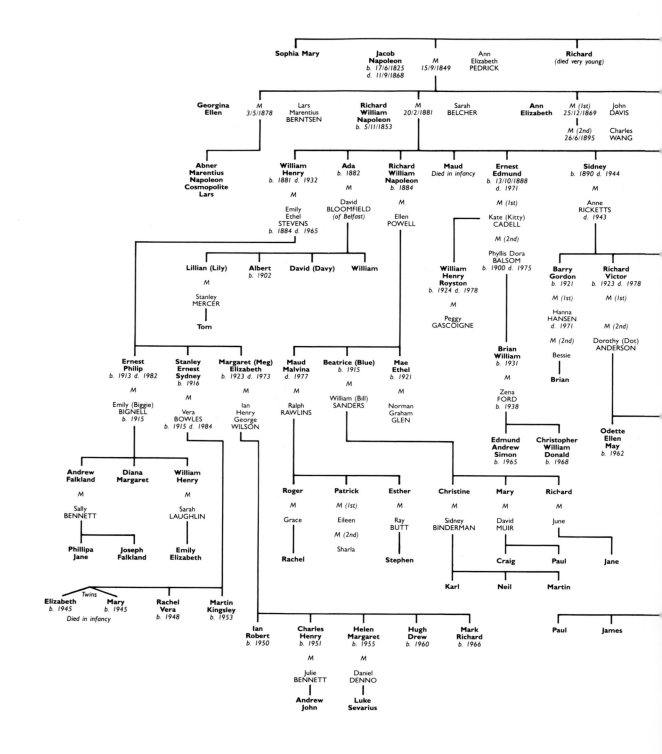

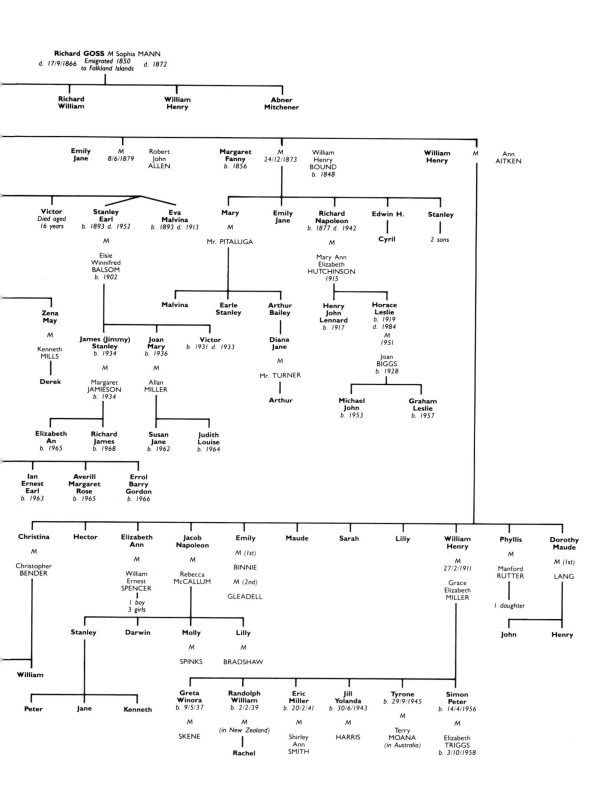

FAMILY TREE No. 4

# Abner Mitchener Goss (U.K.)

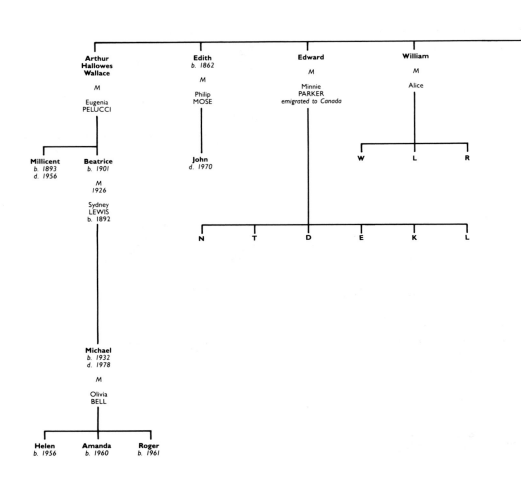

Richard **GOSS** M Sophia MANN

Sophia     Jacob Napoleon     Richard

**Arthur Hallowes Wallace**

M

Eugenia PELUCCI

**Edith** b. 1862

M

Philip MOSE

**Edward**

M

Minnie PARKER emigrated to Canada

**William**

M

Alice

**Millicent** b. 1893 d. 1956

**Beatrice** b. 1901

M 1926

Sydney LEWIS b. 1892

**John** d. 1970

W     L     R

N    T    D    E    K    L

**Michael** b. 1932 d. 1978

M

Olivia BELL

**Helen** b. 1956

**Amanda** b. 1960

**Roger** b. 1961

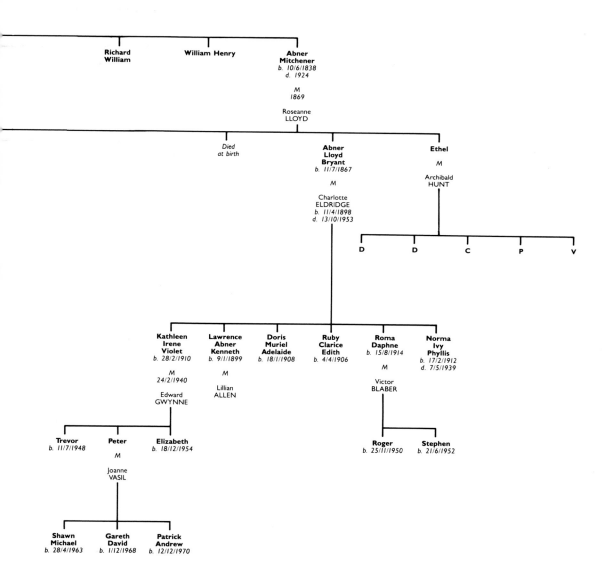

**Richard William**

**William Henry**

**Abner Mitchener**
*b. 10/6/1838*
*d. 1924*

*M*
*1869*

Roseanne LLOYD

*Died at birth*

**Abner Lloyd Bryant**
*b. 11/7/1867*

*M*

Charlotte ELDRIDGE
*b. 11/4/1898*
*d. 13/10/1953*

**Ethel**

*M*

Archibald HUNT

D    D    C    P    V

**Kathleen Irene Violet**
*b. 28/2/1910*

*M*
*24/2/1940*

Edward GWYNNE

**Lawrence Abner Kenneth**
*b. 9/1/1899*

*M*

Lillian ALLEN

**Doris Muriel Adelaide**
*b. 18/1/1908*

**Ruby Clarice Edith**
*b. 4/4/1906*

**Roma Daphne**
*b. 15/8/1914*

*M*

Victor BLABER

**Norma Ivy Phyllis**
*b. 17/2/1912*
*d. 7/5/1939*

**Trevor**
*b. 11/7/1948*

**Peter**

*M*

Joanne VASIL

**Elizabeth**
*b. 18/12/1954*

**Roger**
*b. 25/11/1950*

**Stephen**
*b. 21/6/1952*

**Shawn Michael**
*b. 28/4/1963*

**Gareth David**
*b. 1/12/1968*

**Patrick Andrew**
*b. 12/12/1970*

# FAMILY TREE No. 5
# Sophia Hurlin (U.S.A.)

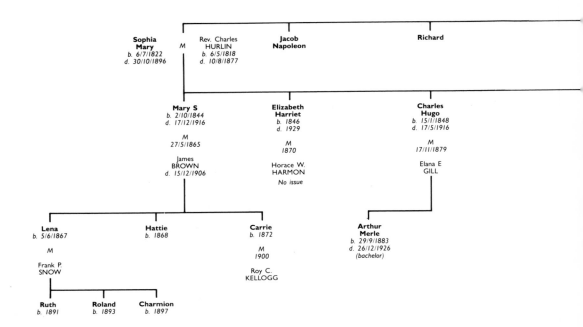

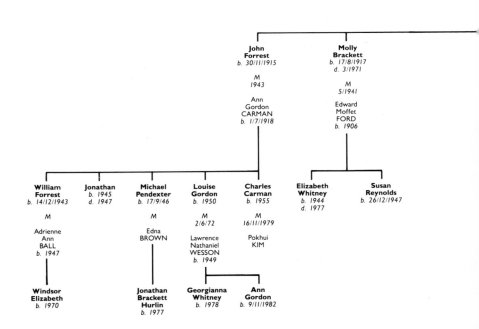

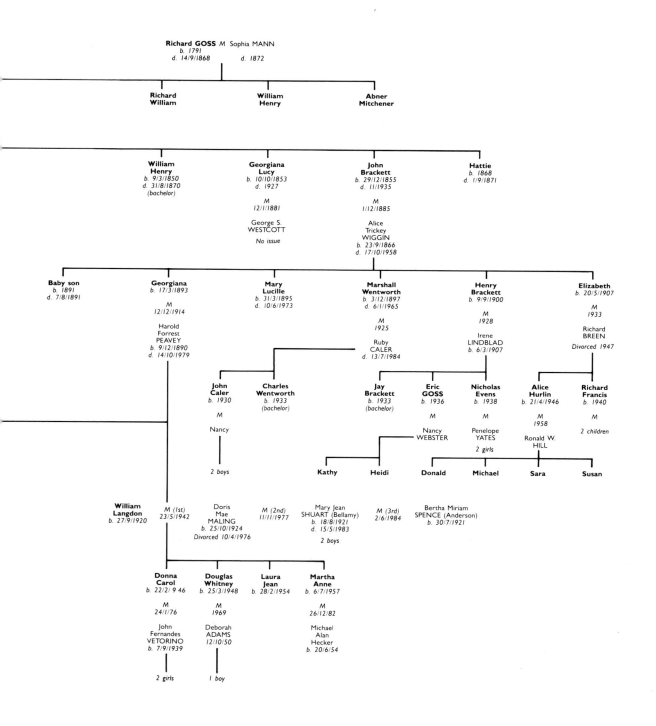

# Goss & Crested China Ltd. are the leading dealers in Heraldic China

We have been buying and selling for over fifteen years and our experienced staff led by Nicholas Pine will be able to answer your questions and assist you whether you are a novice or an experienced collector.

A constantly changing attractively priced stock of some 5,000 pieces may be viewed at our Horndean showrooms which includes Goss cottages, fonts, crosses, shoes, lighthouses, models etc. and the full range of crested ware including military, animals, buildings etc. covering all the other manufacturers.

Visitors are welcome to call during business hours of 9.00-5.30 any day except Sunday. Those travelling long distances are advised to telephone for an appointment so that they may be sure of receiving personal attention upon arrival.

Most of our business is by mail order and we publish *Goss & Crested China*, a monthly 32 page illustrated catalogue containing hundreds of pieces for sale from every theme and in every price range. The catalogue is available by annual subscription; please send for details.

In addition, if you specialise, we will be pleased to offer you particular pieces or crests from time to time as suitable items become available. Please let us know your wants as with our ever-changing stock we will probably have something to suit.

Our service is personal and friendly and all orders and correspondence are dealt with by return. You will find us fair and straightforward to deal with, as we really care about crested china and we hope that this is reflected in our service.

Finally, we are just as keen to buy as we are to sell and offers of individual items or whole collections are always welcome. These will be dealt with by return and the very highest offers will be made.

**Goss & Crested China Ltd,**
**62 Murray Road,**
**Horndean,**
**Hampshire**
**PO8 9JL.**

**Telephone: Horndean (0705) 597440**

# THE MILESTONE RANGE OF
# HERALDIC CHINA REFERENCE BOOKS

### The Price Guide to Goss China
*Nicholas Pine*

A new revised edition of the standard reference work on Goss collecting, this hard-working mine of information lists virtually every piece of Goss known. It is well illustrated and contains no less than 1300 illustrations. Every matching crest is given (where applicable) in addition to the height of every piece.

A short history of the factory and a range of factory marks in addition to no less than 2500 current prices make this book compulsory for either the novice or the experienced collector.

The author is the leading authority on the subject, and this fourth edition now categorises Goss China in first, second and third periods.

### Goss China Arms, Decorations and their values
*Nicholas Pine*

This fascinating book written by the leading authority on the subject, lists, describes and values all the different coats-of-arms and decorations which appear on Goss Models — over 7000 of them.

In addition, market values are given throughout the book showing the premium to be added to a piece for a crest or a decoration.

Its 13 well illustrated chapters include: UK and overseas arms, Royal, Nobility, Educational, Commemorative, Transfer printed, Regimental, Flora and Fauna, Flags, Welsh, Masonic and late decorations. These are further sub-divided into 55 easy-to-use sections — with prices.

### Crested China *Sandy Andrews*

Tells the story of heraldic China and its manufacturers — over 220 of them. Every known factory mark is given and over 4000 pieces are listed.

Profusely illustrated, it is a definite 'must' for every collector, whether budding or learned. Acknowledged as the standard work on the subject.

### The Price Guide to Crested China
*Sandy Andrews and Nicholas Pine*

This guide lists and prices some 6000 pieces, each of which is listed under factory headings further sub-divided into themes such as: Busts, figures, buildings, monuments, animals, birds and World War I Military China.

Also included are the latest revisions and details of new factories and marks to update *Crested China* by Sandy Andrews.

### Take me back to Dear Old Blighty *Robert Southall*

All you ever wanted to know about military crested china. Written in easy-to-read style, it is a valuable reference work, a price guide to military crested china and an exciting history of the Great War and the crested china that was produced as a result. Profusely illustrated, the book features some 430 different pieces as well as many of the original photographs of the World War I armaments and personalities that were modelled in crested china.

### SEND FOR FULL DETAILS OF THESE USEFUL AND INFORMATIVE BOOKS TO:

Milestone Publications
Goss & Crested China Ltd.
62 Murray Road
Horndean
Hants, PO8 9JL
England

*Goss china all purchased at Lands End, Cornwall between 1890-1930*